Developer Experience

* * *

**Navigating Digital Transformation
For Productivity And Satisfaction**

* * *

Marcus Maestri

ISBN

ISBN 9789152765913
ISBN 9789152765814

* * *

ISBN / KB.se
Royal Library of Sweden

Nothing endures but change.

— **Heraclitus**

Preface

***

In the vast ocean of technology, developers are the skilled navigators who chart the course of our digital future. With their ingenuity and expertise, they craft innovative solutions, steering us through uncharted waters and shaping how we interact with the world.

With this maritime spirit in mind, I set sail on a journey to explore the intricacies of developer experience, leading to the creation of this book, "Developer Experience: Navigating Digital Transformation for Productivity and Satisfaction."

Throughout my career, I have marveled at the transformative power of technology and the remarkable accomplishments of developers who harness it to overcome complex challenges, enhance our lives, and redefine the boundaries of what is possible. However, I have also observed that even the most skilled navigators can struggle in stormy seas when their ships are ill-equipped or their crew is not adequately supported. This realization inspired me to delve deeper into the concept of developer experience, seeking to understand how it can be improved to empower developers to reach new heights of productivity and satisfaction.

In this book, I have endeavored to gather the pearls of wisdom, insights, and best practices I have collected from experienced captains of industry, thriving communities of practice, and my adventures navigating the treacherous waters of digital transformation. The chapters within these pages cover a wide range of topics, from fostering collaboration and continuous learning to implementing agile methodologies and leveraging cutting-edge tools and technologies.

This book is a testament to the power of human ingenuity and the spirit of exploration. It is a tribute to the developers who are charting the course of our digital world and a guide to help them navigate the ever-changing currents of digital transformation. I sincerely hope that the insights and strategies presented in this book will inspire, empower, and guide developers toward greater productivity and satisfaction, ultimately unleashing the full potential of their talents and creativity.

As you embark on this journey with me, I invite you to hoist your sails and approach the pages that follow with an open mind, eager to discover new horizons and challenge your assumptions. Together, we will uncover the keys to unlocking the true potential of developers, ensuring that they can continue to navigate our digital future with confidence, creativity, and unparalleled expertise.

Happy reading,
Marcus Maestri

Who This Book Is For

* * *

"Developer Experience: Navigating Digital Transformation for Productivity and Satisfaction" is a comprehensive guide that explores the many facets of developer experience, shedding light on creating an environment that fosters productivity, satisfaction, and innovation. This book is designed to cater to a diverse audience, each of whom can derive valuable insights and practical advice from its pages.

CTOs, CIOs, and IT Executives

As the leaders responsible for guiding their organizations through digital transformation, CTOs, CIOs, and IT executives will find this book a valuable resource. By understanding the importance of developer experience and implementing the strategies and best practices presented in this book, they can ensure that their organization is well-positioned to navigate the challenges of digital transformation and harness the full potential of their development teams.

Team Leads and Project Managers

This book will also benefit team leads and project managers overseeing software development projects. Understanding the developer experience can help them create a work environment that fosters creativity, engagement, and collaboration, ultimately leading to improved project outcomes. The book provides insights into managing teams effectively, promoting open communication, and implementing agile methodologies to enhance productivity and satisfaction.

Developers

At its core, this book is intended for developers of all levels, from novices to seasoned veterans. Developers will find valuable information on best practices, collaboration, continuous learning, and utilizing modern tools and methodologies. By understanding the fundamental principles of developer experience and applying the strategies outlined in this book, developers can optimize their productivity, enhance their satisfaction, and contribute to the overall success of their projects.

Human Resources and Talent Development Professionals

Professionals in human resources and talent development who focus on recruiting, onboarding, and retaining software developers can also gain valuable insights from this book. Understanding the factors contributing to a positive developer experience can help these professionals design more effective hiring processes, create better onboarding programs, and foster a work culture that attracts and retains top talent.

Educators and Mentors

Educators and mentors involved in the training and development of software developers, whether in formal educational settings or through mentorship programs, can benefit from the knowledge and insights shared in this book. By understanding the components of developer experience, educators can tailor their teaching methods and curricula to better prepare students for the challenges they will face in the rapidly evolving world of software development.

Conclusion

"Developer Experience: Navigating Digital Transformation for Productivity and Satisfaction" is a valuable resource for a wide range of individuals who play a role in the software development ecosystem. By understanding and implementing the principles and strategies outlined in this book, readers can enhance their experience, improve their team's performance, and contribute to the overall success of their organization's digital transformation journey.

How To Read This Book

* * *

This chapter is dedicated to helping you get the most out of your reading experience by providing tips and strategies for reading this book.

We first look at the cover of this book for a glimpse of the nautical context that awaits us within its pages. Here, the helm takes center stage – a fitting symbol, as it is the heart of a ship's steering system, guiding the rudder and ultimately directing the vessel on its course. Just as the helm is crucial in navigating the open seas, so too are the platform and tools that drive the evolution and growth of the software development industry.

Fading into the background, we see images of caravels, the iconic ships that once traversed the unknown waters in search of new continents and opportunities for cultural and societal transformation. These vessels serve as a poignant reminder of the spirit of exploration that has long characterized humanity's quest for knowledge and progress. With the same curiosity and determination, we set sail into the uncharted waters of digital innovation.

The compass, another essential element in our nautical theme, represents the importance of having a clear direction and a reliable reference point on our journey. As we face the challenges and uncertainties of an ever-evolving technological landscape, a well-defined path and strong guidance are invaluable in keeping us on course and helping us reach our desired destination.

Drawing inspiration from the rich history of seafaring exploration, this book aims to provide a perspective on the software development industry and the transformative power of digital tools and platforms. By delving into this fascinating world, we aim to capture the spirit of adventure and resilience that marked the voyages of the great explorers, applying their lessons to the challenges and opportunities that lie ahead in our digital odyssey.

The premise of this book is that even the seemingly obvious must be addressed. We will explore a wide range of topics, starting with straightforward yet effective practices like pair programming, which may appear elementary to some seasoned developers and leaders. From there, we will delve into more complex techniques, such as advanced deployments using GitOps on Kubernetes.

Although this book provides a comprehensive list of practices, the vastness of the development world means that some topics may only receive a cursory overview. We aim to emphasize each subject's importance, elucidate its benefits, and spark your curiosity to learn more about the areas that pique your interest.

With that in mind, we encourage you to immerse yourself in the topics discussed herein and determine how they can best serve your organization. Each chapter of this book begins with a heading summarising the following content. Skimming these headings can help you understand each chapter's main topics and themes.

The introduction to this book provides an overview of the content and explains the purpose and scope of the book. It can help you understand the context and background of the material and guide you on how to approach the content.

Taking notes can help you stay engaged with the material and retain your reading. Consider using a notebook, highlighter, or sticky notes to mark important passages or jot down questions or ideas that come to mind as you read.

Reading a book can be time-consuming, so it's important to pace yourself. Consider setting aside a specific amount of time each day or week to read, and stick to that schedule as much as possible.

After reading a chapter or section of the book, take a few minutes to reflect on what you've learned. Ask yourself questions like: What did I find most exciting or surprising? What questions do I still have? How does this relate to other things I've read or experienced?

Don't be afraid to go back and revisit sections of the book if you need clarification or want to review the material. You may find that certain areas become more meaningful or relevant as you progress through the book.

Chapter 1
Setting Sail on a Voyage of Discovery

* * *

In 1500, just as the last sunlight disappeared below the horizon, illuminating Lisbon's harbor in a subdued light, Pedro Álvares Cabral and his determined crew of 1,200 men readied themselves to embark on a journey that would significantly impact the course of history.

This skilled Portuguese navigator had been entrusted with the formidable task of commanding a fleet of 13 majestic ships, each primed and ready to establish new trade routes and extend Portugal's global influence.

The journey took an unexpected turn as Cabral's magnificent fleet set sail. Confronted by the daunting challenge of navigating the powerful winds and unpredictable currents along the African coast, Cabral boldly opted to steer westward, daring to venture further into the uncharted waters before him.

This seemingly innocuous choice would culminate in the accidental discovery of a new land, initially christened Ilha de Vera Cruz. As Cabral and his crew delved deeper into this enigmatic territory, they soon realized it was no mere island but an entirely new continent. They aptly renamed it Terra de Santa Cruz; today, we know this vast, rich land as Brazil.

Drawing inspiration from Cabral's extraordinary expedition, this book invites you on a thrilling and enlightening journey through the deep, tumultuous waters of the enterprise setting. As we navigate this literary adventure's pages, we will confront our mighty winds and swirling currents, propelling us in unforeseen directions.

Yet, as Cabral's awe-inspiring tale vividly illustrates, we often stumble upon the most astonishing discoveries when we courageously face these challenges head-on. Sometimes, we may not obtain what we desire; instead, we uncover what we never knew we needed.

Prepare to be thoroughly entertained and captivated as we embark on this remarkable voyage, charting a course through unexplored territories and making our serendipitous discoveries. With each enthralling chapter, we will delve deeper into infinite possibilities, confronting life's challenges with unwavering courage, insatiable curiosity, and an unyielding sense of adventure.

So, join me now as we hoist the sails and embark on this exhilarating odyssey, kindled by the indomitable spirit of Pedro Álvares Cabral and the untold discoveries that await us just beyond the horizon. Let us wholeheartedly embrace the twists and turns that lie ahead, for it is through life's unpredictable waters that we often unearth our most extraordinary and invaluable treasures.

Like the Portuguese navigators, every developer embarks on a distinct journey characterized by individual experiences, challenges, and triumphs that collectively shape their career in technology.

This book chronicles my odyssey, which commenced on the picturesque south coast of Brazil and ultimately led me to become a driving force in the developer experience domain, collaborating with some of the world's most groundbreaking and innovative companies.

My story is a testament to the power of passion, resilience, and an unwavering commitment to lifelong learning. From humble beginnings and pursuing self-taught programming, I navigated the ever-evolving landscape of software development, embracing new opportunities and overcoming obstacles at every turn. Along the way, I discovered the importance of cultivating a deep understanding of the technical and human aspects of the developer experience, which enabled me to unlock my true potential and contribute meaningfully to the industry.

This book delves into the pivotal moments, hard-earned lessons, and transformative experiences that have shaped my career. It offers an intimate glimpse into the various roles I've assumed, the companies I've had the privilege of working with, and the insights I've gleaned from collaborating with diverse teams across continents.

Beyond a personal narrative, this book aims to inspire and empower those who find themselves at any stage of their journey in the world of technology. It serves as a reminder that regardless of one's background or the challenges faced, with determination, adaptability, and a commitment to growth, it is possible to forge a fulfilling and impactful career in this ever-changing field.

Join me as we explore the twists and turns of my journey, uncovering the wisdom and inspiration that can be found in every step to becoming a successful developer and contributing to the exciting and rapidly evolving world of technology.

Lifelong Learning Commitment

* * *

Since childhood, I knew I wanted to pursue a career in the technology industry, and I was determined to gain the knowledge and skills needed to succeed on my terms. So, I decided to become a self-taught expert.

I started by diving deep into the world of technology, devouring every book, article, and tutorial I could find. I taught myself to code, build websites, and create small software projects to hone my skills. I also delved into business and entrepreneurship, studying successful companies and learning from their successes and failures.

As I continued on my self-taught journey, I developed a unique perspective on technology. Without the constraints of traditional academic programs, I could explore new ideas and think outside the box. I combined my technical skills with my business acumen, creating innovative solutions that helped me stand out in a crowded market.

Despite facing many obstacles along the way, I persevered. I knew that success would not come overnight, but I was willing to work to achieve my goals. As a self-taught kid, I learned to embrace failure as a learning opportunity, and I was always ready to pivot and try something new when things didn't go as planned.

Today, my self-taught journey has led me to a successful career in the technology industry. I have founded multiple companies, and industry experts and customers have recognized my innovative solutions. I have proven that you don't need a traditional education to succeed in technology as long as you have the drive, determination, and willingness to learn on your terms.

If you're considering taking the self-taught route, know it's possible to become a self-taught individual. With a passion for learning, a willingness to embrace failure, and a commitment to hard work, you, too, can achieve great things in the world of technology.

Despite these early setbacks and the challenges they presented, I remained steadfast in my determination to forge a career in technology. Driven by my passion for coding and an insatiable curiosity, I embarked on a journey of self-education, teaching myself the art of programming through online resources, books, and sheer persistence.

* * *

At 22, armed with my newfound programming skills, I took a leap of faith and launched a SaaS invoicing platform. While the venture was modest in its success—barely generating enough revenue to cover my living expenses—it was a crucial starting point in my career. This humble beginning allowed me to gain invaluable hands-on experience in software development and ignited my desire to hone my skills further and expand my knowledge.

This early stage of my journey is a testament to the power of resilience and the importance of embracing unconventional paths when pursuing one's passions. Though obstacles and detours marked the road, they ultimately set the stage for my future technological endeavors and helped shape my career trajectory. This stepping stone, however small, laid the foundation for the successes and experiences that would define my journey as a developer.

* * *

Biohacking

At 25, I felt like I was at a crossroads in my life. While I had achieved some success as a self-taught technology expert, I knew there was still so much more I wanted to accomplish. That's when I started to explore the world of biohacking and nootropics.

Biohacking encompasses the application of scientific and technological advancements to optimize one's physical and mental well-being. In conjunction with nootropics, natural or synthetic compounds purported to boost cognitive performance, I experienced a heightened concentration and mental acuity.

By incorporating it together with my keto and intermittent fasting habits, these approaches have empowered me to elevate my work to unprecedented heights. The impact of these practices and my journey might serve as an intriguing narrative for another book.

With this newfound focus and clarity, I bootstrapped a software consultancy specializing in developing mobile hybrid apps. Our team worked tirelessly to deliver high-quality apps that would appeal to users around the globe. And for a time, it seemed like we were on the path to success.

We successfully delivered 15 mobile hybrid apps to over a million users worldwide, and our client list grew each month. It was an exciting time, with the promise of even greater things.

But despite our hard work and success, it seemed like true success still eluded us. Each of our apps faced challenges, whether failing to generate enough revenue, facing stiff competition, or simply not gaining user traction.

It was a frustrating time. We had poured so much time, effort, and resources into these projects, only to see them fall short of our goals. But instead of giving up, we dug deeper, analyzing our processes, strategies, and approaches to see where we could improve.

Through this process of self-reflection and analysis, we learned some valuable lessons. We discovered that we needed to focus more on user needs and desires rather than simply creating apps we thought were cool. We also realized the importance of marketing and promotion, as even the best app in the world won't succeed if nobody knows about it.

Armed with this new knowledge, we pivoted our approach and began focusing on developing apps that solved real-world problems for our clients and users. We also invested more heavily in marketing and promotion, building relationships with influencers, and leveraging social media to spread the word about our apps.

Slowly but surely, we began to see the fruits of our labor. Our apps began to gain traction with users, generating more revenue and even attracting the attention of potential investors. It was a hard-fought victory, but we knew it was worth it.

Ultimately, I learned that true success is not about how many apps you develop or how much money you make—it's about learning from your failures, pivoting when necessary, and staying true to your goals and values. By leveraging the power of biohacking and nootropics and never giving up on my dreams, I was able to turn my struggles into a true success story.

Moving to Europe

The constant struggle to allocate time for refining my programming skills and keeping pace with the rapidly evolving market proved daunting. Undeterred, I persevered and applied for hundreds of positions in search of new opportunities, but each attempt was rejected. Nevertheless, the lessons I learned from biohacking and nootropics and my unwavering determination motivated my quest for technological growth and success.

One fateful day, while browsing LinkedIn, I came across a post detailing the highest-paying positions in IT for that year. To my surprise, the DevOps Engineer role topped the list. This revelation sparked my interest and fueled my desire to upskill to advance my career in the technology industry.

At this point, I decided to research high-paying positions, such as DevOps Engineer, to understand the requirements and skill set needed to succeed. I immersed myself in courses on building pipelines with tools like Jenkins, Ansible, Docker, Linux, AWS, and more. Within months, my efforts paid off: I was offered a full-time position and a relocation package to Stockholm, Sweden, and one year in, my work in building a customized parallel testing container solution and a pipeline that increased deployment capacity by 15 times earned me a promotion.

Empowered by the expertise I had acquired in CI/CD and DevOps, I felt ready to take on more significant challenges and pursue a more senior role in the industry. My search led me to my dream job as an architect at Red Hat's Open Innovation Labs—a renowned organization dedicated to helping businesses accelerate their digital transformation journeys using Open Source methodologies.

Joining Red Hat's Open Innovation Labs came with a unique blend of work arrangements. I had the flexibility to work from home while also having the opportunity to travel across Europe every week, with all expenses covered. This dynamic work setup allowed me to engage with diverse clients and explore new cultures while maintaining a solid connection to my home base.

Keen to expand my skill set and remain at the cutting edge of technology, I upskilled in Kubernetes and OpenShift—two powerful platforms designed to streamline container orchestration and application deployment. This further refinement of my expertise created opportunities to collaborate on world-class projects with an impressive portfolio of prestigious clients, including private companies such as VP Securities, Emirates, Vodafone, and Volvo, as well as renowned Nordic government agencies. These collaborations allowed me to apply my skills across diverse sectors, solidifying my reputation as a versatile and capable technology professional.

In my role at Red Hat's Open Innovation Labs, I worked closely with these clients, applying my knowledge of CI/CD, DevOps, Kubernetes, and OpenShift to help them navigate their digital transformation initiatives. Together, we developed innovative developer experience solutions that optimized their workflows, accelerated application deployment, and propelled their businesses to new heights.

This period in my career was marked by immense professional growth and the invaluable opportunity to contribute to the success of significant organizations in various industries. The experiences I gained at Red Hat's Open Innovation Labs enriched my understanding of the technology landscape and strengthened my passion for driving meaningful change in software development.

Concentrating on enhancing developer experience and productivity, I delved into the intricacies of GitOps, Continuous Integration (CI), Continuous Deployment (CD), and state-of-the-art tooling. My dedication to mastering these disciplines enabled me to streamline development processes, improve collaboration, and accelerate software delivery.

As I gained recognition for my expertise, I was promoted to the role of Senior Architect. In this capacity, I led high-value enterprise contracts worth €500,000 across the Nordics and Europe. My part involved guiding development teams, optimizing workflows, and ensuring seamless collaboration between developers and operations teams. By implementing GitOps, CI/CD, and modern tooling best practices, I was able to help our clients scale their operations, reduce time-to-market, and achieve their digital transformation goals.

In this journey, I was fortunate to work with diverse teams and industries, expanding my understanding of various business models and tailoring my approach to each client's needs. This hands-on experience allowed me to refine my skills, adapt to emerging technologies, and ultimately, drive meaningful change in the world of software development.

* * *

Then, a transformational event occurred: I became a father. This new and pivotal role brought with it the realization that I needed to prioritize my time at home, nurturing my growing family. The constant travel associated with my previous job was no longer conducive to my desired work-life balance.

Determined to find a position allowing me to spend more time with my loved ones, I searched for opportunities aligned with my values and expertise. As fate would have it, I discovered the perfect match: the Global Head of Developer Experience role at H&M Group.

Joining H&M Group provided me with a salary increase and offered me the flexibility to continue to work from home. This new position allowed me to continue contributing to the world of technology while being present and engaged in my family's daily life.

As the Global Head of Developer Experience, I leverage my extensive knowledge and skills to create an environment where developers can thrive, innovate, and collaborate effectively. My focus on nurturing a positive developer experience helps drive H&M Group's digital transformation and ensures the company stays at the forefront of the industry.

In this new chapter of my life, I found a fulfilling balance between my professional aspirations and responsibilities, proving that it is possible to excel in both realms. The ability to work from home, close to my family, has enriched my life in countless ways and reaffirmed the importance of prioritizing what truly matters.

This book serves as a compelling narrative, illustrating the incredible impact that a strong mindset, unwavering determination, and the power of self-improvement can have on driving digital transformation and crafting an exceptional developer experience. Through sharing my journey and insights, I aim to illuminate the potential within each of us to overcome challenges, embrace growth, and emerge as leaders in the technology field.

However, this book is not based solely on personal observations and opinions but on a solid foundation of evidence-based research. Each topic covered in this book has been carefully researched and analyzed, emphasizing the most current and relevant research findings. I encourage readers to continue studying and exploring the topics covered in this book, as there is always more to learn and discover.

A commitment to continuous learning and self-improvement is essential for success in any field, particularly in the ever-evolving technology field. By embracing a growth mindset and seeking new knowledge and insights, readers can continue to drive digital transformation and cultivate an exceptional developer experience for themselves and their organizations.

I aspire for the experiences and lessons recounted in these pages to inspire and encourage you, the reader, to forge your unique path in technology. By sharing the highs and lows of my journey, I want to demonstrate that it is possible to navigate the industry's ever-evolving landscape and achieve success, even in the face of adversity.

This book is an invitation to relentlessly pursue the dreams that drive your passion for innovation and harness the power of resilience, adaptability, and self-improvement as you embark on your journey. As you delve into the following chapters, may you find the inspiration and motivation to cultivate your exceptional developer experience, push the boundaries of what is possible, and ultimately, contribute to the ongoing digital transformation shaping our world.

Chapter 2
Basic Navigation

* * *

As the tide rises and the salty sea breeze fills our sails, we embark on a thrilling expedition into the world of developer experience. Before we delve into the depths of this vast ocean, it is essential to familiarize ourselves with the basics of navigation. With a firm grasp of key concepts, directions, the current state, and weather, we will be better prepared for the possible turbulent waters.

In this maiden chapter, we will explore the fundamentals of developer experience, drawing inspiration from the world of nautical navigation. By understanding the importance of these foundational elements, we will be well-equipped to steer our organization through the challenging and ever-changing seas of software development and digital transformation.

As I reflect on my journey navigating the enterprise software development world, the beautiful place called the developer experience organization still resonates with me. In this new chapter, we'll focus on the broader IT industry, delving into the importance of understanding its basics and current market trends. Our goal is to establish a solid footing before exploring digital transformation and the challenges that lie ahead in developer experience.

We will venture into the dark clouds of IT, exploring the industry's pain points and challenges developers face. Recognizing these challenges will help us appreciate the importance of a seamless developer experience in overcoming them and their immense impact on the success of any digital transformation initiative.

We'll also examine the ongoing mental model shifts in the IT industry, shaping how developers think and approach their work. Gaining insight into these shifts will allow us to understand better the transformational power of developer experience in fostering innovation and adaptation in a rapidly evolving landscape.

Furthermore, we'll revisit the story of the evolution of the developer experience, exploring its transformative journey over the years. This historical perspective will provide valuable insights into the factors that have contributed to the current state of developer experience and how it has influenced the IT industry.

With this background, we'll be well-equipped to delve deeper into digital transformation, identifying the challenges and opportunities ahead. As organizations strive to adapt and innovate in response to market demands, understanding the critical role of developer experience becomes increasingly essential.

In conclusion, this chapter will serve as a bridge between my journey and the broader context of the IT industry, setting the stage for our exploration of digital transformation and the crucial role developer experience plays. By understanding the foundations of the industry and the ongoing market trends, we'll be better equipped to tackle the challenges ahead and unlock the full potential of developer experience as a powerful weapon in our digital transformation journey.

Navigating The Dark Clouds

* * *

As we explore developer experience, it is crucial first to comprehend the obstacles and difficulties currently afflicting the IT market. This chapter endeavors to illuminate the array of issues contributing to a pervasive negative sentiment within the sector, obstructing innovation, development, and cooperative efforts.

The importance of developer experience in today's rapidly evolving technological landscape cannot be understated. It is the backbone of a thriving IT market, ensuring developers can efficiently and effectively work together, create new solutions, and adapt to ever-changing demands. However, as we delve deeper into the subject, we must acknowledge the numerous hurdles developers and organizations must overcome to optimize their working environments and achieve success.

In this chapter, we will unravel the complex web of challenges that permeate the IT industry, focusing on the factors that stifle creativity, hamper productivity, and undermine the collaborative spirit essential for progress. By examining these issues in detail, we aim to provide a comprehensive understanding of the barriers that must be addressed to foster a more supportive and fruitful developer experience.

Through this analysis, we hope to pave the way for meaningful discussions and innovative solutions to counteract the negativity that currently plagues the IT market. By tackling these challenges head-on and embracing the transformative power of developer experience, organizations can break free from the constraints that hinder their growth and unlock their full potential in the world of technology.

Ineffective team design and cross-team dependencies are frequently at the core of numerous IT challenges organizations face today. When teams are not designed with collaboration and communication in mind, they often struggle to navigate the complexities of their projects efficiently. This is further exacerbated by cross-team dependencies, which can create bottlenecks and hinder the flow of information and resources between different organizational groups.

These issues stem from organizational structures that inadvertently obstruct effective collaboration. Hierarchical arrangements, rigid departmental silos, and unclear roles and responsibilities can all contribute to the fragmentation of efforts, making it difficult for teams to work together cohesively towards a shared goal. This disjointed approach can lead to duplicated work, miscommunication, and slow and cumbersome progress.

Furthermore, when teams cannot collaborate effectively, they may lack a comprehensive understanding of the overall project objectives and the contributions of other teams. This can result in misaligned priorities, with teams working in isolation and making decisions based on incomplete information. This disjointedness impacts the final product's quality and the organization's overall efficiency.

* * *

To overcome these challenges, organizations must prioritize establishing a collaborative culture, breaking down silos, and fostering open lines of communication across teams. This can be achieved through various means, such as adopting agile methodologies, implementing cross-functional teams, and encouraging a culture of knowledge-sharing and continuous learning.

By addressing the root causes of ineffective team design and cross-team dependencies, organizations can create an environment that promotes seamless collaboration, enabling teams to work together more efficiently and accelerate progress. This will lay the foundation for a more positive developer experience, driving innovation and success in the rapidly evolving IT market.

The fear of reprisal for failure is another pervasive issue within the IT industry, with detrimental consequences for creativity and innovation. In an environment where mistakes are met with harsh criticism and blame, individuals and teams may become risk-averse, opting for safe, incremental improvements over bold, transformative ideas. This oppressive atmosphere constrains the potential for groundbreaking advancements and hinders the industry's progress.

This fear-driven mindset can give rise to what is commonly referred to as feature factories. In these settings, teams become trapped in a perpetual cycle of churning out new features to satisfy an ever-growing backlog while neglecting to address the underlying issues that may be causing problems in the first place. The primary focus shifts towards ticking off tasks and meeting short-term goals, often at the expense of long-term vision and strategy.

In a feature factory, emphasizing quantity over quality can lead to a bloated and unmanageable product. New features are continuously added without properly evaluating their necessity or impact on the end-user experience. Moreover, the constant pressure to deliver can result in teams overlooking opportunities for optimization and refinement and dismissing valuable feedback from customers and other stakeholders.

To break free from the feature factory mindset, organizations must foster a culture that embraces failure as an opportunity for learning and growth. This can be achieved by promoting psychological safety, where individuals feel comfortable taking risks, sharing ideas, and admitting mistakes without fear of negative consequences. Encouraging open dialogue, constructive feedback, and continuous improvement can help teams to shift their focus from merely delivering features to addressing the root causes of issues and driving meaningful, sustainable progress.

Organizations can empower their teams to think critically, challenge the status quo, and pursue groundbreaking solutions by creating an environment that supports and celebrates innovation. In doing so, they can cultivate a more positive developer experience and propel the IT industry forward, unlocking new possibilities and fostering lasting success.

In the fast-paced IT industry, it is too familiar for customer voices to become lost amidst internal priorities and competing demands. With limited opportunities for genuine engagement and an insufficient understanding of customer needs, product development can often become disconnected from the people it aims to serve. This disconnection can lead to a slow time to market and a misguided focus on delivering outputs rather than meaningful outcomes that truly benefit the end users.

When organizations fail to prioritize customer input and feedback, they risk developing products misaligned with the target audience's needs, preferences, and expectations. This misalignment can result in wasted resources, missed opportunities, and diminished customer satisfaction. Ultimately, organizations may struggle to gain traction in the market and face an uphill battle to retain customers and secure their loyalty.

To counteract these issues, organizations must emphasize customer-centricity, ensuring that end-users' needs and perspectives are consistently integrated throughout product development. This can be achieved by implementing various practices, such as conducting regular customer interviews, surveys, and focus groups;

involving customers in the early stages of creativity and design; and establishing feedback loops to gather and incorporate user insights continuously.

* * *

Additionally, organizations should strive to shift their focus from simply delivering outputs—such as features, lines of code, or completed tasks—to creating meaningful outcomes that have tangible value to customers. This outcome-oriented approach necessitates the establishment of clear, customer-centric goals and metrics to guide decision-making and track progress. By prioritizing outcomes over outputs, organizations can ensure that their efforts are directed toward solving real problems and delivering genuine value to their customers.

Organizations can bridge the gap between product development and customer needs by fostering a customer-centric culture and focusing intensely on outcomes. This alignment will lead to a more positive developer experience and a faster time to market, increased customer satisfaction, and long-term success in the competitive IT landscape.

Enterprise processes, particularly within large organizations, can often be complex, bureaucratic, and cumbersome. These cumbersome processes may hinder innovation and agility, making it difficult for teams to adapt and respond to evolving market demands and customer needs. This rigidity not only hampers progress but also exacerbates the disconnect between demand and capacity, creating inefficiencies and hindering the effective allocation of resources.

Traditional budgeting and funding processes are prime examples of outdated practices impeding innovation. These processes tend to be inflexible and focused on maintaining the status quo, prioritizing predictable returns on investment over pursuing new, potentially transformative opportunities. In many cases, annual budgets are determined based on historical data and assumptions, which may not accurately reflect the organization's current needs, priorities, or market conditions.

This conventional approach to budgeting and funding can stifle creativity and hinder the development of innovative solutions, as teams are often discouraged from taking risks and exploring uncharted territory. Furthermore, the lack of flexibility in these processes can make it challenging for organizations to reallocate resources in response to emerging opportunities or unforeseen challenges, limiting their ability to pivot and capitalize on new trends.

To overcome these obstacles and foster an environment that supports innovation, organizations must reevaluate their existing processes and adopt more agile, adaptive approaches to budgeting and resource allocation. This can include implementing rolling forecasts, allocating funds based on value delivery, and embracing adaptive budgeting techniques prioritizing outcomes over outputs. By adopting these practices, organizations can cultivate a more flexible and responsive approach to resource management, enabling them to seize opportunities and navigate the ever-changing IT landscape more effectively.

Ultimately, by streamlining enterprise processes and adopting more agile approaches to budgeting and funding, organizations can bridge the gap between demand and capacity, fostering a more positive developer experience and promoting a culture of innovation that drives long-term success.

Also, competing priorities can often lead to a dissonance between technology advancements and organizational progress. As technology progresses, organizations may struggle to keep pace, held back by internal conflicts, outdated processes, and a lack of strategic alignment. This discord can create significant challenges, erasing trust between business and IT departments.

Communication and collaboration suffer when business and IT teams operate in silos with misaligned goals and priorities. This disconnect can result in a lack of shared understanding of each department's objectives, leading to hate, resentment, and mutual suspicion. The business side may perceive IT as an obstacle to progress, slow to deliver solutions, and resistant to change. At the same time, IT may view the business as demanding, unrealistic, and unwilling to invest the necessary resources to drive innovation.

This lack of trust can have far-reaching consequences for the organization. It can lead to inefficiencies, duplicated efforts, and missed opportunities as both sides struggle to work together effectively. Moreover, the resulting tension can create a toxic work environment, stifling creativity and hindering productivity.

Organizations must prioritize aligning their strategic goals and objectives to bridge this divide and foster greater collaboration between business and IT departments. This can be achieved through open communication, cross-functional collaboration, and shared decision-making. Encouraging regular dialogue between departments can help to dispel misunderstandings, clarify expectations, and foster a shared understanding of each other's challenges and priorities.

* * *

Additionally, organizations should consider implementing frameworks such as Agile or DevOps, which promote collaboration, transparency, and shared responsibility between business and IT. These approaches can help break down the silos between departments, enabling teams to work more closely together and focus on delivering value to the organization.

By fostering greater alignment and trust between business and IT departments, organizations can unlock their full potential and ensure they are well-positioned to keep pace with the rapidly changing technology landscape. Embracing collaboration and strategic alignment will improve the developer experience and drive the organization's long-term success and competitive advantage.

The consequences of misaligned priorities, poor communication, and lack of trust between business and IT departments can be far-reaching, ultimately leading to the loss of customers and revenue. As organizations struggle to keep pace with the evolving market demands, they risk falling behind competitors, losing their competitive edge, and experiencing declining customer satisfaction. This creates a sense of urgency to address the underlying issues and challenges, yet many organizations find themselves ill-equipped.

One significant factor that compounds these challenges is the disempowerment of teams, who often lack the autonomy and authority to make decisions and solve problems effectively. This disempowerment can manifest in several ways, including overbearing management, rigid hierarchical structures, and bureaucratic processes that stifle innovation and creativity. When teams feel disempowered, they become less engaged and motivated, leading to lower productivity and decreased job satisfaction.

Moreover, the absence of solid portfolio leadership teams can exacerbate this helplessness. Without influential leaders to set a clear strategic direction, prioritize initiatives, and allocate resources, teams may be adrift in a sea of competing priorities and unclear objectives. This lack of clear leadership can hinder the organization's ability to identify and address the root causes of its challenges, leading to a cycle of stagnation and decline.

To break this cycle and empower teams to tackle the pressing issues, organizations must invest in developing strong portfolio leadership teams and fostering a culture that supports autonomy and decision-making at all levels. This can be achieved by:

- Clearly defining roles and responsibilities within the organization, ensuring everyone understands their contributions and how they fit into the larger strategic picture.
- Implementing a more decentralized decision-making structure empowers teams to make decisions and take ownership of their work.

- Encouraging a culture of trust, transparency, and open communication, where employees feel comfortable sharing ideas, raising concerns, and asking for help.
- Providing ongoing training and development opportunities, equipping employees with the skills and knowledge they need to excel in their roles and contribute to the organization's success.

By empowering teams and fostering strong portfolio leadership, organizations can create an environment where employees feel engaged, motivated, and well-equipped to address their challenges. This leads to improved customer satisfaction and revenue and a healthier, more productive work environment that drives long-term success and growth.

And again, many leaders in the IT industry continue to cling to outdated command-and-control management styles, stifling collaboration and innovation. Teams struggle to align their efforts with business outcomes, widening the gap between IT and the broader organization.

The IT industry's capacity to adapt and evolve in the face of numerous challenges is further hampered by the difficulty of hiring talented professionals and the aging of subject matter experts. As experienced professionals retire or move on, they leave a void in knowledge and expertise that can be difficult to fill. This talent gap poses a significant threat to the industry. Organizations struggle to find and retain the skilled individuals necessary to drive innovation and stay competitive in an ever-changing landscape. Several factors contribute to this talent gap:

- Rapid pace of technological change: The IT industry is characterized by constant innovation and an ever-evolving landscape of tools, platforms, and methodologies. This rapid pace can make it challenging for professionals to keep up with the latest trends and technologies. At the same time, organizations may find identifying and hiring talent with the proper skill set challenging.

- Increasing demand for specialized skills: As technology becomes more complex, organizations require professionals with technical skills to address specific challenges and needs. This increasing demand for specialization can make finding talent with the right combination of expertise and experience challenging.
- Generational shift: The IT industry is experiencing a generational shift as older professionals with deep expertise retire or move on from their roles. This shift can create a knowledge vacuum, as younger professionals may lack the experience and insights of their predecessors.
- Skills gap: The rapid pace of technological change and the increasing demand for specialized skills can lead to a skills gap, where the supply of talent with the necessary expertise fails to meet the demand. This gap can make it challenging for organizations to find and retain talent, resulting in increased competition for skilled professionals and higher costs associated with talent acquisition and retention.

Organizations must prioritize strategic workforce planning and talent management to address this talent gap and ensure the industry's ability to adapt and evolve. This includes:

- Fostering a culture of continuous learning: Encouraging employees to stay current with the latest trends, technologies, and best practices will help organizations maintain a competitive edge and close the skills gap.
- Investing in employee development: Providing ongoing training and development opportunities will ensure that

employees have the skills and knowledge necessary to excel in their roles and contribute to the organization's success.
- Creating mentorship programs: Pairing experienced professionals with younger talent can help bridge the knowledge gap and transfer valuable insights and expertise from one generation to the next.
- Implementing flexible and adaptable hiring practices: Embracing diverse hiring strategies, such as considering candidates with non-traditional backgrounds or leveraging remote work to access a broader talent pool, can help organizations find and retain skilled professionals.
- Developing vital succession planning: Identifying and nurturing high-potential employees for future leadership roles can help organizations ensure continuity and maintain institutional knowledge as experienced professionals retire or move on.

By proactively addressing the talent gap and investing in the development and retention of skilled professionals, organizations can help ensure the IT industry's ability to adapt and evolve in the face of ongoing challenges, fostering innovation and long-term success.

Yikes! That was a doom-and-gloom tour of the IT industry, wasn't it? Don't worry; we've only scratched the surface of the challenges, making it exciting. Now we have the perfect setup for a heroic transformation tale! So, strap in and buckle up because we'll dive into those obstacles head-on in the upcoming chapters.

We'll embark on a thrilling journey, exploring how we can turn the tide on these pesky issues using the mighty power of developer experience as our weapon of choice. Together, we'll forge a path to digital transformation and usher in a new era of IT greatness. Get ready for a rollercoaster of learning, laughter, and—dare I say it—hope for a brighter future in the IT market. Onward!

The Changing Currents

* * *

A focus on resource efficiency and a hierarchical, top-down management approach has long characterized the IT industry. However, in recent years, a new system has emerged that values innovation, collaboration, and a customer-centric focus. This shift has required a fundamental change in how organizations think about and approach technology and has led to a series of mental model shifts that are transforming the industry.

This chapter will explore some essential mental model shifts in the IT industry. From moving from simple to complex to shifting from producer-centric to customer-centric, we will examine how these changes impact the industry and what they mean for developers and organizations alike. We will also discuss the benefits of these shifts and how they can help organizations thrive in an ever-changing technological landscape.

Moving From Simple to Complex:

One example of this mental model shift can be seen in the evolution of software development methodologies. In the early days of computing, waterfall development was the norm, with each phase of the development process completed sequentially.

However, as software systems grew more complex, the limitations of this approach became apparent, leading to the development of more agile methodologies like Scrum and Kanban. These approaches prioritize flexibility, adaptability, and collaboration, allowing development teams to respond more effectively to changing requirements and market conditions.

Another example can be found in the rise of artificial intelligence and machine learning. As these technologies have advanced, they have become increasingly complex, requiring developers to understand algorithms, statistics, and data analysis deeply.

At the same time, these technologies have created new opportunities for innovation and problem-solving, with applications ranging from medical diagnosis to fraud detection.

The shift towards greater complexity is also evident in the move toward cloud computing and containerization. These technologies allow organizations to build and deploy applications at scale but require more excellent technical expertise and team collaboration.

Organizations have developed new tools and practices to address these challenges, such as DevOps and site reliability engineering, prioritizing automation, testing, and continuous improvement.

The move from a simple to a complex IT industry is a clear example of the need for continuous learning and adaptation. As technologies and methodologies evolve, developers and organizations must be willing to embrace new approaches and strategies to stay competitive and drive innovation.

Moving From Resource Efficiency To Flow Efficiency:

Another critical mental model shift in the IT industry is the move from resource efficiency to flow efficiency. In the past, organizations focused on maximizing resource efficiency, often at the expense of flexibility and responsiveness.

However, in today's rapidly changing technological landscape, organizations must prioritize flow efficiency, which values speed, adaptability, and responsiveness. By focusing on flow efficiency, organizations can better meet changing customer demands and achieve better overall results.

Moving From Managing People To Managing The System:

Historically, IT industry management has focused on managing individual workers. However, as the industry has become more complex, there has been a shift toward managing the system.

This involves creating processes and structures that enable teams to work more effectively and efficiently rather than relying on individual heroics. Organizations can create a more collaborative, adaptive culture that can better respond to changing needs by operating the system rather than just the people.

Moving From Producer-centric To Customer-centric:

The shift from producer-centric to customer-centric is another significant mental model shift in the IT industry. In the past, organizations focused primarily on creating products and services that met their own needs rather than the needs of their customers.

However, as technology has evolved, so too have customer expectations. Today, organizations must understand and respond to customer needs quickly and effectively to remain competitive. By shifting to a customer-centric approach, organizations can create products and services that better meet the needs of their customers, leading to greater customer satisfaction and loyalty.

Moving From Top-down Leadership To Servant Leadership By Influence:

The shift from top-down leadership to servant leadership by influence is a critical mental model shift in the IT industry. In the past, organizations were often characterized by rigid hierarchies and top-down decision-making. However, in today's fast-paced, rapidly evolving industry, organizations must be able to adapt quickly to changing circumstances.

Servant leadership by influence encourages leaders to empower their teams and create a culture of collaboration and shared ownership. By doing so, organizations can become more agile and better respond to changing customer needs.

Moving From Production Workers To Knowledge Workers:

As technology has evolved, so too have the roles and responsibilities of workers in the IT industry. In the past, the industry was dominated by production workers focused on building and maintaining technology systems.

However, as technology has become more sophisticated, there has been a shift toward knowledge workers concentrating on problem-solving and innovation. This shift has required new skills and competencies, including collaborating effectively and adapting quickly to changing circumstances.

Moving From Individual Heroes To Team Success:

In the past, the IT industry was characterized by individual heroes who were celebrated for their achievements. However, as the industry has become more complex, there has been a shift towards team success, with organizations recognizing the importance of collaboration and teamwork in achieving results.

By emphasizing team success over individual heroics, organizations can create a more collaborative, adaptive culture that can better respond to changing customer needs.

Moving From Failure = Embarrassment To Failure = Learning Experience:

One of the most critical mental model shifts in the IT industry has been the move from failure as a source of embarrassment to being viewed as a valuable learning experience. In the past, organizations were often focused on minimizing risk and avoiding failure at all costs.

However, this approach often led to a lack of innovation and an inability to adapt to changing circumstances. Today, organizations are encouraged to embrace failure as an opportunity to learn and grow, leading to more incredible innovation and adaptability.

Moving From Large Projects To Small Initiatives:

Another essential mental model shift in the IT industry is the move from large projects to small initiatives. In the past, organizations often focused on large, complex projects that required significant time and resources. However, these projects often lacked flexibility and adaptability, making responding to changing customer needs difficult.

Today, organizations are encouraged to focus on small, manageable initiatives that can be completed quickly and with minimal resources. This approach allows organizations to be more agile and better respond to changing customer needs.

Moving From Annual Budgeting To Continuous Funding:

Traditionally, the IT industry has relied on annual budgeting to fund projects and initiatives. However, this approach can be inflexible and make it challenging to respond to changing circumstances.

Today, organizations are encouraged to adopt a continuous funding model for greater flexibility and adaptability. By continually funding initiatives, organizations can be more responsive to changing customer needs and ensure that resources are allocated to the most critical projects at any time.

Moving From Project Managers To Team Leads:

In the past, project managers were often seen as the driving force behind successful IT projects. However, as the industry has evolved, there has been a shift towards team-based approaches prioritizing collaboration and shared ownership.

Today, team leads are often seen as more effective than project managers, as they can better empower their teams and create a culture of collaboration and shared ownership. This approach allows for greater flexibility and adaptability and can help organizations to be more responsive to changing customer needs.

Moving From Functional Specialists To Generalizing Specialists:

Another essential mental model shift in the IT industry is the move from functional specialists to generalizing specialists. In the past, organizations often relied on specialists in a specific area of technology or business.

However, this approach can lead to silos and a lack of collaboration. Today, organizations are encouraged to adopt a more generalized T-shaped approach, where cross-functional team members have a broad range of skills and competencies. This approach allows for greater collaboration and can help organizations to be more agile and better able to respond to changing customer needs.

The Evolution of Developer Experience

* * *

The history of developer experience (DX) can be traced back to the earliest days of software development, but it has evolved significantly over the years. While not an exhaustive account, this brief history provides a general overview of the critical milestones and trends that have shaped the concept of developer experience.

Early days of programming (the 1940s-1960s):

During this period, programming was primarily done in low-level assembly languages and machine code. Developer experience was not a significant concern, as the focus was mainly on making computers work and solving specific problems. Programmers had to deal with limited memory, slow processing speeds, and a lack of debugging tools. Writing, testing, and deploying code was often laborious and time-consuming.

The emergence of high-level languages (the 1950s-1970s)

High-level programming languages like FORTRAN, COBOL, and LISP emerged, making it easier for developers to write and maintain code. These languages removed some hardware complexities and helped improve the developer experience. With the introduction of compilers and interpreters, developers no longer had to write machine code directly, which allowed them to work more efficiently and focus on problem-solving rather than low-level details. This period also saw the emergence of early integrated development environments (IDEs), such as IBM's VisualAge, which provided a more user-friendly experience for writing, debugging, and testing code.

Structured programming and modular design (the 1960s-1980s):

Concepts like structured programming and modular design led to better software organization and more manageable codebases. This positively impacted the developer experience, making it easier to understand and maintain code.

Pioneered by influential computer scientists like Edsger Dijkstra and Niklaus Wirth, structured programming encouraged well-defined control structures. It discouraged the use of unstructured jumps (e.g., GOTO statements).

Modular design, on the other hand, promoted the separation of code into smaller, reusable components that could be developed and tested independently. This approach made it easier for developers to collaborate, share code, and reduce the complexity of their projects.

The rise of IDEs and developer tools (the 1980s-1990s):

Integrated development environments (IDEs) like Visual Studio, Eclipse, and later JetBrains products provided advanced code editing, debugging, and management capabilities, significantly improving the developer experience.

IDEs combine various tools, such as source code editors, compilers, debuggers, and build automation tools, into a unified interface. This enabled developers to work more efficiently by reducing the need to switch between multiple applications and streamlining the development process.

Furthermore, introducing features like code completion, syntax highlighting, and version control integration helped developers write and manage code more effectively, reducing the chances of errors and enhancing overall productivity.

Open-source movement (1990s-present)

Open-source movement (1990s-present): The growth of the open-source movement led to an explosion of libraries, frameworks, and tools available to developers. This has made it easier for developers to build applications more efficiently and effectively, enhancing their experience.

Open-source projects like Linux, Apache, MySQL, and PHP (collectively known as the LAMP stack) have provided developers with free and powerful tools for building web applications. The open-source community has also fostered a spirit of collaboration and knowledge-sharing, developing countless resources such as tutorials, documentation, and forums to help developers learn and troubleshoot issues.

The widespread adoption of open-source technologies has contributed to a vast ecosystem of software components that can be easily integrated into projects, allowing developers to focus on their unique business logic instead of reinventing the wheel. This has accelerated development and empowered developers to innovate and create more complex and sophisticated applications.

Agile and DevOps methodologies (2000s-present)

Adopting Agile and DevOps methodologies encouraged continuous integration, continuous delivery, and more collaborative development processes, contributing to better developer experiences. Agile methods, such as Scrum and Kanban, shifted the focus from a traditional waterfall approach to iterative and incremental development. This enabled developers to be more responsive to changing requirements, receive regular feedback from stakeholders, and deliver value to end-users more quickly.

DevOps emerged as a cultural movement to bridge the gap between development and operations teams. It emphasized the importance of cross-functional collaboration, automation, and shared responsibility for the entire software development lifecycle. As a result, developers became more involved in deploying and monitoring their applications, gaining a better understanding of the operational aspects and ensuring the smooth functioning of their software in production environments.

The combination of Agile and DevOps practices has led to the widespread adoption of tools and platforms that streamline the development process, such as version control systems (e.g., Git), continuous integration and continuous deployment (CI/CD) tools (e.g., Jenkins, Travis CI, and CircleCI), containerization technologies (e.g., Docker), and infrastructure-as-code (e.g., Terraform). These tools have played a significant role in automating repetitive tasks, reducing manual intervention, and minimizing the risk of human errors, ultimately leading to an enhanced developer experience.

Furthermore, the collaborative nature of Agile and DevOps methodologies has fostered better communication and teamwork among developers, testers, and operations personnel. This has improved the quality of software being developed and created a more supportive and enjoyable working environment for developers, positively impacting their overall experience and job satisfaction.

The rise of web APIs and developer portals (2000s-present)

As APIs (Application Programming Interfaces) became the backbone of modern applications, API providers focused on developer experience by creating comprehensive documentation, interactive API consoles, SDKs (Software Development Kits), and other resources to make it easier for developers to integrate and work with their APIs. This shift was driven by the increasing importance of interoperability and the need for different software systems to communicate with each other effectively.

API documentation emerged as a crucial aspect of developer experience, as clear, concise, and accurate documentation enables developers to understand how to use an API, its available endpoints, and the expected request and response formats. Many API providers have adopted tools such as Swagger, Postman, and Apiary to generate interactive documentation that developers can easily explore and test.

Interactive API consoles have also become a popular feature in developer portals, providing developers with a user-friendly interface to interact with the API directly, experiment with various API calls, and better understand the API's functionality. These consoles often include features like auto-generated code snippets, authentication helpers, and error message explanations, further simplifying the integration process.

SDKs are another valuable resource for developers, offering pre-built libraries and tools to simplify the integration of APIs into various programming languages and platforms. By providing SDKs, API providers can reduce the amount of boilerplate code developers need to write and help them get up and running more quickly.

Developer portals often include additional resources such as sample applications, tutorials, and community forums, which help developers learn how to use the API effectively, troubleshoot issues, and share knowledge with their peers.

In summary, the rise of web APIs and developer portals has emphasized developer experience as API providers strive to create accessible, user-friendly resources that empower developers to integrate their APIs more efficiently and effectively. This focus on developer experience has not only led to better and more reliable software. Still, it has also fostered community and collaboration among developers working with these APIs.

The emergence of low-code/no-code platforms (2010s-present)

Low-code/no-code platforms like Salesforce, OutSystems, and Appian have made it possible for non-developers, sometimes referred to as "citizen developers," to create and deploy applications, greatly expanding the reach of software development and further highlighting the importance of developer experience.

These platforms are designed to be user-friendly and accessible to users with limited or no programming knowledge. They provide visual development environments and drag-and-drop interfaces that enable them to build applications using pre-built components and templates. By simplifying the development process, low-code/no-code platforms empower a more comprehensive range of individuals and teams to create custom software solutions without requiring extensive coding expertise.

This democratization of software development has led to a renewed focus on developer experience as platform providers strive to create intuitive, easy-to-use tools that cater to a diverse user base with varying technical expertise. Critical aspects of developer experience in low-code/no-code platforms include:

Visual development environments enable users to design applications visually, arranging components on a canvas and configuring their properties and behavior through graphical interfaces. This approach allows users to see the structure and layout of their application as they build it, making the development process more intuitive and approachable.

Pre-built components and templates: Low-code/no-code platforms offer a library of pre-built components, such as forms, data tables, and navigation elements, that users can easily add to their applications. These components have built-in functionality and can be customized to suit the application's requirements. Templates for common application types and use cases are also provided, giving users a starting point for their projects and reducing the time it takes to build an application from scratch.

Integration with existing systems and services: To be truly effective, low-code/no-code platforms must integrate seamlessly with existing systems, databases, and APIs. This allows users to leverage the data and functionality of their existing infrastructure while building new applications. Platform providers often offer pre-built connectors and integration tools to simplify this process and ensure a smooth developer experience.

Collaboration and version control: Low-code/no-code platforms often include features that facilitate collaboration among team members and provide version control to track changes to an application over time. This enables users to work together efficiently, share ideas, and roll back to previous versions of the application if needed.

Learning resources and support: To cater to users with diverse skill sets, low-code/no-code platforms often provide a range of learning resources, such as tutorials, documentation, and community forums, as well as dedicated support services to assist users in their development journey.

The emergence of low-code/no-code platforms has not only expanded the reach of software development. Still, it has also highlighted the importance of developer experience for users of all skill levels. By focusing on accessibility, ease of use, and comprehensive support, these platforms enable new developers to create custom software solutions more efficiently and effectively than ever.

The emergence of AI/ML coding assistants (2010s-present)

With chat and terminal interfaces integrated into every part of your workflow, tools such as GitHub Copilot X promises to revolutionize the developer experience by providing a context-aware, intelligent coding assistant that understands your project and codebase.

Context-aware conversations: Employs advanced natural language processing (NLP) techniques to understand and interpret your queries and provide relevant suggestions, considering the context of your project and its requirements. This allows you to engage in more intuitive and productive conversations with the AI assistant, helping you to overcome challenges and move forward with your development tasks more efficiently.

AI-generated content: It can generate various types of content, such as pull request (PR) descriptions, test cases, and code snippets, based on the context and requirements of your project. By leveraging OpenAI GPT-4's powerful language generation capabilities, it can create high-quality content that saves time and enhances the quality of your project documentation and codebase.

Seamless workflow integration: It is designed to be integrated into every part of your development workflow, from code editing and debugging to version control and collaboration. This ensures that the AI assistant is always available to provide insights, suggestions, and support whenever needed, making your development process smoother and more efficient.

The emergence of AI/ML coding assistants, like GitHub Copilot X, represents a significant shift in the developer experience. By harnessing the power of artificial intelligence and machine learning, these assistants can automate and streamline various aspects of the development process, enabling developers to focus on higher-level tasks and creative problem-solving. This leads to more efficient development and fosters innovation and growth in the software industry.

As AI-powered software development tools like OpenAI GPT-4

and Github Copilot X become more sophisticated and widely adopted, the developer experience will be significantly enhanced, allowing developers to work more efficiently and effectively, ultimately leading to the creation of more innovative and impactful software solutions.

Throughout this evolution, the focus on developer experience has continued to grow. Organizations recognize that a positive developer experience is crucial for attracting and retaining top talent, increasing productivity, and fostering innovation.

Chapter 3
Winds Of Change

* * *

Just as sailors must adjust their sails to harness the power of shifting winds, organizations must be agile and adaptable in the face of technological advancements and industry trends. Digital Transformation is a prime example of such a change, which compels organizations to reassess their strategies and embrace new technologies to remain competitive and successful in today's rapidly evolving landscape.

Much like the legendary Viking seafarers who conquered the seas and discovered new lands, organizations today must navigate the uncharted waters of digital transformation. The Vikings were renowned for their incredible ability to traverse vast oceanic distances and reach their destinations with remarkable precision.

One of their most fascinating navigational tools was the enigmatic sunstone. This crystal allowed them to pinpoint the sun's position even in the foggiest conditions, ensuring they stayed on course.

In this chapter, we'll draw inspiration from the Vikings' masterful use of sunstones and apply similar principles to guide your organization through the complex digital transformation journey.

Just as the Vikings relied on sunstones to help them navigate the challenges of the open ocean, we'll cover crucial areas such as organizational mindset, product strategy, and development processes to ensure you have a comprehensive grasp of the digital transformation landscape.

The story of the Viking sunstones teaches us the value of leveraging innovative tools and strategies to stay ahead of the competition and achieve our goals, even in the most challenging circumstances. As we delve into the intricacies of digital transformation, we'll explore how developer experience can serve as your organization's "sunstone," illuminating the path to productivity and satisfaction and ultimately ensuring your organization can successfully adapt, innovate, and thrive in the rapidly evolving digital world.

As we explore digital transformation and developer experience, we will first profoundly dive into the key topics essential to understanding a successful digital transformation journey. We'll cover crucial areas such as organizational mindset, product strategy, and development processes to ensure you comprehensively grasp the digital transformation landscape.

Once we have laid the foundation by covering the basics of digital transformation, we'll shift our attention to a powerful weapon that can propel your organization to new heights: Developer Experience (DX). In the upcoming pages, we will delve into the intricacies of DX, unraveling its many facets and offering valuable insights into its current state.

We will also guide you on recognizing a bad developer experience, which is critical in ensuring your developers remain productive and engaged. Identifying and addressing the pitfalls of a poor DX can pave the way for a more efficient and effective development process.

Lastly, we will take a moment to reflect on the remarkable journey of developers and how they have, over time, gradually conquered the world. Their growing influence has profoundly impacted the tech industry, shaping products, services, and entire markets.

Stay tuned as we embark on this exciting exploration of digital transformation and the powerful role that Developer Experience plays in it. Armed with the knowledge we provide, you'll be well-equipped to harness the full potential of DX and steer your organization toward a successful and transformative journey in the digital world.

Chapter 4
Sailing Through Troubled Waters

* * *

In the unpredictable world of software development, challenges and obstacles are inevitable. In today's rapidly evolving technology landscape, the importance of creating an exceptional developer experience cannot be overstated. The success of a software development organization hinges on its ability to quickly and efficiently deliver high-quality products that meet the needs of its customers. This requires a strong focus on the developer experience, as developers are the ones who are responsible for building the software that powers the business.

However, creating a DX team is not without its challenges. One of the biggest challenges DX teams face is attracting and retaining top talent. The demand for skilled developers is higher than ever, and companies must provide an exceptional working environment that enables developers to do their best work. This means providing access to cutting-edge technology, fostering a culture of innovation, and offering competitive salaries and benefits. In addition, companies must focus on creating an inclusive environment that promotes diversity and encourages collaboration. Failure to do so can result in a lack of talent and an inability to keep up with the competition.

Another challenge faced by DX teams is reducing time to market. In today's fast-paced business environment, companies must be able to deliver new features and products to stay competitive quickly. DX teams are critical in enabling companies to do this by providing developers with the tools and resources to work swiftly and efficiently. This includes providing access to cloud infrastructure, implementing continuous integration and delivery processes, and promoting automation wherever possible. However, failure to prioritize time to market can result in missed opportunities and lost revenue.

Finally, DX teams must work to avoid constant service disruption. Developers rely on the tools and resources the DX team provides to do their jobs effectively, and any disruption can significantly impact productivity. This means that DX teams must focus on ensuring that their services are always available and reliable and have processes in place to address any issues that arise quickly. Failure to do so can result in frustrated developers and decreased productivity.

Companies must invest in creating a strong DX team to address these challenges. This includes hiring the right people, providing the necessary resources, and creating a culture encouraging innovation and collaboration. By doing so, companies can ensure that they can deliver high-quality products quickly and reliably while attracting and retaining top talent.

However, creating a DX team is not a one-time task, and it requires ongoing investment and attention to ensure that it continues to meet the organization's needs. This means continually evaluating the team's performance and adjusting strategies as necessary. It also means creating a feedback loop that enables developers to provide input on the tools and resources they need to do their jobs effectively.

Creating a strong DX team is essential for any organization that wants to succeed in today's fast-paced business environment. By focusing on the developer experience, companies can attract and retain top talent, reduce time to market, and avoid constant service disruption. This can ensure the long-term success and growth of the organization.

Now, let's embark on an intriguing journey to uncover the challenges of building a robust DX organization and transforming your business. As we delve into the nitty-gritty, you'll find this adventure enlightening, equipping you with the knowledge to tackle these challenges head-on. So, join me as we unlock the secrets to enhancing your Developer Experience and driving successful organizational change.

Outdated Organizational Structure

* * *

IT organizations have come a long way over the past few decades, from being seen as a back-office function to becoming an integral part of almost every business. However, some organizations may still be clinging to outdated IT structures that are no longer effective in today's fast-paced, technology-driven world. One such structure is the ITIL framework.

ITIL, or the Information Technology Infrastructure Library, is a set of best practices for IT service management developed in the 1980s and 1990s. While ITIL has undergone some updates over the years, the fundamental structure remains unchanged, focusing on rigid processes and procedures designed to ensure consistency and reliability.

The problem with this approach is that it can be slow and inflexible, making it difficult for IT organizations to keep up with the pace of technological change and business needs. It can also create silos and barriers between IT functions, making collaborating and sharing information harder.

Another issue with the ITIL framework is that it tends to focus on the IT organization rather than the business as a whole. This can lead to a lack of alignment between IT and other departments, making it harder to achieve business goals and deliver customer value.

IT organizations must adopt a more agile and flexible approach to overcome these challenges. This may involve breaking down silos and creating cross-functional teams focused on delivering business outcomes rather than simply following processes and procedures.

Another critical aspect of a modern IT organization is a focus on innovation and continuous improvement. This means being open to new ideas and technologies and constantly looking for ways to improve processes and deliver more value to customers.

Finally, IT organizations must be more customer-centric, focusing on understanding and meeting the business's and customers' needs. This means working closely with other departments to ensure that IT is aligned with the overall business strategy and delivering value where needed most.

In conclusion, while ITIL has served as a valuable framework for IT organizations in the past, it may no longer be the best approach for today's fast-paced and rapidly evolving business environment. To stay competitive and deliver customer value, IT organizations must be more agile, innovative, and customer-centric, focusing on delivering business outcomes rather than simply following processes and procedures.

Painful Enterprise Processes

* * *

Enterprise processes are a vital part of many organizations, helping to ensure consistency, compliance, and efficiency across teams and departments. However, they can also be a significant pain point for employees and create challenges for software development teams.

One of the biggest challenges with enterprise processes is that they are often designed to be rigid and inflexible, making it difficult to adapt to changing business needs or market conditions. This lack of flexibility can lead to frustration and a lack of motivation among employees, particularly those in software development roles, who may feel like cumbersome processes are holding them back.

Another challenge is that enterprise processes can be complex and difficult to navigate, particularly for new employees. This can slow down work and make it harder to get things done efficiently, leading to frustration and delays.

In addition, enterprise processes can create silos and barriers between departments, making collaborating and sharing information harder. This can lead to missed opportunities, duplicated efforts, and a lack of organizational innovation.

To overcome these challenges, software development teams must work closely with other departments within the organization to identify pain points and develop solutions. This may involve streamlining existing processes, creating new processes that are more agile and flexible, or leveraging technology to automate tasks and make workflows more efficient.

It's also essential to ensure that employees are empowered to provide feedback on enterprise processes and are involved in decision-making. This can create a culture of collaboration and innovation within the organization, leading to better outcomes for the company and its customers.

Finally, it's essential to recognize that enterprise processes are not set in stone and should be regularly reviewed and updated to meet the organization's needs. By taking a proactive approach to process improvement and being open to change, software development teams can overcome the challenges posed by enterprise processes and drive innovation and success within the organization.

Command and Control Leadership

* * *

Software organizations must be agile and adaptive to remain competitive in today's rapidly evolving business world. However, many leaders in software organizations still rely on command and control leadership styles, which can be detrimental to the organization's success. This chapter will explore the pitfalls of command and control leadership in software organizations.

Lack of Innovation: Command and control leadership can stifle innovation. When leaders make all the decisions and control all aspects of the organization, there is little room for experimentation or new ideas. This can lead to a lack of innovation, a significant disadvantage in a rapidly evolving market.

Low Morale: Command and control leadership can also lead to low employee morale. When employees feel that they have no say in the decision-making process or that their ideas are not valued, they may become disengaged and demotivated. This can lead to high turnover rates and difficulty attracting and retaining top talent.

Limited Agility: Command and control leadership can also limit agility. When leaders make all the decisions, changes in direction or pivots can be slow and challenging to execute. This can be a significant disadvantage in a market that demands quick adaptation to changing circumstances.

Lack of Ownership: Command and control leadership can also lead to a lack of ownership among employees. When employees are not given the autonomy to make decisions or take ownership of their work, they may become disengaged and less invested in the organization's success.

Limited Creativity: Command and control leadership can also limit creativity. When leaders dictate all aspects of the organization, there is little room for creativity or experimentation. This can lead to a lack of fresh ideas and a stagnant organizational culture.

Limited Empathy: Finally, command and control leadership can limit empathy. When leaders are focused solely on their objectives and goals, they may not take the time to understand the needs and concerns of their employees. This can lead to a lack of trust and a culture of fear and uncertainty.

In conclusion, command and control leadership can be detrimental to the success of software organizations. By stifling innovation, leading to low morale, limiting agility, and creating a lack of ownership, creativity, and empathy, this leadership style can create a culture of fear and uncertainty that is not conducive to success.

To avoid these pitfalls, leaders in software organizations should focus on empowering their employees, fostering a culture of trust and collaboration, and allowing for experimentation and creativity. By doing so, they can create a culture that values innovation and adaptability and is primed for success in today's fast-paced business world.

Limited Customer Voice in Software Development Teams

* * *

Software development teams are constantly striving to create products that meet the needs of their customers. However, despite best intentions, the voice of the customer is often limited or even non-existent in the development process. This can lead to products that don't meet customer needs, resulting in lost revenue and a damaged reputation. In this pessimistic blog article, we will explore why the voice of the customer is often limited in software development teams.

Lack of Communication: One of the biggest reasons the customer's voice is limited is a lack of communication between the development team and the customer. The development team may be working in isolation without understanding the needs and requirements of the customer. This can result in products that miss the mark or, even worse, that customers don't want or need.

Time Constraints: Another reason why the voice of the customer is limited is time constraints. Development teams are often pressured to deliver products quickly, leaving little time for customer feedback and input. This can result in rushed and poorly tested products, leading to poor quality and customer dissatisfaction.

Cost Constraints: In some cases, the voice of the customer may be limited due to cost constraints. Organizations may not want to invest in customer research or feel it is too expensive. This can result in products that are developed without a deep understanding of customer needs, leading to poor product-market fit.

Lack of Customer Representation: In some organizations, there may be no dedicated customer representation in the development process. This means no one can advocate for the customer's needs or provide feedback on the product. This can result in products being developed without consideration for the customer, leading to poor customer experiences.

Limited Customer Engagement: Finally, the voice of the customer may be limited due to limited customer engagement. Development teams may not actively seek out customer feedback, or customers may not be willing to provide feedback. This can result in a lack of understanding of customer needs, leading to products not tailored to them.

In conclusion, the limited voice of the customer in software development teams can have serious consequences. Without a deep understanding of customer needs and input, development teams may create products that don't meet customer needs, resulting in lost revenue and a damaged reputation.

Organizations should prioritize customer engagement, invest in customer research, and ensure dedicated customer representation in the development process to avoid these pitfalls. By doing so, they can create products that meet the needs of their customers and, ultimately, improve their bottom line.

Disempowered Teams

* * *

IT organizations must be agile and adaptive to remain competitive in today's fast-paced business world. However, one of the biggest challenges many IT organizations face is disempowered teams. Disempowerment can take many forms, from limited decision-making authority to a lack of access to critical resources. This chapter will explore the perils of disempowered teams in IT organizations.

Limited Decision-Making Authority: Limited decision-making authority is one of the most common forms of disempowerment. When teams are not empowered to make decisions, they are often unable to solve problems quickly or make the best use of available resources. This can lead to delays in project delivery and missed opportunities for innovation.

Lack of Access to Critical Resources: Disempowerment can also be limited access to critical resources. When teams are not given the resources they need to succeed, they are often forced to make do with what they have, which can limit their ability to solve problems effectively. This can result in suboptimal solutions that don't fully address the underlying issues.

Limited Autonomy: Another form of disempowerment is limited autonomy. When teams are not given the autonomy they need to operate effectively, they are often unable to experiment with new ideas or approaches. This can limit their ability to innovate and result in missed opportunities for growth.

Lack of Trust: Disempowerment can also stem from a lack of trust. When teams are not trusted to make decisions or operate autonomously, they may feel micromanaged or undervalued. This can lead to low morale and high turnover, harming the organization's overall success.

Limited Collaboration: Finally, disempowerment can lead to limited collaboration. When teams are not empowered to work together, they may not be able to leverage each other's strengths or share knowledge effectively. This can result in silos and a lack of cross-functional collaboration, limiting the organization's ability to solve complex problems.

In conclusion, disempowered teams can be a significant obstacle to success in IT organizations. By limiting decision-making authority, access to critical resources, autonomy, trust, and collaboration, disempowerment can lead to missed opportunities for innovation, delays in project delivery, low morale, and high turnover.

To avoid these pitfalls, IT organizations should prioritize empowering their teams by giving them the resources they need to succeed, the autonomy to experiment with new ideas, and the trust to make decisions. By doing so, they can foster a culture of innovation and collaboration that can drive success in today's fast-paced business world.

Feature Factory with Infinite Backlogs

* * *

In many software development organizations, there is a tendency to prioritize feature delivery over everything else. This results in teams becoming feature factories, focusing on churning out new features as quickly as possible. While this may seem like a good idea initially, it can lead to many problems in the long run, especially if the backlog is never-ending. This chapter will explore the pitfalls of a feature factory with infinite backlogs and why it's a bad idea.

Lack of Prioritization: When a team has an infinite backlog, it can be difficult to prioritize which features to work on next. This can lead to the team working on less important features while critical features are left on the backlog for months or even years. This can cause frustration for stakeholders, who may feel that their needs are unmet.

Burnout: The pressure to constantly deliver new features can lead to burnout among team members. When focusing solely on feature delivery, little time or room for experimentation or innovation leads to a monotonous work environment.

Technical Debt: Technical debt can pile up quickly when a team solely focuses on delivering new features. This can lead to an unstable codebase that is difficult to maintain, resulting in long-term problems for the organization.

Lack of Innovation: There is little room for experimentation or innovation when focusing solely on feature delivery. Teams may miss out on opportunities to create new and innovative solutions that could ultimately benefit the organization.

Poor Quality: When the focus is on quantity over quality, the quality of the product can suffer, leading to negative customer experiences, lost revenue, and damaged reputation.

Organizations should focus on delivering value to the customer to avoid these pitfalls rather than churning out new features. They should prioritize features based on customer needs and business goals rather than simply adding them to an endless backlog. This approach helps teams to prioritize their efforts, avoid burnout, reduce technical debt, foster innovation, and ultimately improve the quality of the product.

In conclusion, while it may seem like a good idea to have an infinite backlog and a focus on feature delivery, the pitfalls of a feature factory with infinite backlogs can be severe. Organizations can create a more sustainable and successful software development process by prioritizing value delivery, avoiding burnout, managing technical debt, fostering innovation, and improving product quality.

Delivering Outputs and Not Outcomes

* * *

One of the fundamental principles of Agile software development is to focus on delivering value to the customer. However, many teams get caught up in measuring outputs rather than outcomes, leading to a focus on quantity rather than quality. This can result in teams delivering features that do not meet the customer's needs, wasting time and resources.

Agile teams must focus on delivering outcomes, not just outputs, on overcoming this challenge. This means measuring success based on the value delivered to the customer rather than the number of features or lines of code produced. To achieve this, Agile teams can take several steps:

- Define clear outcomes: Agile teams should define outcomes that align with the business goals and customer needs. These outcomes should be specific, measurable, achievable, relevant, and time-bound (SMART) and communicated clearly to the entire team.

- Engage with customers: Agile teams should engage with customers to understand their needs and priorities. This helps ensure that the delivered outcomes align with customer needs and provide value to the customer.
- Measure success: Agile teams should measure success based on the value delivered to the customer rather than the number of features or lines of code produced. This helps ensure the team delivers outcomes that align with the business goals and customer needs.
- Continuous feedback: Agile teams should continuously gather feedback from customers and stakeholders to ensure they meet their needs and deliver value. This helps teams adapt and adjust their approach to provide the desired outcomes.

In conclusion, Agile teams must focus on delivering outcomes, not just outputs, to ensure they deliver value to the customer. By defining clear outcomes, engaging with customers, measuring success based on value delivered, and continuously gathering feedback, Agile teams can ensure that they deliver outcomes that align with the business goals and customer needs. This approach helps teams to prioritize their efforts, improve the quality of their work, and ultimately, deliver more value to the customer.

Fear and Reprisal for Failure

* * *

Fear of failure is a common problem in many organizations, including those that practice Agile software development. This fear can be exacerbated by a culture of reprisal, where employees are punished or reprimanded for making mistakes or failing to meet expectations. However, this culture can seriously affect team morale, creativity, and innovation.

Failure is an inevitable part of the development process. Teams are encouraged to take risks, experiment, and learn from mistakes. However, the fear of reprisal can stifle creativity and innovation, as team members fear taking risks or trying new things. This can lead to a lack of innovation and, ultimately, project failure.

To overcome this problem, Agile teams need to create a culture of psychological safety where team members feel safe to take risks, make mistakes, and learn from them. This culture is based on trust, respect, and transparency, where team members are encouraged to speak up and share their ideas and concerns without fear of reprisal. Agile teams can take several steps to create a culture of psychological safety, including:

1. Encourage transparency: Agile teams should encourage open communication and transparency, where team members feel comfortable sharing their progress, challenges, and concerns. This helps build trust and respect among team members and fosters a sense of shared ownership.
2. Celebrate failure: Agile teams should celebrate failure as a learning opportunity rather than a source of shame or punishment. Teams should debrief after failures to understand what went wrong and how to improve in the future.
3. Avoid blame: Agile teams should avoid blaming individuals for failures but instead focus on the systemic causes of failure. This helps prevent a culture of fear and reprisal from developing.
4. Emphasize continuous improvement: Agile teams should emphasize continuous improvement, where team members are encouraged to try new things, experiment, and learn from their mistakes. This helps build a culture of innovation and creativity where team members feel safe to take risks and push boundaries.

In conclusion, fear of failure and reprisal can negatively affect Agile teams. To overcome this problem, Agile teams need to create a culture of psychological safety based on trust, respect, and transparency.

By encouraging transparency, celebrating failure, avoiding blame, and emphasizing continuous improvement, Agile teams can foster a culture of innovation, creativity, and collaboration, where team members feel safe to take risks and push boundaries.

Keeping Developers Engaged and Motivated

* * *

In Developer Experience (DX), one of the most crucial challenges is ensuring developers remain engaged and motivated throughout their work. This issue can become particularly pressing when developers encounter roadblocks or feel unmet needs.

Recognizing the factors contributing to developers becoming frustrated and demotivated is essential, as these can significantly impact a team or project's overall performance and success.

First, developers may feel frustrated if they lack access to the necessary tools and resources to perform their tasks efficiently. This could involve anything from outdated or incompatible software to inadequate documentation or knowledge resources. When developers can't access the appropriate tools, their productivity suffers, leading to frustration and disengagement.

Second, developers can become demotivated if they perceive their efforts are not yielding the expected results. This may occur when their work isn't recognized or appreciated or when the goals of a project are unclear or not well-defined. In such situations, developers might struggle to see the value in their contributions, resulting in decreased motivation and job satisfaction.

Moreover, a lack of communication and collaboration within the team or organization can also make developers feel disengaged. When developers are isolated from their colleagues or not involved in decision-making processes, they may feel undervalued or disconnected from the broader goals and objectives of the project.

Additionally, developers may experience frustration when faced with unrealistic expectations or deadlines. Tight deadlines can pressure developers, causing them to rush through tasks and compromise quality. This can lead to disillusionment, as developers may feel they cannot meet their expectations.

In summary, DX teams must acknowledge the challenges of keeping developers engaged and motivated. Factors such as inadequate tools and resources, unclear project goals, poor communication and collaboration, and unrealistic expectations can frustrate and demotivate developers. Recognizing these challenges is an important step in ensuring that developers remain committed to their work and contribute effectively to the team's success and the whole project.

Balancing User Experience with Functionality

***

Maintaining an optimal Developer Experience (DX) can be challenging for teams, especially when it comes to striking the right balance between delivering a great user experience and providing the necessary functionality for developers. This delicate equilibrium can be particularly difficult to achieve when developers have complex requirements that must be addressed.

One of the primary challenges that DX teams face is catering to diverse developers, each with unique preferences, skill sets, and requirements. In some cases, developers prioritize a seamless user experience that allows them to focus on their tasks without distractions. In other cases, they may need access to advanced functionality or customizable features to help them tackle their specific challenges or meet unique project goals.

Another challenge that DX teams may encounter is keeping up with the ever-evolving landscape of development tools and technologies. Developers' requirements and expectations may change rapidly as new and existing technologies evolve. This can make it difficult for

DX teams to stay ahead of the curve and provide a user experience that meets developers' diverse and evolving needs.

Furthermore, budget and resource limitations can also complicate balancing user experience and functionality. DX teams may find themselves in a position where they need to make trade-offs between investing in user experience improvements and ensuring that developers have access to the necessary features and tools. This decision can be challenging, as both aspects are critical for a successful and satisfying developer experience.

Moreover, measuring and evaluating the success of a DX strategy can be a complex process. Quantifying the impact of user experience enhancements or new functionality on developers' productivity, satisfaction, and overall performance may be challenging. This can make it difficult for DX teams to determine whether they are achieving the right balance between user experience and functionality or if adjustments are needed.

In summary, striking the perfect balance between user experience and functionality in Developer Experience is a multifaceted challenge. DX teams must cater to diverse developer preferences and requirements, stay updated on the latest development tools and technologies, manage budget and resource constraints, and accurately evaluate the success of their efforts. Acknowledging these challenges is crucial for DX teams as they strive to create an environment that empowers developers and helps them achieve their full potential.

Managing Competing Priorities

* * *

Managing competing priorities is one of the most significant challenges a Developer Experience (DX) team faces. Developers come with diverse backgrounds, skill sets, and expectations, making it difficult for DX teams to cater to everyone's needs and requirements adequately. The responsibility of prioritizing and addressing these varying demands falls upon the DX team, and finding the right balance can be daunting.

One aspect that complicates this challenge is the ever-changing landscape of software development. Developers' needs and requirements continue to shift as new technologies emerge and development methodologies evolve. Staying current with industry trends and meeting the demands of modern developers can be an ongoing struggle for DX teams.

Additionally, DX teams often have to balance the interests of various stakeholders within an organization. These stakeholders may include product managers, designers, support staff, and even company executives, each with goals and expectations. Navigating these diverse perspectives and finding common ground can be challenging for DX teams.

Another factor contributing to the challenge of managing competing priorities is the need to allocate limited resources effectively. DX teams often face constraints related to time, budget, and personnel, making it essential to prioritize initiatives and allocate resources judiciously. Determining which needs and requirements should take precedence can be a complex decision-making process.

Moreover, DX teams must also consider the long-term impact of their decisions on the developer community. By prioritizing certain needs and requirements over others, they may inadvertently create a negative experience for some developers. Striking the right balance between addressing immediate needs and fostering a sustainable, inclusive developer community can be a delicate process.

In conclusion, the challenge of managing competing priorities is a complex and multifaceted issue faced by DX teams. From keeping up with the rapidly evolving world of software development to balancing the interests of multiple stakeholders and allocating limited resources effectively, DX teams must navigate many challenges to meet developers' diverse needs and requirements.

Recognizing these challenges is essential to understanding the complexities of creating an optimal Developer Experience that caters to a wide range of developers and their unique demands.

As a software developer, I've worked with various teams, each with its unique way of handling competing priorities. One experience that stands out is when I joined a team where the consensus mechanism was based on who could scream louder and convince others.

This was far from the ideal approach to making decisions or managing priorities. It often led to a toxic work environment and poor decision-making, as the most assertive team members would dominate the conversation while other valuable perspectives went unheard.

Thankfully, numerous exercises and methodologies help teams

reach a consensus democratically and collaboratively. By adopting some of these practices, we were able to transform our team's approach to decision-making and ensure that everyone's voice was heard. In this chapter, I want to share some of the most effective practices I've used to manage competing priorities and reach a consensus.

- Dot Voting: This simple yet powerful technique involves providing each team member with a set number of "votes" (represented by dots or stickers) to distribute among various options or priorities. Team members can allocate their votes according to their preferences, and the options with the most votes are deemed the highest priority. Dot Voting encourages democratic decision-making and ensures that everyone's opinion is considered.
- Cost of Delay: This method helps teams prioritize tasks based on the potential cost or impact of not completing them on time. By weighing the urgency and value of each task against the potential consequences of delaying it, teams can make more informed decisions about which tasks should take precedence.
- MoSCoW: This prioritization technique involves categorizing tasks or features into four groups: Must-have, Should-have, Could-have, and Won't-have. By clearly defining the importance of each item, teams can better understand the relative priorities and allocate resources accordingly.
- Impact Mapping: This practice involves creating a visual representation of the relationships between goals, actors, impacts, and deliverables. By mapping out the connections between these elements, teams can better understand the potential impact of each priority and make more informed decisions about where to focus their efforts.

- Kano Analysis: This technique helps teams prioritize features based on their potential to satisfy user needs and create a positive user experience. By considering factors such as performance, excitement, and basic expectations, teams can better decide which features will significantly impact users.

By incorporating these practices into our decision-making process, my team was able to replace the ineffective "loudest voice wins" approach with a more democratic and collaborative method for managing competing priorities.

We found that these techniques fostered a sense of unity and commitment among team members, even when we didn't all agree on the final decisions. By adopting these practices, we learned the value of disagreeing and committing when necessary, ultimately leading to a more efficient and harmonious work environment.

Keeping Up With Technological Changes

* * *

Another significant challenge for DX teams is keeping up with the rapid pace of technology changes. The world of software development is ever-evolving, with new tools, platforms, and frameworks emerging constantly. DX teams must stay on top of these changes and adapt their strategies accordingly to ensure that they provide developers with the latest and most effective tools.

For example, consider the rise of containerization and orchestration tools like Docker and Kubernetes in recent years. These technologies have revolutionized how developers deploy and manage applications, offering greater flexibility and scalability. A DX team that fails to recognize the importance of such tools and integrate them into the developer environment risks limiting their developers' productivity and innovation potential.

To overcome this challenge, DX teams must adopt several strategies to stay informed about the latest developments in the industry. Some of these strategies include:

Building a strong network of industry contacts

A reliable network of peers and experts is crucial for staying informed about new technologies and trends. By engaging in conversations and exchanging insights with these contacts, DX teams can better understand the tools and platforms shaping the industry. Here are some examples of how DX teams can leverage their network to stay up-to-date:

Online Communities: Participating in online forums, Slack channels, or LinkedIn groups dedicated to software development, DevOps, or other relevant topics can provide DX teams valuable information and insights. By engaging with other professionals in these communities, they can learn about emerging tools, platforms, and best practices and discuss challenges and potential solutions.

Example: A DX team member might join a Slack community focused on cloud-native development, where they can connect with other professionals, ask questions, and share knowledge about the latest trends and tools in the space.

Local Meetups and Workshops: Attending local meetups and workshops related to software development, DevOps, or other relevant areas can help DX teams expand their industry contacts and gain firsthand knowledge of new technologies and trends. These events provide learning, networking, and collaboration opportunities in a more informal setting.

Example: A DX team leader could attend a local DevOps meetup to participate in hands-on workshops, learn from expert speakers, and network with other professionals facing similar challenges.

Webinars and Online Events: Participating in webinars and online events related to software development, DevOps, or other relevant topics can help DX teams stay informed about the latest technologies and trends. Industry experts often lead these events and offer valuable insights and actionable advice.

Example: A DX team member might register for a webinar on the latest advancements in container orchestration, where they can learn about new features, best practices, and real-world use cases from industry experts.

Social Media and Blogs: Following industry influencers, thought leaders, and relevant organizations on social media platforms like Medium, Twitter, or LinkedIn, as well as subscribing to blogs, can provide DX teams with a steady stream of information and insights about the latest tools, platforms, and trends.

Example: A DX team member might follow a well-known software development influencer on Medium who regularly shares news, articles, and insights related to emerging technologies and best practices in the field.

By actively engaging with their network of peers and experts, DX teams can stay informed about the latest technologies, trends, and best practices, helping them make better decisions about the tools and platforms they adopt to enhance their developers' experience.

Attending relevant conferences and events:

Attending relevant conferences and events is essential to stay informed about the latest technological advancements and learning from field experts. By participating in these events, DX teams can keep up to date with emerging tools and platforms, gather insights on best practices, and learn strategies for integrating new technologies into their environments. Here are several examples of conferences and events that DX teams might consider attending:

- KubeCon + CloudNativeCon: Organized by the Cloud Native Computing Foundation, this conference is dedicated to Kubernetes and other cloud-native technologies. By attending KubeCon + CloudNativeCon, DX teams can learn about the latest containerization, orchestration, and cloud-native

development trends, helping them stay informed about the tools and platforms shaping the industry.
- GitHub Universe: GitHub Universe is an annual event organized by GitHub, one of the most popular platforms for code collaboration and version control. The conference brings developers, maintainers, and industry leaders together to explore the latest innovations and best practices in software development, open-source collaboration, and DevOps. Attending GitHub Universe can give DX teams valuable insights into leveraging GitHub and its associated tools to improve developer experience and productivity.
- Web Summit: Web Summit is one of the largest technology conferences in the world, attracting a diverse audience of startups, investors, developers, and industry leaders. The event covers various technology-related topics, including software development, AI, IoT, cybersecurity, and more. By attending Web Summit, DX teams can gain insights into the latest trends and innovations across the entire technology landscape, helping them identify emerging tools and platforms that could enhance the developer experience.
- DeveloperWeek: As mentioned earlier, DeveloperWeek is a significant conference that brings together thousands of developers, engineers, and tech executives to discuss the latest trends in software development. Attending DeveloperWeek allows DX teams to learn about emerging tools and platforms, network with industry experts, and attend workshops and presentations on various topics.
- AWS re:Invent: This annual conference, organized by Amazon Web Services, covers a wide range of topics related to cloud computing, including DevOps, serverless computing, containers, and more. By attending AWS

Keeping Up With Technological Changes 79

re:Invent, DX teams can gain insights into the latest innovations in cloud-based tools and platforms and learn how to leverage them for their developers.
- Google I/O: Google's annual developer conference covers various topics related to Google's ecosystem, including Android, Chrome, Google Cloud Platform, and more. Attending Google I/O can provide DX teams with valuable insights into the latest tools and technologies developed by Google and their potential impact on the software development landscape.
- Microsoft Build: Microsoft Build is an annual conference focused on the latest trends in Microsoft technologies, including Azure, .NET, Visual Studio, and more. By attending Microsoft Build, DX teams can gain insights into the latest developments in Microsoft's ecosystem and learn how to utilize these technologies to enhance their developers' experience.
- O'Reilly Software Architecture Conference: This conference focuses on the latest trends and best practices in software architecture, including microservices, DevOps, and more. Attending the O'Reilly Software Architecture Conference can help DX teams learn about emerging architectural patterns and practices that can impact their developers' productivity and effectiveness.

By attending these conferences and events, DX teams can not only stay informed about the latest trends in software development but also network with industry experts and learn from their experiences. This knowledge can prove invaluable when deciding which tools and platforms to adopt, ensuring developers can access the most up-to-date and effective technologies.

Conclusion

By adopting these strategies, DX teams can better equip themselves to navigate the rapidly changing landscape of software development tools and technologies. This, in turn, allows them to provide developers with the most up-to-date and effective tools, enabling them to innovate and excel in their work.

Ensuring Consistency Across Platforms

* * *

Consistency is a crucial aspect of a great developer experience, and DX teams face the challenge of ensuring this consistency is maintained across various platforms and environments. This can be particularly difficult when developers work on multiple projects, each employing different tools and technologies.

For example, imagine a team of developers working on a mobile application project using specific tools and frameworks. At the same time, they are involved in a web development project with a different technology stack. The discrepancy between these two environments can lead to confusion, inefficiencies, and even frustration among developers, as they have to switch between different tools and adjust to the unique requirements of each project.

Another challenge related to consistency is maintaining a uniform experience across different platforms, such as Windows, macOS, and Linux. Ensuring that the development tools and processes work seamlessly on all these platforms can be complex, as each platform has nuances and limitations.

Additionally, DX teams may also need to consider the consistency of the developer experience across various team members with different roles and expertise levels. For example, the tools and processes used by front-end developers may differ significantly from those used by back-end developers or data scientists, making it even more challenging to maintain consistency across the entire development team.

In summary, maintaining a consistent developer experience across different platforms, environments, and projects is a significant challenge faced by DX teams. As developers navigate between various tools and technologies, the lack of consistency can lead to confusion and inefficiencies, ultimately impacting productivity and overall satisfaction. In future chapters of this book, we will explore strategies and best practices for addressing this challenge and ensuring a consistent, high-quality developer experience.

Afterword

* * *

As we conclude our exploration of the challenges facing developer experience teams, it's clear that many hurdles exist to creating a successful DX department. However, it's important to remember that along with these challenges come numerous opportunities to learn, grow, and innovate within the realm of developer experience.

As we advance in this book, we will delve deeper into how to tackle these problems and build a thriving DX organization that will drive digital transformation within your company. We will provide insights, strategies, and best practices for addressing the issues we've discussed so far, as well as unlocking the potential of your DX team.

By learning how to navigate these challenges, you will be better equipped to create an environment that empowers developers, fosters collaboration, and ultimately leads to the delivery of high-quality software products that meet your customers' needs.

So, while the road ahead may be filled with obstacles, the journey also presents many opportunities for growth and success. By embracing the challenges and harnessing the lessons learned throughout this book, you will be well on your way to launching a successful DX organization and playing a pivotal role in your organization's digital transformation.

Chapter 5
Sailing Toward Success

* * *

The modern business landscape constantly evolves, with new technologies and methodologies playing a pivotal role in shaping organizations' success. As the importance of software development continues to grow, the need for a strategic approach to developer experience becomes increasingly crucial.

In this chapter, we'll discuss why developer experience deserves a seat at the leadership table and explore the benefits it brings to the organization.

* * *

The Importance of Developer Experience

In today's fast-paced, technology-driven world, software development is critical to an organization's digital transformation journey. Creating high-quality, innovative, and user-friendly software products is essential to maintaining a competitive edge in the market. However, achieving these goals requires more than just talented developers; it requires an environment that fosters productivity, innovation, and satisfaction among those developers. This is where developer experience comes into play.

Developer experience encompasses the tools, processes, and working conditions contributing to software developers' overall satisfaction and productivity. By prioritizing developer experience, organizations can empower their developers to work more efficiently and effectively, leading to improved product quality, faster time to market, and increased innovation.

Developer Experience at the Leadership Table

While it may not be immediately apparent, developer experience is a strategic function that can have far-reaching effects on an organization's success. By including developer experience at the leadership table, organizations can ensure that the needs and concerns of developers are heard and addressed, ultimately leading to better decision-making and resource allocation. Here are some reasons why developer experience should have a seat at the leadership table:

- Attracting and Retaining Top Talent: The demand for skilled software developers continues to grow, and competition for the best talent is fierce. By prioritizing developer experience, organizations can create a work environment that attracts and retains top talent, ensuring they have the resources necessary to drive innovation and growth.
- Driving Innovation: A positive developer experience fosters creativity and innovation, empowering developers to explore new ideas and technologies. By including developer experience in strategic discussions, organizations can stay ahead of the curve and remain competitive in the rapidly evolving technology landscape.

- Improving Productivity: A well-designed developer experience can significantly improve productivity, as developers can work more efficiently and effectively. By understanding and addressing the needs of developers, organizations can optimize their software development processes and achieve better results.
- Enhancing Collaboration: Developer experience extends beyond just the tools and processes developers use; it also encompasses how developers collaborate and communicate with other teams within the organization. By considering developer experience at the leadership level, organizations can break down silos and promote cross-functional collaboration, leading to better decision-making and problem-solving.
- Supporting Business Goals: Improving developer experience aims to support the organization's broader business objectives. By incorporating developer experience into strategic planning and decision-making, organizations can ensure that their software development efforts are aligned with their overall goals and priorities.

Management Disconnected from The Software Delivery Lifecycle

Throughout my career, I've worked with various organizations as a consultant or employee and have observed a common issue that often arises. Many developers express their frustration with the disconnect between top management and the actual software delivery practices being followed within the company.

This disconnect often results in strategies and decisions that go against the established best practices within the IT industry and those adopted by high-performing software delivery organizations.

I've also heard rumors of similar challenges in other organizations, emphasizing the importance of having someone at the leadership level who understands software delivery from a developer's perspective. By including a representative who is well-versed in developer experience in the boardroom, leadership teams can benefit from a more informed and well-rounded understanding of software delivery.

This representative would bridge developers and top management, ensuring the leadership team is updated on the latest industry practices, trends, and technological advancements. This knowledge would enable the leadership team to make more informed decisions, create strategies that align with current best practices, and ultimately improve the overall developer experience within the organization.

By addressing this disconnect and emphasizing developer experience at the leadership level, organizations can empower their developers to work more effectively and efficiently. In turn, this can lead to improved product quality, faster time to market, and increased innovation—all of which are essential components of a successful digital transformation journey.

Conclusion

In conclusion, developer experience is a crucial aspect of an organization's digital transformation journey, and its importance cannot be overstated. By including developer experience at the leadership table, organizations can ensure that the needs and concerns of developers are taken into account, ultimately leading to a more successful and competitive organization.

The Lighthouse in the Storm

* * *

An exemplary leadership mindset is critical to the success of any digital transformation initiative. As organizations embark on this journey, having strong leadership that cultivates an environment conducive to change, experimentation, and collaboration becomes essential.

This chapter highlights the importance of having the right leadership mindset and discusses how it will be covered in various aspects throughout the book.

By adopting the principles and practices outlined in this chapter, organizations can empower their teams to drive digital transformation effectively and thrive in an increasingly competitive landscape.

Promote a Culture of Experimentation and Collaboration

A successful digital transformation journey requires a culture of experimentation and collaboration. Leaders should encourage their teams to take risks, test new ideas, and learn from successes and failures. By fostering an environment where employees feel safe to experiment, organizations can rapidly innovate and adapt to changing market conditions. Additionally, promoting collaboration across teams and departments helps break down silos, facilitates knowledge sharing, and drives collective problem-solving.

Encourage Transparent and Honest Communications

Transparent and honest communication builds trust and fosters a positive work environment. Leaders should create channels for open dialogue where employees can freely express their opinions, ask questions, and raise concerns. By maintaining open lines of communication and addressing issues proactively, leaders can ensure that everyone is aligned and working towards a shared goal.

Reward the Behaviors You Would Like to See

Leaders play a crucial role in shaping organizational culture by rewarding the behaviors they want to see. Recognizing and celebrating the achievements of teams helps reinforce desired behaviors, such as innovation, collaboration, and resilience. By consistently rewarding these behaviors, leaders can drive positive change and foster a culture that supports digital transformation.

Create a Common Purpose and Vision

A clear and compelling vision is the foundation for successful digital transformation. Leaders should articulate a common purpose that resonates with employees and inspires them to work towards the organization's goals. By sharing this vision and reinforcing its importance, leaders can unite their teams and create a sense of shared ownership in the digital transformation journey.

Empower Decision-Making at the Right Level

Effective leadership involves pushing decision-making down the chain of command and empowering the people closest to the work to make informed decisions. This approach accelerates decision-making and fosters a sense of ownership and accountability among employees. Leaders can create a more agile and responsive organization by trusting their teams and providing them with the necessary information and resources.

Break Down Barriers Between Departments

Leaders must break down unnecessary barriers between departments to drive successful digital transformation. Leaders can eliminate bottlenecks, improve information flow, and enhance organizational efficiency by encouraging cross-functional collaboration and creating opportunities for teams to work together.

Invest in and Encourage Continuous Learning

Continuous learning is crucial for staying ahead in the digital era. Leaders should invest in their employees' growth by providing access to learning resources, training programs, and professional development opportunities. By fostering a learning culture, organizations can ensure that their workforce is equipped with the skills and knowledge needed to navigate the challenges of digital transformation.

Foster a No-Blame Culture

In a rapidly changing environment, mistakes and failures are inevitable. However, leaders need to foster a culture that does not place blame or punish people for failure. Instead, they should encourage their teams to learn from their mistakes and use these experiences to improve processes and drive innovation. Leaders can promote resilience, adaptability, and long-term success by creating a safe space for employees to fail.

* * *

Build Trust

As a DX leader, your mindset significantly influences your team's performance and the overall quality of their work. Building trust with your team members and colleagues is essential for fostering a positive developer experience.

This chapter will explore 12 ways to build trust and cultivate the right mindset to become an effective DX leader.

1. Honor your commitments: Keep your promises, meet deadlines, and follow through on tasks. Honoring your commitments demonstrates reliability and values your team's time and effort.
2. Listen actively to others: Make an effort to understand your team members' perspectives, concerns, and ideas. Practice active listening by giving your full attention, asking questions, and providing feedback to ensure clear communication.
3. Apologize when you are wrong: Nobody is perfect. When you make mistakes or misunderstand something, own up to it and apologize sincerely. This shows humility and that you are willing to learn from your mistakes.
4. Communicate properly: Be clear, concise, and transparent. Ensure to address any questions or concerns and provide updates on project progress. Effective communication is the foundation for building trust and collaboration.
5. Help other people out: Offer assistance to your team members when needed. You demonstrate that you care

about their success and personal growth by supporting and providing resources.
6. Do and say what you believe in. Be true to your values and stand by your convictions. Consistency in your beliefs and actions will make you more credible and trustworthy to your team.
7. Make careful decisions: Take the time to gather all necessary information and consider the potential consequences before making decisions. This demonstrates that you value the input of others and take their concerns into account.
8. Share your feelings openly: Be open about your emotions and the reasons behind your decisions. By being genuine and transparent, you build trust and create a supportive environment for your team.
9. Be honest with others: Always tell the truth, even when it's complicated. Honesty is essential for building trust; your team will appreciate your honesty.
10. Be consistent in your actions: Consistency in your behavior and decisions helps establish predictability and stability. Your team will trust you more if they know what to expect from you.
11. Admit when you make mistakes: Acknowledging your errors shows humility and a willingness to learn. It also encourages your team members to be open about their mistakes, fostering a culture of continuous improvement.
12. Show your authentic self: Be genuine in your interactions with others. Embrace your unique qualities and let your true personality shine through. Being authentic creates deeper connections with your team and cultivates an environment where everyone feels valued and respected.

Adopting these 12 principles will foster a positive developer experience and create a strong foundation of trust with your team. As a DX leader, your mindset and actions will be crucial in building and maintaining a productive, collaborative, and successful team.

Conclusion

An exemplary leadership mindset is key to a successful digital transformation journey. By promoting a culture of experimentation and collaboration, encouraging transparent communication, rewarding desired behaviors, creating a shared vision, empowering decision-making, breaking down barriers, and fostering a no-blame culture, you will be on the right mindset in your transformational journey.

Managing Ego for Effective Leadership

* * *

As a leader, your role in fostering an environment that nurtures creativity, collaboration, and efficiency is paramount. One key aspect of effective leadership is managing one's ego.

Ego refers to an individual's sense of self or self-importance, a psychological construct that drives one's thoughts, emotions, and behaviors. The conscious aspect of our identity helps us navigate the world by providing a sense of individuality and differentiation from others.

While a healthy ego is essential for self-esteem, confidence, and resilience, an unchecked or inflated ego can lead to arrogance, self-centeredness, and resistance to feedback or change.

This chapter will discuss the importance of keeping your ego in check and offer practical advice for leaders to manage their egos for a better leadership style.

The Importance of Managing Ego

Ego-driven leadership often results in inflexible decision-making, strained relationships, and stifled innovation. By contrast, leaders who can manage their egos are better equipped to:

- Foster open communication and collaboration
- Encourage constructive feedback and learning
- Adapt to new ideas and changing circumstances
- Develop empathy and understanding toward team members

Practical Tips for Managing Ego

Cultivate self-awareness: The first step in managing your ego recognizes when it is at play. Regularly take a step back to assess your motivations, emotions, and reactions. Are you putting your personal interests above the team's goals? Are you open to feedback and new ideas, or are you resisting change?

Example: A project manager realizes that their insistence on using a particular technology is driven by their familiarity with it rather than its suitability for the project. By recognizing this bias, they can reevaluate the decision and consider alternative solutions.

Embrace vulnerability: Admitting when you don't know something or make a mistake demonstrates humility and openness to learning. This can build trust among your team and encourage open dialogue.

Example: A team leader admits that they don't fully understand the nuances of a new programming language and asks for input from the team. This creates an opportunity for collective learning and problem-solving.

Encourage feedback: Actively solicit feedback from your team members, both on your performance and the team's overall direction.

This keeps your ego in check and ensures that you are making informed decisions.

Example: An engineering manager schedules regular one-on-one meetings with each team member to discuss their concerns and gather feedback on the team's processes and performance.

Celebrate others' successes: Recognizing and celebrating the achievements of your team members fosters an environment of collaboration and mutual respect. This also helps you stay focused on the collective success of the team rather than your accomplishments.

Example: A product owner organizes a team lunch to celebrate the successful release of a new feature, highlighting the contributions of each team member.

Practice empathy: Put yourself in your team member's shoes and try to understand their perspectives, challenges, and motivations. This can help you be more compassionate and make better decisions that consider the entire team's needs.

Example: A CTO, before deciding on a new technology stack, considers the learning curve for the team and the potential impact on their workload and job satisfaction.

Conclusion

Managing one's ego is critical for effective leadership in developer experience. Leaders can create an environment that nurtures creativity, collaboration, and efficiency by cultivating self-awareness, embracing vulnerability, encouraging feedback, celebrating others' successes, and practicing empathy. In doing so, they pave the way for a better developer experience and long-term success for their organization.

Leadership Philosophical Framework

* * *

In developer experience, effective leadership is instrumental in creating a thriving and supportive work environment. Stoicism, an ancient Greek and Roman school of thought, offers invaluable insights for leaders seeking to optimize their mental operating system.

This chapter will explore how Stoic principles can guide leaders in building a successful organization.

Stoic Principles for Effective Leadership

Focus on what you can control: Stoicism teaches the importance of distinguishing between things within our control and those outside it. As a leader, concentrate your efforts on aspects of the organization that are within your purview, such as setting goals, providing resources, and creating a supportive environment.

Recognize that factors beyond your control, such as market fluctuations or external competition, should not dictate your emotional well-being or decision-making.

Embrace adversity as an opportunity for growth: Stoicism encourages viewing challenges and obstacles as opportunities to learn and grow.

When facing difficulties, adopt a problem-solving mindset and seek to extract valuable lessons. Encourage your team to approach setbacks with resilience and adaptability, fostering a culture that embraces continuous improvement.

Practice emotional intelligence: Stoics believed in the power of reason and emotional mastery. Cultivate self-awareness, empathy, and emotional regulation to understand better and manage your own emotions and those of your team members.

This will enable you to make more informed decisions, maintain a composed demeanor under pressure, and support your team's emotional well-being.

Cultivate virtues and lead by example: Stoicism emphasizes the importance of cultivating virtues such as wisdom, courage, justice, and temperance.

As a leader, embody these virtues in your actions and decisions, setting a positive example for your team. You will inspire trust, loyalty, and respect among your team members by consistently demonstrating solid ethical values.

Practice gratitude and maintain perspective: A Stoic leader maintains a sense of perspective and focuses on the positives. Cultivate an attitude of gratitude by regularly acknowledging and appreciating the achievements and contributions of your team members. This practice will encourage a positive work culture and help keep challenges in perspective.

Encourage reflection and self-improvement: Stoics valued self-examination and personal development. Encourage your team to regularly reflect on their performance, strengths, and areas for growth.

Promoting a culture of self-improvement and learning will foster a more skilled, adaptable, and motivated workforce.

Conclusion

By incorporating Stoic principles into your leadership style, you can develop a resilient and adaptable mindset that will empower you to navigate the complexities of organizational management.

Embracing the tenets of Stoicism, such as focusing on what you can control, facing adversity with resilience, practicing emotional intelligence, and cultivating virtues, can lead to a more successful organization and a positive developer experience.

Embodying these timeless principles will drive your organization's success and inspire and support your team in their personal and professional growth.

The Product Horizon: A New Way of Navigating

* * *

The focus should shift from projects to products in the digital transformation journey. A project-oriented approach often results in short-term gains, whereas a product-centric approach supports long-term growth and adaptability. This chapter highlights the importance of focusing on products and outlines strategies for organizations to make this shift successfully.

Shift the Focus from Projects to Products

Projects are temporary endeavors with defined goals, timelines, and resources. Once a project is completed, its purpose and related activities often end. On the other hand, products are designed to evolve continuously, adapting to changing customer needs, market conditions, and technological advancements. By shifting the focus from projects to products, organizations can build sustainable solutions that deliver ongoing value and drive digital transformation more effectively.

Treat the Product as an Experiment

Organizations must adopt an experimental mindset to thrive in the rapidly changing digital landscape. When developing a new product, it is essential to formulate a hypothesis and then create a prototype to test it. Organizations can quickly validate assumptions, gather valuable user feedback, and iterate on their designs by treating the product as an experiment. This iterative approach enables organizations to identify and address potential issues early in development, ultimately leading to better products and more satisfied users.

Fail Fast, Fail Often, and Learn Always

Embracing failure is a crucial aspect of product development. By adopting a "fail fast, fail often" mentality, organizations can learn from their mistakes, make rapid adjustments, and ultimately create more successful products. It is essential to recognize that not every product will succeed, and some may not meet user expectations.

However, the lessons learned from these failures can be invaluable, informing future product development efforts and driving continuous improvement. To cultivate a culture that embraces failure, organizations should:

- Encourage open communication and transparent sharing of lessons learned from failed experiments.
- Reward risk-taking and experimentation, even if the outcome is not successful.
- Provide resources and support for teams to iterate quickly and learn from their experiences.
- Emphasize User Needs and Feedback

A product-centric approach prioritizes user needs and feedback. Organizations can develop products that genuinely address pain points and deliver value by actively engaging with users, gathering their insights, and incorporating feedback. Regularly soliciting user feedback throughout the product development process ensures that products remain relevant and aligned with user expectations.

Foster Cross-Functional Collaboration

Product development is a collaborative effort that requires input from various stakeholders, including developers, designers, product managers, and users. By fostering cross-functional collaboration, organizations can ensure that different perspectives are considered, resulting in more well-rounded and effective products. Encouraging collaboration across teams also helps break down silos, improving overall organizational agility and responsiveness.

Invest in Continuous Improvement

In the world of product development, there is always room for improvement. Organizations must invest in ongoing refinement and optimization of their products to stay competitive and maintain user satisfaction. By continually iterating on products, organizations can ensure that their solutions remain relevant, effective, and aligned with evolving user needs.

Conclusion

Focusing on products rather than projects is essential for organizations seeking to succeed in their digital transformation journey. Organizations can develop sustainable, adaptable solutions that drive long-term growth and success by embracing an experimental mindset, learning from failure, prioritizing user needs, fostering collaboration, and investing in continuous improvement.

The strategies outlined in this chapter provide a roadmap for organizations looking to shift from a project-oriented to a product-centric approach, setting the stage for a successful and sustainable digital transformation.

Innovating the Development Process

* * *

Innovation is a critical component of the digital transformation journey. A key aspect of innovation lies in optimizing the development process to deliver better products and services more efficiently. This chapter explores the importance of innovation in the development process and offers practical strategies for organizations to adopt in pursuing digital transformation.

Develop Empathy for Other Teams and Users

A successful development process hinges on understanding the needs and perspectives of different stakeholders. Developing empathy for other teams and users enables organizations to create solutions that genuinely address pain points and deliver value. To cultivate empathy, organizations should:

- Encourage open and transparent communication between teams, fostering a shared understanding of the consequences of decisions.
- Involve end-users and other stakeholders in the development process, incorporating their feedback and insights.
- Prioritize user experience (UX) and user-centered design principles to ensure products and services are tailored to users' needs.
- Aim for Rapid Feedback

Rapid feedback is essential for refining and improving products throughout the development process. By focusing on delivering a minimum viable product (MVP) quickly, organizations can gather valuable user feedback and iterate on their designs more effectively. Resisting the impulse to over-engineer ensures that resources are directed towards high-impact features and improvements, maximizing the return on investment (ROI).

Foster a Culture of Curiosity and Inquiry

Cultivating a culture of curiosity and inquiry drives innovation by encouraging employees to ask questions, challenge assumptions, and explore new ideas. Organizations can foster this culture by:

- Providing opportunities for employees to attend conferences, workshops, and other learning events.
- Encouraging cross-functional collaboration and knowledge sharing.
- Celebrating creative problem-solving and recognizing innovative solutions.
- Offer Opportunities to Build Skills and Encourage Creative Problem Solving

*　*　*

Empowering employees to develop new skills and tackle challenges creatively is crucial for driving innovation in the development process. Organizations can support skill-building by:

- Offering access to training programs, online courses, and mentorship opportunities.
- Encouraging employees to explore new technologies, tools, and frameworks.
- Providing time and resources for employees to work on passion projects or tackle complex problems.

*　*　*

Commit to Technical Excellence, Testing, and Continuous Integration

Technical excellence is foundational to the success of any development process. Organizations must prioritize high-quality code, robust testing, and continuous integration to ensure their products are reliable and performant. Key strategies for achieving technical excellence include:

- Adopting best practices in software development, such as code reviews, pair programming, and documentation.
- Implementing a comprehensive testing strategy that includes at least unit, integration, and end-to-end tests.
- Automating testing and deployment pipelines to improve code quality, minimize human error, and increase throughput.

Conclusion

Innovating the development process is crucial for organizations embarking on a digital transformation. Organizations can optimize their development processes and deliver better products more efficiently by fostering empathy, prioritizing rapid feedback, cultivating curiosity, offering skill-building opportunities, and committing to technical excellence.

The strategies outlined in this chapter provide a roadmap for organizations seeking to drive innovation in their development process, laying the foundation for a successful digital transformation journey.

Maintaining Healthy Operations

* * *

As organizations embark on digital transformation, maintaining healthy operations becomes increasingly critical. A successful transformation requires close collaboration between development, product, and operations teams to ensure a smooth transition and minimal impact on existing services. This chapter explores the importance of maintaining healthy operations during digital transformation and offers practical strategies for organizations.

Develop Empathy for Developers and Product Managers

Operational teams play a vital role in the digital transformation journey, often bridging development and product teams. Developing empathy for developers and product managers is crucial to fostering collaboration and ensuring that operational concerns are adequately addressed.

Instead of simply saying "no" to projects or timelines that may be challenging for operations, work closely with development and product teams to find acceptable solutions. This collaborative approach strengthens team relationships and ensures operational needs are considered throughout the transformation process.

Implement Mechanisms for Fault Detection and Determination

Robust monitoring is the foundation of reliability in any system. As organizations undergo digital transformation, it is essential to implement mechanisms for fault detection and determination. By proactively monitoring systems, organizations can identify potential issues before they escalate, minimizing downtime and ensuring a smooth transformation. Key strategies for effective fault detection and determination include:

- Establishing comprehensive monitoring across all technology stack layers, including infrastructure, applications, and services.
- Implementing automated alerting and escalation processes to address potential issues promptly.
- Regularly reviewing and refining monitoring processes to ensure they remain effective as the organization evolves.
- Develop the Technical Understanding to Remediate and Learn from Incidents

Operational excellence requires responding to incidents in a live system while minimizing service disruption. Developing the technical understanding to remediate and learn from incidents is essential for maintaining healthy operations during digital transformation. Organizations can build these capabilities by:

- Investing in ongoing training and skill development for operations teams, ensuring they remain up-to-date with the latest technologies and best practices.
- Encouraging cross-functional collaboration and knowledge sharing, enabling operations teams to draw on the expertise of their development and product counterparts.
- Establishing clear escalation paths and communication channels to ensure incidents are managed effectively and resolved quickly.
- Conduct Post-Incident Analysis with the Goal of Learning, Not Blaming
- Learning from incidents is crucial for improving operations and preventing future issues.

Organizations should conduct post-incident analysis to understand the incident's root cause, identify areas for improvement, and implement corrective actions. It is essential to approach this analysis with a learning mindset, focusing on understanding what happened and why rather than assigning blame.

To conduct effective post-incident analysis, organizations should:

- Establish a structured process for reviewing incidents, including gathering relevant data, conducting a root cause analysis, and identifying corrective actions.
- Involve representatives from all affected teams in the analysis process, ensuring that diverse perspectives are considered, and lessons learned are shared across the organization.
- Implement a continuous improvement mindset, regularly reviewing and refining processes based on the insights gained from post-incident analysis.

Conclusion

Maintaining healthy operations is a critical aspect of the digital transformation journey. Organizations can ensure that their operations remain stable and reliable throughout the transformation process by fostering empathy, implementing robust monitoring, developing the technical understanding to remediate incidents, and conducting post-incident analysis with a learning mindset.

The strategies outlined in this chapter provide a roadmap for organizations seeking to maintain healthy operations while undergoing digital transformation, ultimately enabling them to deliver better products and services more efficiently.

The State of Developer Experience

* * *

The developer landscape has significantly changed in recent years, with new technologies and working models shaping how professionals approach their craft.

Stack Overflow's Developer Survey 2022 provides valuable insights into the current state of developer experience, offering a comprehensive snapshot of emerging trends and preferences.

In this chapter, we'll explore the key findings from the survey and discuss how they can inform your organization's approach to developer experience and digital transformation.

A Growing Interest in Software Engineering

The survey highlights an increasing global interest in software engineerings career paths, such as full-stack, backend, frontend, and DevOps. This surge in interest can be attributed to the growing demand for digital solutions across industries, with organizations increasingly recognizing the value of skilled developers in driving innovation and growth.

The Shift Towards Hybrid and Fully Remote Work

The COVID-19 pandemic has profoundly impacted how developers work, with many organizations adopting a hybrid or fully remote work models. According to the survey, many developers now work remotely within enterprises or startups.

This shift highlights the need for organizations to adapt their developer experience strategies to support remote collaboration, communication, and productivity.

Educational Backgrounds: A Broader Perspective

Traditionally, a Bachelor's degree in computer science or a related field was considered essential for pursuing a career in software development. However, the survey reveals that this requirement is becoming less strict, with many developers finding success without a formal degree in the field. Some specialized roles may still require advanced degrees, but overall, the landscape is becoming more inclusive, allowing individuals to enter the field through alternative educational paths.

Learning Through Technical Documentation, Blogs, Videos, and Online Courses

Developers increasingly turn to alternative learning resources as the industry evolves to stay up-to-date with the latest tools, technologies, and best practices.

The survey shows many developers prefer learning through technical documentation, blog posts, videos, and online courses. This trend highlights the importance of providing accessible, engaging, and up-to-date learning materials to support developer growth and skill development.

The Importance of Linux Proficiency

Regardless of the primary operating system developers use (Windows or macOS), the survey emphasizes the importance of having at least some proficiency in Linux.

Linux is a versatile and powerful operating system widely used in server environments and development workflows. Ensuring developers have a working knowledge of Linux can boost productivity and enable smoother team collaboration.

Conclusion

The findings from the Stack Overflow Developer Survey 2022 offer valuable insights into the current state of developer experience, shedding light on emerging trends and preferences in the industry. By understanding and adapting to these trends, organizations can better support their developers, enabling them to thrive in an increasingly digital world.

As you embark on your digital transformation journey, it's crucial to consider these insights and create a developer experience strategy that aligns with the shifting landscape.

By doing so, you'll be better positioned to attract, retain, and empower top talent, driving innovation and growth within your organization.

State of DX and the Atlassian Developer Survey 2022

* * *

A positive developer experience is essential for attracting and retaining top talent in the software industry. Understanding current trends and developers' preferences helps organizations create an environment conducive to growth, innovation, and job satisfaction.

In this chapter, we look into the state of developer experience based on insights from the Atlassian Developer Survey 2022. We explore key aspects, such as developer autonomy, responsibility, coding preferences, and tooling, to shed light on the evolving landscape of software development.

The Supremacy of Developer Autonomy

The survey reveals that greater autonomy is crucial for developers' happiness at work, with over 80% of developers reporting increased satisfaction despite more frequent context switching and job complexity.

Developers with higher autonomy spend more time coding and

contributing to various products and services. Larger companies (250-1,000 employees) tend to offer higher autonomy levels, emphasizing the need for smaller and very large companies to prioritize granting developers more autonomy in a growing distributed work environment.

Embracing Greater Responsibility

The emergence of the 'You build it, you run it' (YBIYRI) practice has led development teams to take on more responsibility for the code they produce. According to the survey, nearly 60% of developers now work this way, with over 65% believing they should be responsible for a larger portion of the software product lifecycle.

Developers with a high degree of ownership can potentially enhance products and services when closely involved. Engineering leaders must enable development teams to adopt YBIYRI responsibilities, providing the necessary tools, processes, and rituals to succeed.

Navigating Coding and Tooling Preferences

While two-thirds of developers view writing code as the most important skill in their role, 58% believe it won't be required in the future. Some developers foresee the continued importance of writing code, while others predict tools will render it obsolete.

Most developers fall somewhere in between these two perspectives. Managers and team leaders should accommodate developers' preferences rather than imposing a specific approach.

Rethinking the Tooling Approach

Most developers (nearly 70%) use more tools to accomplish their work than before. This trend isn't necessarily negative, as flexibility in tools is crucial. Developers using more flexible tools report simplified work and increased job satisfaction, whereas those adopting inflexible tools risk facing tool sprawl. Instead of concentrating on the number of tools, it's vital to consider the value each tool brings to developers.

Adapting to an Evolving Landscape

There isn't a one-size-fits-all solution for developer experience. Each software developer has unique needs and preferences, and the Atlassian Developer Survey 2022 provides valuable insights to help attract and retain top developer talent.

Embracing greater autonomy, responsibility, and flexibility in tools and coding preferences will pave the way for a thriving developer experience in the ever-changing landscape of software development.

The State of Platform Engineering

* * *

As organizations navigate the digital transformation landscape, the role of platform engineering has become increasingly important. In this chapter, we will explore the state of platform engineering, drawing upon key findings from the "State of Platform Engineering" report by Humanitec.

We will discuss the importance of treating platforms as products, the value of "glue" in operations, salary trends, and the predominant technologies and working setups in the field.

Platform as a Product

The concept of treating platforms as products has gained traction in recent years. This approach involves applying product management principles to the development and maintenance of internal platforms, focusing on delivering value to users—developers in this case.

Platform engineering teams can create more efficient and satisfying work environments by centering the developer experience (DevEx) and continuously iterating based on feedback.

The Value of Glue

Platform engineering teams often play a crucial role as the "glue" that holds an organization's setup together, integrating and connecting various parts of the toolchain. While not directly contributing to customer-facing features, this glue is essential for streamlining processes and improving DevEx.

By embracing this function and promoting its value internally, platform engineers can drive standardization by design and enhance self-service capabilities within the organization.

Salary Trends in Platform Engineering

According to the report, platform engineers earn higher average salaries than their DevOps engineer counterparts, with a 9.4% gap in North America and a 19.4% gap in Europe. This discrepancy highlights the increasing demand for platform engineering skills and the growing recognition of the value these professionals bring to an organization.

Technology and Skillsets

The report identifies the following key technologies and skillsets among platform engineers (multiple selections possible)::

- Docker and Kubernetes (66%)
- Infrastructure as Code (IaC) tools, such as Terraform and Pulumi (60.4%)
- Continuous Integration/Continuous Deployment (CI/CD) tools, such as Jenkins and ArgoCD (58.5%)
- Database and Storage (24.5%)

- Networking (22.6%)

The prominence of Kubernetes and IaC tools reflects the trend of building platforms as a layer on top of clusters and infrastructure, which streamlines configuration management and orchestration.

Working Setups for Platform Engineers

Platform engineers are also leading the way in remote work, with 83.3% of respondents in the US working fully remotely and 16.7% in hybrid arrangements. In Europe, 37.9% work fully remotely, while 62.1% operate in hybrid setups. This flexibility highlights the adaptability of platform engineers and the potential for distributed collaboration in this field.

Conclusion

As organizations continue to embrace digital transformation, the importance of platform engineering cannot be overstated. By treating platforms as products, valuing the "glue" they provide, and fostering a culture of continuous learning and improvement, platform engineers are positioned to drive innovation and enhance the developer experience.

As remote work gains traction, the demand for skilled platform engineers is expected to grow, shaping the future of software development and digital transformation.

Insights from the Stack Overflow Developer Survey

***

In the previous chapter, we provided an overview of the developer community based on Stack Overflow's research insights. This chapter will delve deeper into various aspects of the developer experience, focusing on their profiles, technologies, and work-related trends. This information can help organizations better understand the preferences and needs of their developers, which is crucial for creating an optimal developer experience.

Developer Profile

Most professional developers possess a Bachelor's degree, indicating that formal education continues to play a crucial role in laying the groundwork for a prosperous career in software development.

However, the rapidly evolving nature of technology and the software development landscape requires developers to stay up-to-date with the latest tools and methodologies. As a result, developers increasingly rely on alternative learning resources such as blog posts, videos, and online courses to supplement their formal education.

This growing reliance on diverse and up-to-date learning materials highlights the importance of providing developers easy access to a wide range of resources. Organizations looking to improve developer experience should consider investing in platforms that offer a curated selection of learning materials or developing partnerships with educational institutions and online learning providers.

By enabling developers to learn and grow continuously, organizations can foster a culture of continuous improvement, leading to higher levels of innovation and adaptability.

Full-stack Development

The survey results reveal a growing trend among developers to expand their skill sets and specialize in full-stack development. Full-stack developers comprehensively understand the different layers of software development, from front-end user interfaces to back-end infrastructure.

This breadth of knowledge allows them to work effectively across various aspects of a project, making them highly valuable assets for organizations.

Full-stack developers can bring unique perspectives and problem-solving abilities to a team, as they can navigate the entire development process and understand the interdependencies between different system components. This versatility can lead to more efficient collaboration and communication within the development team, resulting in a better overall developer experience.

Organizations aiming to optimize their developer experience should recognize the value of full-stack developers and consider investing in training and resources that support their growth.

By nurturing the skills and expertise of full-stack developers, organizations can build more agile, adaptable, and efficient development teams capable of tackling complex projects and driving digital transformation success.

Technology

Thanks to its versatility in front and backend development, JavaScript continues to be the most popular programming language among developers. Its widespread use in web development and the growth of server-side frameworks like Node.js have cemented its status as a go-to language for many projects. Python, another highly popular language, is widely used in data science, machine learning, and web development, making it a favorite among developers seeking a versatile and powerful language.

* * *

Most Loved and Wanted Languages

Developers have shown a strong affinity for languages like Rust, Elixir, Clojure, and TypeScript. These languages offer unique benefits and capabilities that set them apart from more traditional languages. Rust, for example, is known for its focus on safety, performance, and concurrency, while Elixir offers powerful support for concurrent and distributed systems.

Clojure, a functional programming language, emphasizes simplicity and immutability, while TypeScript enhances JavaScript with static typing for better maintainability and error detection. As developers seek to expand their skill sets and explore new technologies, these languages are becoming increasingly attractive.

Mobile Application Development

The survey suggests that native mobile application development using languages like Kotlin and Swift remains popular among developers. These languages provide high performance and seamless integration with their respective platforms, ensuring a smooth user experience.

However, a growing interest is also in cross-platform development using frameworks like React Native and Flutter.

These frameworks allow developers to build applications for multiple platforms, such as iOS and Android, using a single codebase, streamlining the development process and reducing the need for platform-specific expertise.

Databases and Cloud Providers

Relational databases like MySQL and PostgreSQL remain popular for developers due to their reliability, scalability, and robust feature sets. NoSQL databases like MongoDB and Redis are also gaining traction, offering more flexible data models and easier horizontal scaling for certain use cases.

In cloud providers, Amazon Web Services (AWS), Microsoft Azure, and Google Cloud Platform (GCP) dominate the market; providing a wide range of services and resources to support various development needs. Alternative providers like Heroku, DigitalOcean, and Tanzu maintain a strong presence, offering developers additional choices and flexibility when selecting the right provider for their projects. As developers embrace cloud technologies, understanding and navigating these platforms become even more critical for delivering a seamless developer experience.

Work-Related Trends

Most survey participants identified themselves as full-time employees, emphasizing the industry's stable and growing demand for professional developers.

This trend reflects the importance of software development in modern businesses and the value organizations place on developers as key drivers of innovation and digital transformation.

The shift towards remote work has become increasingly popular among developers, with many organizations embracing remote and hybrid work models. Developers appreciate remote work's flexibility and autonomy, enabling them to balance their personal and professional lives more effectively.

Additionally, remote work allows developers to collaborate with colleagues and contribute to projects from virtually anywhere in the world, broadening the pool of talent and resources available to organizations.

Organizations looking to improve developer experience should consider the benefits of remote and hybrid work models and how they can adapt their culture and processes to support developers working from various locations.

Coding Outside of Work

A significant percentage of professional developers (88%) reported writing code outside of work, with 73% treating it as a hobby. This passion for coding beyond professional obligations demonstrates a strong intrinsic motivation among developers to learn, innovate, and contribute to the field of software development.

Developers who engage in coding outside work will likely stay current with the latest tools, technologies, and best practices, ultimately benefiting their employers and projects. Furthermore, developers who are intrinsically motivated to code often bring a sense of enthusiasm and creativity to their work, resulting in higher-quality output and increased innovation.

To support and encourage developers' passion for coding, organizations can provide opportunities for professional development, including access to learning resources, internal workshops, and time for personal projects. By nurturing their developers' interests and skills, organizations can create a more engaged and productive development team, further enhancing the developer experience and driving success in their digital transformation journey.

Processes, Tools, and Programs

Organizations must constantly adapt and implement new processes, tools, and programs to stay competitive and provide the best developer experience in the ever-evolving software development landscape. Based on the findings from the Stack Overflow research, we can identify several key areas where organizations are investing in their development ecosystems:

Continuous Integration and Continuous Delivery (CI/CD): Most professional developers (69.79%) report having CI/CD available at their organization. CI/CD enables faster and more reliable software releases by automating the building, testing, and deployment of code changes. By implementing CI/CD pipelines, organizations can reduce the time it takes to deliver new features and bug fixes, improving both the developer experience and the overall quality of their products.

DevOps Function: Nearly 60% of developers report that their organizations have a dedicated DevOps function. DevOps is an approach that aims to bridge the gap between development and operations teams, streamlining the software development lifecycle and promoting collaboration, communication, and shared responsibility. A well-functioning DevOps team can improve the developer experience by facilitating faster deployments, more stable environments, and better feedback loops.

Automated Testing: Automated testing is reported as being available in 58.09% of organizations. This practice involves using software tools to automatically run tests against your code, identifying issues, and ensuring that new changes do not break existing functionality. Automated testing helps to improve the developer experience by providing fast feedback on code quality and reducing the time spent on manual testing.

Microservices: Nearly half of the surveyed developers (48.97%) work with microservices, a software architecture that breaks applications into smaller, independent services that can be developed, deployed, and scaled independently. Microservices can enhance the developer experience by promoting modularity, flexibility, and faster development cycles.

Developer Portal: Despite the many advantages, only 38.18% of developers report having a portal or a central place to find tools and services. A developer portal can significantly improve the developer experience by making it easy to discover, access, and utilize the tools and resources necessary for their work.

Observability Tools: About 37.07% of developers report having access to observability tools, which provide insights into the performance, reliability, and health of software systems. These tools help developers monitor and troubleshoot issues, improving their applications' stability and user experience.

Inner-source Initiative: Promote open-source practices within an organization is relatively rare, with only 16.31% of developers reporting their availability. Innersource can enhance the developer experience by fostering collaboration, knowledge sharing, and code reuse across teams.

Conclusion

The detailed insights from the Stack Overflow Developer Survey offer valuable information about the developer community's preferences, needs, and trends. By understanding these factors, organizations can create a developer experience that caters to their developers' unique requirements and preferences, ultimately driving innovation and success in their digital transformation journey.

Recognizing Bad Developer Experience

* * *

Throughout my journey in software development, I've encountered various instances of poor developer experience. In this chapter, I'll share some examples of a bad developer experience and how to address these issues to create a more seamless and enjoyable development process.

NordicAPIs, an international community of API practitioners, asked their Twitter followers what they thought constituted a bad developer experience. The responses they received highlighted several key pain points:

- Documentation in Non-Standardized Formats: Poorly formatted or inconsistent documentation can create confusion and frustration for developers who rely on clear, concise, and standardized information to complete their tasks.
- Lack of Examples: When documentation lacks practical examples, diagrams, test environments, or logs,

developers can struggle to understand how to implement APIs and other tools effectively.
- Manual Integration: If APIs or other systems require extensive manual integration, this can slow down development processes and create a frustrating experience for developers.
- Lack of Consistency: Inconsistent APIs or other tools can lead to confusion and extra work for developers who must adapt to different conventions and practices.
- Lack of OpenAPI Specifications: OpenAPI is a widely adopted standard for describing and documenting APIs. A lack of OpenAPI specifications can make it difficult for developers to understand and work with APIs, leading to confusion and inefficiencies.
- Questionable Deployment Options: Limited or inflexible deployment options can create roadblocks for developers who need to adapt to different environments or requirements.
- Restricted Access to Documentation: Developers can become frustrated when access to essential documentation is limited or requires jumping through hoops.

In addition to the previously mentioned issues, several other factors can contribute to a poor developer experience. I've encountered these in my professional journey, and they are worth discussing to help organizations identify and address these challenges.

- Too Much Interference from Other Areas: When developers are frequently interrupted by issues related to network or hardware, it can create a disjointed and frustrating development process. Streamlining team communication and collaboration can minimize these disruptions and improve the developer experience.

- Overbearing Mandates: Excessive enforcement or mandating certain practices can hinder developers' ability to innovate and find creative solutions to problems. Striking a balance between providing guidance and allowing flexibility is essential to fostering a positive developer experience.
- Poorly Designed Environments: Poor development environments can impede productivity and contribute to a negative developer experience. Better tools, infrastructure, and overall environment design can significantly improve developers' satisfaction and productivity.
- Slow and Outdated Hardware: Developers rely on efficient hardware to complete their tasks quickly and effectively. Slow and outdated hardware can result in frustration and delays. Regularly updating hardware and ensuring developers access the needed resources can vastly improve their experience.
- Fixed Mindset: A fixed mindset within an organization can limit growth, innovation, and learning. Encouraging a growth mindset and providing continuous learning and improvement opportunities can foster a more positive developer experience.
- Blaming and Excuses Culture: An organizational culture that focuses on blame and excuses rather than addressing the root causes of issues can be detrimental to the developer experience. Promoting a culture of accountability, ownership, and collaboration can help create a more supportive and productive developer environment.
- Lack of community: A small or unengaged developer community that can make it difficult to find answers, share knowledge, or collaborate on projects.

- Self-Victimization: One topic often neglected politely in discussions surrounding developer experience is the problem of self-victimization. In some cases, developers may fall into the trap of self-victimization, feeling that external factors are always to blame for their struggles. This mindset can lead to a negative work environment and hinder the developer experience.

A typical example of self-victimization in the context of developer experience could be a developer who consistently blames the lack of adequate tools, documentation, or support from other teams for their inability to deliver high-quality code or meet deadlines. Instead of seeking solutions, collaborating with colleagues, or learning new skills, the developer might focus on complaining about the perceived obstacles and externalizing responsibility.

This self-victimizing behavior can harm the individual developer's growth and the team's morale and productivity. By avoiding taking responsibility for their part in the situation, the developer misses opportunities to improve their skills and contribute positively to the team's success.

Organizations can create a more positive and productive developer experience by recognizing and addressing these additional factors. This will increase job satisfaction and improve the organization's overall quality and efficiency of software development.

How Developers Have Conquered the World

***

In the early 2000s, Microsoft was at the pinnacle of its power, dominating the tech landscape with its Windows operating system and a suite of software products. In 2000, Steve Ballmer took the reins as CEO following Bill Gates' decision to step down. Ballmer, known for his energetic and animated personality, was determined to lead Microsoft into a new era where developers played a central role in driving the company's success.

The "Developers! Developers! Developers!" presentation took place at a Microsoft event in 2001, intended to convey Ballmer's commitment to the developer community. He recognized the importance of developers in creating applications, tools, and platforms that leveraged Microsoft's technologies, and he wanted to ensure that they knew they were valued and supported.

As Ballmer took the stage, his excitement and passion were palpable. Sweating profusely and with an intensity rarely seen in corporate presentations, he began to chant "Developers! Developers! Developers!" while energetically bouncing around the stage. This passionate display quickly caught the audience's attention and, later, the world's. The moment became one of tech history's most memorable and parodied episodes.

His spirited performance and its message made Ballmer's presentation unforgettable. In an era when the tech landscape was rapidly evolving, Ballmer understood that Microsoft's continued success hinged on its ability to attract, support, and retain talented developers. Ballmer believed the company would maintain its edge in an increasingly competitive market by cultivating a thriving ecosystem of developers who built applications and solutions using Microsoft's technologies.

Though the presentation may have been unorthodox, the underlying sentiment proved prescient. Today, developers are widely regarded as the driving force behind technological innovation and progress, shaping the way we live, work, and interact with one another. Today's tech giants, including Microsoft, continue to invest heavily in fostering a vibrant developer community, recognizing that their contributions are essential for sustained growth and success.

If you haven't had the chance to watch this iconic presentation, don't miss out. Head to YouTube and search for "Steve Ballmer Developers" to experience the unforgettable moment that forever linked developers' passion with their impact on the world. This display of unbridled enthusiasm for the development community is a testament to developers' power and influence in shaping our modern world.

* * *

This chapter will explore how developers have risen to prominence, shaping the modern world through creativity, innovation, and collaboration. As Ballmer's exuberant chant suggests, developers are not just individuals who write code; they are the architects of our digital lives, laying the foundation for the technologies that have transformed every aspect of our society.

In the digital age, developers have emerged as the driving force behind the rapid transformation of industries, economies, and societies. As software continues to "eat the world," developers have become the new rockstars, shaping how we live, work, and interact.

This chapter celebrates the achievements of developers and explores the exciting opportunities that lie ahead for those who choose to join this dynamic and influential profession.

The Rise of the Developer

The developer's rise as a driving force in the global economy can be traced back to the rapid expansion of the internet and the proliferation of digital technologies. As businesses and organizations recognized the need to innovate and adapt to the digital landscape, developers became the key players in building the software and applications that power our modern world.

Developers are at the forefront of emerging technologies, such as artificial intelligence, machine learning, and the Internet of Things, driving change and shaping the future.

Developers As the New Rockstars

Developers have become the new rockstars, possessing the power to transform industries and redefine our lives. Their creativity, technical expertise, and problem-solving abilities have led to groundbreaking innovations that have reshaped the world.

From creating revolutionary products and services to disrupting traditional business models, developers have demonstrated their ability to turn ideas into reality and challenge the status quo.

Some of the most iconic companies of the digital age, such as Google, Facebook, and Apple, were founded by developers who dared to dream big and change the world. These visionaries have left an indelible mark on society and have become role models for aspiring developers worldwide.

Google: Founded by Larry Page and Sergey Brin, two developers who met at Stanford University, Google has become synonymous with search and has revolutionized how we access and organize information.

With products like Gmail, Google Maps, and the Android operating system, Google's impact on our daily lives is undeniable. It is a shining example of how developers can use their skills to improve the world.

Facebook: Mark Zuckerberg, a developer with a vision to connect the world, created Facebook in his Harvard dorm room. Today, Facebook is one of the largest social media platforms globally, connecting billions of people and transforming how we communicate, share information, and interact. Facebook's success is a testament to the power of developers to bring people together and create new opportunities for connection and collaboration.

Apple: Steve Jobs and Steve Wozniak, two developers passionate about technology and design, founded Apple in a garage in Silicon Valley.

Apple has since become one of the most valuable companies in the world, known for its cutting-edge products like the iPhone, iPad, and MacBook. Apple's innovative spirit and commitment to excellence have inspired countless developers to push the boundaries of what's possible and create products that delight and empower users.

These iconic companies and their developer-founders have redefined the game's rules, proving that developers can change the world with the right combination of creativity, technical expertise, and determination.

The success stories of Google, Facebook, and Apple demonstrate the transformative power of developers and serve as a reminder that anything is possible when you dare to dream big and think differently.

As the new rockstars of the digital age, developers play a pivotal role in shaping the future and driving progress across industries.

By embracing the spirit of innovation and challenging the status quo, developers can leave a lasting impact on the world and inspire others to join them in their quest to create a better tomorrow.

The Exciting World of Developer Opportunities

Being a developer today offers unparalleled opportunities for creativity, impact, and personal growth, making it a truly extraordinary profession. The ever-evolving landscape of technology presents developers with the chance to work on cutting-edge projects that have the potential to transform lives and create a lasting impact on society. The possibilities are limitless, and developers are presented with a vast array of exciting avenues to explore:

Build the next generation of software applications and platforms: Developers can create game-changing software and platforms that redefine industries and shape the future.

From designing intuitive and powerful user interfaces to developing innovative algorithms that drive efficiency and automation, developers are at the forefront of technological progress, pushing the boundaries of what's possible.

Create innovative solutions to address pressing global challenges: Developers play a critical role in tackling some of the world's most pressing challenges, such as climate change, poverty, and inequality.

By harnessing the power of technology, developers can create solutions that drive sustainable development, promote social justice, and improve living conditions for millions of people across the globe. This noble pursuit not only delivers a sense of purpose and fulfillment but also highlights the immense potential of developers to make a meaningful difference in the world.

Revolutionize industries by leveraging emerging technologies: Developers have the chance to pioneer groundbreaking technologies, such as blockchain, virtual reality, and quantum computing. These cutting-edge technologies can disrupt traditional business models and create new opportunities for growth and innovation. Developers who embrace these emerging technologies can redefine entire industries, creating novel applications and services that were once considered the stuff of science fiction.

Drive social change through the development of accessible and inclusive digital tools and services: Developers have the power to foster social change by creating digital tools and services that are accessible and inclusive for all.

By designing software that caters to diverse user needs and promotes equity, developers can help bridge the digital divide and empower marginalized communities. This important work not only drives positive social change but also serves as a testament to the transformative potential of the developer profession.

In summary, being a developer today is an extraordinary experience, filled with endless opportunities for creativity, impact, and personal growth. With the power to shape the future and drive positive change in various aspects of life, developers are truly at the helm of a technological revolution.

By seizing these opportunities and embracing the potential to make a tangible difference, developers can leave an indelible mark on the world and inspire future generations to join this exhilarating journey.

The Power of Developer Communities

Developers have also harnessed the power of community to share knowledge, collaborate on projects, and support one another in their pursuit of excellence. Platforms such as GitHub, Stack Overflow, and developer forums have fostered a global network of developers who learn from one another, contribute to open-source projects, and drive innovation collectively.

These communities have become a breeding ground for creativity and collaboration, propelling the profession forward and amplifying the impact of individual developers.

The Future Belongs to Developers

As the world continues to evolve at a breakneck pace, the role of developers in shaping our future has never been more apparent. With their unique blend of creativity, technical prowess, and problem-solving skills, developers are well-positioned to tackle the challenges of the digital age and unlock new opportunities for growth and progress.

As the new rockstars of the global economy, developers have the power to change the world for the better and inspire future generations to follow in their footsteps.

Raising children to become developers equips them with the skills to excel in a rapidly changing world and instills in them the ability to contribute meaningfully to society. The developer profession offers numerous benefits, including:

A rewarding and fulfilling career: Developers have the opportunity to work on projects that impact millions of lives, making a real difference in the world. By teaching children to become developers, we encourage them to pursue a career fostering creativity, innovation, and a sense of accomplishment.

A secure and high-demand profession: The demand for skilled developers continues to rise, and this trend is not expected to slow down anytime soon. Raising children to become developers ensures a secure and prosperous future in a high-demand profession.

Opportunities for lifelong learning: The technology field is ever-evolving, and developers must continually learn and adapt to new advancements. Encouraging children to become developers instills in them the values of lifelong learning and intellectual curiosity.

Developers have made significant contributions to the world, improving it. Some notable examples include:

Tim Berners-Lee: As the inventor of the World Wide Web, Berners-Lee revolutionized how people access and share information, connecting the world in previously unimaginable ways.

Linus Torvalds: Creator of the Linux operating system, Torvalds made a significant impact on the world of technology, offering a free and open-source alternative to proprietary systems, driving innovation, and enabling countless other developers to build upon his work.

Ada Lovelace: Often recognized as the world's first computer programmer, Lovelace's work on Charles Babbage's Analytical Engine laid the foundation for modern-day computing.

The developers behind life-saving medical applications: Developers have contributed to the creation of applications that assist in diagnosing and treating various medical conditions, helping to save lives and improve patient outcomes.

In conclusion, raising children to become developers is an extraordinary and inviting prospect, equipping them with the skills to thrive in an ever-changing world and empowering them to positively impact society. By embracing the potential of the developer profession, future generations can continue to shape our world for the better and inspire others to join this exciting journey.

Conclusion

Developers have conquered the world, emerging as the driving force behind the digital transformation that has reshaped our lives in countless ways. As the new rockstars of the global economy, developers have demonstrated their ability to innovate, disrupt, and transform, leaving an indelible mark on the world.

The exciting world of developer opportunities offers boundless potential for creativity, impact, and personal growth, making it an exhilarating time to be a developer. By embracing the power of developer communities and looking toward the future with optimism and ambition, developers can continue to shape our world for the better and inspire others to join them on this exciting journey.

A F$#@!ing Word For Developers

* * *

Once upon a time, there were two types of coders in the land of programming: the middle-grounders and the elite. The middle-grounders were the ones who stayed in their comfort zones, while the elite dared to venture into uncharted territories.

But what secret sauce set these elite coders apart from their more mundane counterparts? Surprisingly, one answer lay in the profanities that peppered their code.

Jan Strehmel, a curious programmer from the Karlsruhe Institute of Technology, couldn't help but notice a peculiar pattern in the world of elite coding. He observed that swear words were common in the code of elite programmers.

Intrigued by this, he conducted a research study, analyzing over 10,000 code repositories and comparing those with swear words to the starred repositories.

Strehmel employed the open-source software benchmarker to rate each repository. The results were pretty interesting. As it turns out, the repositories that incorporated swear words had a higher code concentration at the upper echelons of the software scale.

The significantly high concentration around the 7-point mark appears to be an outlier, but concentrations above were still higher than those of the starred repositories. So, what gives?

The $#@!ing Hypothesis

Strehmel postulated that swearing in code indicated a deep emotional involvement on the programmer's part. This emotional connection, he argued, led to a more thorough, critical, and dialectic code analysis process. In short, the more you give a shit, the better your code.

So, do you have to start swearing like a sailor in your code to become an elite programmer? Not exactly. Instead, the key takeaway from Strehmel's study is to abandon any inhibitions you have when it comes to your code and find passion in the process. It's not about the swear words but the emotions and dedication they represent.

In Conclusion: Let Developers Give a $#@!

If you want to have developers in the ranks of elite coders, heed this simple advice: give a shit. Be emotionally invested in your work, and strive to create the best code possible. You might find that adding a few well-placed expletives is a small price to pay for programming greatness. So let your passion (and the occasional curse word) flow through your code – it might just be the ticket to becoming a $#@!ing legend.

Chapter 6
Steering By The Stars

* * *

In the annals of history, few events have been as transformative and consequential as the Age of Discovery. Among these pivotal moments was the accidental discovery of Brazil by Pedro Álvares Cabral and his crew, chronicled by the fleet's scribe, Pero Vaz de Caminha, in his insightful "Letter of the Discovery of Brazil."

Like the detailed letter Caminha presented to King Manuel I of Portugal, this chapter aims to lay the foundation for understanding the key aspects of creating a successful developer experience organization.

Caminha's letter provides a comprehensive account of the fleet's journey, the land they discovered, and their initial interactions with the indigenous people. His keen observations of the landscape, vegetation, and resources revealed the potential for future colonization and trade.

Similarly, this book will explore the uncharted territories of developer experience, unveiling the untapped potential within every organization. Just as Caminha's letter highlighted the importance of understanding the new land and its people, this chapter will emphasize the significance of grasping the intricacies of developer experience.

As sailors of old relied on celestial navigation to guide them on their voyages, leaders can analyze the various elements that constitute a successful developer experience organization. We can unlock invaluable insights that will guide our journey toward digital transformation.

As we embark on this exciting adventure, we will navigate through the deep waters of technology, strategy, and collaboration, much like Cabral's fleet did in its pursuit of new trading routes. Our ultimate goal is to provide a clear and actionable roadmap for building a thriving developer experience organization, empowering your team to harness the full potential of your digital endeavors.

* * *

So, join me now as we set sail on this incredible journey, inspired by the spirit of Pero Vaz de Caminha and the remarkable discoveries that await us. Together, we will chart the course of developer experience and unlock the secrets to creating a flourishing organization that drives digital transformation and success.

In the previous chapter, we discussed the context of the industry, the challenges of the market, and the right mindset needed to start driving digital transformation. Now, let's move on to more practical steps of creating a DX organization.

The first step is understanding why your organization needs a developer experience team and what you aim to achieve. We will also explore how you can drive and sustain this team and a suggested leadership model for driving the organization.

One of the most critical aspects of creating a successful DX organization is fostering the perfect environment where a 10x developer can exist and evolve. We will explore what it takes to create such an environment, the role of the organization, and the individual.

Moving on to planning, we will discuss the importance of choosing the right team structure and understanding what doesn't work. We will also define your DX organizational chart, including areas and teams.

We will dive deep into each of the areas and teams, understanding their principles, key responsibilities, and even job descriptions for each team. We will also cover emerging topics such as Platform Engineering and Developer Portals.

Next, we will explore teams fitting the DX domain, such as Developer Tools, Performance, Test Enablement, Collaboration Tools, and Engineering Culture. In detail, we will discuss how each of these teams contributes to a successful DX organization.

We will then move on to Ways of Working and how to master them for an exceptional developer experience. We suggest a practical framework adopted by several large enterprises worldwide, such as Volkswagen, UNICEF, Delta, Airbus, World Health Organization, Red Hat, and Santander. We will also introduce the Open Practice Library, a directory with many practices to help you in your daily life as a practitioner and leader of the DX organization.

Finally, we will discuss how to train and become a master practitioner and deliver outcomes to your organization. We will suggest practices such as functional and non-functional requirements, metrics-based process mapping, and event storming.

It's also essential to be aware of anti-patterns that you might be tempted to accept as a leader in traditional IT organizations. We will discuss some of the most common anti-patterns and how to avoid them.

So, climb aboard and join me on this remarkable voyage as we navigate the uncharted waters of developer experience. Together, we will learn to master the art of navigation, charting a course for success and steering our organization towards a brighter, more innovative future. With the right knowledge and tools, we will be ready to brave the tumultuous seas of software development and emerge triumphant on the other side.

Finding Purpose

* * *

Companies must provide seamless and intuitive developer experiences to keep up with the competition in today's fast-paced world. Companies that fail to invest in developer experience risk losing top talent and innovation.

In response, many organizations are considering building Developer Experience areas to manage their infrastructure, including Kubernetes clusters and tools for engineers. However, creating a successful Developer Experience team requires a clear identity, aligned priorities, and a deep understanding of customer pain.

This chapter will explore how we define Developer Experience, starting with the "why." We will discuss the importance of a clear purpose and how it guides some organizations' operations and evolution.

Starting with the "why"

Years ago, Simon Sinek's video on the power of "why" sparked a revolution in marketing and branding. The idea was simple: great companies start with a clear purpose or "why" that guides everything they do, and this purpose shapes what they execute and how they operate and evolve.

Simon Sinek discusses the difference between leaders and those who lead. He argues that people don't follow leaders because they have to but because they want to. Those who lead inspire us because they start with "why." Sinek discusses the law of diffusion of innovation and how attracting those who believe what you believe in achieving mass-market success is important.

To understand the power of "Start With Why," we first need to grasp the concept of the Golden Circle, a simple yet powerful model introduced by Simon Sinek. The Golden Circle comprises three concentric circles: Why, How, and What.

* * *

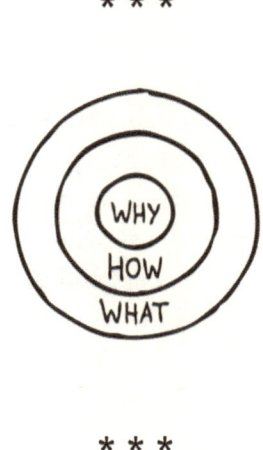

* * *

- **Why** - The core purpose, belief, or cause that inspires and drives an individual or organization.

- **How** - The strategies, processes, or methods used to realize the Why.
- **What** - The tangible products, services, or results in an organization offers.

Most people and organizations focus on the What and How aspects, often neglecting the crucial question of Why. By flipping this conventional approach and putting the Why at the center, we can unlock the full potential of our ideas and work. Incorporating the "Start With Why" practice empowers leaders to:

1. Inspire and engage: Articulating the Why behind a project, initiative, or organization can inspire and engage stakeholders, creating a sense of shared purpose and motivation.
2. Build trust: When people understand the Why, they are likelier to trust the How and What. This trust can lead to increased collaboration, improved decision-making, and accelerated progress.
3. Foster innovation: By focusing on the underlying purpose or belief, teams can stay open to innovative approaches that might not have been considered if they were merely focused on the How and What.
4. Drive long-term success: Teams that lead with Why are more likely to achieve long-term success, as their purpose-driven approach encourages continuous improvement, adaptability, and resilience.

A recommended approach for organizations seeking clarity on their purpose is to ask essential questions such as, "Why does our organization exist?" and "Who are our customers?" Determining the appropriate work to undertake, aside from tool or domain-specific tasks, can be challenging without a clear purpose.

This ambiguity can also hinder alignment on cross-domain priorities and make it difficult for leadership to comprehend the organization's impact on engineering or the business. Organizations should strive to see and define themselves as cohesive entities to maximize their potential.

What makes a good purpose statement?

A good purpose statement should be emotional, inspiring, simple, meaningful, in plain language and easy to understand. Further, it should be stable and able to last as long as the organization does. To ensure we identified a purpose that resonated with our customers and stakeholders, we assembled a working group of individuals from our teams and began researching.

Adopting a customer-driven perspective is recommended to define an organization's purpose. This can be achieved by interviewing people across all customer teams to understand their pain points and gather context on how they addressed specific problems.

Additionally, meeting with stakeholders and leadership provides insights into their long-term concerns, critical projects, or initiatives that must succeed. Reviewing backlogs, roadmaps, and plans helps understand the desired direction of customers and leadership over the next 12 months.

Asking the leadership team questions such as, "What keeps you up at night?" can reveal current concerns and provide context on the duration and impediments of these issues.

Inquiring about critical projects or initiatives that must succeed can help understand what is visible to senior leadership and link future investments to what matters most to them.

Organizations should gather input from customers and stakeholders to align priorities and create a clear identity. For instance, defining Developer Experience as "making it easy for engineers to ship high-quality code quickly and securely" can guide everything from a team's priorities to daily operations.

This approach allows organizations to align with cross-domain priorities and create a clear identity that customers and stakeholders can understand.

With a unified purpose established, the next step is determining the methods and actions required to achieve the desired outcomes.

Driving the How and What

* * *

In "Drive: The Surprising Truth About What Motivates Us," bestselling author Daniel H. Pink challenges traditional assumptions about motivation and presents a new paradigm that focuses on intrinsic motivation. This chapter examines the key ideas from Pink's book and explores their implications for individuals, teams, and organizations.

Rethinking Motivation

Pink argues that the conventional carrot-and-stick approach to motivation, which relies on extrinsic rewards and punishments, is outdated and ineffective. He introduces a new framework for understanding motivation, comprising three elements:

- **Autonomy:** The desire to direct our own lives.
- **Mastery:** The urge to get better at something that matters.

- **Purpose:** The yearning to do what we do in the service of something larger than ourselves.

Pink says these intrinsic motivators drive our behavior more effectively and sustainably than extrinsic rewards or punishments.

Autonomy is controlling our work, time, tasks, and team. When people have autonomy, they feel a sense of ownership and responsibility for their actions. Pink highlights four aspects of autonomy:

- Task autonomy: The freedom to choose what tasks to work on.
- Time autonomy: The flexibility to decide when to work on tasks.
- Technique autonomy: The liberty to choose how to approach and complete tasks.
- Team autonomy: The ability to select who we collaborate with.

Organizations that promote autonomy tend to have more engaged and productive employees and higher job satisfaction and well-being.

Mastery is the desire to improve and develop our skills continually. It involves embracing challenges, learning from mistakes, and seeking growth opportunities. Pink identifies three key elements for achieving mastery:

- Mindset: Adopt a growth mindset, which emphasizes the belief that abilities can be developed through effort and learning.
- Deliberate practice: Engage in focused, goal-oriented practice that targets areas for improvement and includes feedback.
- Persistence: Recognize that mastery requires time, effort, and resilience in the face of setbacks.

Organizations that support mastery create an environment where employees feel empowered to learn, grow, and excel.

Purpose is the understanding that our work contributes to something greater than ourselves. It connects our efforts to a broader mission or cause, fostering a sense of meaning and significance. Pink suggests two ways to cultivate a sense of purpose:

- Connect to a higher cause: Align individual and organizational goals with a larger, meaningful purpose. This can be a social, environmental, or humanitarian cause that resonates with employees.
- Practice servant leadership: Encourage leaders to focus on serving and supporting employees, prioritizing their growth and well-being. This approach can inspire a sense of shared purpose and commitment to the organization's mission.

Organizations emphasizing purpose can enjoy higher employee engagement, loyalty, and performance.

Applying the Principles of Drive

To tap into the power of intrinsic motivation, individuals, teams, and organizations can take the following steps:

Encourage autonomy: Provide opportunities for people to make choices and take ownership of their work. This can include offering flexible work arrangements, encouraging self-organized teams, and promoting a culture of trust and accountability.

Support mastery: Create an environment where people can develop and hone their skills. Offer training, mentoring, and resources for personal and professional growth, and encourage a culture of continuous learning and improvement.

Foster purpose: Help people connect their work to a larger

mission or cause. Communicate organizational values and goals, and demonstrate how individual efforts contribute to the overall purpose.

Rethink rewards: Shift the focus from extrinsic rewards, such as bonuses or promotions, to intrinsic rewards that foster autonomy, mastery, and purpose. For example, instead of offering a financial bonus for completing a project, consider providing opportunities for skill development or increased autonomy.

Nurture well-being: Recognize that intrinsic motivation is closely linked to overall well-being. Encourage work-life balance, create a supportive and inclusive work environment, and promote physical and mental health.

Leading a Developer Experience Team

* * *

The Developer Experience (DX) team plays a crucial role in shaping how developers interact with tools, processes, and systems within an organization.

As a leader of a DX team, your goal is to create an environment where developers can work effectively, efficiently, and with a high degree of satisfaction. Intent-Based Leadership, a concept popularized by David Marquet, offers a powerful approach to achieving this goal.

By implementing Intent-Based Leadership principles, you can improve your DX team's performance and influence the rest of the organization by serving as a role model.

In this chapter, we will explore the principles of Intent-Based Leadership and how to apply them to lead a DX team effectively.

The Story - Turn The Ship Around!

The story of intent-based leadership begins with David Marquet, a former submarine commander in the US Navy. In his book, "Turn the Ship Around!", Marquet shares his experience of leading the USS Santa Fe, a submarine struggling with poor performance and low morale.

When Marquet assumed command of the submarine, he quickly realized that the traditional top-down leadership model was not working. Instead, he adopted a new approach called "intent-based leadership."

Under Marquet's leadership, the crew of the USS Santa Fe was empowered to make decisions based on the commander's intent. This meant that instead of waiting for orders, the crew was encouraged to think critically and act based on what they believed was the best way to achieve the desired outcome.

This approach improved the submarine's performance and created a culture of innovation, collaboration, and ownership among the crew.

Since the publication of "Turn the Ship Around!" intent-based leadership has gained popularity in both the military and the business world. Organizations such as Google, Amazon, and Toyota have adopted this approach, recognizing the benefits of empowering their teams to make decisions and take ownership of their work.

Intent-based leadership is not just a leadership philosophy but also a mindset and a set of practices. Leaders who adopt this approach must be willing to let go of control, trust their teams, and provide a clear direction and purpose. Teams must be encouraged to think critically, take risks, and learn from failure.

Understanding Intent-Based Leadership

Intent-Based Leadership empowers team members to make informed decisions and take ownership of their work. This leadership style emphasizes trust, competence, and clarity as its foundation. The key principles of Intent-Based Leadership include the following:

- Giving control: Empower your team members to make decisions and take responsibility for their actions.
- Developing competence: Invest in the professional development of your team members and help them acquire the necessary skills and knowledge.
- Encouraging clarity: Ensure your team members understand the organization's goals, priorities, and work context.

Building a Culture of Trust and Ownership

A vital component of Intent-Based Leadership is fostering a culture where team members feel trusted and take ownership of their work. To achieve this, consider the following strategies:

- Delegate authority: Give your team members the autonomy to make decisions within their areas of expertise. This demonstrates trust in their capabilities and encourages them to take responsibility for their actions.
- Encourage open communication: Promote a culture where team members feel comfortable sharing their ideas, concerns, and feedback. This helps create an environment where everyone can contribute to the decision-making process and feel valued.
- Recognize and celebrate success: Acknowledge your team members' achievements and successes, reinforcing the sense of ownership and motivating them to deliver excellent results.

Developing Competence in Your DX Team

You must invest in their professional development to enable your DX team to perform at their best. Some ways to develop competence within your team include:

- Providing training opportunities: Offer training courses, workshops, and conferences to help your team members acquire new skills and stay current with industry trends.
- Encouraging knowledge sharing: Promote a culture of knowledge sharing within the team by organizing regular knowledge-sharing sessions, creating internal documentation, and encouraging team members to collaborate and learn from each other.
- Offering mentorship and coaching: Pair experienced team members with less experienced ones to facilitate knowledge transfer and skill development.

Clarifying Goals, Priorities, and Context

Help your DX team understand the organization's goals, priorities, and work context. This clarity will enable them to make better decisions and focus on the right tasks. To provide clarity, consider the following approaches:

- Communicate organizational objectives: Clearly articulate the organization's goals and priorities to your team members. This helps them understand how their work contributes to the bigger picture.
- Define team goals: Set specific, measurable, achievable, relevant, and time-bound (SMART) goals for your team. This helps them focus on the right tasks and measure their progress.

- Share context: Provide your team with the necessary context to understand the decisions made within the organization. This allows them to make more informed decisions and contribute more effectively to the organization's success.

Cultivating 10x Developers

* * *

Pursuing highly productive "10x Rockstar Ninja" developers is a common objective for organizations seeking top-notch talent. Regardless of the role or level of experience, the ability to perform focused, deep work is essential for success in technology.

Drawing inspiration from Cal Newport's book, Deep Work, this chapter will explore how cultivating the skill of deep work can help create many 10x developers in your organization, leading to a thriving, in-demand team.

The 10x Developer

We've all heard about the legendary developer who can get things done faster and with higher quality than anyone else.

These developers have become known as the 10x developers, and they are the ones who make a significant impact on the industry. In this chapter, I will share real-life examples of 10x developers and explore what makes them stand out.

First, let's define what a 10x developer is. The term "10x" refers to a developer's productivity compared to an average developer. A 10x developer can deliver ten times the value in the same time as an average developer.

These developers are highly skilled and efficient, have a deep understanding of their craft, and possess the ability to solve complex problems quickly.

One example of a 10x developer is Linus Torvalds, the creator of Linux. Torvalds developed Linux as a college student in 1991 and continued to refine and enhance it for years.

His Linux kernel development has profoundly impacted the industry and is widely regarded as one of the most significant contributions to open-source software. Torvalds is known for his passion, determination, and focus, all critical traits of a 10x developer.

Another example of a 10x developer is John Carmack, id Software's lead programmer, and co-founder. Carmack developed the game engines for games such as Wolfenstein 3D, Doom, and Quake.

He is known for his relentless pursuit of performance optimization, leading to significant game engine technology advancements. Carmack is also highly skilled in mathematics and physics, which helped him create realistic simulations in his games.

Another example of a 10x developer is Martin Fowler, the Chief Scientist at ThoughtWorks. Fowler is a renowned software engineer and author of many influential books on software development.

He is known for his ability to break down complex problems into simple solutions and has been a significant contributor to the agile methodology development. Fowler is also highly skilled in software architecture and has developed several well-known design patterns widely used in the industry.

In conclusion, a 10x developer possesses exceptional skills, knowledge, and work ethic. They deeply understand their craft and are highly efficient at solving complex problems.

Examples like Linus Torvalds, John Carmack, and Martin Fowler show us that becoming a 10x developer takes time, effort, and a strong commitment to continuous learning and improvement. While not everyone may become a 10x developer, we can all strive to improve our skills and become better at our craft.

Embrace the Creative Nature of Programming

Programming is often misunderstood as a purely technical and logical activity. However, it is essential to recognize and embrace the creative nature of programming to foster a thriving environment for your developers. By acknowledging the artistic potential within the craft of coding, you can inspire your developers to innovate, grow, and excel in their roles.

Encourage your developers to approach programming with an open, creative mindset. Empower them to explore new ideas, experiment with different techniques, and push the boundaries of conventional thinking. This creative mindset will lead to unique solutions, improved problem-solving skills, and better software.

Promote a culture of collaboration and idea-sharing among your developers. Please encourage them to share their ideas, learn from one another, and work together to solve complex problems. This exchange of knowledge and perspectives will inspire creative thinking and lead to innovative solutions.

Recognize and celebrate instances where your developers have employed creative problem-solving or developed unique solutions to challenges. By highlighting these successes, you reinforce the importance of creativity and inspire your team to continue embracing the artistic side of programming.

Allow your developers to pursue personal projects or explore their passions outside their primary responsibilities. These pursuits can inspire creativity, spark new ideas, and lead to valuable skill development that can be applied to their work within your organization.

The work environment plays a crucial role in fostering creativity. Provide your developers with a comfortable, inspiring, and flexible workspace that encourages innovation and collaboration. Ensure they can access the necessary tools and resources to unleash their creative potential.

As with any creative endeavor, practice is vital for growth and improvement. Encourage your developers to engage in focused, deep work, dedicating uninterrupted time to hone their programming skills. They can refine their craft and unlock their creative potential by practicing deliberately and effectively.

By embracing the creative nature of programming and supporting your developers in their artistic pursuits, you can cultivate a team of highly skilled, innovative, and passionate individuals. This creative environment will lead to better software and contribute to your organization's overall success and growth.

Foster a Growth Mindset Among Developers

The concept of a 10x developer, while often cited as an example of exceptional programming talent, can inadvertently lead to the belief that these developers possess innate abilities that cannot be cultivated.

Fostering a growth mindset among your developers is crucial to dispel this misconception. By emphasizing that the ability to produce high-quality work efficiently can be nurtured and honed with practice and training, you create a culture of continuous learning and improvement within your team.

Promote the idea that all developers can achieve mastery in their craft through dedication and persistence. Encourage your team members to view their skills as a constantly evolving work in progress rather than a fixed attribute.

Reinforce the importance of effort and persistence in achieving success. Celebrate instances where developers have put in the hard work to overcome challenges and improve their skills, regardless of whether they are junior or senior team members.

Offer regular opportunities for your developers to learn new technologies, languages, and methodologies. This can include workshops, conferences, online courses, or dedicated time for self-study. By giving your team the resources to grow, you encourage the belief that skills can be developed over time.

Foster a culture that embraces curiosity and encourages developers to ask questions, explore new ideas, and experiment with different approaches. When team members are willing to take risks and learn from their mistakes, they cultivate a growth mindset that leads to continuous improvement.

Help your developers set realistic, achievable goals that challenge them to grow and improve. Track their progress and celebrate their successes, large and small, to reinforce the notion that hard work and dedication pay off.

Encourage your developers to collaborate and share their knowledge, skills, and experiences. This collaborative environment facilitates learning and reinforces that everyone has something valuable to contribute, regardless of their current skill level.

Offer regular, constructive feedback to help your developers identify areas for improvement and growth. Please support them in their efforts to improve, providing guidance, resources, and encouragement as needed.

Teach your developers to view setbacks and failures as opportunities for growth rather than insurmountable obstacles. Please encourage them to analyze their mistakes, learn from them, and apply this newfound knowledge to future challenges.

By fostering a growth mindset among your developers, you create an environment where individuals are empowered to develop their skills, embrace challenges, and continuously improve. This leads to a more skilled and adaptable team and contributes to your organization's success and growth.

Help Your Team Prioritize and Manage Distractions

Promoting deep work and focus within your team is essential for achieving high-quality results. Helping your team manage distractions effectively creates an environment where developers can prioritize tasks, set boundaries, and eliminate potential interruptions. Here are some strategies to help your team achieve a distraction-free work environment.

Empower your developers by teaching effective time management skills. Introduce techniques such as time blocking, the Pomodoro Technique, or the Eisenhower Matrix to help them prioritize tasks and allocate their time efficiently.

Set expectations around communication, such as using specific channels for urgent matters, setting "Do Not Disturb" hours, or implementing regular check-ins to address questions and concerns. This will help minimize interruptions and allow team members to focus on their work.

Provide a workspace that minimizes distractions by offering private offices, quiet areas, or noise-canceling headphones. Encourage developers to personalize their workspaces to create a comfortable, focused environment.

Teach your team the importance of setting boundaries and saying "no" when necessary. This can include turning off notifications during deep work sessions, setting expectations with colleagues, and establishing personal routines to maintain a healthy work-life balance.

Provide your team access to productivity apps and tools to help them stay organized, manage their time, and eliminate distractions. This can include task management software, calendar apps, or website blockers to help them maintain focus during work hours.

Promote the importance of taking regular breaks and engaging in physical activity to maintain focus and productivity. This can include encouraging team members to step away from their desks, go for a walk, or engage in other forms of exercise to refresh their minds.

Introduce focused work sessions, such as "no-meeting days" or designated "deep work" hours, where team members can concentrate on high-priority tasks without interruptions.

Promote mindfulness practices, such as meditation or deep breathing exercises, to help your team develop greater focus and concentration. Encourage open discussions about productivity challenges and share strategies for overcoming distractions.

Offer workshops, seminars, or coaching to help your team develop the skills to manage distractions effectively. Encourage ongoing learning and provide support as they implement new strategies.

Helping your team prioritize and manage distractions creates an environment that fosters focus, productivity, and deep work. This leads to higher-quality outcomes and contributes to your organization's success and growth.

The Art of Saying "No"

* * *

As an engineering leader, you constantly face balancing your team's workload and maintaining healthy relationships with other departments.

In this chapter, we will explore the importance of knowing how to say "no" as an engineering leader, taking inspiration from Mark O'Neill, Gartner Chief of Research for Software Engineering, who discussed this topic in a Twitter post about the research.

It is not uncommon for software engineering leaders to struggle with saying "no." Empathy and a desire to support Sales or Product departments often lead to taking on work that might be unrealistic or unsustainable for the team. However, learning to say "no" is crucial for maintaining your team's well-being, efficiency, and overall success.

To help you navigate this delicate balance, we present the concept of the "assertive no." This approach enables engineering leaders to decline requests while maintaining positive relationships and reputational objectives. The "assertive no" communicates respect and consideration for the requestor and their goals, fostering a mutual understanding that paves the way for a constructive resolution. Here are some steps to deliver the "assertive no" effectively:

- Listen actively: Take the time to understand the requestor's perspective and the potential business value they see in their proposal. For instance, when a Product team requests a new feature that could impact DX negatively, listen to their rationale and consider the trade-offs between the feature's benefits and the potential impact on developer productivity. Demonstrating that you genuinely consider their needs will help you empathize with their situation and facilitate open communication.
- Communicate empathy: Adapt to each stakeholder and situation, expressing empathy for the requestor's objectives and challenges. For example, if a Sales team asks for customizations that could overburden developers and slow the overall development process, acknowledge the importance of meeting customer needs while highlighting the potential risks to DX. By expressing empathy, you can help defuse potential conflicts and encourage reciprocal empathy between both parties, leading to a more collaborative atmosphere.
- Provide a clear rationale: Offer a valid business or resource-related reason for your "no." For instance, if a request could significantly increase technical debt or affect the developers' ability to maintain a clean and modular codebase, explain how this could negatively impact the project's long-term success. By presenting a well-informed decision, you show that you prioritize both DX and the organization's overall goals, making it easier for the stakeholder to accept your decision.

- Be concise: Strive for brevity in your explanation, but avoid being too brief. When communicating your reasons for saying "no," provide enough context and information for the stakeholder to understand your perspective while not overwhelming them with excessive details. For example, when discussing the impact of a request on DX, you could briefly mention the additional workload it would place on developers or how it could affect the overall development timeline.

By incorporating these steps into your approach as an engineering leader, you can maintain a healthy balance between the needs of stakeholders and the importance of fostering an exceptional Developer Experience.

The "assertive no" empowers you to make informed decisions that prioritize the well-being and productivity of your team while demonstrating a commitment to the organization's broader objectives.

In conclusion, saying "no" is essential for engineering leaders who strive to provide a positive Developer Experience while managing stakeholder expectations. By mastering the "assertive no" technique, you can cultivate an environment where developers can thrive, leading to more successful and sustainable projects in the long run.

Embrace the power of "no" and unlock your potential as an engineering leader who champions Developer Experience and your organization's broader goals.

Overcoming The Fear of Saying "No"

Saying "no" can be daunting for many people, personally or professionally. The fear of disappointing others or being perceived as uncooperative can cause us to agree to things that may not align with our goals or values.

However, learning to say "no" is essential for maintaining a healthy work-life balance, setting boundaries, and making empowered decisions. This chapter will explore strategies to help you overcome the fear of saying "no" and embrace the power of setting limits.

Understand the Value of Your Time and Priorities

The first step in overcoming the fear of saying "no" is recognizing the importance of your time and priorities. Understand that your time is valuable, and you have the right to protect it by making conscious choices about spending it. Prioritize tasks and activities that align with your goals and values, and be willing to decline those that do not.

Reflect on Your Motivations and Fears

Take time to reflect on your fear of saying "no." Are you worried about disappointing others, damaging relationships, or facing potential conflict? By understanding the root causes of your fear, you can better address and overcome these concerns.

Recognize the Consequences of Always Saying "Yes."

Saying "yes" to everything can lead to overcommitment, burnout, and a diminished ability to focus on your most important tasks. Acknowledge the potential negative consequences of always saying "yes," and use this awareness to empower yourself to say "no" when necessary.

Practice Assertiveness and Clear Communication

Develop assertive communication skills to help you convey your "no" in a confident, respectful manner. Be clear and concise in your response, and avoid the temptation to over-explain or apologize excessively. Remember that saying "no" is not inherently aggressive; it is simply a statement of your boundaries and priorities.

Offer Alternatives When Possible

If you must decline a request, consider offering an alternative solution or compromise when appropriate. This can help maintain positive relationships while still asserting your boundaries.

Build Your Self-confidence

Cultivate self-confidence by acknowledging your strengths, accomplishments, and capabilities. A strong sense of self-worth can help you overcome the fear of saying "no" by reinforcing the belief that your opinions and decisions are valid and valuable.

Seek Support From Others.

Discuss your fears and challenges with trusted friends, colleagues, or mentors who can offer guidance, encouragement, and support. Surround yourself with people who respect your boundaries and can be role models for assertive communication.

Practice Saying "No" in Low-stakes Situations

Build your confidence by practicing saying "no" in situations where the stakes are lower, and the potential consequences are minimal. As you become more comfortable with saying "no," you'll find it easier to apply this skill in higher-stakes situations.

Overcoming the fear of saying "no" is vital for personal and professional growth. By understanding the value of your time and priorities, reflecting on your motivations and fears, and developing assertiveness and clear communication, you can learn to set boundaries and make empowered decisions. Embrace the power of saying "no" and unlock your potential for greater success and fulfillment in all aspects of your life.

Building a Magnet for Talent

* * *

As an engineering leader aspiring to excel in Developer Experience, one of your key challenges is to create an organization that attracts and retains top talent. In today's competitive landscape, offering competitive salaries and benefits is no longer enough.

You must create a compelling developer-experience-driven employee value proposition to stand out truly. This chapter will guide you through the essential steps to build an organization that becomes a magnet for talent.

- Craft a compelling developer-experience-driven employee value proposition: Your employee value proposition (EVP) is the unique combination of benefits, rewards, and opportunities your organization offers its employees. To attract top developers, your EVP should emphasize an exceptional Developer Experience, with a strong focus on growth opportunities, autonomy, cutting-edge technology, and positive work culture.

- Align with the market in roles, architecture, and technologies: Stay ahead of the curve by keeping up with the latest trends in software development roles, architectures, and technologies. This alignment ensures that your organization remains relevant and competitive and signals to the prospective talent that you are committed to innovation and continuous improvement.
- Modernize your tech stack and work with world-class tools: Top developers are attracted to organizations that use cutting-edge technology and tools. Modernizing your tech stack and adopting the best tools available demonstrate your commitment to quality and efficiency, making your organization more appealing to prospective talent.
- Deliver experiences that customers love by adopting outcome-based strategies: Emphasize a customer-centric approach in your development process, focusing on delivering solutions that truly meet customers' needs. This approach not only results in better products but also increases developers' motivation and satisfaction, as they can see the direct impact of their work on customer success.
- Develop an obsession with design and quality: Instill a culture of excellence within your organization with a strong focus on design and quality. Encourage your developers to take pride in their work and continuously strive to improve. To support this, invest in building a robust digital immune system, incorporating practices such as autonomous testing, chaos engineering, and observability.
- Be international: Embrace diversity and inclusivity by fostering an international mindset within your organization. This helps you attract talent worldwide,

enriches your work culture, and promotes innovation through diverse perspectives.

By following these steps, you can create a developer-experience-driven organization that attracts and retains the best talent in the industry. Remember, the key to becoming a magnet for talent is to provide an exceptional Developer Experience, enabling your team members to thrive and unlock their full potential.

With the right strategies, you will attract top talent and create an environment where they can flourish, ultimately driving your organization's success in your digital transformation journey.

Aligning Your Digital Transformation with Value Streams

* * *

This chapter will explore the importance of aligning your digital transformation efforts with a value stream strategy and how Developer Experience (DX) can support this alignment. A well-executed digital transformation can unlock significant value for your business, but it requires a thoughtful approach and a focus on delivering value at every process step.

As organizations navigate the ever-evolving digital transformation landscape, a deep understanding of value streams becomes crucial to success. The concept of value streams represents the interconnected series of activities and processes that contribute to creating and delivering value to customers.

In the context of digital transformation, a value stream strategy is an approach that aligns digital initiatives with these value streams to maximize the impact of transformation efforts. This chapter will explore a value stream strategy's essence and role in guiding digital transformation.

The Foundations of a Value Stream Strategy

A value stream strategy is built upon thoroughly understanding the organization's existing value streams. It involves mapping out the flow of activities and resources that create and deliver customer value.

This process allows leaders to identify bottlenecks, inefficiencies, and misalignments that may hinder the organization's ability to meet customer needs and achieve business objectives.

Aligning Digital Transformation Initiatives with Value Streams

Once the organization's value streams have been identified and assessed, aligning digital transformation initiatives with these streams becomes possible. This alignment ensures that digital initiatives are targeted, efficient, and focused on delivering the maximum possible value to the business.

By investing in digital initiatives that directly support the optimization of value streams, organizations can improve customer experiences, drive innovation, and achieve a competitive advantage in the marketplace.

Developing a Value Stream-Based Roadmap for Digital Transformation

A value stream strategy serves as a roadmap for digital transformation, guiding the organization's efforts and ensuring that resources are allocated effectively.

This roadmap includes prioritizing digital initiatives based on their impact on value streams and aligning them with the organization's objectives. It also involves setting clear, measurable goals for each initiative and monitoring progress toward achieving them.

Creating a Culture of Continuous Improvement

A key component of a successful value stream strategy is fostering a culture of continuous improvement within the organization. This involves regularly assessing value stream performance, identifying improvement areas, and implementing targeted initiatives to optimize them.

By continuously monitoring and refining value streams, organizations can remain agile and adaptable in changing market conditions and customer needs.

Real-world Examples of Value Stream Strategy in Action

To illustrate the power of a value stream strategy in digital transformation, consider the example of a global e-commerce company that wanted to improve its customer experience. The company identified inefficiencies in its order fulfillment process by mapping out its value streams.

The company then prioritized digital initiatives to streamline this process, invest in automation technologies, and optimize its supply chain.

As a result, the company significantly reduced order fulfillment times, increasing customer satisfaction and higher revenues.

In conclusion, a value stream strategy is a powerful tool that can guide organizations through the complexities of digital transformation. By aligning digital initiatives with value streams, organizations can ensure that their transformation efforts are targeted, efficient, and focused on delivering maximum value to customers and the business.

By embracing a value stream strategy, organizations can unlock the full potential of digital transformation and emerge as leaders in their respective industries.

The Role of Developer Experience (DX) in Supporting a Value Stream-Aligned Strategy

Developer Experience (DX) enables and supports a value stream-aligned digital transformation strategy. By focusing on DX, you can ensure your developers have the tools, processes, and environment to innovate, collaborate, and deliver value quickly and efficiently. Here are some ways that DX can support a value stream-aligned digital transformation strategy:

- Streamlining development processes: A strong focus on DX involves implementing streamlined development processes that minimize friction and waste. This enables developers to work more efficiently and deliver value faster, ultimately supporting your digital transformation goals.
- Emphasizing collaboration and communication: A key aspect of DX is fostering a culture of collaboration and open communication among development teams and other stakeholders. By breaking down silos and encouraging cross-functional collaboration, you can ensure that your digital transformation initiatives align with your organization's value streams and that all stakeholders work towards a common goal.
- Investing in the right tools and technologies: Providing your developers with cutting-edge tools and technologies is essential for driving innovation and enabling them to deliver value quickly. Make sure that your technology stack is modern and flexible and supports the needs of your development teams as they work on your digital transformation initiatives.
- Encouraging continuous improvement: A culture of continuous improvement is a hallmark of value stream-aligned strategies and successful DX. By fostering a

constant learning, experimentation, and iteration mindset, you can ensure that your digital transformation efforts are agile and responsive to changing customer needs and market conditions.

In conclusion, aligning your digital transformation efforts with a value stream strategy is crucial for unlocking maximum value and ensuring the long-term success of your initiatives. By focusing on Developer Experience, you can create an environment that empowers your development teams to innovate, collaborate, and deliver value quickly and efficiently, ultimately supporting your organization's digital transformation journey.

Involve UX Early and Often

* * *

I remember vividly the day I received the call to lead me on an incredible journey to Norway. I was tasked with leading project delivery, or residency as we called it, for a prestigious Norwegian agency responsible for managing the national register and data source for the digital exchange of information. I could feel the anticipation and excitement bubbling inside me as I prepared to embark on this adventure.

Upon arrival, I was greeted by the breathtaking beauty of Norway and the enormous challenge ahead. Our mission was to create a state-of-the-art platform-as-a-service (PaaS) offering to revolutionize developer experience and productivity.

This platform would be the backbone for the country's next generation of registry services, catering to internal and external developers.

Equipped with a wealth of UX research capabilities and a strong belief in collaboration, our team set out to listen actively to our internal customers, the developers. We discovered a fundamental problem: the agency had numerous internal proprietary tools, many created by a single "hero" developer who had since left the company. This left the organization a challenging environment to debug, evolve, and scale.

Our solution hinged on a community-based approach. By exploring the cloud-native landscape and engaging departments across the organization, we began to engineer a platform based on the UX research we conducted with stakeholders. This new PaaS would be the foundation for the future, built on usability, adaptability, and growth principles.

As the project progressed, we witnessed an incredible transformation. The once fragmented and inefficient environment evolved into a cohesive, well-oiled machine. Error correction became more efficient, and developers saw faster implementation times. The outcome was a future-proof platform treated as a product designed to serve the organization for years.

But the true measure of our success was not just the platform itself. Once struggling with outdated tools and disjointed practices, the development team was empowered with the right mindset and tools to excel. They had become a force to be reckoned with, capable of delivering an exceptional developer experience and laying a solid foundation for the future.

As we embarked on our mission to transform the developer experience for the Norwegian agency, I knew that our approach had to be thorough and effective. To achieve this, we turned to an extensive list of Discovery, UX, and Research practices to guide our efforts. I invite you to join me on this journey as I recount how these practices contributed to our success and provided invaluable insights into the hearts and minds of our users.

Empathy Mapping: As we delved into the world of our users, we realized the importance of truly understanding their experiences. We gathered our team and dedicated time to empathy mapping sessions, where we discussed and documented the developers' thoughts, feelings, and needs using the platform. We analyzed their daily routines, struggles, and aspirations, which allowed us to identify pain points and areas where we could make a significant impact. This exercise fostered a deeper connection with our users and ensured their voices were at the heart of our decisions.

How Might We: To foster a creative and collaborative environment, we introduced the "How Might We" (HMW) approach to our brainstorming sessions. This powerful question inspired our team to think beyond the constraints of the current situation and imagine innovative solutions to our challenges. By reframing problems as opportunities, the HMW technique unleashed our collective creativity and led to ideas that would have otherwise remained untapped.

Lean UX and the Double Diamond: The principles of Lean UX and the Double Diamond framework became the cornerstone of our development process. The Double Diamond consists of four phases: Discover, Define, Develop, and Deliver. This approach allowed us to explore ideas widely during the Discover and Develop phases and narrow our focus during the Define and Deliver phases. Lean UX encouraged us to iteratively test and validate our ideas through rapid prototyping and user feedback. This combination ensured we were continually moving in the right direction, learning from our users and refining our concepts to create a platform that resonated with them.

Non-functional Requirements: Beyond the functional capabilities of the platform, we recognized the importance of addressing non-functional requirements, such as scalability, security, and reliability. We dedicated resources to ensure these critical aspects were considered from the outset, laying a solid foundation for the platform's future. By addressing non-functional requirements early in the development process, we safeguarded the platform's ability to evolve and meet the demands of a growing user base while maintaining a secure and stable environment.

Proto Personas: To better understand the diverse needs of our user base, we created proto personas - fictional representations of different user groups. These archetypes helped us empathize with various user perspectives and preferences, ensuring we considered various experiences and expectations. By developing these proto-personas, we could tailor the platform's features and functionality to meet the unique needs of each user group, resulting in a more inclusive and accessible experience for all.

Stakeholder Map: Recognizing the importance of engaging all relevant parties, we began by mapping out the key stakeholders and their relationships. This visual representation enabled us to identify the organization's interests, concerns, and expectations. By involving and aligning these stakeholders throughout our journey, we fostered a collaborative atmosphere and ensured that our platform addressed the needs of everyone involved. This approach helped us build a strong foundation of support for our project and secured buy-in from all levels of the organization.

Start at the End: To maintain focus on our ultimate goal, we adopted the "Start at the End" strategy. We envisioned the ideal state of the platform and user experience, imagining what success would look like for our users and the organization. This vision was a guiding star, helping us make informed decisions and prioritize our efforts effectively. By keeping our end goal in mind, we could navigate the complexities of the project and ensure that each step brought us closer to realizing our desired outcome.

Impact Mapping: To align our actions with our objectives, we employed impact mapping – a strategic planning technique that visually represents the connections between our goals, the actors involved, and the specific actions required to achieve those goals. This exercise explained how our efforts would contribute to the desired outcomes and allowed us to prioritize activities based on their potential impact. With impact maps as our guide, we were better equipped to make data-driven decisions and stay on course toward delivering a successful platform.

Target Outcomes: Establishing clear, measurable target outcomes was essential for tracking our progress and determining the success of our platform. These targets helped us quantify the impact of our efforts, allowing us to identify areas of improvement and celebrate our achievements. Setting realistic and attainable goals created a sense of shared purpose and motivation within our team, inspiring everyone to strive for excellence.

Usability Testing: Ensuring our platform met user needs and expectations was paramount. To achieve this, we conducted usability tests at various stages of the development process. These tests involved real users interacting with our prototypes and providing valuable feedback on their experiences. This iterative approach allowed us to identify and address usability issues, refine our platform's design, and validate our ideas. Through continuous usability testing, we delivered a platform that met and exceeded user expectations, paving the way for a seamless and enjoyable user experience.

When presenting this project, I often compare the value we aimed to deliver to our users to how Linux releases a new version of their OS. It should feel like a gift, carefully designed and delivered to meet their needs, unlike Microsoft's forceful approach with Windows updates, which can feel rushed and disruptive.

*   *   *

Of course, our journey would not have been complete without the powerful technology that fueled our endeavor. We carefully selected a suite of tools that facilitated our work and brought joy to our development process. We created a robust and efficient platform that exceeded expectations by leveraging cutting-edge technologies such as OpenShift, Tekton, ArgoCD, and GitOps.

OpenShift: This container orchestration platform provided a solid foundation for deploying, managing, and scaling our applications. Built on Kubernetes, OpenShift offered an enterprise-ready solution that simplified application development and streamlined deployment. Its user-friendly interface and extensive features allowed us to focus on delivering value to our users while OpenShift took care of the underlying infrastructure.

Tekton: As a cloud-native CI/CD solution, Tekton played a vital role in automating our build, test, and deployment processes. Its Kubernetes-native architecture allowed us to create flexible and scalable pipelines that supported the rapid iteration and continuous improvement we sought. Tekton's integration with other tools in our technology stack further enhanced our ability to deliver a seamless developer experience.

ArgoCD: This declarative, GitOps-based continuous delivery tool proved invaluable in managing the deployment of our applications. ArgoCD enabled us to define our desired application state using Git repositories, ensuring that our deployments were consistent, version-controlled, and auditable. By automating application deployment and management, ArgoCD empowered our team to focus on feature development and innovation while maintaining a stable, reliable platform.

GitOps: Embracing the GitOps methodology allowed us to maintain a single source of truth for our platform's infrastructure and application configuration. By storing all configuration data in Git repositories, we ensured our platform was transparent and easily reproducible. This approach enabled our team to collaborate more effectively, track changes, and maintain a clear history of our platform's evolution. GitOps provided the foundation for a robust, auditable, and efficient development process crucial to our project's success.

By harnessing the power of these innovative technologies, we were able to create a platform that not only addressed the needs of our users but also provided a delightful experience for our development team. These tools enabled us to work efficiently and collaboratively, ultimately delivering a robust, scalable, and future-proof solution.

These practices were instrumental in creating a user-centric, future-proof platform that delighted our customers and empowered our development team. By leveraging these methodologies and tailoring them to your context, you, too, can impact your organization and ensure you deliver what your customers truly want.

My time in Norway was about solving a technical problem and changing how an organization approached development. It was about fostering a culture of collaboration and innovation, and above all, it was about understanding the crucial role UX plays in creating a seamless developer experience.

This Norwegian adventure will always hold a special place in my heart, as it is a powerful reminder of the impact we can make when we listen, collaborate, and innovate.

Inner-Sourcing and Open Source

* * *

Once upon a time, in the magical realm of technology, the open-source movement emerged like a phoenix from the ashes of proprietary software. It was a force that would revolutionize the world of software development, becoming a powerful weapon in the digital transformation journey.

As the open source movement gained momentum, it unlocked the hidden power of Developer Experience (DX), transforming how developers collaborated and co-created solutions.

In the early days of software development, proprietary software ruled the land. Developers were confined within the four walls of their organizations, unable to freely share their knowledge and innovations. The world was fragmented, and collaboration was a distant dream.

This was until a group of visionary developers, led by the wise wizard Linus Torvalds, took a bold stand and initiated the open-source movement.

These pioneers believed in the power of collaboration and the importance of open access to knowledge. They knew that, together, they could create a better digital world. The open-source movement spread like wildfire, igniting the spark of innovation in every developer who encountered it. The result was an explosion of creativity that changed the world of technology forever.

And so, the open-source movement became the cornerstone of the Developer Experience. The movement fostered an environment where developers could thrive, collaborate, and grow. The walls that once divided them crumbled, and a new era of innovation was born.

* * *

But how did open-source unleash the true power of DX? The answer lies in its core principles. The open-source movement promoted transparency, collaboration, and community-driven development. It encouraged developers to share their code, learn from each other, and build upon existing solutions. This created a global ecosystem where developers could collectively contribute, learn, and grow.

Open-source enabled developers to access a vast library of tools, frameworks, and resources at their fingertips. This enabled them to focus on solving problems instead of reinventing the wheel. This newfound efficiency and convenience spurred the rapid adoption of open source, and soon enough, it became the backbone of the software industry.

The open-source movement didn't stop there. The spirit of openness and collaboration extended beyond the boundaries of public projects, giving birth to the concept of inner source. This powerful idea took the best practices of open source and applied them within the walls of an organization.

Inner-source innovation can be fostered even within an organization's boundaries. Developers were encouraged to contribute to each other's projects, breaking down silos and fostering cross-functional collaboration. This created a breeding ground for innovation, improved efficiency, and streamlined processes, further fueling the growth of the Developer Experience.

The impact of open source and inner source on Developer Experience was extraordinary. It accelerated innovation, fostered a global community, and transformed how developers worked individually and as a team. Today, open source and inner source stand as the pillars of the digital transformation journey, empowering developers to create the future with the full potential of their talents and expertise.

And so, the story of the open source movement and its impact on the Developer Experience is a testament to the power of collaboration, community, and shared knowledge. It is a story of how openness and togetherness can unlock the true potential of developers, paving the way for a brighter, more innovative future in the magical realm of technology.

Inner Source In Detail

Inner-sourcing is adopting open-source collaboration principles within an organization to encourage knowledge sharing, code reuse, and cross-team collaboration. By leveraging internal resources and expertise, inner-sourcing fosters a culture of innovation reduces duplication of effort, and accelerates software development. Key benefits of inner sourcing include:

- Improved code quality and consistency
- Increased developer engagement and collaboration
- Faster problem-solving and innovation
- Reduced reliance on external dependencies

**

Inner-sourcing offers numerous advantages for organizations, including:

a. Enhanced collaboration: Inner-sourcing encourages teams to collaborate, share ideas, and contribute to projects beyond their immediate responsibilities. This increased collaboration leads to innovative solutions and a more unified organizational culture.

b. Improved code quality: By allowing developers to review and contribute to code across projects, inner-sourcing promotes better code quality and facilitates identifying and resolving issues earlier in the development process.

c. Faster development: Inner-sourcing accelerates the development process by enabling teams to leverage existing code, reducing duplication of effort, and streamlining the integration of new features and bug fixes.

d. Increased knowledge sharing: By providing access to code repositories and documentation, inner-sourcing fosters a knowledge-sharing culture that helps developers learn from one another and build on existing expertise.

e. Better resource utilization: Inner-sourcing allows organizations to tap into the skills and knowledge of their entire workforce, leading to more efficient resource allocation and better overall project outcomes.

* * *

While inner sourcing offers numerous benefits, it also presents challenges that organizations must consider and address:

a. Cultural change: Adopting inner sourcing requires a cultural shift within the organization, moving away from a siloed approach to software development and embracing transparency, collaboration, and shared ownership.

b. Intellectual property concerns: As developers contribute to projects across teams and departments, organizations must have clear policies to protect intellectual property and maintain compliance with regulatory requirements.

c. Coordination and governance: Inner sourcing requires coordination across teams and departments, as well as the establishment of clear governance structures to ensure consistent code quality, security, and adherence to organizational standards.

d. Training and support: Developers need guidance and support to navigate the inner-sourcing ecosystem, including training on tools, processes, and best practices.

Best Practices for Successful Inner-Sourcing

To maximize the benefits of inner sourcing and overcome potential challenges, organizations should follow these best practices:

a. Establish a clear inner-sourcing strategy: Define the goals, objectives, and scope of inner-sourcing within the organization, and communicate this strategy to all stakeholders.

b. Encourage a culture of collaboration: Foster an organizational culture that values transparency, collaboration, and knowledge sharing. Recognize and reward employees who contribute to inner-sourcing initiatives.

c. Implement the right tools and infrastructure: Provide developers with the tools, platforms, and infrastructure to facilitate inner sourcing, such as version control systems, code repositories, and collaboration tools.

d. Create clear guidelines and governance structures: Develop guidelines for code contribution, review, and approval, as well as governance structures to ensure consistent quality and security.

e. Provide training and support: Offer ongoing training and support to help developers navigate the inner-sourcing ecosystem and adopt best practices.

Setting Sail with Kubernetes

* * *

In the ever-evolving realm of technology, innovations emerge as beacons of hope, guiding us through the turbulent waters of digital transformation. One such beacon is Kubernetes, a powerful and versatile container orchestration platform that has revolutionized how we develop, deploy, and manage applications.

Like Pedro Álvares Cabral's groundbreaking voyage, Kubernetes has charted a course that has forever altered the landscape of software development and has become a critical component in the journey toward digital transformation.

The Genesis of Kubernetes: A Voyage of Discovery

Kubernetes' journey began in the hallowed halls of Google, where engineers Brendan Burns, Joe Beda, and Craig McLuckie embarked on a mission to develop a solution that would address the growing challenges of managing containerized applications at scale.

Their combined expertise and unwavering determination culminated in the creation of Kubernetes, first released as an open-source project in 2014.

The open-source nature of Kubernetes fostered a vibrant, collaborative community that has since contributed to its rapid evolution and widespread adoption. As organizations worldwide recognized the potential of containerization to accelerate software delivery and streamline operations, Kubernetes emerged as the de facto standard for container orchestration.

Kubernetes at the Helm: Commanding the Fleet of Digital Transformation

As digital transformation redefines the competitive landscape, organizations are under immense pressure to modernize their operations, embrace cloud-native technologies, and deliver exceptional user experiences.

Kubernetes has proven to be an invaluable ally in this quest, providing a robust and extensible platform that empowers organizations to navigate the complexities of the digital age.

Simplifying the Application Lifecycle: Kubernetes streamlines the deployment, scaling, and management of containerized applications, enabling organizations to respond swiftly to changing market dynamics and user demands. This agility is crucial in a digital transformation journey, as it fosters innovation, accelerates time-to-market, and helps maintain a competitive edge.

Ensuring Resilience and High Availability: Kubernetes' built-in fault tolerance and self-healing capabilities ensure that applications remain operational and highly available, even in the face of hardware failures or unexpected traffic spikes. This resilience is critical in the age of digital transformation, where downtime and performance issues can have severe consequences on a company's reputation and bottom line.

Facilitating Multi-Cloud and Hybrid Deployments: Kubernetes' platform-agnostic design enables organizations to embrace a multi-cloud or hybrid cloud strategy, providing the flexibility to deploy applications across diverse environments while avoiding vendor lock-in. This freedom is essential in a digital transformation journey, as it allows organizations to harness the full potential of cloud computing while mitigating the risks associated with relying on a single provider.

Accelerating DevOps Adoption: Kubernetes promotes a culture of collaboration between development and operations teams, facilitating adopting of DevOps practices and fostering continuous integration and continuous delivery (CI/CD) pipelines. By breaking down silos and streamlining workflows, Kubernetes accelerates software delivery and paves the way for a more agile and responsive organization.

Comparing Kubernetes and Vendor-Specific Cloud Providers

Vendor-specific cloud providers like AWS, Microsoft Azure, and GCP offer proprietary container orchestration services such as Amazon Elastic Kubernetes Service (EKS), Azure Kubernetes Service (AKS), and Google Kubernetes Engine (GKE), respectively.

These managed services are built on top of Kubernetes but provide additional features, integrations, and optimizations tailored to their specific cloud environments.

One of the primary advantages of Kubernetes over vendor-specific cloud providers is its open-source nature. Kubernetes is maintained and developed by a diverse community of contributors from various organizations, ensuring that a single vendor's interests do not dictate its growth and evolution. This democratization of development leads to a more robust and innovative platform, benefiting from the expertise of developers across the globe.

In contrast, vendor-specific cloud providers are proprietary platforms, subject to their parent companies' strategic decisions and business goals. While these companies contribute to the Kubernetes project, their primary focus is optimizing their managed services for their specific cloud environments, which can lead to a more constrained and less adaptable experience.

Kubernetes offers a high degree of flexibility and portability, allowing developers to run their applications on any cloud infrastructure, including on-premises data centers and hybrid clouds. This flexibility is particularly valuable in a multi-cloud world, where organizations often leverage multiple cloud providers for different aspects of their business.

Vendor-specific cloud providers, on the other hand, inherently encourage vendor lock-in. While they offer seamless integration within their respective ecosystems, migrating applications to other cloud providers can be complex and time-consuming. This lock-in can also lead to increased costs and reduced negotiating power as organizations rely heavily on a single provider.

Kubernetes' open-source nature and modular architecture enable developers to easily extend and customize the platform to meet their needs. A rich ecosystem of third-party tools, plugins, and integrations is available, further enhancing the capabilities of Kubernetes.

While vendor-specific cloud providers also offer customization options, these are generally limited to the offerings provided by the respective vendor. This can result in a more rigid and less adaptable experience, with developers potentially missing out on innovative solutions and tools in the broader Kubernetes ecosystem.

By choosing Kubernetes, leaders can avoid vendor lock-in, tap into a vibrant ecosystem of third-party tools and integrations, and build applications that can run on any cloud infrastructure.

Furthermore, the widespread adoption of Kubernetes has led to a growing talent pool of experienced developers and engineers familiar with the platform. This ensures organizations can find and onboard skilled team members more easily, strengthening the case for Kubernetes as the container orchestration platform of choice.

As organizations increasingly embrace cloud-native architectures and seek to avoid over-reliance on proprietary solutions, Kubernetes stands out as the most future-proof and versatile option. By choosing

Kubernetes over vendor-specific cloud providers, engineering leaders can unlock the full potential of containerization and microservices, ensuring their applications' continued growth, innovation, and success.

Embarking on the Kubernetes Adventure

As we embark on our digital transformation journey, Kubernetes serves as a steadfast compass, guiding us through uncharted waters and helping us navigate the challenges.

By harnessing the power of Kubernetes, organizations can chart a course toward greater agility, resilience, and innovation, weathering the storms of digital disruption and emerging stronger than ever.

In the chapters to come, we will explore the intricacies of Kubernetes in greater detail, delving into its best practices and real-world success stories.

Together, we will unlock the secrets of this remarkable platform and learn how to harness its full potential in our quest for digital transformation and improve the developer experience.

Infrastructure as Code

* * *

Developer experience (DX) is a crucial aspect of software development that refers to the ease with which developers can create, maintain, and deploy code. A vital element that contributes to an enhanced DX is the practice of defining infrastructure as code (IaC). This chapter will explore the importance of IaC in improving the developer experience and its connection to the GitOps model, which will be discussed in the next chapter.

Infrastructure as Code (IaC) is managing and provisioning computing resources and infrastructure through machine-readable definition files rather than manual hardware configuration or interactive configuration tools. IaC helps ensure that the infrastructure is consistent, repeatable, and more manageable, making it an essential part of modern software development practices.

IaC offers numerous advantages that lead to an improved developer experience. By defining infrastructure as code, developers can maintain consistency across different environments (e.g., development, staging, and production). This consistency reduces the likelihood of encountering environment-specific issues and makes it easier to reproduce problems and resolve them more efficiently.

When infrastructure is defined as code, it can be stored in a version control system like Git, allowing developers to track changes, collaborate, and review modifications. This enables better visibility into the infrastructure's evolution and promotes a more collaborative development process.

IaC enables automation of infrastructure provisioning and management, reducing the need for manual intervention. This saves time and minimizes the risk of human error, leading to a more stable and reliable infrastructure.

IaC makes scaling infrastructure up or down easier based on application needs. As developers modify the infrastructure code, the changes can be easily applied across multiple environments and resources, allowing for greater flexibility and adaptability.

The History of Infrastructure as Code

The concept of Infrastructure as Code has its roots in the evolution of computing and software development practices. Let's briefly examine the history of IaC and how it has grown to become an essential component of modern development workflows.

In the early days of computing, infrastructure management was primarily manual, with system administrators configuring individual servers, networking devices, and storage systems. As organizations began to scale their computing resources, the need for a more automated approach to managing infrastructure became apparent.

This led to development of various scripting languages and automation tools to automate repetitive tasks, such as configuring servers or deploying applications. While this approach was an improvement over manual configuration, it still had limitations. Scripts were often specific to a particular environment, and managing infrastructure changes were challenging.

As the complexity and scale of infrastructure continued to grow, configuration management tools like Puppet, Chef, and Ansible emerged in the mid-to-late 2000s. These tools allowed developers and system administrators to define infrastructure components and their desired state using a domain-specific language (DSL) or data serialization format (like YAML or JSON).

Configuration management tools enabled more efficient and standardized management of infrastructure. However, they still relied on mutable infrastructure, meaning that changes were applied to existing resources rather than recreating them from scratch.

The concept of immutable infrastructure emerged as a response to the limitations of mutable infrastructure. Immutable infrastructure treats infrastructure components as disposable and replaceable, with changes made by creating new resources rather than modifying existing ones.

Around the same time, cloud computing and virtualization technologies were becoming increasingly popular, further emphasizing the need for more efficient infrastructure management practices. Infrastructure as Code (IaC) was born out of these developments, enabling developers to define infrastructure using code and version control systems to manage changes, automate provisioning, and maintain consistency across environments.

The growth of cloud computing has led to the development of a new generation of IaC tools and platforms, such as AWS CloudFormation, Azure Resource Manager (ARM), Google Cloud Deployment Manager, and Terraform. These tools and platforms have made managing infrastructure across multiple cloud providers and on-premises environments easier using a single, unified approach.

The Declarative Power

The declarative approach to software development and infrastructure management has emerged as a powerful and effective paradigm, offering numerous benefits over traditional, imperative methods. By specifying the desired end state of a system rather than outlining the exact steps to achieve that state, the declarative approach simplifies complex processes. It promotes consistency, scalability, and maintainability. Below are some key benefits of adopting a declarative approach:

The declarative approach abstracts away the low-level details and complexities of implementing a specific system or configuration. Instead, developers define the desired outcome, allowing the underlying tools and platforms to handle the implementation details.

This simplification enables developers to focus on high-level objectives and functionality, improving productivity and reducing the cognitive load associated with managing intricate processes.

By defining the desired state of a system in a declarative manner, developers can maintain consistency across different environments and stages of the development process.

This consistency reduces the likelihood of encountering environment-specific issues, as the declarative definitions can be easily reproduced in various contexts. As a result, debugging and troubleshooting become more efficient, further enhancing the developer experience.

Declarative definitions can be stored in version control systems like Git, allowing developers to track changes, collaborate, and review modifications. This approach enables better visibility into the evolution of a system or infrastructure and promotes a more collaborative development process. By storing declarative definitions in a version control system, development teams can maintain a history of changes and easily revert to previous states if needed.

A declarative approach lends itself well to automation, as the underlying tools and platforms can automatically enforce the desired state. By removing the need for manual intervention and detailed step-by-step instructions, the declarative approach minimizes the risk of human error, leading to a more stable and reliable system.

Declarative definitions provide a higher level of abstraction, making it easier to scale systems and adapt to changing requirements. By modifying the desired state of a system, developers can easily apply changes across multiple environments and resources. This flexibility enables development teams to more readily adapt to evolving business needs and maintain the agility required in today's fast-paced software development landscape.

In conclusion, the declarative approach significantly benefits software development and infrastructure management. By focusing on the desired end state and abstracting away implementation details, developers can achieve greater simplicity, consistency, and scalability. By embracing the declarative approach, development teams can enhance their overall experience, streamline workflows, and deliver more reliable and adaptable solutions.

Infrastructure as Code and declarative are powerful approach that significantly enhances the developer experience by providing consistency, reproducibility, version control, automation, and scalability. When combined with GitOps, IaC further streamlines the development and deployment process, fostering a culture of collaboration and shared responsibility. As you move on to the next chapter, you'll explore the link between Infrastructure as Code and GitOps in more detail, enabling you to make the most of these practices to improve your developer experience.

Increasing Reliability with GitOps

* * *

GitOps, my favorite pattern, is arguably one of the most powerful paradigms in software development. It stands out as the most advanced workflow designed with DevOps principles in mind. It effectively addresses the challenges faced by modern development teams by streamlining deployment processes, automating infrastructure management, and fostering a culture of collaboration and shared responsibility It's a paradigm that leverages Git as the single source of truth for declarative infrastructure and application configuration, automating the deployment process using continuous delivery pipelines.

This chapter will explore the principles of GitOps, its benefits and challenges, best practices, and how to get started with implementing GitOps in your organization.

GitOps is an operational framework built on Git, a distributed version control system, and Kubernetes, a container orchestration platform. By using Git as the central point for managing infrastructure and application configurations, GitOps streamlines the deployment process, ensuring consistency and reliability across environments. The GitOps approach is built on four key principles:

a. Declarative configuration: Infrastructure and application configurations are defined using a declarative language, allowing teams to specify the desired state of their systems without detailing the steps to achieve that state.

b. Version control: All configurations are stored in a Git repository, providing a single source of truth, version control, and an audit trail for all changes made to the system.

c. Continuous delivery: Changes to infrastructure and application configurations are automatically applied to the target environment through continuous delivery pipelines, eliminating manual intervention and reducing human error.

d. Observability: The system's current state is continuously monitored and compared to the desired state defined in the Git repository, ensuring that discrepancies are detected and resolved quickly.

Advantages

GitOps offers several advantages for organizations, including:

1. Increased reliability: By automating deployments and eliminating manual intervention, GitOps reduces the risk of human error and ensures consistency across environments.
2. Enhanced collaboration: GitOps promotes collaboration between development and operations teams by using familiar Git workflows and processes, making it easier to track, review, and approve changes
3. Improved audibility: Storing all infrastructure and application configurations in a Git repository provides a complete audit trail of changes, facilitating compliance with regulatory requirements and simplifying identifying and resolving issues.

4. Faster deployments: GitOps accelerates the deployment process by automating the application of changes, reducing the time it takes to deliver new features and bug fixes to production.

Challenges

While GitOps offers numerous benefits, it also presents some challenges that organizations should consider:

a. Learning curve: Adopting GitOps requires teams to learn new tools, processes, and workflows, which can be a significant investment in time and resources.

b. Security concerns: Storing sensitive configuration data in a Git repository can introduce security risks. Organizations must ensure proper access controls and encryption to protect sensitive data.

c. Integration with existing systems: Integrating GitOps with existing systems and tools can be complex and may require customization or the development of additional tooling.

Best practices

To successfully implement GitOps in your organization, consider the following best practices:

Start small: Begin by implementing GitOps on a small scale, such as a single application or environment, and incrementally expand its adoption as your team becomes more comfortable with the approach.

Standardize workflows: Establish standardized workflows for managing infrastructure and application configurations, including branching, merging, and pull request processes. This consistency will make it easier for teams to collaborate and ensure that best practices are followed across the organization.

Automate everything: Automate the deployment process from end to end, including testing, validation, and rollback capabilities, to ensure consistency and reliability across environments. Automation speeds up the deployment process, reduces the risk of human error, and makes it easier to maintain your infrastructure.

Monitor and observe: Continuously monitor the state of your systems and compare them to the desired state defined in your Git repository, alerting you on discrepancies and automatically triggering remediation actions when necessary. This approach ensures that your infrastructure remains desired and any issues are detected and resolved quickly.

Emphasize security: Take steps to secure your Git repository and its configurations. This includes implementing proper access controls, using encryption for sensitive data, and regularly reviewing and auditing access logs to detect and prevent unauthorized access.

Train your team: Ensure members know GitOps principles, tools, and processes. Provide ongoing training and support to help them adopt the new approach and work more effectively within the GitOps framework.

Establish clear governance: Define roles and responsibilities for team members involved in the GitOps process. This includes specifying who can make configuration changes, who is responsible for reviewing and approving changes, and who is responsible for monitoring and maintaining the system's overall health.

Document your process: Thoroughly document your GitOps processes and best practices, making it easy for team members to understand the approach and contribute effectively. This documentation should include guidelines on managing infrastructure and application configurations and step-by-step instructions for common tasks and workflows.

Encourage collaboration: GitOps promotes collaboration between development and operations teams, which can lead to better communication and more efficient processes. Encourage team members to actively participate in the GitOps process, share their knowledge and expertise, and work together to solve problems and improve the overall system.

Continuously improve: Regularly review and evaluate your

GitOps processes to identify areas for improvement. By continuously iterating and refining your approach, you can ensure that your organization stays current with the latest GitOps best practices and benefits from the ongoing improvements in the field.

Popular Tools

A key aspect of GitOps is using specialized tools designed to manage the deployment and synchronization of infrastructure and application code based on Git repositories. Two prominent tools in the GitOps ecosystem are ArgoCD and Flux, and both are open-source projects and have been widely adopted by development teams for implementing GitOps workflows.

ArgoCD, a project under the Cloud Native Computing Foundation (CNCF), is a declarative, GitOps-based continuous delivery tool for Kubernetes. It leverages Git repositories as the single source of truth for Kubernetes resources and automates the process of deploying and managing applications. ArgoCD supports various configuration management tools, such as Kustomize, Helm, and Jsonnet, providing flexibility in defining Kubernetes manifests.

Flux, also a CNCF project, is another popular GitOps tool for managing Kubernetes deployments. Flux automatically synchronizes the desired state defined in a Git repository with the current state of the Kubernetes cluster. It supports a range of deployment strategies, including Canary and Blue/Green deployments, and works seamlessly with Helm charts for packaging and deploying Kubernetes applications. Additionally, Flux provides features such as automatic updates and rollback capabilities, ensuring a robust and resilient deployment process.

ArgoCD and Flux are powerful tools that help organizations implement GitOps workflows, streamline infrastructure and application deployments, and improve the overall developer experience. By leveraging these tools, development teams can enforce best practices, simplify deployment processes, and maintain consistency across different environments.

Templating with Helm Charts

In the context of Kubernetes-based applications, Helm charts play a significant role in streamlining the deployment process and improving the developer experience. This chapter will focus on the benefits of using Helm charts for managing Kubernetes resources and their connection to the GitOps model, which emphasizes using Git as a single source of truth for both application and infrastructure code.

Helm is a package manager for Kubernetes that simplifies deploying, managing, and upgrading applications on Kubernetes clusters. Helm charts are the packaging format used by Helm, containing all the necessary Kubernetes resource definitions, metadata, and configurable values required to run an application. Helm charts enable developers to define, version, share, and reuse application configurations across different environments, making them an invaluable tool for enhancing the developer experience.

Helm charts offer numerous advantages that contribute to an improved developer experience. Helm charts provide a standardized way of defining and deploying Kubernetes applications, encapsulating complex configurations into a single, easy-to-use package. This simplification enables developers to focus on writing application code rather than wrestling with the intricacies of Kubernetes resource definitions.

Helm charts can be versioned and stored in Helm repositories, allowing developers to maintain a history of application configurations and share them across teams. This promotes the reusability of configurations and encourages collaboration within the development community.

Helm charts support templating, which allows developers to create dynamic Kubernetes resource definitions based on configurable values. This enables the customization of application deployments according to the requirements of different environments, further enhancing the developer experience.

Helm provides built-in support for managing application rollbacks and upgrades, making it easier for developers to maintain and update their applications on Kubernetes clusters. This reduces the risk of deployment issues and ensures that applications remain stable and reliable.

Helm Charts in the GitOps Context

In the GitOps model, Helm charts can be utilized as a part of the infrastructure and application management process. By storing Helm charts in a Git repository, development teams can leverage the benefits of GitOps, such as version control, collaboration, and automation, to enhance the developer experience further:

GitOps tools like ArgoCD and Flux can be configured to work with Helm charts, automating the deployment and synchronization of applications on Kubernetes clusters. This ensures that the desired application state, as defined in the Helm chart, is always in sync with the actual state of the Kubernetes cluster, reducing the need for manual intervention.

By storing Helm charts in a Git repository, development teams can collaborate on application configurations, perform code reviews, and track changes over time. This promotes a culture of shared responsibility and encourages the adoption of best practices for Kubernetes resource management.

When Helm charts are used in conjunction with GitOps, it becomes easier to monitor and observe changes in application configurations. As all modifications to Helm charts are tracked in the Git repository, development teams can quickly identify and resolve issues, further enhancing the developer experience.

Helm charts play a crucial role in improving the developer experience by simplifying the deployment and management of Kubernetes-based applications. When used in the GitOps context, Helm charts can further streamline the development process, fostering a culture of collaboration, shared responsibility, and best practices. By leveraging Helm charts and GitOps, development teams can achieve a more efficient, reliable, and enjoyable development experience.

As you continue to explore the world of GitOps and Kubernetes, consider incorporating Helm charts as part of your application deployment strategy. By doing so, you will enhance the developer experience and ensure that your applications are consistently managed and deployed across various environments. This will lead to more stable, secure, and scalable applications, ultimately benefiting both your development team and the end users who rely on your software.

Leveraging OKRs and KPIs

* * *

Organizations must constantly evolve to stay ahead of the competition in today's rapidly changing digital landscape. One key component of successful digital transformation is the developer experience (DX).

Setting clear objectives and measuring progress using Objectives and Key Results (OKRs) and Key Performance Indicators (KPIs) is essential to ensure that your organization's DX remains a powerful weapon in your digital transformation journey.

This chapter will explore the importance of OKRs and KPIs in driving a successful developer experience and how they contribute to digital transformation. We'll discuss setting meaningful objectives, selecting the right KPIs, and monitoring progress to achieve your goals.

* * *

Understanding OKRs and KPIs

Objectives and Key Results (OKRs): A widely-used goal-setting framework helps organizations articulate, track, and measure their strategic objectives. The OKR framework is designed to maintain a razor-sharp focus on the desired outcomes and to create alignment within the organization. The two main components of OKRs are:

- Objectives: These are high-level, qualitative goals clearly defining the organization's goals. Objectives are meant to be ambitious, inspiring, and time-bound, serving as a rallying point that unifies and motivates teams to work together towards the larger goal.
- Key Results: These are quantitative, measurable outcomes that indicate progress toward the corresponding objective. Key Results must be specific, achievable, and time-bound, ensuring that teams can track their progress effectively and adjust as needed.

The OKR framework is distinct from traditional goal-setting methods in its emphasis on setting ambitious targets and prioritizing outcomes over activities. This outcome-oriented approach encourages teams to think beyond their immediate tasks, fostering innovation and pushing them to explore new ways of achieving their objectives.

One of the most powerful aspects of the OKR framework is its ability to align individual, team, and organizational goals. By cascading OKRs down from the organizational level to individual contributors, a clear line of sight is created between each team member's work and the organization's strategic objectives. This alignment ensures that everyone in the organization works together towards a shared vision, making it easier to achieve large-scale success.

The OKR framework offers organizations a structured and effective approach to setting and tracking strategic objectives. By focusing on ambitious, outcome-driven goals and fostering alignment across all levels of the organization, OKRs help create a shared sense of purpose and drive teams to work together to pursue their shared objectives.

* * *

Key Performance Indicators (KPIs): These are measurable metrics used to evaluate the performance of an organization, team, or individual against predefined targets. These quantifiable metrics serve as valuable tools for tracking progress, pinpointing areas for improvement, and assessing the effectiveness of various strategies and initiatives. To ensure KPIs accurately represent progress and contribute to driving desired outcomes, they should adhere to the SMART criteria, which stands for Specific, Measurable, Achievable, Relevant, and Time-bound.

Throughout this book, we will explore various examples of KPIs, exploring their significance in different contexts and illustrating how they can be effectively utilized to enhance the developer experience, optimize workflows, and support digital transformation efforts. By examining these KPIs in detail, you will better understand how to select and implement the most appropriate performance indicators for your organization's unique needs and goals. Some of the KPI examples we will cover in this book include the following:

- Developer satisfaction: This KPI gauges the overall satisfaction of developers within an organization, which can be measured using surveys, feedback, and interviews. By tracking developer satisfaction, organizations can gain insights into the effectiveness of their developer experience initiatives and make improvements as needed.
- Code quality: Monitoring metrics like code coverage, defect density, and code review feedback can help

organizations assess code quality, an essential component of a positive developer experience. Improving code quality can lead to more efficient development processes, fewer bugs, and better product outcomes.
- Deployment frequency: Measuring the frequency of code deployments to production can provide insights into the efficiency of development processes and the developer experience. Frequent deployments indicate a streamlined and efficient development pipeline.
- Mean time to resolution (MTTR): Tracking the average time taken to resolve issues and bugs can help organizations identify bottlenecks in their development processes and make improvements to enhance the developer experience.

By exploring these and other KPIs in-depth, this book aims to provide readers with the knowledge and tools to select, implement, and track their organization's most relevant performance indicators.

By better understanding KPIs and their role in driving developer experience and digital transformation, organizations can make data-driven decisions, optimize their processes, and ultimately achieve their strategic objectives.

Chapter 7
Charting The Course

* * *

Navigating the uncharted waters of software development often resembles the journey of explorers and navigators from the past: the path is rarely direct, and unforeseen challenges frequently arise. However, the importance of planning cannot be overstated.

Maps, route patterns, interactions, training, experience, and leadership awareness increase the likelihood of reaching a destination successfully. This chapter will delve into the essential aspects of planning for an exceptional developer experience within an organization.

Providing an outstanding developer experience is paramount for any enterprise striving to create high-quality software efficiently. Organizations must establish the right team structure, implement effective working methods, and address cognitive load challenges to achieve this.

By doing so, they create an environment where developers can thrive, innovate, and drive the digital transformation essential in today's competitive landscape.

In this chapter, we will explore the following key elements of planning for a successful developer experience:

The Right Team Structure

Suggested team structure: We will discuss the recommended team structure for enterprises to follow, ensuring the most efficient and productive environment for developers.

Teams and their key responsibilities: We will outline the suggested teams, their primary responsibilities, and how they contribute to the organization's overall success.

Roles and role descriptions: We will delve into the suggested roles within these teams and provide role descriptions to clarify expectations and responsibilities.

Ways of Working

Principles of Agile: In this section, we will discuss the principles of Agile, focusing on its benefits and how it can improve the developer experience by promoting collaboration, adaptability, and continuous improvement.

Anti-patterns of DevOps: We will cover common anti-patterns that can hinder developer experience and negatively impact software development processes.

Important Things to Consider

Cognitive load: In this section, we will explore the concept of cognitive load and its impact on developer experience. We will discuss strategies for managing cognitive load and maintaining a balance between the work demands and the developers' capabilities.

Conclusion

Planning for an excellent developer experience is critical to any organization's software development process. By considering the right team structure, implementing efficient ways of working, and addressing cognitive load challenges, organizations can create an environment that supports and empowers developers to produce high-quality software.

Join me as we embark on this exciting journey, drawing on the wisdom of explorers and navigators who have come before us. By meticulously planning for the challenges ahead, we can chart a course toward a future where our organization's developer experience is exceptional.

With the right planning and execution, we can transform our organization into a beacon of innovation and success in the ever-evolving world of software development.

A Better Team Structure

* * *

Selecting the ideal DevOps team structure or topology for an organization hinges on several key factors:

- The organization's product portfolio: Fewer products lead to simpler collaboration, as there will be fewer natural silos, in line with Conway's Law.
- The quality, potency, and efficacy of technical leadership and the shared goals between Development and Operations teams.
- The organization's capability and willingness to transform its IT Operations department from focusing on tasks such as 'racking hardware' and 'configuring servers' to aligning with the value stream and ensuring operational features are prioritized by software teams.
- The organization's ability and expertise in addressing operational concerns.

While there are various topologies and types, they should serve as a reference guide or heuristics for evaluating suitable patterns. A mixture of multiple patterns or transitioning from one pattern to another often yields the most effective results.

So, what team structure allows DevOps to thrive? No single configuration or team topology will fit all organizations. Nonetheless, it is beneficial to categorize a limited number of different models for team structures, with some being more suitable for certain organizations than others.

By examining the strengths and weaknesses of these team structures (or 'topologies'), we can determine the team structure that best supports DevOps practices in our organizations, considering Conway's Law.

In this chapter, we acknowledge the valuable contributions of several experts in the field of DevOps, who have significantly shaped our understanding of team structures and topologies.

Lawrence Sweeney of CollabNet, for instance, has provided crucial insights in a comment on Ben Kepes's blog. The DevOps-Guys have compiled a comprehensive list of Twelve DevOps Anti-Patterns, which has informed our discussion.

Furthermore, the thoughts and ideas shared by Jez Humble, Gene Kim, Damon Edwards, and other prominent voices have contributed to developing DevOps practices and topologies.

The foundation of this chapter is largely based on the work of these industry leaders, and we extend our gratitude for their contributions.

We would also like to highlight the DevOps Topologies collection of patterns (diagrams and descriptions) by Matthew Skelton and Manuel Pais as an indispensable resource for understanding various team structures and determining the most suitable approach for your organization.

Recognizing Anti-Patterns in Team Structures

* * *

In this chapter, we will explore various anti-patterns in team structures that can hinder the successful implementation of DevOps practices. By understanding these pitfalls, organizations can avoid them and create an environment where collaboration and integration improve efficiency and effectiveness.

Anti-Type A: Dev and Ops Silos

The classic 'throw it over the wall' split between Development and Operations teams results in software operability issues. Developers lack context for operational features, while Operations teams do not engage developers to address problems before the software goes live. Although this topology is widely recognized as problematic, there are worse scenarios.

* * *

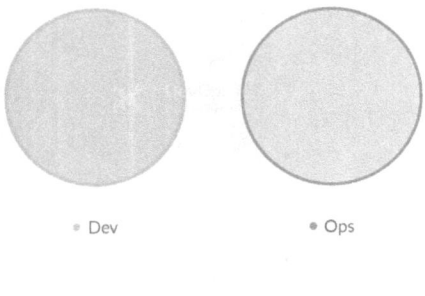

* * *

Anti-Type B: DevOps Team Silo

This anti-pattern emerges when an organization creates a separate DevOps team to incorporate "a bit of this DevOps thing." The DevOps team members form another silo, further distancing Development, and Operations. A separate DevOps team makes sense only when it is temporary, with the specific goal of bringing Development and Operations closer together.

* * *

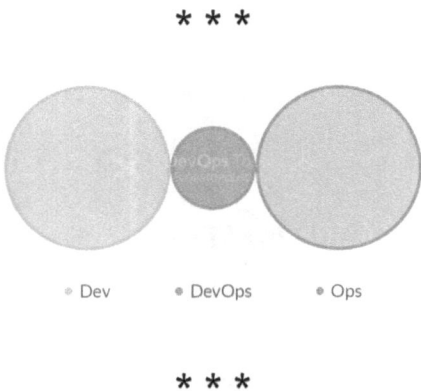

* * *

Anti-Type C: Dev Don't Need Ops

When developers and development managers underestimate the complexity and importance of operational skills and activities, they

Recognizing Anti-Patterns in Team Structures

assume they can manage without them. This topology typically requires a Type 3 (Ops as IaaS) or Type 4 (DevOps-as-a-Service) topology when operational activities overwhelm development time.

* * *

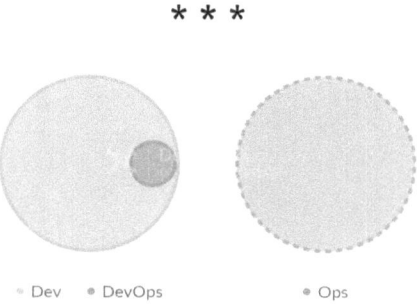

Anti-Type D: DevOps as Tools Team

A DevOps team is created to work on tooling while Operations teams work in isolation. Although this team can improve the toolchain, the lack of early Operations involvement and collaboration in the application development lifecycle remains an issue.

* * *

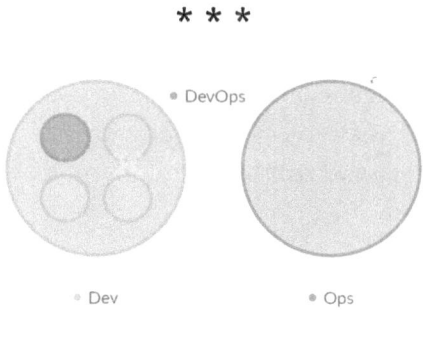

* * *

Anti-Type E: Rebranded SysAdmin

This anti-type is common in organizations with low engineering maturity that view IT as a cost center rather than a core business driver. They "do DevOps" by hiring "DevOps engineers" for their Ops teams, but this is simply a rebranding of the SysAdmin role, with no real cultural or organizational change taking place.

* * *

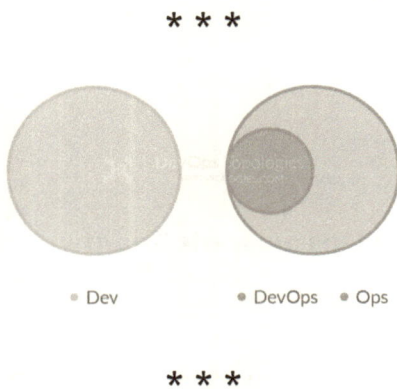

* * *

Anti-Type F: Ops Embedded in Dev Team

In this anti-pattern, development teams take responsibility for infrastructure, managing environments, and monitoring. However, treating these tasks as a project or product-driven responsibility leads to subpar approaches and half-baked solutions.

* * *

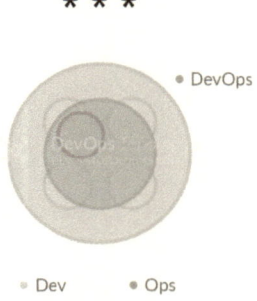

Recognizing Anti-Patterns in Team Structures

* * *

Anti-Type G: Dev and DBA Silos

Prominent in medium-to-large companies, this anti-pattern stems from a dedicated Database Administrator (DBA) team acting as a gatekeeper for database changes, hindering small and frequent deployments. The lack of early involvement in application development leads to data problems discovered late in the delivery cycle.

* * *

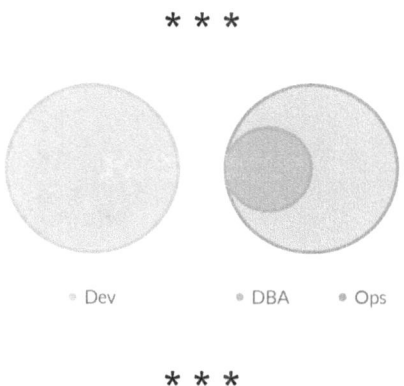

- Dev   - DBA   - Ops

* * *

Anti-Type H: Fake Site Reliability Engineering (SRE)

This is a form of Anti-Type A (Dev and Ops Silos) but with a twist. Ops engineers are now called SREs, but the fundamental issues remain. Software operability suffers due to the lack of collaboration between developers and SREs, leading to persistent problems.

* * *

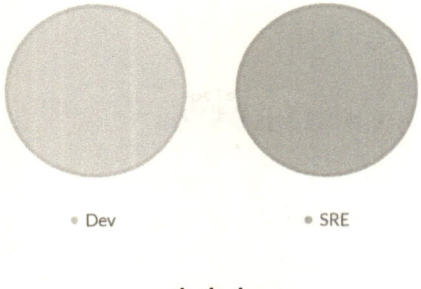

* * *

Organizations can create a more conducive environment for successfully adopting and implementing DevOps practices by understanding and avoiding these anti-patterns in team structures.

The Team API Template Exercise

* * *

In your digital transformation journey, creating a positive developer experience is crucial for the success of your organization. An essential aspect of achieving this lies in structuring your teams effectively and enabling seamless collaboration.

In this chapter, we will explore the Team API Template, a powerful tool for defining a Team API, inspired by the ideas in the book Team Topologies by Matthew Skelton and Manuel Pais.

By implementing this template, you can establish clear communication and collaboration channels, improving team dynamics and overall productivity.

The Team API Template is a structured approach to defining a Team API (Application Programming Interface) that outlines the interactions and responsibilities of each team within an organization. This template helps to create a shared understanding of how teams should collaborate, communicate, and support each other while minimizing dependencies and fostering autonomy. The Team API Template comprises the following key components:

Team Purpose: Clearly articulate the primary goal or mission of the team. This should be aligned with the organization's broader objectives and serve as the foundation for the team's decision-making and prioritization.

Services and Capabilities: Identify the core services and capabilities the team is responsible for providing the organization. This includes the systems, applications, or components the team owns and maintains.

Team Dependencies: Highlight any dependencies on other teams or external resources. This helps to identify potential bottlenecks and areas where collaboration or coordination is necessary.

Team Interaction Modes: Outline the preferred methods and channels for communication and collaboration, both within and with other teams. This may include tools, meeting formats, or communication protocols.

Service Level Objectives (SLOs): Define the expected levels of performance and availability for the team's services and capabilities. These objectives should be measurable and agreed upon by all stakeholders.

APIs and Integration Points: Document the APIs and integration points the team provides for other teams to interact with their services and capabilities. This ensures a clear understanding of how teams can collaborate and leverage each other's work.

Team Evolution: Describe how the team's purpose, services, and capabilities may evolve, considering the organization's strategic direction and growth plans.

Implementing the Team API Template

To successfully implement the Team API Template, follow these steps:

Gather Input: Engage with team members and stakeholders to gather input on the team's purpose, services, dependencies, and interaction modes. This ensures that the Team API accurately reflects the current state and needs of the team.

Document the TEAM API: Create a comprehensive Team API document for each team within your organization using the input gathered. This document should be easily accessible and regularly reviewed and updated.

Share and Communicate: Share the Team API documents with all relevant parties, ensuring that everyone clearly understands their roles and responsibilities and the expectations of others.

Review and Iterate: Regularly review and update the Team API documents to reflect any changes in team structure, services, or organizational goals. This ensures that the Team API remains accurate and relevant, fostering a culture of continuous improvement.

Measure and Monitor: Track the success of the Team API implementation by monitoring key performance indicators (KPIs), such as team productivity, collaboration effectiveness, and service level objective achievement. Use these metrics to identify areas for improvement and make any necessary adjustments.

* * *

Example of Team API Template

[Team Name] Team API

- *Date:*
- *Team name and focus:*
- *Team type:*
- *Part of a Platform? (y/n) Details:*
- *Do we provide a service to other teams? (y/n) Details:*
- *What kind of Service Level Expectations do other teams have of us?*
- *Software owned and evolved by this team:*
- *Versioning approaches:*

- *Wiki search terms:*
- *Chat tool channels:* #_____ #_____
  #_____
- *Time of daily sync meeting:*
- *Team type: (Stream-Aligned, Enabling, Complicated Subsystem, Platform)*

What we're currently working on

- *Our services and systems:*
- *Ways of working:*
- *Wider cross-team or organizational improvements:*

Teams we currently interact with:

- *Team name/focus*
- *Interaction Mode*
- *Purpose*
- *Duration*
- *Team Interaction Modes: (Collaboration, X-as-a-Service, Facilitating)*

Teams we expect to interact with soon:

- *Team name/focus*
- *Interaction Mode*
- *Purpose*
- *Duration*

Structuring Your Developer Experience Organization

* * *

A well-structured Developer Experience (DX) organization is crucial for driving digital transformation. This chapter will discuss how a typical DX organization might look, including its teams, team structure, roles, responsibilities, and suggested ways of working. We'll also provide example job descriptions for key roles to help you start hiring in minimal time.

A DX organization can be structured into areas and product teams. The area is a higher-level grouping, while product teams work within specific areas to deliver on their goals.

Area: Platform Engineering

Platform Engineering is a critical area in the DX organization, providing the technology foundation for the entire organization. This area is divided into two sub-teams: Container Platform and Platform Applications.

* * *

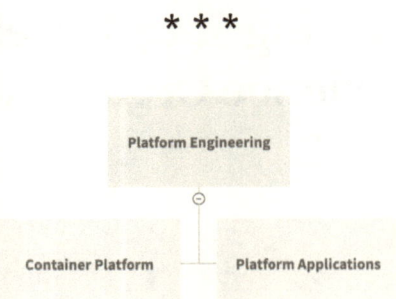

Team: Container Platform

The Container Platform team manages containerization technologies, orchestration tools, and infrastructure. This team ensures the development and deployment processes are seamless, secure, and scalable. Key roles within this team include:

- Container Platform Engineer
- Infrastructure Architect
- DevOps Engineer

Team: Platform Applications

The Platform Applications team builds and maintains internal application templates, APIs, and services that power the developer experience. Key roles within this team include:

- Application Developer

- API Developer
- Backend Engineer

In addition to the Platform Engineering area, other teams contribute to the overall DX. These teams can include, but are not limited to:

Developer Tools

This team manages and maintains developer tools like GitHub, binaries, and Copilot. They ensure that developers have access to the tools they need and are secure, reliable, and efficient. Key roles within this team include:

- Developer Tools Engineer
- Source Control Administrator
- Build and Release Engineer

Engineering Culture

The Engineering Culture team drives the adoption of guardrails and acts as an enabling team, supporting the entire DX. They promote best practices and ensure that the organization follows established engineering standards. Key roles within this team include:

- Engineering Coach
- Agile Coach
- Software Development Process Expert

Test Enablement

The Test Enablement team is responsible for driving quality engineering, test automation capabilities, reducing cognitive load, and evangelizing Test-Driven Development (TDD), Behavior-Driven

Development (BDD), and the shift-left concept. Key roles within this team include:

- Quality Assurance Engineer
- Test Automation Engineer
- Test Architect

Performance Engineering

The Performance Engineering team is responsible for performance testing, building performance into the technology stack, and ensuring that performance is considered during the early stages of the Software Development Life Cycle (SDLC). Key roles within this team include:

- Performance Engineer
- Load and Stress Tester
- Performance Architect

Collaboration Tools

The Collaboration Tools team manages collaboration tools such as JIRA and Confluence, ensuring these platforms are available, secure, and optimized for the organization's needs. Key roles within this team include:

- Collaboration Tools Administrator
- Atlassian Administrator
- Knowledge Management Specialist

Suggested Way of Working

To maximize the efficiency of the DX organization, it is crucial to foster a culture of collaboration, continuous learning, and shared

Structuring Your Developer Experience Organization   251

responsibility. The teams should work in an agile and iterative manner, constantly adapting to the organization's changing needs. Cross-functional collaboration between teams should be encouraged to facilitate knowledge-sharing and problem-solving.

We will examine each of these teams in detail in the following chapters. Let's go.

Platform Engineering

* * *

An important area within the Developer Experience domain is Platform Engineering. It's a rapidly evolving technology approach that aims to accelerate application delivery and enhance business value.

By improving the developer experience and productivity, platform engineering offers self-service capabilities with automated infrastructure operations. This approach is gaining popularity due to its potential to optimize the developer experience and expedite product teams' delivery of customer value.

The Emergence of Platform Engineering

Platform engineering has emerged in response to the growing complexity of modern software architectures. Nowadays, non-expert end-users often need to operate a collection of intricate, arcane services.

To assist end-users and reduce friction for their valuable work, forward-thinking companies have started building operating platforms between the end-user and the underlying services they depend on.

Gartner predicts that by 2026, 80% of software engineering organizations will establish platform teams as internal providers of reusable services, components, and tools for application delivery. Consequently, platform engineering will address the central collaboration challenge between software developers and operators.

Platform Engineering in Action

Platform engineering is a modern trend designed to revolutionize enterprise software delivery, particularly for digital transformation. A dedicated product team develops and maintains the engineering platform to support software developers and other users by offering common, reusable tools and capabilities while interfacing with complex infrastructure.

An engineering platform's specific features depend entirely on its end-users needs. The platform is a product built by experts and offered to customers such as developers, data scientists, or end-users. Platform teams must understand the requirements of their user groups, prioritize tasks, and build a platform that meets the target audience's needs.

Initial platform-building efforts often start with internal developer portals (IDPs), as these are more mature. IDPs provide a curated set of tools, capabilities, and processes selected by subject matter experts and packaged for easy consumption by development teams.

Collaborating closely with the developers they support, the platform team must determine the best approach for their unique circumstances.

The Goal and Advantages of Platform Engineering

The primary objective of platform engineering is to create a frictionless, self-service developer experience that offers the right capabilities to enable developers and others to produce valuable software with minimal overhead.

The platform should enhance developer productivity while reducing cognitive load. It should include everything development teams require and present it in a manner that aligns with the team's preferred workflow.

The development of a new generation of tools has made platform engineering a hot topic within the DevOps community. These tools aim to simplify the process of building and maintaining platforms.

Conclusion

Platform engineering is poised to become a critical component in the future of application delivery. By providing a streamlined developer experience and promoting collaboration between software developers and operators, platform engineering has the potential to revolutionize how organizations deliver software and create value. As more companies adopt platform engineering, their role in driving innovation and digital transformation will grow.

A Journey to Platform Engineering

* * *

In modern software development and deployment, container platforms have become indispensable for achieving operational efficiency, scalability, and reliability. This chapter will guide you through the evolution of container platforms, starting from the most primitive stage, Cloud Thanos, to the most desired state, Container Native.

We will discuss why Kubernetes and container platforms are necessary, the problems they solve, and how platform engineering is the best approach to delivering container-native solutions.

Cloud Thanos - The Primitive State

Initially, Cloud Thanos was characterized by manual deployment, network and storage dependencies, manual service discovery, and a brittle, big-ball-of-mud architecture.

This primitive state lacked the agility and resilience needed in today's rapidly changing technology landscape. Deployments were slow and error-prone, and the lack of automation led to inconsistencies and operational inefficiencies.

Cloud Ready - The Journey Begins

As organizations recognized the limitations of Cloud Thanos, they began to transition toward a Cloud Ready state. At this stage, well-defined services or monoliths were designed, with automated deployment processes.

Configurations were tailored to suit cloud environments, making applications more adaptable to the demands of modern technology. However, this stage still fell short regarding fault tolerance and operational consistency.

Cloud Native - The Turning Point

The Cloud Native stage ushered in a new era of software development, characterized by independently deployable services, fault tolerance, and suitable configuration and discovery mechanisms.

This approach enabled organizations to build and deploy applications as a collection of small, loosely coupled services, making it easier to scale, update, and maintain applications over time. However, while this stage offered substantial improvements over its predecessors, it still left room for further optimization in terms of operational consistency and focus on business logic.

Container Native - The Most Desired State

Container Native represents the zenith of container platform evolution, where the focus is on business logic and the use of platform-provided services such as service discovery, configuration, Horizontal Pod Autoscaling (HPA), Pod Disruption Budgets (PDB), and observability.

This state achieves operational consistency by relying on

container orchestration platforms like Kubernetes, which automates containerized applications' deployment, scaling, and management.

In the Container Native stage, organizations can harness the full power of containerization and Kubernetes to deliver highly scalable, resilient, and efficient applications.

By leveraging platform engineering, businesses can streamline their container-native solutions, ensuring that infrastructure, tooling, and processes are in place to support the development and deployment of containerized applications.

Conclusion

The journey from Cloud Thanos to Container Native has been transformative, with each step bringing new capabilities and improvements to the software development and deployment process.

Kubernetes and container platforms are now essential for organizations looking to maximize operational efficiency, scalability, and reliability in their applications.

By adopting a platform engineering approach, businesses can reach the most desired state of Container Native and fully realize the benefits of modern containerization and orchestration technologies.

DevOps, SRE, and Platform Engineering

* * *

As the digital landscape evolved and businesses increasingly relied on technology, new approaches to software development and operations emerged to address the growing complexities and demands of modern applications.

In the previous chapter, we explored the journey to platform engineering. Now, we will delve into the nuances of DevOps, SRE, and Platform Engineering, outlining their differences and how each plays a vital role in shaping the developer experience.

The Emergence of DevOps

DevOps, a term coined by Patrick Debois and Andrew Shafer at the Agile conference in 2009, aimed to bridge the gap between software development and operations. The duo recognized the need for a more collaborative culture and shared responsibility for the entire software development lifecycle. DevOps was born from the realization that siloed development and operations teams were hindering the potential for faster and more efficient software delivery.

The DevOps movement aimed to break down these barriers by fostering an environment where development and operations teams worked closely together, sharing knowledge, tools, and processes. This revolutionary approach enabled organizations to iterate on their software rapidly, respond more effectively to customer needs, and continuously improve their systems.

The Rise of Site Reliability Engineering (SRE)

While DevOps gained traction, another innovative approach to managing complex systems took shape at Google. In the early 2000s, Google pioneered Site Reliability Engineering (SRE) to address operational challenges in managing large-scale, complex systems.

The company needed to maintain high levels of reliability and efficiency, so they developed SRE practices and tools, such as the Borg cluster management system and the Monarch monitoring system.

SRE sought to apply software engineering principles to operations, transforming the traditional role of the system administrator. By automating repetitive tasks, monitoring system performance, and setting reliability targets, SRE engineers could focus on more strategic work that improved Google's services' overall stability and performance.

The SRE philosophy centered on balancing the need for rapid innovation with maintaining the reliability of systems, coining the term "error budget" to manage risk and set expectations.

The Evolution to Platform Engineering

Platform Engineering, a more recent concept, builds on the foundations of SRE and DevOps. While its precise origins are less clear, Platform Engineering is generally understood to be an extension of

DevOps and SRE practices, focusing on delivering a comprehensive platform for product development that supports the entire business perspective.

Platform Engineering teams take a holistic view of the organization's technology stack, ensuring it is robust, reliable, and scalable. These teams are responsible for building, maintaining, and evolving platforms that empower development teams to build, test, and deploy software efficiently.

This includes infrastructure, tooling, shared services, and establishing best practices and guidelines for development teams.

Platform Engineering recognizes that a positive developer experience is crucial to the success of any digital transformation journey. By providing developers with a consistent, reliable, and efficient platform, these teams can significantly reduce cognitive load, increase productivity, and ultimately accelerate innovation across the organization.

DevOps, SRE, and Platform Engineering are distinct yet complementary approaches to managing modern software development and operations. DevOps emphasizes collaboration and shared responsibility, SRE applies software engineering principles to operations, and Platform Engineering provides a comprehensive platform for product development.

Together, they form a powerful trifecta for optimizing the developer experience and driving digital transformation success. In the following chapters, we will explore these concepts more thoroughly, revealing their unique contributions and best practices.

Platform Engineering: Guiding Principles

* * *

Platform engineering organizations are at the heart of modern technology companies, enabling the rapid development and deployment of software applications across various platforms. The field of platform engineering has grown in importance as businesses increasingly rely on digital products and services to remain competitive.

This chapter will explore the guiding principles of platform engineering organizations, which are essential for driving innovation, efficiency, and consistency across an organization's technical infrastructure.

- Scalability: One of the primary goals of a platform engineering organization is to build systems that scale effortlessly. Platform engineers must consider scalability's horizontal and vertical dimensions to achieve this. The organization should prioritize creating modular and adaptable components, facilitating seamless growth as the company expands and evolves.

- Collaboration: Effective collaboration is critical for platform engineering teams within and across the organization. Cross-functional communication and collaboration should be encouraged to ensure that diverse perspectives are incorporated into the design and development process. This will lead to a better understanding of user needs, requirements, and potential challenges.
- Automation: Platform engineering organizations must prioritize automation to streamline processes, reduce human errors, and increase efficiency. Implementing continuous integration and continuous deployment (CI/CD) pipelines, automated testing, and monitoring tools are essential for rapid, reliable, and consistent software delivery.
- Observability: Understanding the health and performance of a platform is crucial for proactive issue resolution and continuous improvement. Platform engineering organizations should prioritize observability by implementing monitoring, logging, and tracing tools that provide comprehensive insights into system performance and behavior.
- Security: Platform engineering organizations must prioritize security as the backbone of a company's digital infrastructure. This includes implementing robust security measures, such as encryption, access controls, and regular security assessments, and fostering a culture of security awareness throughout the organization.
- Reliability: A platform's reliability is paramount for maintaining user trust and satisfaction. Platform engineering teams should prioritize the development of fault-tolerant systems that can gracefully handle unexpected issues and minimize downtime.

- Modularity: Encouraging modularity in platform design allows for the creation reusable components and promotes flexibility in the development process. By leveraging modular components, platform engineering organizations can more easily adapt to changing requirements and scale more efficiently.
- Documentation: Thorough and up-to-date documentation is vital for efficient collaboration, onboarding new team members, and reducing the complexity of the platform. A platform engineering organization should prioritize creating and maintaining comprehensive documentation, ensuring it remains accurate and relevant.
- Continuous Improvement: Platform engineering organizations should foster a culture of continuous improvement in processes and technical skills. Encouraging team members to stay current with industry best practices, participate in training and conferences, and continuously refine processes will drive innovation and maintain a competitive edge.
- User-centricity: At the core of every successful platform engineering organization is a focus on the end user. By prioritizing user needs and experiences, the platform engineering team can ensure they build solutions that address user pain points and drive overall satisfaction.

Ramping up a Platform Engineering Area

* * *

A platform engineering organization is crucial in accelerating application delivery and streamlining the developer experience. To effectively create and maintain a robust platform engineering organization, it is vital to establish well-defined teams with clear responsibilities and strong collaboration. In this chapter, we will discuss the structure and functions of two primary teams within a platform engineering organization:

- Container Platform
- Platform Applications

We will explore each team's definitions, key responsibilities, and collaboration with other teams. To help you establish these teams within your organization, we will also provide pro tips and outline team compositions, including the job descriptions for each role. By understanding the roles and dynamics of these two teams, you will be better equipped to create and maintain an efficient platform engineering organization that empowers developers and drives innovation.

Naturally, both teams must excel in their agile skills and take advantage of numerous foundational practices highlighted in the Open Practice Library, such as Infrastructure as Code, Test-Driven Development (TDD), Behavior-Driven Development (BDD), and more.

Infrastructure as Code manages and provides an infrastructure through code instead of manual processes. By adopting IAC, teams can increase efficiency, reduce human error, and maintain consistency across environments.

Additionally, IAC facilitates collaboration between developers and operations, leading to a smoother development process and a more positive developer experience.

Test-Driven Development is an agile software development technique that involves writing tests before writing the actual code. This approach ensures that code meets the defined requirements and promotes clean, maintainable code.

TDD encourages developers to think critically about their code and helps them identify potential issues early in the development process, leading to a more efficient and enjoyable developer experience.

Behavior-Driven Development is a software development methodology emphasizing collaboration between developers, testers, and business stakeholders. BDD encourages using a shared language, bridging the gap between technical and non-technical team members.

This approach helps ensure that the software meets the needs of its users and reduces the risk of miscommunication and misunderstandings. By fostering collaboration and communication, BDD enhances the developer experience and leads to a more cohesive and efficient development process.

In conclusion, both teams must excel in agile skills and leverage these foundational practices from the Open Practice Library. These practices help create a more efficient and enjoyable development process, ultimately contributing to a better developer experience.

By integrating Infrastructure as Code, Test-Driven Development, and Behavior-Driven Development into their workflows, teams can foster a more collaborative and agile environment that drives success in their digital transformation journey.

Platform Engineering: Container Platform

* * *

The Container Platform Team plays a crucial role in the Developer Experience domain, focusing on building and maintaining a robust, scalable, and efficient container platform that empowers development teams to deliver high-quality software with speed and agility.

In this chapter, we will outline the scope of the Container Platform Team within the context of Platform Engineering and the Developer Experience domain.

Key Responsibilities of the Container Platform Team

1.1 Container orchestration and management: The team is responsible for implementing and managing container orchestration solutions, such as Kubernetes, to ensure seamless deployment, scaling, and management of containerized applications.

1.2 Platform infrastructure: The Container Platform Team designs, builds, and maintains the underlying infrastructure required for the container platform, including networking, storage, and compute resources.

1.3 Security and compliance: The team ensures that the container platform adheres to security best practices and complies with relevant industry standards and regulations.

1.4 Monitoring and observability: The Container Platform Team implements monitoring, logging, and tracing solutions to provide visibility into the performance and health of the container platform and the applications running on it.

1.5 Platform automation: The team develops and maintains automation tools and scripts to streamline deployment, configuration, and management processes, enhancing the developer experience and reducing manual intervention.

Collaboration with Other Teams

2.1 Development teams: The Container Platform Team works closely with development teams to understand their requirements, provide guidance on best practices, and ensure that the container platform meets their needs.

2.2 Infrastructure and operations teams: The team collaborates with infrastructure and operations teams to ensure the container platform is seamlessly integrated with other components of the organization's technology stack.

2.3 Security teams: The Container Platform Team works with security teams to implement and maintain security controls, ensuring the platform's protection against potential threats.

Continuous Improvement and Innovation

3.1 Staying up-to-date with industry trends: The Container Platform Team must keep abreast of the latest containerization technologies, tools, and best practices, ensuring the platform remains cutting-edge and aligned with industry standards.

3.2 Continuous improvement: The team should actively seek opportunities to optimize and enhance the container platform, incorporating user feedback and proactively addressing any issues or areas for improvement.

Pro Tips

1.1 Embrace GitOps: GitOps is an operational framework that uses Git as the single source of truth for declarative infrastructure and applications. By adopting GitOps, the Container Platform Team can simplify deployment, rollback, and configuration management, increasing transparency and improving team collaboration.

1.2 Leverage ArgoCD for Continuous Delivery: ArgoCD is a declarative, GitOps-based continuous delivery tool for Kubernetes. Integrating ArgoCD into the container platform's continuous delivery pipeline enables the team to automate application deployments, ensuring consistency and minimizing errors.

1.3 Utilize Crossplane for Infrastructure Management: Crossplane is an open-source Kubernetes add-on that allows the Container Platform Team to manage infrastructure resources using familiar Kubernetes APIs. By adopting Crossplane, the team can streamline infrastructure provisioning and management, making deploying and managing applications on the container platform easier.

Typical Team Structure and Composition

A typical team structure and composition for a Container Platform Team in the context of Platform Engineering and the Developer Experience domain can consist of the following roles:

Head of Container Platform: This individual leads the Container Platform Team, setting the team's strategic direction, managing resources, and ensuring that the container platform meets the needs of development teams across the organization.

Container Platform Architects / Platform Engineers: These engineers are responsible for designing and implementing the overall architecture of the container platform, ensuring that it is robust, scalable, and efficient. They work closely with development teams to understand and incorporate their requirements into the platform design.

Container Platform Developers / DevOps Engineers: These team members are responsible for building and maintaining the container platform's infrastructure, automating processes, and integrating the platform with development pipelines and tools. They work closely with the platform architects to implement their designs and ensure the platform functions optimally.

Site Reliability Engineers (SREs): The SREs on the team focus on the platform's reliability, performance, and security. They monitor the platform, troubleshoot issues, and implement improvements to enhance its stability and resilience.

Security Engineers: Security Engineers ensure that the container platform complies with organizational security policies and industry best practices. They work with the team to identify potential vulnerabilities and implement security measures to protect the platform and its applications.

Quality Assurance (QA) / Test Engineers: These engineers are responsible for validating the container platform's functionality, performance, and reliability. They develop and execute test plans, identify and report issues, and collaborate with the team to ensure the platform meets quality standards.

Technical Writers: Technical Writers create and maintain documentation for the container platform, including architecture diagrams, user guides, and troubleshooting guides. They collaborate with the team to ensure the platform's documentation is accurate, up-to-date, and accessible to development teams and stakeholders.

Product Owners / Business Analysts: These individuals work closely with development teams and stakeholders to understand their requirements and priorities. They help the Container Platform Team to plan, prioritize, and track work items, ensuring that the platform evolves to meet the organization's needs.

This team structure and composition can be adapted based on the specific needs of the organization and the size of the Container Platform Team. Cross-functional collaboration and open communication among team members is essential for building and maintaining a successful container platform that enhances the developer experience.

Job Description for the Head of Container Platform

[Company Name] is a leading [Industry] organization committed to delivering cutting-edge solutions and driving digital transformation. We seek an experienced Head of Container Platform to join our Developer Experience domain and lead our Container Platform Team. This team is crucial in building and maintaining a robust, scalable, and efficient container platform that empowers development teams to deliver high-quality software with speed and agility.

Responsibilities:

As the Head of Container Platform, your responsibilities will include the:

1. *Leading the Container Platform Team in designing, developing, and maintaining a scalable, secure, and efficient container platform.*
2. *Collaborating with development teams to understand their requirements and ensure the container platform meets their needs.*
3. *Defining and implementing containerization best practices and standards across the organization.*
4. *Ensuring the container platform's reliability, performance, and security through proactive monitoring, optimization, and incident management.*

5. Developing and maintaining documentation on the container platform architecture, processes, and procedures.
6. Collaborating with other teams within the Developer Experience domain and the broader organization to drive continuous improvement and innovation in the container platform.
7. Staying up-to-date with industry trends, emerging technologies, and best practices related to containerization and platform engineering.
8. Managing the Container Platform Team's budget, resources, and timelines to ensure successful project delivery.

Requirements:

- Bachelors or Master's in Computer Science, Engineering, or similar experience.
- Proven experience in leading a container platform or platform engineering team.
- Strong expertise in containerization technologies like Docker, Kubernetes, and OpenShift.
- Knowledge of cloud platforms and services like AWS, Azure, or Google Cloud Platform.
- Familiarity with CI/CD pipelines, Infrastructure as Code, and other DevOps practices.
- Excellent leadership, communication, and collaboration skills.
- Strong problem-solving abilities and a keen eye for detail.
- Ability to adapt to changing priorities and work in a fast-paced, dynamic environment.

As the Head of Container Platform, you will play a critical role in shaping the future of our container platform and enhancing the developer experience at [Company Name]. If you are a passionate and expe-

rienced leader with a strong containerization and platform engineering background, we encourage you to apply for this exciting opportunity.

Suggested Ways of Working:

The Container Platform Team, as part of the Developer Experience domain, should adopt an agile way of working focused on delivering outcomes and ensuring a fast flow of work. To achieve this, the team can follow these suggested practices:

Embrace Agile and Lean principles: The team should adopt Agile methodologies, such as Scrum or Kanban, to manage their work effectively. By following these principles, the team can continuously improve, adapt to change, and maintain a focus on delivering value to the organization.

Use Kanban for fast flow: Kanban is an ideal framework for managing workflow in the Container Platform Team. By visualizing the team's work on a Kanban board, the team can quickly identify bottlenecks, prioritize tasks, and ensure that work is moving smoothly through the process.

Foster cross-functional collaboration: Encourage open communication and collaboration between team members with different roles and expertise. This will help the team make better decisions, learn from one another, and deliver high-quality outcomes.

Implement Continuous Integration and Continuous Deployment (CI/CD): By automating the integration, testing, and deployment processes, the team can ensure that new features and improvements are delivered quickly and efficiently. This approach also helps to minimize the risk of errors and reduces the time spent on manual tasks.

Establish clear goals and metrics: Define the outcomes the team is working towards and establish metrics to measure progress. This will help the team focus on delivering value and continuously improving performance.

Conduct regular retrospectives: Periodically review the team's performance, processes, and collaboration to identify areas for improvement. Use the findings from these retrospectives to implement changes and continuously improve the team's working methods.

Encourage a culture of learning and experimentation: Provide opportunities for team members to learn new skills, experiment with new tools and techniques, and share their knowledge with others. This will help the team to stay up-to-date with the latest developments in container technology and foster a culture of continuous improvement.

Prioritize work based on value and impact: Use techniques such as impact mapping and value slicing to prioritize tasks and ensure that the team focuses on the most valuable and impactful work items.

Implement a transparent and inclusive decision-making process: Involve team members, ensuring everyone's perspectives and expertise are considered. This will help the team to make better decisions and foster a sense of ownership and commitment.

By adopting these suggested ways of working, the Container Platform Team can excel in Agile and outcome delivery, creating a robust, scalable, and efficient container platform that enhances the developer experience and drives the organization's digital transformation journey.

Conclusion

The Container Platform Team is an essential component of the Developer Experience domain, responsible for providing a scalable, secure, and efficient container platform that supports the needs of development teams throughout the software development lifecycle.

By understanding and addressing the various aspects of the container platform's scope, the team can contribute to a positive developer experience, enabling faster, more reliable software delivery and driving overall business success.

Platform Engineering: Platform Applications

* * *

This team plays a crucial role in streamlining the onboarding and development processes for developers within the organization. Their primary objective is to create and maintain a set of templates and workflows that adhere to best practices and enhance the developer experience.

Ensuring compliance with established guardrails, help minimize potential risks and maintain consistency across projects. In addition, this team focuses on reducing manual toil, thus allowing developers to concentrate on their core responsibilities without getting bogged down by repetitive tasks.

The Platform Applications efforts are typically based on container technology and guided by cloud-native principles. This approach facilitates a more efficient and scalable development process, enabling developers to work in a modern, agile environment. The following are some key aspects of their role:

- Standardized Templates: The platform engineering team creates standardized templates for various application components, such as container configurations, infrastructure-as-code templates, and CI/CD pipelines. These templates serve as a foundation for developers, helping them quickly set up their development environment and adhere to best practices.
- Workflow Automation: By automating workflows, the team ensures that developers can efficiently build, test, and deploy their applications without manual intervention. Automation helps reduce human error, speeds up the development process, and ensures consistent application of best practices across the organization.
- Compliance and Guardrails: This team codifies the guardrails to ensure that the development process complies with organizational policies, security requirements, and industry standards. These guardrails may include automated checks and enforcement mechanisms integrated into the development workflows, helping maintain consistency and mitigate risks.
- Continuous Improvement: The Platform Applications team continuously evaluates and refines the templates and workflows to keep up with evolving best practices, industry trends, and organizational needs. This commitment to continuous improvement ensures developers access the most efficient and effective tools and processes.
- Education and Support: Besides providing the necessary templates and workflows, the Platform Applications team offers guidance and support to developers as they onboard and adapt to the container-based and cloud-native development environment. This may involve training sessions, documentation, and ongoing assistance

to address any challenges or questions during development.

By focusing on these key aspects, the team is vital in optimizing the developer experience, ensuring that developers can quickly and efficiently build, test, and deploy applications while adhering to best practices and organizational requirements. This approach enhances productivity and promotes a culture of collaboration, innovation, and continuous improvement.

The Principles of Container-Native Development

Container native development is a modern approach focusing on leveraging containers as the primary unit for deploying and managing applications.

This paradigm shift has significantly improved developer experience by enabling developers to focus on application development and simplifying operational tasks. This chapter will explore the key principles of container-native development and how they contribute to an enhanced developer experience.

Focus on the Application, Not the Platform

One of the core principles of container native development is prioritizing the application over the platform. This means that developers should concentrate on building, testing, and deploying applications while the container runtime and orchestration systems handle the underlying platform concerns. This approach allows developers to work more efficiently and focus on delivering value to users without worrying about the platform's intricacies.

Focus on the Development Approach

Container native development emphasizes the importance of adopting modern development practices, such as continuous integration, continuous deployment, and infrastructure as code. By embracing these practices, developers can streamline the development process, reduce errors, and ensure their applications are always up-to-date and ready for deployment.

Focus on the Operational Approach

In a container native environment, operational tasks are simplified through container orchestration systems, such as Kubernetes. These systems automate many operational aspects, such as scaling, updates, and monitoring, allowing developers to focus on building and improving their applications. At the same time, the platform takes care of operations.

Avoid NIH (Not Invented Here) Syndrome

Container native development encourages developers to avoid the "Not Invented Here" syndrome by leveraging existing tools, libraries, and frameworks instead of building everything from scratch. By utilizing proven technologies, developers can reduce the time and effort required to develop and maintain applications, leading to a more efficient and enjoyable development experience.

Utilize Platform Features

Container native platforms offer a variety of features that can enhance the developer experience, such as self-healing capabilities, automated rollouts, and rollbacks. By leveraging these features, developers can create more resilient and scalable applications without investing significant time and effort in developing custom solutions.

Use 3rd Party Services, Managed via Operators

Container native development encourages third-party services to offload common tasks like data storage, caching, or messaging. These services can be managed using operators, and custom Kubernetes resources that automate these services' deployment, scaling, and management. Using operators, developers can focus on their application logic and rely on managed services to handle specific tasks, resulting in a more streamlined and efficient development process.

Strive to Remove Manual Interaction as Much as is Feasible

Automating manual tasks is a critical aspect of container native development. By minimizing manual interactions, developers can reduce the potential for human error and improve the overall reliability of their applications. Automation also leads to more consistent processes, making it easier for developers to collaborate and share knowledge.

Conclusion

Embracing container native principles can significantly enhance the developer experience by simplifying application development and operational tasks. Developers can create more efficient, scalable, and resilient applications by focusing on the application, adopting modern development and operational approaches, leveraging existing tools and technologies, and automating manual tasks.

Ultimately, these principles lead to a more enjoyable and productive development experience that enables developers to deliver value to users more effectively.

Ingredients of Container Native Application

* * *

In container-native development, it's crucial to understand the typical ingredients that make up a well-designed and robust container-native application. This chapter will discuss the essential components of a container native application managed by a Platform Application team and how these ingredients contribute to a seamless developer experience.

Application Endpoints

Application endpoints play a vital role in managing and monitoring container-native applications. These endpoints provide visibility into the application's health and performance, allowing developers and platform teams to identify issues and optimize performance. Some key application endpoints include:

1.1 Prometheus Metrics Scraping: Prometheus is a popular monitoring and alerting tool for container-native applications.

Applications expose metrics using a Prometheus format, which is then scraped and collected for monitoring and alerting purposes.

1.2 Probes - Liveness/Readiness: Liveness and readiness probes are essential for Kubernetes to determine the health of your application. Liveness probes indicate if the application is running, while readiness probes determine if the application is ready to receive traffic.

1.3 Software Version: Exposing the software version through an endpoint enables easy identification of the running application version, simplifying troubleshooting and maintenance.

1.4 Dynamic Logging: Dynamic logging endpoints allow developers to adjust logging levels at runtime, enabling them to investigate issues without restarting the application.

1.5 OpenAPI/Swagger: OpenAPI and Swagger provide a standardized way to describe RESTful APIs, making it easier for developers to understand and interact with the API.

Metrics

Monitoring application metrics is essential for understanding application performance and identifying potential issues. Key metrics to monitor include:

2.1 Connection Pools: Monitoring connection pool usage helps identify potential bottlenecks and ensure optimal resource utilization.

2.2 Last Request Timestamp: Tracking the timestamp of the last request provides insight into application activity and can help detect potential issues.

2.3 Request/Error/Thread Counts: Monitoring request, error, and thread counts provide visibility into application performance and can help identify potential problems.

2.4 Garbage Collection (if applicable): Tracking garbage collection metrics helps developers understand memory usage and optimize application performance.

Configuration

Proper configuration management is essential for maintaining a flexible and maintainable container-native application. Key configuration aspects include:

3.1 Runtime Flags: Runtime flags like JVM -D allows developers to configure application behavior at runtime.

3.2 ConfigMaps/Secrets/Env Vars: Kubernetes ConfigMaps, Secrets, and environment variables enable developers to store and manage configuration data separately from application code.

3.3 Service Serving Secrets: Service Serving Secrets are a secure way to store and manage sensitive data, such as API keys and certificates.

3.4 Feature Flags: Feature flags enable developers to toggle features on and off at runtime, allowing for controlled rollouts and testing.

3.5 Known Ports: Defining known ports for HTTP, debug, and other services simplifies application deployment and management.

3.6 Helm Templates: Helm templates provide a standardized way to package and deploy Kubernetes applications.

3.7 Metadata: Metadata, such as labels and annotations, helps organize and manage applications within Kubernetes.

Logging

Consistent and effective logging is crucial for troubleshooting and monitoring application performance. Key logging aspects include:

4.1 Consistent Format: Using a consistent log format makes analyzing and troubleshooting issues easier.

4.2 Correlation Ids: Correlation Ids enable developers to trace requests across multiple services, simplifying debugging in distributed systems.

4.3 Default to stdout: Logging to stdout enables easy log collection and aggregation by tools like Fluentd or Logstash.

Resiliency

Resiliency is fundamental to container-native applications, ensuring that applications can recover from failures and continue functioning effectively. By incorporating the following resiliency features into their applications, developers can create systems that are more robust and fault-tolerant:

5.1 Shutdown Signal Handlers

Shutdown signal handlers enable graceful shutdowns by allowing applications to intercept termination signals and perform cleanup operations before shutting down. This ensures that resources are released, and ongoing transactions are completed, reducing the risk of data corruption or loss.

5.2 Circuit Breakers Status

Circuit breakers are a design pattern used to prevent cascading failures in distributed systems by monitoring the health of dependencies and temporarily disabling them if they become unhealthy. By exposing the status of circuit breakers, developers can monitor the health of their application's dependencies and react accordingly to minimize the impact of failures.

5.3 Timeouts and Exponential Backoff

Incorporating timeouts and exponential backoff into applications helps to ensure they remain responsive even when dependencies are experiencing issues.

Timeouts ensure that requests do not hang indefinitely. At the same time, exponential backoff algorithms gradually increase the delay between retries, allowing the system to recover without being overwhelmed by a sudden influx of requests.

Challenges of Building Container-Native Applications

* * *

In the previous chapter, we discussed the principles of building container-native applications and how adopting these principles can improve the developer experience. However, as with any new approach, there are challenges to be overcome when building container-native applications. In this chapter, we will explore these challenges and provide insights into how developers can navigate these complexities while ensuring the delivery of high-quality applications.

It's More Than Just Code: Complexity in the Process

Building container-native applications is not just about writing code; delivering these applications can be complex and requires a solid understanding of various tools, platforms, and technologies.

Developers need to manage containerization, orchestration, networking, security, and other aspects of the application lifecycle, which can be daunting, especially for those new to container native development.

Embracing continuous learning and staying up-to-date with best practices can help developers overcome this challenge and become more effective in delivering container-native applications.

It's User-Centered: Building Relevant and Long-lasting Applications

Container native applications should be built with end users in mind to ensure they are relevant and long-lasting. This user-centered approach demands a deep understanding of user needs, preferences, and pain points, which can be challenging for developers who may be more focused on technical aspects. To overcome this challenge, developers should collaborate closely with UX designers, product managers, and other stakeholders, incorporating user feedback throughout the development process to create applications that truly meet users' needs.

It's Always Changing: Adapting to an Evolving Landscape

The world of container native development is continually evolving, with new technologies, tools, and best practices emerging regularly. Yesterday's approaches may be limited, and today's options can be overwhelming.

Developers must be adaptable and willing to learn and embrace new technologies and methodologies to stay ahead in this fast-paced environment. To navigate this challenge, developers should invest time in continuous learning, participate in industry events, and stay connected with the developer community to keep abreast of the latest trends and best practices.

It's Essential to Your Business: Meeting Customer Expectations and Staying Competitive

Container native applications play a crucial role in the success of modern businesses. Customers demand more features and better experiences delivered sooner. Competitors are continually innovating and moving quickly, increasing the pressure on developers to deliver high-quality applications rapidly.

To overcome this challenge, developers should focus on adopting agile development methodologies, automating processes, and leveraging container native principles to enable faster delivery cycles and improve application quality. By doing so, developers can better meet customer expectations and ensure their businesses remain competitive in an increasingly demanding market.

Job Description: Head of Platform Applications

We seek a forward-thinking and experienced Head of Platform Applications to join our organization. The Head of Platform Applications will play a pivotal role in enhancing our developer experience by driving our platform applications' development, implementation, and maintenance.

This team ensures compliance with established guardrails, minimizes potential risks, and maintains consistency across projects while focusing on reducing manual toil, allowing developers to concentrate on their core responsibilities.

As the Head of Platform Applications, you will lead a team of skilled engineers working with container technology and adhering to cloud-native principles. You will foster a culture of innovation, collaboration, and continuous improvement within the team, enabling developers to work in a modern, agile environment.

Key Responsibilities:

1. *Develop and implement a strategic vision for the Platform Applications Team, aligned with the organization's goals and objectives.*
2. *Lead and manage a team of skilled engineers, fostering a collaborative and inclusive working environment.*
3. *Drive the adoption of container technology, cloud-native principles, and best practices throughout the organization.*
4. *Ensure compliance with established guardrails, minimizing potential risks and maintaining project consistency.*
5. *Focus on reducing manual toil by automating repetitive tasks and streamlining processes to enable developers to concentrate on their core responsibilities.*
6. *Collaborate with other teams and stakeholders to optimize the developer experience and drive continuous improvement.*
7. *Track and measure the success of platform applications and drive improvements based on key performance indicators.*
8. *Stay current with industry trends and technologies, ensuring the organization remains competitive and innovative.*

Qualifications:

- *Bachelor's or Master's degree in Computer Science, Engineering, or similar experience.*
- *Proven experience in a leadership role within a Platform Engineering or similar team.*
- *Strong knowledge of container technology, cloud-native principles, and best practices.*
- *Excellent communication and interpersonal skills, with the ability to collaborate effectively across different teams and stakeholders.*

- *A strong track record of managing and delivering complex projects on time and within budget.*
- *Demonstrated ability to lead, motivate, and mentor a team of skilled engineers.*
- *A solid commitment to continuous improvement, innovation, and learning.*

As the Head of Platform Applications, you will be crucial in transforming our development process and driving our organization's digital transformation journey. We would love to hear from you if you have a passion for innovation, a solid technical background, and the ability to lead and inspire a high-performing team.

Conclusion

Building container-native applications presents various challenges, from navigating a complex development process to adapting to an ever-changing landscape and meeting customer expectations.

By embracing continuous learning, adopting user-centered design, staying current with industry trends, and leveraging agile methodologies, developers can overcome these challenges and deliver high-quality applications that meet user needs and support business success.

By addressing these challenges head-on, developers can ultimately enhance their development experience and contribute to the long-term success of their organizations.

Internal Developer Portals (IDPs)

* * *

Internal Developer Portals (IDPs) are becoming increasingly popular in organizations focusing on software development. These portals act as a central hub for developers within the organization, providing them access to a wide range of tools and resources that help them build, test, and deploy software applications.

IDPs are typically designed and maintained by internal teams within an organization and provide a range of benefits to developers, including:

- Access to a centralized source of documentation and knowledge sharing
- Self-service access to APIs and other tools
- Streamlined workflows for development and deployment
- Increased collaboration and communication between teams

In this chapter, we will explore the key features and benefits of

Internal Developer Portals and how they can improve the efficiency and productivity of software development teams.

Key Features of Internal Developer Portals

Several key features are common to most Internal Developer Portals, including:

- Documentation and Knowledge Sharing: One of the primary functions of an IDP is to provide developers with access to a centralized source of documentation and knowledge sharing. This can include coding standards, best practices, and guidelines for using different tools and technologies.
- API and Tool Access: IDPs provide developers with self-service access to various APIs and other tools. This includes testing frameworks, development environments, and other resources that help streamline the development process.
- Workflow Management: IDPs provide streamlined workflows for development and deployment, helping to automate the development process and reduce errors and inconsistencies.
- Collaboration and Communication: IDPs also provide a range of collaboration and communication tools, such as forums, chat rooms, and project management tools. This help to facilitate communication between teams and improve collaboration on development projects.

Benefits of Internal Developer Portals

There are several key benefits of Internal Developer Portals, including:

- Improved Efficiency and Productivity: By providing developers with self-service access to resources and tools, IDPs help to reduce the time and effort required to develop, test, and deploy software applications. This can lead to significant improvements in efficiency and productivity.
- Better Collaboration and Communication: IDPs provide a range of collaboration and communication tools that help to improve communication between teams and facilitate collaboration on development projects. This helps reduce errors and inconsistencies and ensures that projects are completed on time and within budget.
- Streamlined Workflows: IDPs provide streamlined workflows for development and deployment, helping to automate the development process and reduce errors and inconsistencies. This can improve software application quality and reduce the time and effort required to complete development projects.
- Increased Developer Satisfaction: By providing developers with access to a centralized source of documentation and knowledge sharing, self-service access to APIs and other tools, and streamlined workflows, IDPs can help to improve the satisfaction and engagement of developers within the organization.

Implementing an Internal Developer Portal

* * *

In the previous chapter, we discussed the importance of developer portals in the digital transformation journey. When implemented effectively, these portals serve as a foundational tool to scale knowledge and leadership across the organization, ultimately leading to increased developer productivity, satisfaction, and talent retention.

Implementing an Internal Developer Portal requires careful planning and execution. The following steps can help organizations successfully implement an IDP:

Identify Key Requirements: The first step in implementing an IDP is to identify the key requirements of the portal. This includes the types of resources and tools that will be provided, the workflows that will be supported, and the collaboration and communication tools that will be used.

Choose the Right Platform: A range of platforms are available for implementing IDPs, including open-source solutions and commercial offerings. Choosing a platform that meets the organization's specific needs is important.

Design and Build the Portal: Once the requirements and platform have been identified, the next step is to design and build the portal. This chapter will explore the key considerations when implementing a developer portal.

Engaging Engineering Teams

For a developer portal to be successful, engineering teams must be fully engaged from the outset. This means involving them in the planning, design, and implementation processes. By doing so, you ensure that the portal is designed with the needs of its users in mind and promote a sense of ownership among developers.

Adopting a Product Mindset

A developer portal should be treated like any other product, focusing on continuous improvement and iteration. This means identifying key performance indicators (KPIs), setting goals, and regularly measuring progress. By treating the portal as a product, you can ensure that it remains relevant, up-to-date, and aligned with the needs of its users.

Researching Developer Pains

Understanding your developers' pain points and challenges is essential to creating a valuable developer portal. This can be achieved through surveys, interviews, or focus groups. By identifying these pain points, you can prioritize features and resources significantly impacting developer productivity and satisfaction.

Securing Leadership Sponsorship

Obtaining executive leadership's support is crucial to your developer portal's success. This sponsorship will provide the necessary resources and budget and send a strong message to the organization about the importance of developer experience. Be prepared to make a compelling case for the portal by demonstrating its potential impact on productivity, innovation, and talent retention.

Incrementally Adding to the Portal

Take an iterative approach by incrementally adding features, content, and tools based on feedback and priorities. This allows you to refine and improve the portal over time, making it more valuable to its users and easier to maintain.

Fostering Shared Ownership and Inner Source

A successful developer portal requires a sense of shared ownership among its users. Encourage contributions from developers across the organization by promoting inner source practices. This could include documentation, code samples, reusable components, or other resources. By creating a culture of collaboration and openness, you can ensure that the portal remains relevant and valuable to its users.

Providing High-Quality Starter Kits and Templates

One of the most significant benefits of a developer portal is the ability to provide developers with high-quality starter kits and templates. These resources can dramatically speed development, reduce errors, and promote best practices. Invest time creating these assets, ensuring they are up-to-date, well-documented, and easy to use.

Ensuring Visibility and Awareness

A developer portal is only as valuable as the number of people who use it. Be proactive in promoting the portal within your organization, using various communication channels such as newsletters, company meetings, and internal social media platforms. Additionally, consider offering training sessions, workshops, or webinars to help developers make the most of the available resources.

Conclusion

A developer portal can profoundly impact your organization's developer experience, increasing productivity, satisfaction, and talent retention. By carefully considering the points outlined in this chapter, you can ensure that your portal is a valuable resource for developers and a key component of your digital transformation journey.

SaaS Developer Portal Solutions

* * *

The previous chapter discussed the critical considerations for implementing a developer portal in your organization. With many developer portal solutions in the market, choosing the right one for your needs can be challenging.

This chapter will compare four popular developer portal solutions: OpsLevel, GetPort.io, Cortex, and Compass. By understanding the features and capabilities of each platform, you can make an informed decision about which solution best fits your organization's requirements.

OpsLevel

OpsLevel, a popular operations platform, offers a powerful solution through its developer portal that streamlines operations management and enhances the developer experience.

This chapter will delve into the features and benefits of the

OpsLevel developer portal and explore how it contributes to a seamless developer experience.

The OpsLevel developer portal is a centralized, user-friendly platform that consolidates various aspects of operations management for developers. With its wide range of features and integrations, the portal simplifies managing services, infrastructure, and deployments, ensuring that developers can focus on writing code and delivering value to their customers.

GetPort.io

Getport.io, an innovative developer portal, offers a comprehensive solution that enhances the developer experience by providing a unified platform for managing APIs, services, and applications. In this chapter, we will explore the features and benefits of the Getport.io developer portal and discuss how it contributes to a seamless developer experience.

The Getport.io developer portal is an intuitive, user-friendly platform designed to consolidate various API and service management aspects for developers.

With its extensive range of features and integrations, the portal simplifies the process of managing APIs, services, and applications, allowing developers to focus on delivering value to their customers and improving overall productivity.

Cortex

The Cortex developer portal boasts extensive features to enhance developer experience and streamline development. The platform includes Scorecards, which provide a detailed overview of the performance and health of individual services and applications, allowing developers to identify areas for improvement.

The Service Catalog offers a centralized repository of all available services, simplifying navigation and access for developers. On the other hand, the Resource Catalog serves as a comprehensive inventory of infrastructure resources and components, enabling developers to manage their technology stack better.

In addition, the Cortex developer portal offers a Scaffolder that automates the process of creating new services and applications, significantly boosting engineering efficiency. The Teams feature promotes collaboration and clear service ownership by assigning responsibilities and roles to specific team members, fostering a sense of accountability.

Lastly, the Query Builder allows developers to quickly and easily generate queries for retrieving data from various services, reducing the time and effort required to access crucial information. By addressing challenges in engineering efficiency, automation, production readiness, service ownership, and security migrations, the Cortex developer portal empowers developers to work more effectively and deliver outstanding project results.

Atlassian Compass

Compass is a developer experience platform and component catalog that brings your distributed software architecture and the teams collaborating on them together in a single, unified place.

Compass includes a powerful extensibility engine called "apps" to extend and customize the Compass experience to meet each team's unique needs. Their open-toolchain approach brings information across disparate SaaS tools like code, CI/CD, observability, incident management, APM, and security into Compass to build a developer experience that matches how each team works and the tools they use.

Conclusion

When selecting a developer portal solution, it's essential to consider your organization's unique needs and requirements. OpsLevel, GetPort.io, Cortex, and Compass each offer distinct features and capabilities that cater to different aspects of the developer experience.

By evaluating the features and benefits of each platform in the context of your organization's specific goals and requirements, you can make an informed decision about which developer portal solution best fits your needs. Remember that choosing the right platform is just the beginning; successful implementation and adoption of a developer portal also require ongoing engagement, iteration, and support from your organization's leadership and development teams.

Backstage - An Open Source Developer Portal

* * *

An efficient and comprehensive developer portal is essential to enhance Developer Experience (DX) as a key component of a successful digital transformation journey. One such popular open-source option is Backstage, a developer portal developed by Spotify.

Backstage aims to simplify and streamline the work of developers by unifying various tools, services, and documentation into a single, user-friendly platform.

The Story of Backstage

Backstage was born out of Spotify's need to manage the increasing complexity that emerged as its software development ecosystem expanded. As Spotify grew, so did the number of tools, services, and teams involved in their development processes.

This rapid growth led to fragmentation and inefficiencies, as developers had to navigate multiple platforms and resources to accomplish their tasks.

Realizing the potential benefits of a unified platform, Spotify began developing Backstage to streamline the developer experience. By consolidating all developer resources, including tools, services, and documentation, into a single, integrated platform, Backstage aimed to minimize friction and enable developers to work more efficiently.

The platform provided developers with a unified interface to access and manage all aspects of software development, making it easier to find information and collaborate with other teams.

In 2020, Spotify decided to share the advantages of Backstage with the wider developer community by open-sourcing the platform. This move allowed organizations outside Spotify to leverage Backstage's innovative features and capabilities to enhance developer experiences.

By making Backstage open-source, Spotify also benefited from the contributions and feedback of a diverse community of developers, helping to refine further and improve the platform for all users.

The open-source model enabled Backstage to evolve and adapt to the needs of various organizations, making it a valuable solution for companies looking to streamline their software development processes and improve Developer Experience.

Potential Benefits of Backstage

Unified Interface: Backstage consolidates various tools, services, and documentation, creating a single access point for developers. This simplifies navigation and reduces the cognitive load on developers, enabling them to focus on writing high-quality code.

Extensibility: Backstage's plugin architecture allows organizations to easily extend and customize the platform to suit their needs. By leveraging plugins, developers can integrate their preferred tools and services, tailoring the platform to their unique requirements.

Enhanced Collaboration: Backstage fosters collaboration and communication by providing a shared platform for all development teams. This facilitates knowledge sharing, reduces silos, and enables teams to work together more efficiently.

Improved Onboarding: The unified interface of Backstage simplifies the onboarding process for new developers by providing easy access to all necessary tools, services, and documentation, shortening the learning curve and speeding up the integration of new team members.

Potential Challenges of Backstage

Implementation Effort: As an open-source platform, Backstage requires organizations to invest time and effort in setting up, customizing, and maintaining the platform to ensure it aligns with their specific needs and workflows.

Learning Curve: While Backstage aims to simplify the developer experience, it may introduce a learning curve for developers unfamiliar with its interface and functionalities. Training and support may be required to help developers adapt to the platform.

Integration Limitations: While Backstage offers a wide range of plugins to integrate with various tools and services, there may be instances where specific integrations are not yet available. Organizations may need to invest additional resources in developing custom plugins or workarounds in such cases.

In conclusion, Backstage has the potential to significantly enhance the Developer Experience by providing a unified, extensible platform for managing tools, services, and documentation. By understanding the potential benefits and challenges of adopting Backstage, organizations can make informed decisions about whether it's the right solution to support their digital transformation journey.

Developer Tools

* * *

A "Developer Tools" team within a Developer Experience department focuses on creating, maintaining, and enhancing the tools, frameworks, and environments developers use to build, test, and deploy software. The primary goal of this team is to improve the overall developer experience, making it more efficient, productive, and enjoyable. Key responsibilities of a Developer Tools team include:

Toolchain Management: Select, maintain, and upgrade the tools and technologies developers use, such as integrated development environments (IDEs), version control systems, build tools, and dependency management systems.

Framework Development: Develop and maintain internal frameworks, libraries, and templates to streamline the software development process, ensuring consistency and adherence to best practices across projects.

Continuous Integration and Continuous Deployment (CI/CD): Implement and maintain CI/CD pipelines to automate the building, testing, and deployment of software, reducing manual effort and ensuring a consistent delivery process.

Documentation and Knowledge Sharing: Create and maintain comprehensive documentation for tools, frameworks, and best practices, ensuring that developers have access to up-to-date, accurate information. Encourage knowledge sharing through internal workshops, presentations, and training sessions.

Developer Onboarding: Develop and maintain onboarding materials and processes to help new developers become familiar with the tools, frameworks, and environments they will be using, reducing their time to become productive team members.

Performance Monitoring and Optimization: Monitor and analyze the performance of tools, frameworks, and development processes, identifying areas for improvement and implementing optimizations to enhance the developer experience.

Collaboration with Other Teams: Work closely with other teams, such as product, engineering, and quality assurance, to ensure that the developer tools meet their needs and facilitate efficient collaboration across teams.

Developer Support: Support developers encountering issues or difficulties with the tools, frameworks, and environments, helping them troubleshoot and resolve problems quickly.

Staying Up to Date with Industry Trends: Continuously research and evaluate new tools, technologies, and best practices in the industry, identifying opportunities to incorporate them into the existing developer experience.

Advocating for Developer Experience: Champion the importance of a positive developer experience within the organization, promoting a culture that values efficiency, productivity, and collaboration.

The Role of Performance Engineering in Developer Experience

* * *

In the digital transformation era, businesses rapidly adapt to ever-changing technology landscapes. In this context, Developer Experience (DX) fosters a culture of collaboration, innovation, and productivity.

One often overlooked aspect of DX is the importance of having a performance engineering team. This chapter will explore the significance of performance engineering in your digital transformation journey and how it contributes to a superior developer experience.

Why Performance Engineering Matters in DX

Performance engineering is an essential component of DX, as it directly impacts the application's user experience, system reliability, and overall efficiency.

By incorporating a performance engineering team, you can ensure your software applications are designed and optimized for peak performance. This allows developers to focus on building features, knowing that a dedicated team of experts takes care of performance.

Key Components of Performance Engineering

Performance Modeling and Simulation: For instance, consider an e-commerce platform that experiences a sudden surge in traffic during a holiday sale event. The performance engineering team can create a virtual representation of the platform and simulate different levels of user traffic to test its responsiveness and identify potential bottlenecks.

This approach enables them to predict how the system might behave under real-world conditions and make necessary adjustments to handle the increased load.

Another example is a financial institution planning to migrate its customer-facing applications to a new cloud infrastructure. Using performance modeling and simulation, the team can compare the performance of different cloud providers and assess the impact of the migration on the application's performance, ultimately choosing the best option for their needs.

Load and Stress Testing: A popular social media platform might use load testing to simulate millions of users accessing the platform simultaneously, posting updates, and interacting with others. By analyzing the system's response time, throughput, and resource utilization under these conditions, the performance engineering team can identify areas where the platform may struggle to handle the increased load and address them proactively.

On the other hand, stress testing might involve pushing the platform's infrastructure beyond its expected capacity to uncover potential breaking points. For example, the team could simulate a sudden influx of users caused by a viral post, examining how the platform's database, caching, and networking systems respond to the extreme load.

Monitoring and Profiling Tools: Monitoring and profiling tools can be used to gather valuable data on the performance of a software system. For example, a SaaS company offering a project management tool might use monitoring tools like New Relic, Datadog, or AppDynamics to track various performance metrics, such as response times, error rates, and CPU usage.

In addition, profiling tools like Java VisualVM or Py-Spy can be employed to examine the internal workings of the application's code, pinpointing areas where resource consumption is high or execution time is slow. By leveraging these tools, the performance engineering team can identify performance bottlenecks, optimize resource usage, and improve overall application performance.

Performance Optimization Techniques: Performance optimization techniques can take many forms, depending on the nature of the application and its underlying architecture. For example, a video streaming service might optimize its video encoding algorithms to reduce latency and improve playback quality.

Similarly, a database-driven web application could implement caching strategies to reduce the load on its database servers and improve response times for end-users.

In another case, a machine learning application might benefit from hardware-specific optimizations, such as utilizing GPUs for parallel processing or optimizing the application to take advantage of cloud-based hardware accelerators like Google's Tensor Processing Units (TPUs).

By applying these and other optimization techniques, the performance engineering team can ensure that applications run smoothly and efficiently, even under heavy loads or in complex, resource-constrained environments.

The Synergy of Perf. Engineering and DX

A robust performance engineering team not only optimizes applications for peak performance but also enhances the developer experience by:

Providing Actionable Insights and Recommendations to Developers: A performance engineering team can offer valuable insights and recommendations to developers, enabling them to make informed decisions about application design and implementation. For example, the team might identify a database query causing slow page load times.

They can then suggest specific changes to the query, such as adding an index, re-writing the query, or employing caching strategies to optimize performance.

In another scenario, the performance engineering team might discover that certain API calls are causing latency issues due to excessive data transfer. They could recommend more efficient data serialization methods, such as protocol buffers or compressing the data, to minimize the latency and improve the overall user experience.

Streamlining the Development Process: By identifying performance bottlenecks early in the development lifecycle, the performance engineering team can help streamline the development process, reducing the need for costly and time-consuming rework.

For instance, the team might conduct performance simulations during the design phase to identify potential issues before writing any code. This proactive approach allows developers to address potential performance issues before they become deeply embedded in the application, saving time and resources.

Moreover, by integrating performance testing into the continuous integration and continuous delivery (CI/CD) pipeline, developers can receive immediate feedback on the performance impact of their changes, allowing them to quickly adjust and optimize their code as needed.

Facilitating Communication and Collaboration: A performance engineering team can facilitate communication and collaboration between different teams within the organization, such as development, operations, and quality assurance. By acting as a bridge between these teams, the performance engineering team can help break down silos and foster a culture of continuous improvement.

For example, the performance engineering team might work closely with the operations team to monitor application performance in production, sharing insights and data to identify and resolve performance issues.

Similarly, the team can collaborate with quality assurance to develop performance test plans, ensuring that applications meet performance requirements and are thoroughly tested before release.

By fostering open communication and collaboration, the performance engineering team can create a feedback loop where teams work together to identify and address performance issues, ultimately leading to more efficient, scalable, and reliable software applications.

Conclusion

Incorporating a performance engineering team into your DX strategy is crucial for building scalable, efficient, and reliable software applications. By focusing on performance from the outset, your organization can minimize the risk of performance issues, improve user satisfaction, and ultimately enhance the developer experience. In the competitive digital transformation landscape, performance engineering can be a powerful weapon to help you stay ahead of the curve.

Collaboration Tools

* * *

Developer Experience (DX) is at the heart of a successful software development organization. A vital aspect of DX is the establishment of a Collaboration Tools Team, responsible for providing the necessary tools, workflows, and configurations that enable seamless communication, collaboration, and organization within the development ecosystem.

In this chapter, we will look into the key roles and responsibilities of the Collaboration Tools Team and the significance of maintaining a robust collaboration toolset, including the popular Atlassian suite, JIRA, and Confluence.

Administering and Maintaining Collaboration Tools

The foundation of the Collaboration Tools Team's work is to administer and maintain essential collaboration tools. They must ensure that these tools are reliable, secure, and performant, thus providing an exceptional experience for all developers and stakeholders.

The team creates a robust environment that nurtures collaboration and allows for efficient issue tracking, documentation, and project management.

Two major collaboration tools often used in development organizations are JIRA and Confluence, both part of the Atlassian suite. JIRA is a project and issue tracking system, while Confluence is a team collaboration platform for creating, organizing, and sharing information. The Collaboration Tools Team must maintain these systems, keep them up-to-date, and ensure that all users can access and utilize them effectively.

Aligning Workflows with Organizational Processes

To fully leverage the capabilities of collaboration tools like JIRA and Confluence, the Collaboration Tools Team must work closely with other teams to understand their workflows, processes, and standards. This understanding is crucial in creating and maintaining custom fields, configurations, and workflows that align with the organization's requirements.

A well-aligned system fosters efficiency, reduces friction, and helps minimize miscommunications. The Collaboration Tools Team must proactively engage with teams to gather feedback, make adjustments, and ensure that the tools and configurations meet their evolving needs.

Continuous Monitoring and Evaluation

The Collaboration Tools Team must be committed to continuously monitoring and evaluating collaboration tool usage. By examining patterns, they can identify areas for improvement, such as the need for additional custom fields, improvements in workflow configurations, or addressing performance bottlenecks.

Regular monitoring also allows the team to proactively detect and address any security vulnerabilities or potential risks, ensuring the confidentiality, integrity, and availability of the tools and their data.

Staying Current with the Latest Features and Best Practices

In a rapidly evolving technological landscape, the Collaboration Tools Team must stay current with the latest features, updates, and best practices in collaboration tools. This knowledge enables them to optimize tool usage, incorporate new features that enhance the DX, and guide other teams on best practices.

By staying informed and continuously adapting, the Collaboration Tools Team plays a pivotal role in driving innovation and improving developer experience across the organization.

Conclusion

The Collaboration Tools Team is a cornerstone of a successful developer experience organization. They play a crucial role in fostering a collaborative and efficient development environment by administering and maintaining tools, aligning configurations with organizational processes, monitoring usage, and staying current with best practices.

Their work ultimately contributes to the success of the organization as a whole, driving innovation and empowering developers to create high-quality software.

Test Enablement

* * *

The Test Enablement team plays a crucial role in ensuring the delivery of high-quality software products by promoting quality engineering and test automation capabilities.

This team is committed to reducing the cognitive load for developers, enabling them to focus on delivering value to customers while maintaining the highest standards of quality.

In addition, the team actively champions Test-Driven Development (TDD), Behavior-Driven Development (BDD), and the shift-left concept to enhance the overall software development process further.

The shift-left concept in software testing involves incorporating testing activities earlier in the software development lifecycle (SDLC). The aim is to identify and address potential issues or defects as soon as possible, reducing the likelihood of costly and time-consuming fixes later in development.

This approach contrasts with traditional testing practices, where testing typically occurs in the final stages of development. Shift-left testing promotes a proactive and collaborative approach to quality assurance, involving developers, testers, and other stakeholders from the beginning of a project.

One significant advantage of the shift-left approach is the potential for faster and more efficient resolution of defects. By identifying and addressing issues early in the development process, teams can avoid the costly and time-consuming process of fixing problems discovered late in the cycle.

This not only saves resources but also results in a more reliable and higher-quality end product. Furthermore, by involving testers and other stakeholders throughout the SDLC, the team better understands the project requirements and can more effectively address potential issues as they arise.

Shift-left testing also promotes a culture of collaboration and shared responsibility for quality assurance. By involving all team members in testing activities, developers gain a deeper understanding of the importance of writing testable and maintainable code.

This encourages a focus on quality from the beginning of the development process, leading to more robust and reliable software products.

Additionally, the shift-left approach fosters improved communication between developers, testers, and other stakeholders, creating a more cohesive and efficient development team. Overall, adopting the shift-left concept in software testing can lead to significant improvements in both the quality and efficiency of the software development process.

In the context of Team Topologies, a test enablement team should act as an enabling force, providing expertise, guidance, and support to other teams within the organization. This approach allows the test enablement team to share best practices, tools, and techniques, fostering a culture of quality assurance and continuous improvement across the entire organization.

By working closely with other teams, the test enablement team can help identify gaps in testing capabilities, recommend appropriate solutions, and promote the adoption of effective testing strategies, such as the shift-left concept.

As an enabling team, the Test Enablement team should focus on empowering other teams to become self-sufficient in their testing activities. This involves sharing knowledge and expertise and providing hands-on support and mentorship.

By helping other teams build their testing competencies, the test enablement team can ensure that quality assurance becomes an integral part of the software development process across the organization.

One of the key roles within the Test Enablement team is the Quality Assurance Engineer. These professionals are responsible for designing, implementing, and maintaining test plans and test cases that verify software applications' functionality, performance, and reliability.

They collaborate closely with other team members to identify defects, recommend improvements, and ensure that the final product meets or exceeds the established quality standards.

Another critical role within the team is the Test Automation Engineer. These individuals specialize in creating, maintaining, and executing automated test scripts to expedite the testing process and reduce manual effort. By leveraging various automation tools and frameworks,

Test Automation Engineers increase the efficiency and accuracy of the testing process, ensuring that any issues are identified and resolved more quickly.

Finally, the Test Architect is responsible for defining and implementing the overall test strategy, ensuring it aligns with the organization's goals and objectives. This role involves selecting the most appropriate testing methodologies, tools, and frameworks and establishing best practices for the team.

Test Architects also work closely with other stakeholders, such as developers, product owners, and project managers, to ensure that quality is embedded throughout the entire software development lifecycle.

By fostering a culture of quality engineering and test automation, the Test Enablement team contributes significantly to the success of software development projects. By advocating for TDD, BDD, and the shift-left concept, this team ensures that quality is considered from the earliest stages of development, leading to more reliable, efficient, and robust software products.

Developers may hold several typical fallacies about testing and development practices, and these misconceptions can hinder the adoption of effective testing strategies and negatively impact software quality. In the following paragraphs, we will discuss some of these fallacies, provide examples, and suggest techniques to overcome them.

Not My Responsibility

One common fallacy is the belief that testing is solely the responsibility of the Quality Assurance (QA) team. This mindset can lead to a lack of ownership of the code quality by developers and create silos within the organization.

Organizations should encourage a culture of shared responsibility for quality assurance to overcome this fallacy. Implementing practices like Test-Driven Development (TDD) and Behavior-Driven Development (BDD) can help instill this mindset by requiring developers to write tests before writing the actual code, ensuring that testing is an integral part of the development process.

Manual Testing Is Sufficient

Another fallacy is the belief that manual testing is sufficient to ensure software quality. While manual testing is an essential component of the testing process, it is not enough on its own. Relying solely on manual testing can be time-consuming, error-prone, and costly.

To overcome this fallacy, developers should be encouraged to adopt test automation practices. Automated testing can complement manual testing efforts by increasing the speed, efficiency, and accuracy of the testing process, allowing for faster feedback and more reliable results.

We'll do It Later

A third fallacy is that testing can wait until the end of the development cycle. This misconception can lead to the discovery of defects late in the process when they are often more expensive and time-consuming to fix.

Organizations should promote the shift-left concept to overcome this fallacy, integrating testing activities earlier in the development lifecycle. This approach enables developers to identify and address potential issues as soon as possible, reducing the likelihood of costly and time-consuming fixes later on.

If the Code Compiles, It Works

The belief that code that compiles is automatically error-free is another common fallacy. While successful compilation indicates that the code is free of syntax errors, it does not guarantee the absence of logical errors, performance issues, or other defects.

To overcome this fallacy, organizations should emphasize the importance of thorough testing practices, including unit testing, integration testing, and end-to-end testing. By implementing a comprehensive testing strategy, developers can ensure their code is free of syntax errors and functions as intended in various scenarios and environments.

By addressing these fallacies and fostering a culture of quality assurance, organizations can improve the overall software development process, resulting in more reliable, efficient, and robust software products.

Fighting Resistance

Test Enablement teams may encounter strong resistance in organizations not inherently focused on software development. Consequently, the test enablement team must be persuasive and effectively communicate the significance of testing practices.

They must articulate and defend the importance of testing, even when faced with strong opposing opinions from developers.

Some teams may be reluctant to prioritize testing practices, believing that they do not add value and only serve to delay the development of their seemingly endless feature backlog. It is crucial to empower the Test Enablement team to challenge this mindset.

Emphasizing the importance of delivering high-quality code and striving for excellence, measured by metrics such as code coverage, is vital for the organization's overall success.

One potential solution to overcome this resistance is to adopt a manager escalation strategy. If the Test Enablement team encounters uncooperative product teams, they should feel encouraged to communicate their concerns clearly to the respective product owners.

These product teams must understand that they are expected to either comply and advance their test-driven development skills or risk being identified as a team that is diverging from the organization's quality practices standards.

It is crucial, however, to approach this process with tact and diplomacy. Avoid shaming anyone during these discussions, and instead, focus on reasoning and purpose for the betterment of the organization.

By fostering open communication and emphasizing the importance of testing practices, the Test Enablement team can help create a culture of quality assurance that benefits the entire organization.

Engineering Culture

* * *

An Engineering Culture team fosters an organization's healthy, collaborative, and innovative environment, ensuring that developers and other technical teams can work effectively and efficiently.

The key responsibilities of an Engineering Culture team often intersect with the enabling role described in the Team Topologies framework. In this context, an Engineering Culture team supports and empowers other teams by providing guidance, resources, and tools to help them navigate and thrive within the organization's engineering ecosystem. Key responsibilities of an Engineering Culture team may include:

Promoting best practices: The Engineering Culture team helps disseminate and encourage the adoption of best practices in software development, DevOps, and other technical areas. This includes sharing knowledge, providing training, and offering support to help teams adopt proven methodologies and techniques.

Facilitating communication and collaboration: The team works to create an environment that fosters open communication and collaboration among developers and other stakeholders. This might involve organizing regular meetings, workshops, or other events to encourage knowledge sharing, teamwork, and cross-team collaboration.

Supporting team autonomy: Engineering Culture teams help empower development teams by promoting autonomy and self-organization. This includes assisting teams in defining clear goals, removing obstacles, and providing resources to help them make independent decisions and manage their work effectively.

Fostering a growth mindset: The team encourages a culture of continuous learning and improvement, supporting team members in acquiring new skills, exploring new technologies, and staying up-to-date with industry trends. This might involve organizing training sessions, encouraging conference attendance, or providing access to resources such as books or online courses.

Nurturing a psychologically safe environment: The Engineering Culture team helps create an environment where team members feel comfortable sharing ideas, raising concerns, and admitting mistakes without fear of retribution. This involves promoting trust, empathy, and open communication among team members.

Advocating for diversity and inclusion: The team ensures that the organization's engineering culture is inclusive and welcoming to people of diverse backgrounds, experiences, and perspectives. This might involve implementing diversity and inclusion initiatives, providing training, and setting up support systems to help team members feel included and valued.

Aligning teams with organizational goals: The Engineering Culture team helps technical teams understand and work toward the organization's broader goals and objectives. This may involve clarifying priorities, setting expectations, and providing regular feedback to help teams align their work with the company's mission and vision.

In the context of Team Topologies, the Engineering Culture team acts as enabling by providing support, guidance, and resources to other teams. They work closely with development and other enabling and platform teams to create a healthy and efficient engineering ecosystem that drives innovation and supports the organization's overall success.

Mastering Ways of Working for an Exceptional Developer Experience

* * *

In the quest for digital transformation, an organization's approach to working is a critical factor in achieving success. With the right methodologies and practices, the Developer Experience (DX) can be optimized, allowing teams to thrive and deliver exceptional results. This chapter will delve into key concepts and tools that shape effective working methods within the DX realm.

The Mobius Loop: A Flexible and Outcome-Driven Agile Framework

The Mobius Loop is an agile framework that delivers continuous value through a cyclical process of discovery, options, and outcomes. This flexible approach enables teams to better adapt to change and navigate the complexities of the digital landscape. We'll explore the key principles, benefits, and best practices of implementing the Mobius Loop in your DX organization.

The Open Practice Library: A Treasure Trove of Agile Techniques

The Open Practice Library is a comprehensive, community-driven repository of practices and techniques that empowers teams to navigate the agile journey. From collaboration exercises to problem-solving tools, we'll discuss how the Open Practice Library can enrich your team's work and enhance the overall DX.

Building a Backlog Like a Master: Prioritization and Clarity

A well-organized and prioritized backlog is essential for ensuring efficient delivery and alignment with strategic objectives. We'll discuss best practices for creating and managing a backlog, including techniques for prioritization, scoping, and refining work items, to help your team navigate the development process with ease.

The Importance of Non-Functional Requirements: Building Robust and Scalable Solutions

Non-functional requirements determine a software solution's quality, performance, and reliability. We'll examine the significance of non-functional requirements in the context of DX, including how to identify, prioritize, and incorporate them into your development process.

Metrics-Based Process Mapping: Streamlining Workflows and Identifying Opportunities for Improvement

Metrics-Based Process Mapping (MBPM) is a powerful technique that helps organizations visualize, analyze, and optimize their workflows. We'll explore how MBPM can be applied within the DX organization to identify bottlenecks, inefficiencies, and opportunities for improvement, ultimately enhancing team performance and productivity.

Agile Anti-Patterns: The Perils of SAFe and Other Misconceptions

While Agile methodologies have revolutionized the software development landscape, the misapplication of these principles can lead to counterproductive outcomes. We'll discuss common Agile anti-patterns, such as the Scaled Agile Frameworks, and explore how to recognize and avoid these pitfalls to ensure your organization reaps the full benefits of Agile practices.

By understanding and implementing these essential concepts and tools, your organization will be well-equipped to navigate the ever-evolving digital transformation landscape and create a powerful, seamless, and effective Developer Experience. Let's go into detail for each of these.

The Mobius Loop Agile Framework

* * *

Agile software development has been around for over two decades and has proven effective in delivering high-quality software in a fast-paced environment.

However, traditional Agile frameworks can still have limitations, such as difficulty integrating feedback from end-users or stakeholders and a lack of emphasis on continuous improvement. This is where the Mobius Loop Agile Framework comes in as a superior approach to software development.

The Mobius Loop Agile Framework is an iterative and adaptive software development methodology emphasizing continuous learning and feedback loops. The framework's name comes from the Mobius strip, a geometric figure with only one surface and one edge that loops back onto itself. Similarly, the Mobius Loop Agile Framework is a continuous loop of Plan-Do-Check-Act (PDCA) cycles that continually loops back onto itself.

The Mobius Loop Agile Framework is an extension of the Agile Manifesto and principles, which emphasizes the following:

- Individuals and interactions over processes and tools
- Working software over comprehensive documentation
- Customer collaboration over contract negotiation
- Responding to change over following a plan

How Does the Mobius Loop Agile Framework Work?

The Mobius Loop Agile Framework consists of six stages that repeat in a continuous cycle:

- Discovery: In this stage, the team identifies the project goals, objectives, and requirements. This stage includes gathering user stories and creating a product backlog.
- Exploration: In this stage, the team explores possible solutions, conducts research, and creates prototypes to test with users.
- Adaptation: In this stage, the team uses user feedback to refine and adapt the solution.
- Development: In this stage, the team continuously develops and tests the solution to ensure it meets the requirements.
- Release: In this stage, the team releases the solution to users and collects feedback.
- Reflection: In this stage, the team reflects on the process, learns from it, and uses that learning to inform the next cycle.

The Mobius Loop Agile Framework also emphasizes continuous improvement by encouraging teams to reflect on their processes and incorporate what they learn into their work. The framework also encourages teams to prioritize collaboration and communication to ensure everyone is aligned with the project's goals and objectives.

Red Hat Open Innovation Labs, a division of the renowned software company Red Hat, has put forth its unique perspective on the

Mobius Loop framework by incorporating an additional topic known as "Foundation." By integrating the Foundation topic, Open Innovation Labs aims to enhance this framework's effectiveness and efficiency.

* * *

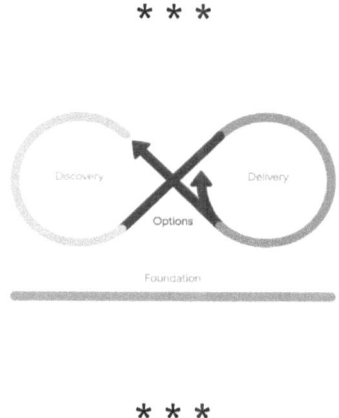

* * *

The Foundation topic sits beneath the Mobius Loop, a strong support structure for the entire process. It encompasses essential practices promoting a more agile, effective, and collaborative software development environment. Some of these practices include:

- Continuous Integration (CI): This practice involves frequently merging code changes from multiple developers into a shared repository. By doing so, CI helps identify and address integration issues early on, reducing the chances of complex, time-consuming problems arising at later stages of the development process.
- Continuous Delivery (CD): Building upon CI, CD automates the process of delivering software updates and new features to production environments. This practice ensures that the software is always in a releasable state, allowing for quicker deployment of updates and reduced time-to-market for new features.

- Everything as Code (EaC): This practice advocates treating all aspects of the software development process as code, including infrastructure, security, and documentation. By doing so, EaC enables version control, collaboration, and automation across the entire development lifecycle, promoting consistency, efficiency, and traceability.
- Psychological Safety: Recognizing the importance of a healthy work environment, the Foundation topic also emphasizes the need for psychological safety within software development teams. This practice involves creating a culture where team members feel comfortable expressing their thoughts, ideas, and concerns without fear of negative consequences. By fostering a psychologically safe environment, teams can encourage open communication, innovation, and effective problem-solving.

This addition aims to provide a robust underlying support structure that bolsters the effectiveness and efficiency of the software development process, ultimately enabling organizations to innovate and deliver better software solutions.

Why is the Mobius Loop Agile Framework Superior?

The Mobius Loop Agile Framework is superior to traditional Agile frameworks because it strongly emphasizes feedback loops and continuous improvement. By incorporating feedback from users and stakeholders at every stage, the framework ensures that the end product meets the users' needs and expectations.

The Mobius Loop Agile Framework also encourages teams to continuously learn and improve their processes, which can lead to higher-quality software, faster development cycles, and happier users.

Finally, the Mobius Loop Agile Framework prioritizes collaboration and communication, which helps ensure that everyone is aligned with the project's goals and objectives. The framework encourages teams to work together to achieve a common goal by focusing on individuals and interactions over processes and tools.

In conclusion, the Mobius Loop Agile Framework is a superior approach to software development that emphasizes continuous learning, feedback loops, and collaboration. By adopting this framework, teams can deliver higher-quality software faster and more efficiently, resulting in happier users and stakeholders.

The Open Practice Library

* * *

The Open Practice Library (OPL) is a treasure trove of information that provides a comprehensive guide to help organizations improve their working methods. The library contains numerous practices and techniques that have proven effective in different domains and industries.

The OPL is particularly relevant for those looking to enhance their understanding of the Mobius Loop, as it provides essential resources to help navigate the continuous discovery and delivery process. This chapter will explore the OPL, its relationship with the Mobius Loop, and how to utilize the library to upgrade your knowledge of working methodologies.

Understanding the Open Practice Library

The Open Practice Library is an open-source collection of practices curated and contributed to by a global community of practitioners. These practices address various aspects of product development, team collaboration, and problem-solving and are designed to help organizations achieve better outcomes faster.

The OPL is structured around several key categories that are relevant to the Mobius Loop, including:

- Discover Practices to help teams identify opportunities, validate assumptions, and understand user needs.
- Define Practices to set clear objectives, prioritize work, and create a shared understanding of the problem to be solved.
- Deliver Practices to develop, test, and deploy high-quality solutions while iterating based on user feedback.
- Reflect Practices to evaluate progress, gather insights, and identify areas for improvement.

The Relationship between the OPL and the Mobius Loop

As we've seen before, the Mobius Loop is an outcome-driven framework enabling continuous discovery and delivery in software development. It emphasizes the importance of focusing on outcomes rather than outputs and encourages iterative cycles of experimentation and learning.

The OPL and the Mobius Loop are intrinsically connected, as the practices within the OPL support and enhance the Mobius Loop framework. By offering a curated set of practices and techniques, the OPL provides teams with the tools to navigate the different stages of the Mobius Loop effectively.

Using the Open Practice Library to Upgrade Your Ways of Working

The OPL offers extensive practices that can help organizations optimize their working methods. To make the most of the library, follow these steps:

- Assess Your Current Knowledge: Begin by evaluating your existing knowledge of working methodologies and identifying areas where you require improvement or additional information.
- Explore the OPL: Browse the OPL's categories and practices to familiarise yourself with the available resources. Consider the most relevant practices to your organization's needs and challenges.
- Experiment and Iterate: Start incorporating selected practices into your workflow, and monitor their impact on your team's performance. Be open to adjusting and iterating as you learn what works best for your unique context.
- Contribute and Collaborate: As you gain experience with the practices, consider contributing your insights and experiences to the OPL community. This collaborative approach will help refine the library and promote knowledge sharing among practitioners.

Conclusion

The Open Practice Library is a valuable resource for organizations seeking to optimize their working methods and make the most of the Mobius Loop framework. By understanding the relationship between the OPL and the Mobius Loop, and actively engaging with the library's practices, you can upgrade your knowledge and drive continuous improvement within your team. Embrace the OPL, experiment with new practices, and unlock your organization's potential.

Building a Backlog

* * *

A well-structured backlog is the foundation of any successful software development project. It helps prioritize work, align team members, and ensure that development efforts focus on delivering value.

Involving developers in the planning process enhances their experience and fosters a sense of ownership and commitment toward the development. In this chapter, we will discuss building a masterful backlog by leveraging practices from the Open Practice Library while keeping developer experience at the core of the process.

Start at the End and Target Outcomes

The first step in building a masterful backlog is defining your target outcomes. Start by envisioning the end state and identifying the project's desired outcomes. This will help you set clear goals and determine the metrics that will be used to measure success. Some examples of target outcomes might include:

- Improving user engagement by 25% within six months
- Reducing the average time taken to complete a transaction by 40% within a year
- Increasing revenue by 15% in the next two quarters
- Enhancing system stability and reducing downtime by 50% within six months

Involving developers in defining target outcomes ensures that their perspectives are taken into account and that they clearly understand the project objectives. This collaboration creates a sense of ownership among developers and fosters a shared vision for the project. Some benefits of engaging developers in this process include the following:

- Gaining insights into potential technical challenges and opportunities for innovation
- Ensuring the feasibility and practicality of the target outcomes
- Enhancing developers' motivation and commitment to the project by making them feel heard and valued
- Fostering a culture of collaboration and open communication among team members

Defining target outcomes and involving developers in the process lays the groundwork for a successful project and creates a strong sense of ownership and alignment within the team.

Priority Sliders

Once the target outcomes are defined, it's essential to prioritize features and tasks based on their importance and potential impact. Priority sliders can visually represent the relative importance of various aspects of the project, such as performance, security, usability, and maintainability.

By engaging developers in the priority sliders exercise, you can ensure their expertise and knowledge are considered when making prioritization decisions. This collaborative approach helps align the team's priorities and fosters a shared understanding of the project's direction.

Impact Mapping

Impact mapping is a powerful technique for visualizing the relationships between project goals, deliverables, and stakeholders. It helps identify the most impactful features and tasks and ensures the backlog focuses on delivering value. An example of impact mapping for an e-commerce application might involve the following steps:

1. Define the project goal: Increase revenue by 20% in the next year.
2. Identify the actors involved: Customers, customer support, marketing team, and developers.
3. Determine the impacts for each actor:
4. Customers: Improved shopping experience, personalized recommendations, and faster checkout.
5. Customer support: Streamlined communication channels, better access to customer data, and improved issue resolution.
6. Marketing team: Enhanced customer analytics, better targeting capabilities, and improved marketing campaign management.
7. Developers: Simplified development processes, faster deployment, and improved collaboration.
8. Outline the deliverables/features to achieve the impacts:
9. Improved search functionality
10. Personalized product recommendations
11. Enhanced mobile app experience
12. Streamlined checkout process

13. Integration with customer support tools
14. Marketing analytics dashboard

Involving developers in the impact mapping process allows them to contribute their insights and expertise, ensuring that the backlog reflects the team's collective wisdom. This collaborative approach empowers developers to take ownership of the project's success and drives a deeper understanding of how their work contributes to achieving the desired outcomes. The benefits of engaging developers in the impact mapping process include the following:

- Ensuring that technical feasibility is considered when identifying features and tasks
- Encouraging a shared understanding of the project's goals and priorities among team members
- Promoting cross-functional collaboration and breaking down silos between development, product, and other stakeholders
- Creating a more accurate and comprehensive backlog that incorporates the team's collective knowledge and expertise

By leveraging impact mapping and involving developers in the process, you can create a more focused and impactful backlog that drives value and helps your team achieve its project goals.

Event Storming

Event storming is a collaborative workshop that brings developers, domain experts, and stakeholders together to explore complex business processes and identify key events, commands, and aggregates. This process helps uncover hidden dependencies, identify potential bottlenecks, and streamline development. An example of event storming for an online ordering system might involve the following steps:

1. Gather diverse participants, including developers, domain experts, and stakeholders.
2. Define the scope of the process, such as the entire order lifecycle, from placing an order to delivery.
3. Identify key events (e.g., Order Placed, Payment Received, Order Shipped) and place them on a timeline.
4. Explore the commands that trigger these events (e.g., Place Order, Process Payment, Ship Order) and the responsible actors (e.g., Customer, Payment Gateway, Shipping Provider).
5. Discover aggregates or entities (e.g., Order, Customer, Inventory, Shipping).
6. Identify potential issues, dependencies, and opportunities for improvement.

By involving developers in event storming, you create an opportunity for them to contribute their unique perspectives and technical expertise. This fosters a sense of ownership and commitment, enhances the developer experience, and ensures the resulting backlog is technically sound and aligned with business objectives. Benefits of engaging developers in event storming include:

- Promoting a shared understanding of the domain and the system's behavior among team members
- Encouraging cross-functional collaboration and knowledge sharing
- Uncovering hidden complexities, assumptions, and risks that might otherwise be overlooked
- Ensuring that the resulting backlog reflects a deep understanding of the system's requirements and constraints

By incorporating event storming into your backlog planning process and actively involving developers, you can create a more accurate, comprehensive, and valuable backlog that addresses technical and business concerns. This approach fosters a sense of ownership and commitment among developers, ultimately enhancing the developer experience and driving project success.

User Story Mapping and Value Slicing

User story mapping is a visual technique for organizing and prioritizing user stories based on their relationship to user goals and journeys. Value slicing involves breaking down larger features or epics into smaller, manageable pieces that can be developed and delivered incrementally. An example of user story mapping and value slicing for a travel booking app could include:

1. Identify user goals: Find the perfect destination, book flights, book accommodations, and plan activities.
2. Map user journeys for each goal, including the steps users take to achieve them.
3. Create user stories for each step, describing the desired functionality from the user's perspective.
4. Prioritize user stories based on their importance, dependencies, and potential value.
5. Slice larger stories or features into smaller, manageable pieces that can be developed incrementally.

Engaging developers in user story mapping and value slicing ensures that their insights are incorporated into the backlog and that the development process remains focused on delivering value. This involvement helps developers feel connected to the end users' needs and fosters a sense of ownership and pride in their work.

Benefits of involving developers in user story mapping and value slicing include:

- Ensuring that technical feasibility is considered when prioritizing and breaking down user stories
- Fostering a deeper understanding of user needs and goals, which can lead to more innovative and user-centric solutions
- Encouraging collaboration and communication between development, product, and other stakeholders
- Facilitating the delivery of high-value features and improvements more rapidly and efficiently

Engaging developers in user story mapping and value slicing can create a more accurate, comprehensive, and user-focused backlog that addresses technical and business concerns. This collaborative approach improves the developer experience and ensures that the development process remains focused on delivering value to end users, ultimately driving project success.

Conclusion

Building a masterful backlog is about prioritizing tasks and features, engaging developers, and enhancing their experience throughout the planning process.

You can create a backlog that reflects the team's collective wisdom and expertise by incorporating practices such as defining target outcomes, using priority sliders, impact mapping, event storming, and user story mapping and value slicing.

Involving developers in these practices fosters a sense of ownership, commitment, and pride in their work, ultimately contributing to the overall success of your digital transformation journey.

The Importance of Non-Functional Requirements

* * *

The previous chapter discussed the significance of involving developers in building the backlog. In this chapter, we will delve into the importance of defining non-functional requirements, mapping functional requirements, and incorporating them into practices such as the definition of done. Addressing these aspects is crucial for delivering high-quality products that meet user needs and business objectives.

Non-Functional Requirements: Why They Matter

Non-functional requirements (NFRs) are essential aspects of a software system that define its characteristics, such as performance, reliability, security, and usability. These requirements are critical in determining the system's quality, user experience, and operational efficiency.

Some reasons why NFRs are important to include:

- Ensuring a positive user experience: Meeting non-functional requirements, such as responsiveness and user-friendliness, is key to satisfying the user experience.
- Enhancing system reliability: Properly addressing NFRs related to reliability and fault tolerance helps create a stable and dependable system.
- Strengthening security: Addressing security-related NFRs can protect sensitive data and minimize the risk of security breaches.
- Facilitating scalability and maintainability: Meeting NFRs concerning scalability and maintainability enables the system to grow and evolve along with the business requirements.

Mapping Functional Requirements

Functional requirements describe the features and capabilities of a software system, defining what it is supposed to do. Mapping functional requirements involves identifying, documenting, and organizing them to ensure they are well-understood and can be translated into actionable development tasks.

Some steps for mapping functional requirements include:

- Gather input from stakeholders: Interview and collaborate with stakeholders, including users, developers, and domain experts, to collect their expectations and needs.
- Define user stories: Create user stories that describe the desired functionality from the user's perspective.
- Prioritize requirements: Rank the functional requirements based on factors such as business value, dependencies, and risk.

- Validate and refine: Review and refine the functional requirements with the help of stakeholders and developers to ensure accuracy and completeness.

Incorporating NFRs and Functional Requirements into the Definition of Done

The definition of done (DoD) is a set of criteria that must be met before a task or feature can be considered complete. Incorporating functional and non-functional requirements into the DoD ensures that developers deliver a high-quality product that meets all expectations.

Some ways to include NFRs and functional requirements in the DoD are:

- Specify NFRs as part of the acceptance criteria: Define the NFRs that must be met for each feature, such as performance benchmarks or security standards, and include them in the acceptance criteria.
- Create a checklist: Develop a comprehensive checklist covering both functional and non-functional requirements, and use it to verify that each feature or task is completed satisfactorily.
- Perform reviews and testing: Conduct thorough reviews, including code reviews, performance tests, security audits, and usability evaluations, to ensure that functional and non-functional requirements are met.
- Encourage cross-functional collaboration: Involve team members from different disciplines, such as developers, QA, operations, and UX, in the DoD definition process to ensure that all aspects of the product are considered.

By defining non-functional requirements, mapping functional

requirements, and incorporating them into practices such as the definition of done, you can ensure that developers deliver a high-quality product that meets user needs and business objectives. This approach improves the developer experience and contributes to the success of your digital transformation journey.

Metrics-Based Process Mapping: A Fundamental Practice for Developer Experience Teams

* * *

In the previous chapter, we explored the importance of defining non-functional requirements, mapping functional requirements, and incorporating them into practices such as the definition of done. This chapter will delve into metrics-based process mapping (MBPM) and its significance for developer experience teams.

Metrics-based process mapping is an analytical technique for visualizing and measuring the performance of processes within an organization. This method enables teams to identify inefficiencies, bottlenecks, and areas for improvement, ultimately leading to more streamlined processes and better overall performance. For developer experience teams, MBPM is a vital practice that can help optimize the development process and enhance the overall developer experience.

Understanding Metrics-Based Process Mapping

Metrics-based process mapping involves the following steps:

- Define the process: Identify the process you want to analyze and define its boundaries, including its start and end points.
- Identify process steps: Break down the process into individual steps or activities.
- Determine performance metrics: Establish relevant metrics for each process step, such as cycle time, wait time, or work in progress.
- Create the process map: Visualize the process steps and their associated metrics using a flowchart or other diagramming tool.
- Analyze and improve: Evaluate the process map to identify areas for improvement and implement changes to optimize the process.

Benefits of Metrics-Based Process Mapping for Developer Experience Teams

MBPM offers numerous benefits for developer experience teams, including:

- Enhanced visibility: MBPM provides a clear visualization of the development process, making it easier for team members to understand the workflow and identify potential areas for improvement.
- Data-driven decision-making: By quantifying process performance using metrics, MBPM enables teams to make more informed decisions about where to focus their improvement efforts.

- Continuous improvement: The ongoing practice of MBPM promotes a culture of continuous improvement within the team, helping them to identify and address inefficiencies proactively.
- Collaboration: MBPM encourages collaboration and communication among team members as they work together to identify and address process issues.
- Improved developer experience: By optimizing the development process, MBPM helps create a more efficient and enjoyable working environment for developers, ultimately leading to higher productivity and job satisfaction.

Implementing Metrics-Based Process Mapping in Developer Experience Teams

To successfully implement MBPM in a developer experience team, consider the following tips:

- Involve team members: Engage developers and other team members in the MBPM process to ensure their insights and expertise are considered.
- Prioritize processes: Focus on mapping and optimizing processes significantly impacting the developer experience.
- Regularly review and update: Revisit and update the process map periodically to ensure it remains accurate and reflects any changes in the development process.
- Communicate results: Share the findings of the MBPM analysis with the entire team and discuss potential improvements to encourage a culture of continuous improvement.

In conclusion, metrics-based process mapping is a powerful tool for developer experience teams to optimize processes, drive continuous improvement, and enhance the overall developer experience. By implementing MBPM, organizations can empower their development teams to work more efficiently, effectively, and enjoyably, ultimately contributing to the success of their digital transformation journey.

Scaled Agile Frameworks

* * *

Scaled Agile Frameworks have become popular for organizations seeking to adopt agile methodologies at scale. However, as with any framework, it has its limitations. This chapter will critically examine how they fall short of fostering a positive developer experience, ultimately hindering digital transformation and diminishing productivity and satisfaction.

This chapter critically analyzes, highlighting its limitations and challenges. While some can offer advantages for large organizations and be useful when considered part of a journey, it is essential to be aware of its potential issues and make informed decisions when adopting it.

In Detail: A Critical Examination of the Scaled Agile Framework:

Agile does not require uniform measurement of work units (i.e., story points) across teams. Scaled Agile Framework's attempt to standardize story points can lead to larger batch sizes and misunderstanding of the purpose of story points.

- Technical debt may increase in organizations due to management-level prioritization, resulting in slower, riskier, and more fragile systems.
- Applying it to operational functions can cause conflicts between delivery and support functions. Support teams need to work responsively or on shorter cycles than the Scaled Agile Frameworks Programme Increment cycle time.
- It focuses on deliverables and accountability can discourage teams from assisting one another, as their success is measured by individual productivity and delivery.
- It relies on "ideal dev days" for estimating is flawed. A more accurate approach is to examine past similar deliverables and their completion times.
- It can compromise the concept of "value" by emphasizing delivery volume and management-imposed deadlines over actual user needs.
- Retrospective activities within Scaled Agile Frameworks PI planning are insufficient. Shorter, more frequent retrospective feedback loops are needed.
- Top-down, large-batch planning contradicts Agile's principles, emphasizing small, iterative feedback loops.
- Describing Scaled Agile Frameworks as a transition stage without outlining steps for transitioning away from it is misleading.
- Most organizations do not need Scaled Agile Frameworks, as their projects and products are not large enough to warrant such an extensive solution.

Ultimately, it tends to overlook that those closest to work may be best suited to make decisions about it. Scaling down the problem is more effective than scaling up the process. Scaled Agile Frameworks should adapt to the organizational structure rather than impose its structure on the organization.

The bonus point, courtesy of Matt Skelton of Team Topologies, notes that the Scaled Agile Frameworks enforced Program Increment approach can lead to unwarranted temporal coupling of teams, which may further result in architectural coupling.

Another aspect that supports the critique of the Scaled Agile Framework is its position in Gartner's trough of disillusionment, where Enterprise Scaled Agile Frameworks are found at a low point. This suggests that the initial excitement surrounding SAFe has diminished as organizations have come to terms with its limitations and challenges.

Gartner's trough of disillusionment is part of their Hype Cycle, which represents the maturity, adoption, and social application of various technologies and methodologies. When a technology or method lands in the trough of disillusionment, the initial enthusiasm wanes, and people become more aware of its shortcomings.

This position for Enterprise Scaled Agile Frameworks, including SAFe, demonstrates that organizations must approach these frameworks cautiously and understand that they may not be the ideal solution for every situation.

Tom Gerathy, a leading voice in Agile and Psychological Safety, has contributed to the critique of SAFe. His insights have inspired the content of this chapter, offering a critical perspective on the framework.

While the Scaled Agile Framework may be an attractive solution for organizations seeking to scale agile practices, it is crucial to be aware of its potential pitfalls regarding developer experience. SAFe may inadvertently stifle creativity, autonomy, and innovation by focusing too heavily on process and hierarchy.

To promote a positive developer experience and achieve true digital transformation, organizations must strike a balance between structure and flexibility, while maintaining a steadfast commitment to the core values of Agile.

Chapter 8
Key Considerations for DX Leaders

* * *

As a Developer Experience (DX) leader, understanding the nuances of your team dynamics and addressing the factors that impact their productivity and well-being is essential. In this chapter, we'll introduce the critical considerations every DX leader should know to create an environment that fosters growth, innovation, and success. We'll touch upon topics such as:

- The correlation between developer productivity and developer happiness
- The importance of understanding cognitive load on developers
- The significance of adopting a team-first principle and ensuring stable teams
- The importance of adapting to changes in teams

In the following chapters, we'll delve deeper into these topics, providing actionable insights and best practices to help you cultivate a thriving DX organization.

Developer Productivity and Happiness: The Vital Connection

A positive correlation exists between developer productivity and happiness. Recognizing this connection and cultivating a positive work environment can significantly impact your team's performance and overall success. As a DX leader, it's crucial to keep this relationship in mind and prioritize productivity and well-being to create a well-rounded, high-performing team.

Cognitive Load: A Crucial Factor in Developer Efficiency

Cognitive load refers to the mental effort required to process and retain information. In software development, an excessive cognitive load can lead to reduced productivity, increased errors, and burnout. As a DX leader, it's essential to understand the impact of cognitive load on your team and implement strategies to minimize it, ensuring that developers can work efficiently and effectively.

Adopting a Team-First Principle and Ensuring Stable Teams

A team-first principle emphasizes creating a cohesive, collaborative environment where team members feel valued and supported.

Additionally, maintaining stable teams helps establish trust, streamline communication, and enhance overall productivity. DX leaders can create a foundation for success by prioritizing team dynamics and stability, allowing their teams to excel in their digital transformation journey.

Key Considerations for DX Leaders

In the upcoming chapters, we'll explore these critical considerations in more detail, providing practical guidance and strategies to help you, as a DX leader, create an exceptional Developer Experience that drives your organization's digital transformation journey forward.

Happiness and Productivity

* * *

In today's rapidly evolving technological landscape, the productivity of software engineers has never been more critical. While numerous factors influence productivity, one aspect that has garnered significant attention in recent years is the happiness of software engineers.

This chapter considers the correlation between happiness and productivity in software engineering, examining the underlying reasons for this relationship and offering practical strategies to foster a happier and more productive workforce.

The correlation between happiness and the productivity of software engineers has been a topic of interest in recent years. While many may assume that paying employees well and providing good benefits will result in a happy and productive workforce, the reality is much more complex.

Research has shown that factors such as autonomy, purpose, and mastery are crucial to fostering happiness and, in turn, increasing productivity among software engineers.

Autonomy

Autonomy is the degree to which an employee has control over their work and the ability to make decisions. In software engineering, this can mean having the freedom to choose which tasks to work on, how to approach them, and when to work on them.

Research has shown that autonomy is critical to job satisfaction and employee happiness. Employees feel empowered and motivated to do their best work when they have autonomy.

One study conducted by Harvard Business Review found that employees who had more control over their work reported higher levels of job satisfaction, were more committed to their organizations, and were less likely to experience burnout.

In software engineering, autonomy can lead to increased creativity and innovation as employees are encouraged to think outside the box and explore new approaches to problem-solving.

Purpose

Another critical factor in employee happiness and productivity is having a sense of purpose. Employees who feel that their work is meaningful and contributes to a larger goal are more likely to feel fulfilled and engaged. This is particularly important for software engineers who often work on complex projects that require significant time and effort.

One study by the University of Warwick found that happy employees are 12% more productive than their unhappy counterparts. When employees feel a sense of purpose in their work, they are more likely to go above and beyond what is expected of them, leading to increased productivity and better outcomes.

Mastery

Mastery refers to the degree to which employees feel they are developing their skills and growing in their roles. For software engineers, this can mean having opportunities to learn new technologies, work on challenging projects, and collaborate with others to solve complex problems. Research has shown mastery is critical to employee engagement and overall job satisfaction.

A Society for Human Resource Management study found that employees with opportunities to develop their skills and learn new things were likelier to feel engaged in their work and committed to their organizations.

In software engineering, mastery can lead to increased creativity and innovation as employees are encouraged to take on new challenges and push the boundaries of what is possible.

Creativity

Finally, creativity is essential to happiness and productivity among software engineers. When employees are encouraged to think outside the box and explore new approaches to problem-solving, they are more likely to feel fulfilled and engaged in their work. This can lead to increased innovation and better outcomes for the organization.

Research has shown that providing employees with opportunities to be creative can increase job satisfaction and overall happiness. In software engineering, this can mean allowing employees to experiment with new technologies or encouraging them to collaborate with others to find creative solutions to complex problems.

Cognitive Load

Another important consideration regarding happiness and productivity among software engineers is cognitive load. Cognitive load refers to the mental effort required to complete a task. When employees are overloaded with tasks or find their work overly complex, it can increase stress and decreased productivity.

Research has shown that reducing cognitive load through strategies such as simplifying tasks or providing additional support can lead to increased productivity and improved job satisfaction. In software engineering, this can mean providing employees with tools and resources to streamline their workflow or breaking down complex projects into smaller, more manageable tasks.

In the next chapter, let's delve deeper into Cognitive Load.

Cognitive Load

* * *

When planning the new organization, it's important to consider many factors, including the cognitive load for developers. Cognitive load is the mental effort to process and retain information during problem-solving or learning activities. For developers, this load can significantly impact productivity and happiness.

This chapter explores the concept of cognitive load, its various forms, and how it affects developers' performance and well-being. It also delves into strategies for managing cognitive load to improve productivity and happiness in the development process.

Understanding Cognitive Load

Cognitive load can be categorized into three primary types:

- Intrinsic cognitive load: This is the inherent difficulty of a task or concept. It is determined by the complexity of the

subject matter and the learners or problem-solvers' expertise.
- Extraneous cognitive load: This load results from ineffective instructional or problem-solving strategies requiring unnecessary mental effort to process information.
- Germane cognitive load: This is the mental effort devoted to constructing and automating schemas or mental representations of knowledge.

Cognitive Load and Developers' Productivity

High cognitive load can negatively impact developers' productivity in several ways, as it considerably strains their mental resources.

When developers are overwhelmed by complex tasks or inundated with information, their ability to perform effectively and efficiently can be severely compromised. The consequences of high cognitive load on developers' productivity include:

- Reducing focus and concentration: High cognitive load can make it challenging for developers to maintain focus and concentration on the task at hand. This can lead to frequent context switching, which increases the time it takes to complete tasks and reduces overall productivity.
- Slowing problem-solving and decision-making abilities: With limited mental resources available, developers may struggle to analyze problems effectively or make informed decisions promptly. This can result in delays and hinder the overall progress of a project.
- Increasing the likelihood of errors and bugs: When the cognitive load is high, developers are more prone to making mistakes as their attention is divided among multiple tasks or sources of information. This can lead to

the introduction of errors and bugs in the code, which can have severe consequences for the project's quality and stability.
- Decreasing overall code quality: High cognitive load can impede developers' ability to think critically and creatively about their code, resulting in a decline in code quality. Developers may resort to shortcuts, suboptimal solutions, or neglect best practices when faced with an overwhelming cognitive load, which can negatively impact the software's maintainability, scalability, and performance.

Organizations can improve productivity, reduce errors, and ensure high-quality software development by addressing the cognitive load developers face. Leaders need to recognize the impact of cognitive load on their teams and implement strategies to minimize it, such as simplifying processes, providing adequate resources and support, and fostering a culture that encourages collaboration and knowledge sharing.

Strategies for Managing Cognitive Load in Development

Effectively managing cognitive load is crucial for enhancing developers' productivity and ensuring the delivery of high-quality software. This section will introduce several strategies to manage cognitive load in development. As you progress through this book, we'll dive deeper into these strategies and provide actionable insights and best practices to help you create a more efficient and productive development environment.

Simplify and modularize code: Breaking down complex tasks into smaller, manageable components can help reduce cognitive load by allowing developers to focus on one aspect of a problem at a time.

Modular code also promotes reusability, maintainability, and scalability, enhancing overall development. We'll explore techniques for simplifying and modularizing code in future chapters.

Develop expertise: Encouraging continuous learning and skill development can help developers better understand the technologies and concepts they work with, reducing the cognitive load associated with unfamiliar or complex tasks. In later chapters, we'll discuss approaches for fostering a culture of learning and growth within your development team.

Implement effective documentation: Providing clear, concise, and accessible documentation can help developers quickly grasp essential information, reducing the cognitive load of deciphering poorly documented code or systems. In upcoming chapters, we'll explore best practices for creating and maintaining effective documentation.

Encourage collaboration: Promoting knowledge sharing and teamwork can help distribute cognitive load across the team, allowing developers to leverage each other's expertise and tackle complex problems more efficiently.

In subsequent chapters, we'll explore techniques for fostering collaboration and building a supportive development environment.

Automate repetitive tasks: Utilizing tools and technologies to streamline the development process can help reduce cognitive load by automating repetitive tasks and freeing up mental resources for more complex problem-solving. As we progress through this book, we'll discuss various automation tools and strategies that can be employed to optimize your development process.

In the following chapters, we'll delve deeper into these strategies and provide practical guidance on effectively managing cognitive load in your development team, ultimately creating a more efficient and productive environment that supports your organization's digital transformation journey.

The Relationship Between Cognitive Load and Happiness

The cognitive load experienced by developers plays a significant role in their overall happiness and well-being. High cognitive load can negatively impact developers' happiness in various ways, including:

Causing frustration and stress: When developers are overwhelmed by complex tasks or large amounts of information, they may experience increased stress and frustration, which can negatively affect their happiness and job satisfaction.

Lowering job satisfaction: Struggling to manage a high cognitive load can make developers feel less competent or satisfied with their work, ultimately affecting their overall happiness and engagement.

Contributing to burnout and mental fatigue: Continuous exposure to high cognitive load can lead to burnout and mental fatigue, causing developers to feel emotionally and mentally drained, significantly impacting their happiness and well-being.

Impacting work-life balance: When developers are consistently burdened with a high cognitive load, it can be challenging to maintain a healthy work-life balance, which may lead to decreased happiness and increased stress in their personal and professional lives.

In future chapters, we'll explore several actionable ways to improve developers' happiness and mental capacity, enabling them to be more creative and drive quality engineering effectively.

By addressing the cognitive load experienced by developers, we can create a more supportive and nurturing environment that fosters happiness, well-being, and high performance, ultimately contributing to the success of your organization's digital transformation journey.

Strategies for Promoting Happiness Through Cognitive Load Management

Effectively managing cognitive load improves developers' productivity and happiness and well-being. In this section, we'll introduce several strategies for promoting happiness through cognitive load management. As you progress through this book, we'll explore these strategies in greater depth, discussing technological practices, architectural frameworks, and best practices to help you successfully manage cognitive load in your development team.

Foster a positive work environment: Encouraging open communication and a supportive culture can help alleviate the stress associated with high cognitive load and create a more positive and enjoyable work environment. In future chapters, we'll delve deeper into techniques for fostering a positive and collaborative atmosphere within your team.

Provide opportunities for growth and development: Offering training, mentorship, and career advancement opportunities can help developers build the skills and knowledge needed to manage cognitive load effectively, ultimately improving their happiness and job satisfaction.

As we progress through this book, we'll explore various approaches to promoting your organization's growth and development.

Encourage work-life balance: Establishing flexible work hours, remote work options, and mental health support can help developers maintain a healthy work-life balance, reducing the strain of high cognitive load and promoting happiness. In subsequent chapters, we'll discuss strategies for supporting work-life balance and mental well-being in your team.

Recognize and reward hard work: Offering incentives, promotions, and recognition for achievements can boost developers' morale and motivation, helping them cope with the challenges associated with a high cognitive load. In later chapters, we'll explore effective recognition and reward systems to acknowledge and celebrate your team's accomplishments.

This is a hint of what we'll cover in the upcoming chapters. As you continue through this book, we'll provide a comprehensive examination of the technological practices, architectural frameworks, and best practices that can help you effectively manage cognitive load in your development team, ultimately leading to happier, more productive developers and a successful digital transformation journey.

Case Studies and Best Practices

In our journey exploring Developer Experience and its crucial role in digital transformation, it is important to understand the impact of cognitive load on developers. To illustrate this point, let us delve into the story of a company that, despite its best intentions, created a nightmarish developer experience, ultimately hindering its progress and growth.

The company, an established player in the tech industry, was determined to maintain a tight grip on security and minimize the risk of data leaks. With a strong command and control approach, they adopted outdated ITIL practices, enforcing a traffic interception system on every developer machine to monitor and control all connections.

The developers at the company soon found themselves grappling with SSL errors in nearly every request they made from their development environment, whether it was through command lines or IDEs. The misconfigured certificates created an incredibly frustrating and demoralizing experience for the development team.

Developers could not pinpoint the problem's cause as the SSL errors persisted. Many attributed the issue to their code, hardware configurations, or the latest OS update.

This uncertainty led them on a wild goose chase to find solutions, consuming valuable time and mental resources that could have been spent on developing the company's core business logic.

To seek answers, developers turned to Google or Stack Overflow, searching for solutions to their mysterious SSL errors. This process added a layer of complexity to their workflow and diverted their attention from the business logic they were originally working on.

After countless hours of searching and troubleshooting, some developers eventually discovered that the problem stemmed from the company's traffic interception system. They could add a certificate authority to their machines to remedy the issue. However, this revelation came at a high cost to their time, energy, and cognitive capacity.

The unfortunate reality for this company was that their stringent security measures created a heavy cognitive burden on their developers.

Each day, the developers wasted precious time and mental resources navigating the maze of SSL errors, detracting from their primary focus: building and improving the company's products.

This tale exemplifies how misaligned priorities and a lack of understanding of cognitive load can stifle innovation and productivity. In the following chapters, we will explore various strategies for managing cognitive load to ensure that developers can focus on delivering exceptional value in their digital transformation journey.

Cognitive load plays a crucial role in developers' productivity and happiness. Developing teams can significantly enhance their performance and well-being by understanding the concept of cognitive load and implementing strategies to manage it. Ultimately, recognizing the impact of cognitive load on developers is an essential step toward fostering a more productive, efficient, and enjoyable work environment.

Assess and Address Cognitive Load Issues

As an engineering leader, I understand the importance of addressing cognitive load issues daily. Regularly assessing and addressing these issues can increase productivity, reduce stress, and a more enjoyable work environment for everyone involved.

In this chapter, I'll share my experiences measuring cognitive load and provide insights into how the Cognitive Loadometer can help teams optimize their processes and tools.

In my experience, surveys are an effective way to measure cognitive load. By regularly asking team members to rate their perceived cognitive load on different tasks, you can gather valuable data highlighting areas of concern.

This feedback helps you identify which aspects of your team's workflow contribute to excessive cognitive load and take appropriate action to address them.

Another approach to measuring cognitive load is analyzing insights and analytics from tools like Microsoft Workplace Analytics. For example, you can monitor deep focus time when developers can work on complex tasks without interruption. By keeping track of deep focus time and identifying trends, you can pinpoint areas that need improvement and take steps to create a more conducive work environment.

One tool I've found particularly useful for managing cognitive load is the Cognitive Loadometer from the Open Practice Library. This tool is designed to help teams evaluate the cognitive load associated with specific tasks or processes.

To use the Cognitive Loadometer, our team first identifies a task or process we want to evaluate. Next, we rate the task or process on a scale of 1 to 10 for each type of load (intrinsic, extraneous, and germane). We then combine the scores to obtain an overall cognitive load score. This information allows us to pinpoint areas to reduce extraneous load and streamline our processes, ultimately optimizing our workflow and minimizing stress and burnout.

For example, after using the Cognitive Loadometer, we discovered that our code review process had a high cognitive load score. We then worked together to refine the process, implementing tools and techniques that helped reduce the extraneous load. As a result, our team experienced less stress during code reviews, and our overall productivity improved.

In conclusion, regularly assessing and addressing cognitive load issues is crucial for creating a healthy and efficient work environment. By measuring cognitive load through surveys and workplace analytics and employing tools like the Cognitive Loadometer, teams can identify areas of concern and take the necessary steps to optimize their processes and tools. Ultimately, these efforts can reduce stress, improve productivity, and a happier, more successful team.

Chapter 9
The Team-First Principle

* * *

Stable teams offer numerous benefits that contribute to a positive developer experience. These benefits arise from the robust behavioral and working dynamics that develop over time, fostering higher levels of transparency, trust, and collaboration among team members.

In this section, we will explore the advantages of stable teams in greater detail and discuss their impact on the developer experience.

Robust Behavioral and Working Dynamics

Stable teams can develop a deep understanding of each other's strengths, weaknesses, and working styles. This familiarity allows team members to effectively coordinate their efforts, streamline communication, and resolve conflicts more efficiently.

As a result, stable teams can better adapt to changes and tackle complex tasks, leading to more efficient and productive work.

Enhanced Transparency and Trust

In stable teams, team members feel more comfortable sharing ideas, concerns, and feedback, leading to increased transparency. This openness helps build trust among team members, essential for fostering a collaborative environment.

Trust enables team members to rely on each other, delegate tasks more effectively, and take calculated risks, all of which contribute to a positive developer experience.

Improved Collaboration

Stable teams benefit from a shared history and a strong sense of camaraderie. This familiarity makes it easier for team members to collaborate on projects, share knowledge, and learn from each other.

Effective collaboration is crucial for delivering high-quality software and ensuring the team stays aligned with project goals and objectives.

Increased Performance and Creativity

Stable teams are better equipped to find innovative solutions and overcome challenges when facing complexity. Confidence within the team drives increased performance levels and creativity as team members feel more comfortable sharing and exploring new ideas.

This environment of support and open communication allows for developing novel approaches and continuous improvement in the team's processes and practices.

Intrinsic Quality of the Product

Stable teams are more likely to take ownership of the products they develop, leading to higher intrinsic quality. When team members are invested in a project, they are more motivated to ensure that the final product meets or exceeds expectations. This commitment to quality translates to fewer defects, better performance, and a more satisfying end-user experience.

Conclusion

Stable teams provide a solid foundation for a positive developer experience by fostering robust behavioral and working dynamics, transparency, trust, and collaboration among team members. These qualities contribute to increased performance, creativity, and product quality, making stable teams essential to successful software development. Organizations can create an environment that promotes growth, innovation, and long-term success by understanding and nurturing these advantages.

Team Composition, Dynamics, and Fostering Effective Teamwork

* * *

While talented individuals are essential for a team's success, team composition and dynamics play an even more significant role in overall performance.

A team's ability to work together often outweighs its members' skills. This section will explore the importance of team composition and dynamics and discuss strategies for creating a supportive environment that promotes effective teamwork.

The Importance of Team Composition

Team composition refers to a team's mix of skills, experience, and personalities. A well-balanced team should include members with diverse skill sets, backgrounds, and perspectives to provide expertise and promote innovative problem-solving. A diverse team is better equipped to approach challenges from different angles and develop well-rounded solutions.

Understanding Team Dynamics

Team dynamics are the behavioral and relational patterns that emerge within a group. These patterns can significantly influence a team's ability to collaborate, communicate, and solve problems. Healthy team dynamics are characterized by open communication, trust, mutual respect, and a shared sense of purpose. On the other hand, poor team dynamics may result in misunderstandings, conflicts, and reduced productivity.

Strategies for Creating a Supportive Environment

Creating a supportive environment that encourages open communication, collaboration, and continuous improvement is crucial to foster effective teamwork. Here are some strategies to consider:

1. Encourage Open Communication: Create a safe space for team members to share their ideas, concerns, and feedback without fear of judgment or retribution. Encourage active listening and ensure that everyone has the opportunity to contribute during discussions.
2. Promote Psychological Safety: Psychological safety is the shared belief that taking interpersonal risks within a team is safe. Encourage team members to voice their opinions, ask questions, and admit mistakes without fear of negative consequences. Recognize and reward vulnerability as an essential component of growth and learning.
3. Build Trust and Accountability: Foster trust among team members by setting clear expectations, providing regular feedback, and holding each other accountable for their commitments. Celebrate successes as a team and address setbacks as opportunities for improvement.

4. Emphasize Collaboration: Encourage team members to work together on tasks and projects, leveraging each other's strengths and expertise. Provide opportunities for cross-functional collaboration and knowledge-sharing to break down silos and promote a collective understanding of the team's objectives.
5. Develop Team Norms and Rituals: Establish a set of shared norms and rituals that govern how the team works together. These can include guidelines for communication, decision-making, conflict resolution, and other aspects of teamwork. Regularly review and adjust these norms as needed to ensure they continue to support the team's growth and success.

Creating high-performing teams goes beyond simply assembling a group of talented individuals. By focusing on team composition, understanding team dynamics, and fostering a supportive environment for effective teamwork, organizations can unlock the full potential of their teams and achieve greater success in their software development efforts.

Practical Tips for Maximizing Team Performance

* * *

Organizations can implement practical tips and strategies to maximize team performance and enhance the developer experience.

This section will explore these tips in greater detail, covering aspects such as embracing diversity, creating a conducive environment, managing cognitive load, and fostering a team-first mindset.

Embrace Diversity and Ownership

Regarding skills, experiences, and perspectives, diversity within a team leads to more innovative problem-solving and well-rounded solutions. Encourage team members to take ownership of their work and contribute their unique strengths. This sense of ownership promotes individual growth and contributes to the team's success. Here are five examples of how to embrace diversity and ownership:

Cross-functional collaboration: Form teams with members from different functional backgrounds, such as developers, designers, product managers, and quality assurance specialists. This diversity in expertise allows the team to address a broader range of challenges and fosters creativity in problem-solving.

Multicultural teams: Encourage the formation of multicultural teams with members from various cultural backgrounds and experiences. This diversity promotes open-mindedness, adaptability, and innovation as team members bring unique perspectives and approaches to problem-solving.

Skill development opportunities: Provide opportunities for team members to learn new skills and expand their knowledge, such as through training programs, workshops, or mentorship initiatives. This investment in personal growth can lead to new insights and ideas, benefiting both the individual and the team.

Inclusive decision-making processes: Involve team members, valuing each person's input and perspective. This inclusive approach ensures a variety of viewpoints are considered and fosters a sense of ownership and commitment among team members.

Recognition and reward systems: Implement recognition and reward systems that appreciate collective achievements. By acknowledging the unique strengths and accomplishments of the team, you encourage ownership and inspire continued growth and success.

Design Physical and Virtual Environments for Focused Interactions

Create physical and virtual workspaces that facilitate collaboration and focused interactions. Ensure that team members have access to the necessary tools, resources, and spaces for individual and group work.

Use communication and collaboration platforms in virtual settings that enable seamless information sharing and efficient teamwork. Here are some examples of how to achieve this:

Dedicated team spaces: In a physical office setting, provide dedicated team spaces where members can collaborate, brainstorm, and hold meetings. These spaces should be comfortable, well-lit, and equipped with necessary resources like whiteboards, monitors, and office supplies.

Private work areas: Offer private work areas or quiet zones for team members who need to focus on individual tasks without distractions. These spaces should be separate from collaborative areas to balance collaboration and focused work.

Flexible seating arrangements: Encourage flexible seating arrangements, such as hot-desking or adjustable workstations, to allow team members to choose where they work based on their needs and preferences.

Remote-friendly infrastructure: For remote or hybrid teams, ensure that team members have access to reliable internet connections, VPNs, and other necessary tools to work effectively from home or other remote locations.

Video conferencing tools: Utilize high-quality video conferencing tools for virtual meetings, enabling clear communication and face-to-face interactions among team members, regardless of location.

Collaboration platforms: Use collaboration platforms like Slack, Microsoft Teams, or Google Workspace to facilitate seamless communication, file sharing, and project management among team members. These platforms should be easily accessible, user-friendly, and well-integrated with other tools used by the team.

Virtual whiteboards and brainstorming tools: Implement virtual whiteboards or brainstorming tools, such as Miro or MURAL, to enable team members to collaborate visually and share ideas, even when working remotely.

Document and knowledge sharing: Utilize cloud-based document storage and knowledge-sharing platforms, such as Google Drive, Dropbox, or Confluence, to ensure team members have easy access to necessary information and resources.

Regular virtual team-building activities: Organize virtual team-building activities, such as online games, workshops, or casual catch-ups, to foster a sense of camaraderie and connection among remote team members.

Restrict Team Responsibilities to Match Cognitive Load

Avoid overloading team members with tasks and responsibilities beyond their cognitive capacity. Delegate tasks according to each team member's skills and expertise while ensuring a balanced workload. This approach helps maintain a sustainable pace and prevents burnout, improving productivity and team morale.

Limit the Number and Type of Domains per Team

Allocate a manageable number of domains to each team, taking into account their skills, expertise, and cognitive capacity. Employing a Domain-Driven Design (DDD) approach can help achieve this by focusing on the core business problems and aligning software design with the underlying domain complexities.

Domain-Driven Design is a software development methodology emphasizing collaboration between domain experts and software developers to create solutions reflecting core business concepts and logic. By breaking down the overall system into smaller, manageable domains, DDD allows teams to focus on specific areas of responsibility and reduces cognitive load.

Using DDD to allocate domains to teams offers several benefits:

- Enhanced focus: Teams can concentrate on specific areas of the system, leading to more efficient work processes and better results.
- Reduced cognitive load: By limiting the number of domains per team, DDD helps prevent cognitive overload, allowing team members to maintain a sustainable workload and avoid burnout.
- Improved collaboration: DDD fosters collaboration between domain experts and software developers, promoting a shared understanding of the business context and enabling more effective problem-solving.

- Greater adaptability: By isolating domain-specific complexities, DDD allows teams to respond more quickly to changes in business requirements, making the overall system more adaptable and resilient.

When allocating domains to teams using DDD, consider the following steps:

- Identify the core domains: Analyze the business requirements to identify the primary domains that represent the essential parts of the system.
- Define bounded contexts: Create bounded contexts for each domain, which are self-contained areas of the system that encompass the domain's logic, data, and interactions.
- Assign teams to domains: Allocate teams to specific domains based on their skills, expertise, and cognitive capacity. Ensure each team has the resources and knowledge to effectively address the domain's complexities.
- Encourage collaboration: Promote collaboration between domain experts and software developers, enabling a shared understanding of the domain's requirements and challenges. This collaboration can help teams create solutions that are more aligned with business needs and easier to maintain and evolve.

Provide a Team-First Working Environment

Cultivate a working environment that prioritizes the needs and goals of the team over individual interests. Encourage team members to support and help each other, share knowledge, and collaborate on tasks. This team-first mindset creates a sense of unity and purpose that can drive success.

Team-based objectives: Set shared goals and objectives for the entire team rather than individual targets. This approach encourages team members to work together, collaborate, and focus on collective success rather than competing against one another.

Collaborative problem-solving: Encourage team members to tackle challenges and problems together, pooling their expertise and knowledge to find the best solutions. This collaborative approach fosters a sense of shared ownership and responsibility for the team's outcomes.

Knowledge-sharing sessions: Organize regular sessions where team members can present their work, share insights, and learn from each other. This practice promotes a learning culture and helps build trust and camaraderie among team members.

Peer recognition: Implement a system of peer recognition where team members can acknowledge and appreciate each other's contributions, efforts, and achievements. This practice reinforces the value of teamwork and encourages a supportive and collaborative environment.

Team-building activities: Organize team-building activities, both within and outside the workplace, to strengthen bonds among team members and foster a sense of unity. These activities range from group workshops, brainstorming sessions, and team lunches to offsite retreats or team sports events.

Minimize Team Distractions

Reduce distractions and interruptions during work hours to allow team members to focus on their tasks. Set clear boundaries and expectations for communication, meeting times, and availability to maintain a healthy work-life balance and improve productivity. Here are some examples of how to achieve this:

Designated quiet hours: Establish specific periods during the day when team members can work without interruptions, such as phone calls, emails, or instant messages. This allows individuals to concentrate on their tasks and progress without constant distractions.

Clear communication guidelines: Set guidelines for communication within the team, specifying preferred channels (e.g., email, chat, or phone) and response time expectations. This helps reduce the pressure to respond immediately and allows team members to plan their work accordingly.

Scheduled meetings: Schedule regular meetings, such as daily stand-ups or weekly progress updates, to discuss project status and share updates. Avoid impromptu meetings or last-minute requests that disrupt team members' focus and workflow.

Meeting-free days or time blocks: Designate specific days or time blocks as meeting-free, allowing team members to dedicate their full attention to their tasks without interruptions.

Availability status: Encourage team members to update their availability status on communication platforms, indicating whether they are available for collaboration, in a meeting, or focused on a task. This helps set expectations and reduces the likelihood of interruptions during focused work time.

Work-life balance boundaries: Encourage team members to set boundaries between their work and personal lives. For example, they should avoid working outside of regular hours or responding to work-related messages during personal time.

Encourage breaks: Promote regular breaks during the workday for team members to recharge and avoid burnout. Short breaks can improve focus and productivity in the long run.

Noise-canceling headphones: If the work environment is noisy, consider providing noise-canceling headphones for team members to minimize distractions and improve focus.

Facilitate Team Interactions for Trust, Awareness, and Learning

Organize regular team meetings, workshops, and informal gatherings to facilitate interaction and relationship-building among team members.

These interactions help build trust, raise awareness of individual strengths and weaknesses, and promote collective learning.

Mentor New or Less Experienced Team Members

Encourage experienced team members to mentor and support new or less experienced colleagues. This mentorship can help bridge knowledge gaps, accelerate onboarding, and foster a supportive environment that benefits both the individual and the team.

Conclusion:

Organizations can maximize team performance and improve the developer experience by implementing these practical tips. Emphasizing diversity, creating a conducive working environment, managing cognitive load, and fostering a team-first mindset are essential for successful software development teams. By prioritizing these factors, organizations can create a positive environment that promotes growth, innovation, and long-term success.

Patterns and Behaviors that Hinder Team Performance

* * *

This section will discuss patterns and behaviors that can hinder team performance and negatively impact the developer experience. Recognizing and addressing these issues is crucial to creating a productive and enjoyable work environment for your team.

Shuffling team members regularly: Constantly moving team members between different teams can disrupt the development of stable working relationships and team dynamics. It takes time for team members to build trust, rapport, and understanding of each other's strengths and weaknesses. Organizations may inadvertently hinder team cohesion and performance by shuffling team members frequently.

Multiple team membership: Assigning team members to multiple teams simultaneously can lead to divided attention, reduced focus, and increased stress. Team members may struggle to manage their workload and commitments effectively, resulting in reduced productivity and a decline in the quality of their work.

Too many handovers: Excessive handovers between teams or

team members can result in a loss of knowledge and context, leading to errors, delays, and miscommunication. A more streamlined and efficient approach is to limit handovers and ensure clear documentation and communication throughout the development process.

Unclear boundaries: When teams lack clearly defined boundaries regarding responsibilities, roles, and domains, they may experience confusion, duplication of effort, and inefficiencies. Establishing clear boundaries and expectations can help teams work more effectively and cohesively.

Partial allocations to teams: Assigning team members to a project or team only part-time can result in a lack of focus and commitment, leading to reduced productivity and a decline in the quality of work. Where possible, it is preferable to allocate team members to projects on a full-time basis, allowing them to dedicate their attention and resources to the task at hand.

Ad hoc team design: Forming teams without carefully considering team composition, skills, expertise, and domain knowledge can lead to suboptimal team performance. Organizations should take the time to design teams thoughtfully, considering each project's unique needs and requirements and team members' strengths.

Embracing Change With Dynamic Reteaming

* * *

In her groundbreaking book, "Dynamic Reteaming: The Art and Wisdom of Changing Teams," Heidi Helfand offers valuable insights and practical guidance on managing team composition in a rapidly changing business landscape effectively.

Drawing on her extensive experience as a coach and consultant, Helfand presents a compelling case for embracing change and fostering a culture of adaptability, growth, and continuous learning.

Key Concepts from Dynamic Reteaming

Dynamic Reteaming, a concept introduced by Heidi Helfand, explores the idea that teams can evolve and adapt by changing their composition and structure in response to the needs of the organization and the project at hand.

By understanding the five patterns of dynamic reteaming, organizations can more effectively manage team changes and improve their productivity and collaboration.

One by One: This pattern involves adding or removing individual team members as needed. This could be in response to a change in project requirements, skill set needs, or team member availability. One by One adjustment allows teams to maintain flexibility and adapt quickly to changing circumstances while minimizing the disruption caused by larger-scale reorganizations.

Grow and Split: In this pattern, a team is allowed to expand until it becomes too large and unwieldy, at which point it is divided into smaller, more focused groups. This process can help maintain efficiency and productivity, as smaller teams can often collaborate more effectively and respond faster to new challenges. Growing and splitting teams can also create opportunities for leadership development, as new team leads may be needed to manage the resulting sub-teams.

Merging: This pattern involves combining two or more teams to form a new, larger team. This can be done to consolidate resources, share knowledge, or streamline processes. Merging teams can help organizations leverage their strengths better and address gaps in skills or expertise. However, care must be taken to manage potential conflicts and ensure the merged team can function cohesively and effectively.

Switching: In this pattern, individuals are moved between teams to address specific needs or challenges. Switching can effectively promote cross-team collaboration, share knowledge, and build a more versatile workforce. However, it can also be disruptive, so it is important to consider the potential impact on the individual and the teams involved.

Isolation: This pattern involves separating a team from the larger organization to focus on a particular project or initiative. By providing the isolated team with the autonomy and resources they need to work independently, organizations can promote innovation and enable the team to move quickly and efficiently. However, it is crucial to maintain open lines of communication with the larger organization to avoid creating silos or disconnects between the isolated team and the rest of the company.

By understanding and leveraging these five patterns of dynamic reteaming, organizations can more effectively manage team changes, foster collaboration, and adapt to the ever-evolving needs of their projects and initiatives.

The Importance of Psychological Safety: A key component of successful dynamic reteaming is creating an environment where team members feel safe to express their ideas, concerns, and questions without fear of retribution. Psychological safety fosters open communication, collaboration, and innovation.

Embracing Change as a Constant: Rather than viewing team changes as disruptive events, Helfand encourages organizations to embrace change as an ongoing, natural part of the development process. This mindset shift allows teams to become more resilient, adaptable, and open to new ideas.

The Role of Leadership: Effective leadership is critical in facilitating dynamic reteaming. Leaders must be able to recognize when team changes are necessary, communicate the reasons for those changes, and provide support and guidance throughout the transition process.

Practical Strategies for Implementing Dynamic Reteaming

Establish a Shared Vision: Ensure all team members understand the organization's goals and values and how their work contributes to achieving those objectives. A shared vision can provide a sense of stability and purpose amid change.

- Foster a Culture of Feedback: Encourage open and honest feedback among team members regarding their performance and the team's overall dynamics. Regularly assess team health and satisfaction to identify areas for improvement.

- Encourage Skill Development: Support team members in developing their skills and expertise within their current roles and in areas that may benefit the organization. This can help ensure teams have the necessary resources to adapt and grow.
- Be Transparent and Communicative: Communicate the reasons for any team changes and provide support and guidance to help team members navigate the transition. Encourage open dialogue and address any concerns or questions that arise.
- Celebrate Success and Learn from Failure: Acknowledge and celebrate the achievements of teams and individuals while recognizing that failure is an opportunity for learning and growth. This can help build a culture of resilience and adaptability.

Conclusion

Heidi Helfand's "Dynamic Reteaming" offers valuable insights and strategies for embracing change and fostering a culture of adaptability and growth in organizations.

By understanding the patterns of team change, creating an environment of psychological safety, and providing effective leadership, organizations can successfully navigate the challenges of dynamic reteaming and unlock their full potential.

Combining Team Topologies, Dynamic Reteaming, and Tuckman's Model

* * *

In previous chapters, we discussed the importance of adopting the team topologies principle of team-first and stable teams and embracing change through dynamic reteaming. These concepts provide valuable insights into how organizations can structure their teams to optimize collaboration and adaptability in the face of evolving business needs.

In this chapter, we will further enhance our understanding of effective team management by introducing Tuckman's model for group development. By integrating Tuckman's model with team topologies and dynamic reteaming principles, organizations can create a comprehensive framework for managing team structures and driving successful digital transformation.

Tuckman's model for group development outlines five key stages that teams typically progress through:

1. Forming: In this initial stage, team members become acquainted with one another and their objectives. They

start to define their roles and responsibilities and establish working relationships.
2. Storming: As team members start working together, conflicts may arise due to differences in opinions, working styles, and personal values. This stage is characterized by tension and disagreements as team members vie for influence and establish their positions within the group.
3. Norming: In this stage, team members resolve their conflicts and develop a shared understanding of their goals and working methods. Trust and collaboration improve, increasing cohesion and creating a more harmonious working environment.
4. Performing: As the team becomes more aligned and efficient, they reach the performing stage, where they can effectively work together to accomplish their objectives. The team has a strong sense of unity and mutual accountability, enabling them to deliver high-quality results.
5. Adjourning: The final stage occurs when a project is completed, or a team is disbanded. Team members reflect on their experiences, celebrate their achievements, and prepare for the next challenge.

By combining the insights from team topologies, dynamic reteaming, and Tuckman's model, organizations can create a powerful framework for guiding their teams through the challenges and opportunities of digital transformation. This comprehensive approach enables leaders to provide the right structure, foster collaboration, and support their teams as they deliver meaningful work.

In conclusion, equipping your organization with these three complementary models can help you navigate the complexities of team management and optimize the developer experience. By fostering a culture of adaptability, collaboration, and continuous improvement, you can position your organization for success in the digital transformation journey.

The Model-Coach-Care Framework

* * *

In this chapter, we will delve into the Model-Coach-Care (MCC) framework, a powerful approach to managing and supporting software development teams on their digital transformation journey. The MCC framework emphasizes three key components: modeling desired behaviors, coaching team members, and providing care to foster a positive and productive work environment.

By understanding and applying the principles of the MCC framework, organizations can create a supportive and empowering developer experience, ultimately accelerating their digital transformation efforts.

Model

The first component of the MCC framework involves modeling desired behaviors and practices. Leaders and managers should demonstrate the values, work habits, and communication styles they expect from their teams. By setting a positive example, leaders can inspire their team members to adopt these behaviors and foster a culture of professionalism, collaboration, and innovation.

Key elements of effective modeling include:

- Transparency: Be open and honest about goals, challenges, and decision-making processes. This encourages trust and collaboration within the team.
- Continuous learning: Emphasize the importance of ongoing professional development and be willing to learn from team members and adapt to new technologies and methodologies.
- Collaboration: Work closely with team members, actively participate in team activities, and promote a culture of collaboration and open communication.

Coach

The second component of the MCC framework focuses on coaching. Coaching is an essential aspect of team management that involves guiding, mentoring, and supporting team members in their personal and professional growth. Effective coaching can help developers acquire new skills, overcome challenges, and achieve their full potential.

Key elements of effective coaching include:

- Regular feedback: Provide constructive feedback consistently to help team members understand their strengths and areas for improvement. Celebrate successes and use setbacks as learning opportunities.
- Skill development: Identify skill gaps and provide resources and support for team members to develop new capabilities. Encourage developers to attend workshops, conferences, and training programs to enhance their skillset further.

- Goal setting: Work with team members to set clear, achievable, and measurable goals. Monitor progress and adjust goals as needed, providing support and guidance.

Care

The final component of the MCC framework is care. Providing care involves creating a supportive and nurturing work environment where team members feel valued, respected, and empowered. A caring and inclusive environment can help reduce stress, improve job satisfaction, and boost overall team performance.

Key elements of effective care include:

- Psychological safety: Foster an atmosphere where team members feel comfortable expressing their ideas, concerns, and opinions without fear of judgment or retribution.
- Work-life balance: Encourage team members to maintain a healthy work-life balance by respecting their time and promoting flexible work arrangements.
- Recognition and rewards: Acknowledge and celebrate team achievements, and provide tangible rewards that reflect the value of their contributions.

The Model-Coach-Care framework is a comprehensive approach to managing and supporting software development teams in their digital transformation journey.

Powerful Enterprise Tools

* * *

In the previous chapter, we discussed the concept of cognitive load and its significance in managing developers' productivity and overall well-being. We also explored various strategies for effectively managing cognitive load, allowing developers to focus on delivering exceptional value in their digital transformation journey.

As we continue to delve into Developer Experience, this chapter will introduce a range of enterprise tools that can further optimize the developer experience.

We will briefly mention these tools, such as Stack Overflow and GitHub, and explore how they can streamline the development process, reduce cognitive load, and foster collaboration among developers. We will closely examine each tool in the upcoming chapters and provide a more in-depth analysis.

In software development, various enterprise tools can help streamline the development process, reduce cognitive load, and improve collaboration among developers. Some of these tools include:

Stack Overflow: A popular platform for knowledge sharing and collaboration among developers. It allows developers to ask questions, find answers, and learn from their peers, reducing the time spent on troubleshooting and research.

GitHub: A widely-used version control and collaboration platform that provides developers a seamless way to collaborate on code, track changes, and manage projects. GitHub's powerful features can help reduce cognitive load by streamlining the development process and fostering a culture of collaboration and knowledge sharing.

In the following chapters, we will explore more tools in detail, delving into their features, benefits, and best practices for integrating them into your development workflow. By leveraging these enterprise tools, your organization can optimize the developer experience and empower your development team to focus on delivering exceptional value in their digital transformation journey.

StackOverflow Enterprise: An In-Depth Look

* * *

StackOverflow Enterprise is a private, secure version of the widely popular Q&A platform StackOverflow, specifically designed for internal use within organizations. It offers a powerful and collaborative environment where developers can work together, share knowledge, and find solutions to problems efficiently.

Throughout my journey across various organizations, one tool that has consistently proven invaluable is Stack Overflow Enterprise. As a developer, I can attest to the countless times it had saved me when I was knee-deep in technical challenges.

It's no secret that large enterprises undergo multi-year technology transformations, grappling with hiring, onboarding, reselling, retention, and managing distributed environments. In this chapter, I will share my experiences with Stack Overflow Enterprise and how it can enhance your developer community and overall experience.

* * *

The Power of Democratizing Knowledge Access

One of the most significant challenges in any organization is breaking down knowledge silos that can hinder collaboration and innovation. Stack Overflow Enterprise enables a cultural shift by encouraging team members to seek and contribute knowledge actively. This approach has numerous benefits, including boosting team productivity, fostering cross-departmental collaboration, and reducing the burden on Subject Matter Experts.

In my experience, Stack Overflow Enterprise has consistently helped bridge these knowledge gaps. A centralized platform where developers can ask questions and receive answers from colleagues empowers individuals to share their expertise and learn from one another. In turn, this creates a more engaged and knowledgeable community of developers.

A Real-World Use Case Study

At one organization I was part of, we saw some impressive results after implementing Stack Overflow Enterprise:

Developer Satisfaction: Stack Overflow quickly became the most loved tool among our developer community. It allowed developers to find answers to their questions efficiently without disrupting other team members' workflow.

Improved Knowledge Reusability: We created a growing knowledge base that could be easily searched and referenced by archiving questions and answers. This helped reduce the time spent on recurring issues and allowed developers to focus on new challenges.

Cross-Silo Collaboration: We found that 64% of all questions asked on our Stack Overflow Enterprise instance were by a user from a different department. This statistic demonstrates how effectively the platform facilitated collaboration across organizational boundaries.

Reduced Ticket Escalations: With Stack Overflow Enterprise,

developers could quickly find answers to their questions, reducing the need to escalate issues to higher-level support. As a result, we saw a 25% reduction in ticket escalations.

Why Stack Overflow Enterprise Deserves a Place in Your Digital Transformation

Based on my experiences across various organizations, I wholeheartedly recommend Stack Overflow Enterprise as a powerful tool to enhance your developer community and experience.

It can help your organization overcome common challenges associated with large-scale technology transformations by fostering a culture of collaboration, knowledge sharing, and continuous learning. By implementing Stack Overflow Enterprise, you can improve developer satisfaction, streamline workflows, and ultimately accelerate your digital transformation journey.

One of the primary advantages of StackOverflow Enterprise is the ease with which developers can search for and find answers to their questions.

This reduces the time spent troubleshooting, allowing developers to focus on more critical tasks and increasing overall productivity. Furthermore, by having a centralized repository of information, developers can avoid duplicating efforts and leverage the expertise of their colleagues to solve problems more effectively.

StackOverflow Enterprise fosters collaboration and teamwork by enabling developers to solve problems and share best practices. Developers can ask questions, provide answers, upvote helpful responses, and engage in discussions to gain insights and learn from their peers.

This collaborative approach promotes continuous learning, ensures the effective use of resources, and helps to maintain a strong and cohesive team.

* * *

Customized experience

Organizations have the flexibility to customize StackOverflow Enterprise to suit their specific needs. They can create tags, categories, and custom branding to reflect their organization's identity and focus on relevant topics.

Additionally, administrators can manage user access, define roles and permissions, and monitor activity to ensure a secure and well-organized environment. This level of customization allows organizations to tailor the platform to their unique requirements, making it an invaluable resource for their development teams.

In conclusion, StackOverflow Enterprise offers a powerful tool for organizations looking to enhance their developer experience by promoting knowledge sharing, collaboration, and customization. By adopting StackOverflow Enterprise, companies can build a thriving community of developers who work together to solve challenges, share their expertise, and drive innovation.

GitHub Enterprise: An In-Depth Look

GitHub Enterprise is a powerful, organization-centric version of the renowned code hosting and version control platform GitHub.

It offers a secure and feature-rich environment for managing code, tracking changes, and collaborating on software development projects. In this section, we'll delve into the key features and benefits of using GitHub Enterprise:

Code management

GitHub Enterprise simplifies collaborating on code by allowing developers to create and manage branches and track changes using pull requests. This makes it easy for teams to work on multiple features or bug fixes simultaneously while maintaining a clean and organized codebase. Additionally, the platform supports code reviews, enabling developers to provide feedback and suggest improvements to ensure high-quality code.

Security

Security is a top priority for organizations, and GitHub Enterprise delivers advanced security features designed to protect your code and data. These features include SAML single sign-on, two-factor authentication, and granular access control, enabling organizations to manage user access and permissions effectively. Moreover, GitHub Enterprise includes built-in security vulnerability scanning and automated dependency updates, helping to identify and address potential security issues before they become critical.

Integration

GitHub Enterprise is designed to work seamlessly with various tools throughout the software development lifecycle. It integrates with popular CI/CD pipelines, project management systems, and code review platforms, creating a streamlined developer workflow. This integration allows organizations to consolidate their development tools and processes, improving efficiency and reducing potential errors.

Customization and flexibility

With GitHub Enterprise, organizations can customize their environment to suit their needs. Depending on their security and compliance requirements, they can create custom integrations using the GitHub API, develop Organization-specific workflows, and even deploy GitHub Enterprise on-premises or in a private cloud.

Artificial Intelligence

Productivity and efficiency are crucial factors in delivering high-quality software on time in software development. GitHub Enterprise Copilot is an AI-powered coding assistant designed to revolutionize the developer experience by simplifying the coding process and boosting productivity. In this chapter, we will explore the features and benefits of GitHub Enterprise Copilot and how it can transform how developers write code.

GitHub Enterprise Copilot is an advanced AI-driven coding assistant that helps developers write code faster and more efficiently. Built on OpenAI's Codex, a large-scale AI model trained on a vast amount of public code, Copilot leverages machine learning to understand and generate code in real time, providing developers with relevant suggestions and insights as they type.

GitHub Enterprise Copilot's primary feature is its ability to automatically suggest code snippets and complete lines of code as developers type. By understanding the context of the written code, Copilot can provide accurate and relevant suggestions, saving developers time and reducing the likelihood of errors.

Copilot is designed to support various programming languages and frameworks, making it a versatile tool for developers working in various environments. From popular languages like Python, JavaScript, and Ruby to niche languages and frameworks, Copilot offers a comprehensive solution for developers of all backgrounds.

One of the most powerful aspects of GitHub Enterprise Copilot is its ability to learn from the context of the written code. As developers work on a project, Copilot adapts to their coding style and preferences, providing increasingly personalized and accurate suggestions over time.

As a part of the GitHub Enterprise ecosystem, Copilot seamlessly integrates with the platform's other features and tools. This allows developers to take full advantage of Copilot's capabilities while using familiar tools and workflows, ensuring a smooth and productive experience.

In addition to generating code suggestions, GitHub Enterprise Copilot can assist with the documentation. The AI-powered assistant can provide developers with explanations of code snippets, function signatures, and other helpful information, making it easier to understand complex code and maintain well-documented projects.

GitHub Enterprise Copilot represents a significant leap forward in developer experience, offering a powerful and intelligent coding assistant that can streamline the software development process. By harnessing the power of AI and machine learning, Copilot helps developers write code faster, reduce errors, and focus on high-level problem-solving. GitHub Enterprise Copilot is a game-changing tool for organizations looking to boost productivity and enhance the developer experience.

In summary, GitHub Enterprise is an invaluable tool for organizations looking to enhance their developer experience by providing a secure, integrated, and customizable platform for code management and collaboration. By adopting GitHub Enterprise, companies can empower their development teams to work more efficiently, improve code quality, and drive innovation.

JIRA and Confluence: The Power of Collaboration

* * *

JIRA and Confluence are two powerful tools developed by Atlassian that, when used together, create a seamless environment for managing software development projects and fostering collaboration among team members.

This section will explore the key features and benefits of using JIRA and Confluence in your organization.

* * *

JIRA: Project Management and Issue Tracking

JIRA is a robust project management and issue-tracking tool designed to help teams plan, track, and release high-quality software. Its key features include:

- Customizable workflows: JIRA allows you to create tailor-made workflows to suit your team's specific

processes, ensuring that tasks flow smoothly from inception to completion.
- Advanced reporting: JIRA provides a wide range of reporting options, including customizable dashboards, burn-down charts, and velocity charts, helping teams gain insights into their progress and identify areas for improvement.
- Integration with development tools: JIRA seamlessly integrates with other development tools, such as GitHub, Bitbucket, and Jenkins, creating a streamlined and efficient development process.
- Scalability: JIRA can easily scale to accommodate growing teams and projects, making it a suitable choice for organizations of all sizes.

Confluence: Collaboration and Documentation

Confluence is a comprehensive wiki and documentation platform that provides a collaborative space for teams to create, organize, and discuss documentation, meeting notes, and project plans. Its key features include:

Rich content creation: Confluence supports various content types, including text, images, videos, and code snippets, making it easy for teams to create engaging and informative documentation.

Version control: Confluence tracks changes made to documents, enabling users to view the history of a document and revert to a previous version if necessary.

Powerful search functionality: Confluence's search functionality allows users to locate relevant documents and information quickly, improving productivity and reducing time spent searching for information.

Integration with JIRA: Confluence integrates seamlessly with JIRA, enabling teams to link project documentation to relevant JIRA issues and track progress in a centralized location.

JIRA and Confluence: The Power of Collaboration

By leveraging the combined power of JIRA and Confluence, organizations can improve their developer experience by providing a cohesive, integrated platform for managing projects and fostering collaboration. Using these tools in tandem can help teams work more efficiently, enhance communication, and deliver high-quality software.

Postman Enterprise: Streamlining API Development and Testing

* * *

Postman Enterprise is a powerful platform designed to streamline designing, developing, and documenting APIs. By providing a comprehensive suite of tools to help developers collaborate, test, and monitor APIs, Postman Enterprise improves efficiency and reduces the risk of errors in API development. This section will explore the key features and benefits of using Postman Enterprise in your organization.

Collaboration

Postman Enterprise facilitates seamless collaboration among team members working on API development. Its key collaboration features include:

Shared API collections: Developers can easily share API collections and environments with their team members, ensuring everyone can access the most up-to-date information and reducing the risk of miscommunication.

Centralized documentation: Postman Enterprise automatically generates and updates API documentation as changes are made, making it easy for teams to maintain accurate and up-to-date documentation.

Access control: Administrators can manage access to API collections and environments, ensuring only authorized users can make changes.

Testing

Postman Enterprise provides robust tools for testing APIs, ensuring they function correctly and meet performance requirements. Key testing features include:

Automated tests: Developers can write and run automated tests for APIs using JavaScript, enabling them to validate API functionality and performance quickly and consistently.

Test reporting: Postman Enterprise generates detailed test reports, providing insights into test results and helping teams identify areas for improvement.

Integration with CI/CD pipelines: Postman Enterprise can be integrated with continuous integration and continuous deployment (CI/CD) pipelines, ensuring that API tests are run automatically as part of the development process.

Monitoring

Real-time monitoring of APIs is a crucial aspect of maintaining high-quality services. Postman Enterprise offers powerful monitoring features, such as:

API performance monitoring: Postman Enterprise tracks the performance of APIs, alerting developers to potential issues and helping them optimize API performance.

Error detection: The platform automatically detects and alerts developers to errors in API responses, enabling teams to address issues before they impact users.

Customizable alerts: Developers can set up customized alerts based on specific conditions, ensuring they are notified of potential issues in real-time.

By leveraging Postman Enterprise, organizations can streamline their API development process and improve the developer experience. The platform's collaboration, testing, and monitoring features ensure that teams can deliver high-quality, reliable APIs to meet the needs of their users.

Red Hat OpenShift: Simplifying Container Management and Deployment

* * *

Red Hat OpenShift is a powerful Kubernetes-based container platform that streamlines containerized applications' deployment, scaling, and management.

By providing a robust and secure environment for developers to build, deploy, and run applications, OpenShift supports a wide range of languages, frameworks, and databases. This section will explore the key features and benefits of using Red Hat OpenShift in your organization.

Developer Productivity

OpenShift is designed to enhance developer productivity by providing an array of tools and features that simplify the application development process. Key productivity features include:

Developer Console: OpenShift's built-in developer console offers a user-friendly interface for managing and deploying applications, giving developers a comprehensive view of their projects and resources.

Command-Line Tools: OpenShift includes powerful command-line tools that allow developers to perform various tasks directly from the command line, such as building and deploying applications.

Source-to-Image (S2I): OpenShift's S2I feature automates the process of building container images from source code, enabling developers to focus on writing code without worrying about the complexities of containerization.

Scalability

OpenShift is designed to handle the scaling needs of modern applications, automating the process of scaling applications to meet demand. Key scalability features include:

Automatic Scaling: OpenShift can automatically scale applications based on demand, ensuring optimal resource utilization and performance.

Load Balancing: The platform provides built-in load balancing capabilities, distributing traffic evenly across application instances and ensuring high availability.

Resource Management: OpenShift allows developers to define resource quotas and limits for applications, ensuring that resources are allocated efficiently and preventing resource overconsumption.

Security

Security is critical for any application development platform, and OpenShift is no exception. The platform offers a variety of advanced security features, such as:

Role-Based Access Control (RBAC): OpenShift's RBAC capabilities allow administrators to define and enforce granular access policies, ensuring users have appropriate permissions for their roles.

Network Isolation: OpenShift supports network isolation

between projects, preventing unauthorized access and ensuring data privacy.

Automated Security Updates: The platform automatically updates the underlying infrastructure, ensuring that applications run in a secure and up-to-date environment.

By leveraging Red Hat OpenShift, organizations can simplify the management and deployment of containerized applications while ensuring optimal performance, security, and scalability. The platform's developer-centric features and robust security capabilities make it an ideal choice for organizations looking to improve their developer experience and accelerate application delivery.

Understanding and Finding Code

* * *

In today's fast-paced and highly interconnected world, understanding and locating code across an organization is paramount. As organizations grow and their codebases expand, it becomes increasingly difficult for developers to maintain an accurate mental map of the entire system.

This can lead to inefficiencies, missed opportunities for collaboration, and reduced overall productivity. In this chapter, we will explore the importance of understanding and finding code across the whole organization and introduce Sourcegraph as a powerful tool to facilitate this process.

The Importance of Understanding Code

Understanding code is crucial for developers, enabling them to work effectively within their organization's codebase. When developers have a comprehensive understanding of the code, they can:

- Quickly identify dependencies and potential issues
- Make informed decisions regarding refactoring, optimization, and architectural changes
- Collaborate more effectively with their peers, reducing the chances of redundant work or conflicting changes
- Facilitate smoother onboarding of new team members by providing a clear picture of the organization's codebase

The Challenge of Finding Code Across the Organization

As organizations grow, so do their codebases, which often lead to an increasingly complex landscape of repositories, languages, and frameworks.

Navigating this landscape can be daunting for developers, who often rely on incomplete or outdated documentation, tribal knowledge, and time-consuming manual searches. Some of the challenges developers face when searching for code across the organization include:

- Identifying relevant repositories and branches
- Searching through multiple programming languages and frameworks
- Dealing with outdated or incomplete documentation
- Lack of visibility into code changes made by other team members

Sourcegraph: A Powerful Solution

Sourcegraph is a powerful tool that helps developers overcome the challenges of finding and understanding code across their organization.

It provides a unified code-search interface that enables developers to easily search, navigate, and understand their organization's codebase, regardless of the size or complexity. Some of the key features and benefits of Sourcegraph include the following:

- Fast, powerful code search: Sourcegraph's search engine lets developers quickly find code across all repositories, languages, and frameworks. Developers can perform complex, regex-based searches and filter results by repository, file type, language, and more.
- Code intelligence and navigation: Sourcegraph provides code intelligence features, such as hover tooltips, go-to-definition, and find-references, to help developers quickly understand and navigate the codebase.
- Real-time tracking of code changes: Sourcegraph tracks code changes in real-time, providing developers with an up-to-date view of their organization's codebase. This visibility helps developers stay informed about changes made by their peers and avoid potential conflicts.
- Integration with popular development tools: Sourcegraph seamlessly integrates with popular development tools, such as GitHub, GitLab, and Bitbucket, making it easy for developers to incorporate Sourcegraph into their existing workflows.

Conclusion

Understanding and finding code across the organization is crucial for developer productivity and collaboration. Sourcegraph offers a powerful solution to help developers overcome the challenges of navigating and understanding complex codebases.

By leveraging Sourcegraph's powerful search capabilities, code intelligence features, and real-time tracking of code changes, developers can work more efficiently, make informed decisions, and collaborate effectively with their peers.

Visualization and Monitoring with Grafana

* * *

In today's competitive landscape, engineering leaders must continuously drive innovation while ensuring a positive developer experience. Grafana, a powerful open-source analytics and visualization platform, offers engineering leaders valuable insights to make informed decisions and improve their team's productivity and satisfaction.

This chapter will explore how Grafana benefits engineering leaders and contributes to an enhanced developer experience.

What is Grafana?

Grafana is an open-source analytics, monitoring, and visualization platform that allows users to create interactive, customizable dashboards. By integrating with various data sources such as Graphite, Elasticsearch, and Prometheus, Grafana enables engineering leaders to visualize and understand complex data from multiple sources, providing valuable insights into applications, infrastructure, and business metrics.

Grafana's Impact on Engineering Leaders

a. Data-driven Decision Making: Grafana empowers engineering leaders to make informed decisions by providing a clear and comprehensive view of their team's performance. By visualizing key performance indicators (KPIs), leaders can identify bottlenecks, allocate resources effectively, and prioritize tasks based on real-time data.

b. Enhanced Collaboration: Grafana's shared dashboards facilitate better communication and collaboration among team members. Engineering leaders can use these dashboards to align their teams on goals and objectives, creating a shared understanding of metrics and progress.

c. Proactive Problem Solving: Grafana's real-time monitoring and alerting features enable engineering leaders to detect and address issues before they escalate. By identifying patterns and trends in the data, leaders can proactively implement strategies to improve performance and prevent potential problems.

d. Continuous Improvement: Grafana's visualizations help engineering leaders identify areas for improvement in their teams' processes and workflows. By analyzing trends and understanding the impact of changes, leaders can drive continuous improvement and optimize their team's efficiency.

e. Resource Optimization: Engineering leaders can use Grafana to monitor resource usage, such as CPU, memory, and storage, across their infrastructure. This visibility allows them to make data-driven decisions on resource allocation, ensuring optimal performance and cost efficiency.

f. Developer Satisfaction and Retention: By leveraging Grafana's insights, engineering leaders can create a more positive developer experience. By addressing bottlenecks, improving processes, and optimizing resources, leaders can foster an environment where developers feel productive, satisfied, and engaged, ultimately contributing to higher retention rates.

Real-World Applications of Grafana for Engineering Leaders

a. Monitoring Application Performance: Engineering leaders can use Grafana to track the performance of their applications, ensuring optimal user experience and identifying areas for improvement.

b. Infrastructure Monitoring: Grafana allows engineering leaders to keep a close eye on their infrastructure's health, enabling them to detect and resolve issues before they impact users.

c. Business Metrics and Analytics: Engineering leaders can use Grafana to visualize business metrics, such as revenue, user engagement, and customer satisfaction, helping them make informed decisions to drive growth and success.

d. Incident Management: Grafana's alerting features can be integrated with incident management tools, streamlining incident response and reducing downtime.

Conclusion

Grafana is an invaluable tool for engineering leaders, providing insights and capabilities that enhance the developer experience. By leveraging Grafana's powerful visualization and monitoring features, engineering leaders can make data-driven decisions, improve collaboration, and drive continuous improvement, ultimately leading to higher productivity and satisfaction within their teams.

Static Code Analysis and SonarQube

* * *

In the previous chapter, we discussed the importance of understanding and finding code to optimize the developer experience. In this chapter, we will delve into the significance of static code analysis and explore the benefits of using a tool like SonarQube to provide actionable insights for code quality improvement.

The Importance of Static Code Analysis

Static code analysis examines source code without executing it to identify potential issues, such as coding errors, security vulnerabilities, and performance bottlenecks. Integrating static code analysis into the development process offers several benefits:

Early detection of issues: By identifying problems early in the development cycle, developers can fix them before they become more complex and costly.

Improved code quality: Regular code analysis promotes adherence to coding standards, resulting in cleaner and more maintainable code.

Enhanced security: Security vulnerabilities can be detected and resolved before they become exploitable, protecting your application and users.

Increased developer productivity: By automating the process of identifying issues, developers can focus on writing code and addressing more critical tasks.

Knowledge sharing: Static code analysis helps promote best practices and consistency across the team, enhancing the overall developer experience.

SonarQube: A Comprehensive Solution for Static Code Analysis

SonarQube is an open-source platform for continuously inspecting code quality that supports over 25 programming languages. It offers a comprehensive and customizable approach to static code analysis by providing actionable insights and helping teams manage their code's technical debt. Here are some key features that make SonarQube an invaluable tool for developers:

Code Quality Metrics: SonarQube tracks various metrics, including code complexity, duplications, coding standards violations, and test coverage. This comprehensive analysis enables teams to focus on areas that need improvement.

Security Vulnerability Detection: With its built-in security rules and vulnerability detection features, SonarQube helps identify and prioritize security risks in the codebase.

Integration with CI/CD pipelines: SonarQube can be seamlessly integrated with widespread continuous integration and continuous delivery (CI/CD) tools like Jenkins, Travis CI, and Azure DevOps, ensuring code analysis becomes an integral part of the development process.

Customizable Rules and Quality Profiles: SonarQube allows

teams to create custom rules and quality profiles tailored to their specific coding standards and project requirements, ensuring that the analysis is relevant and actionable.

Collaborative Environment: SonarQube's web-based interface offers a collaborative platform for developers to review issues, assign tasks, and track progress. This fosters team communication and accountability in addressing code quality concerns.

Historical Analysis and Trend Visualization: SonarQube maintains a history of code analysis results, enabling teams to track improvements over time and visualize trends in code quality metrics.

Conclusion

Incorporating static code analysis and a tool like SonarQube into your development process is crucial for enhancing developer experience and maintaining high-quality code. By providing actionable insights, promoting best practices, and integrating seamlessly with your existing workflow, SonarQube empowers developers to create robust, secure, and maintainable applications while reducing technical debt and fostering a culture of continuous improvement.

Chapter 10
Software Delivery Paradigms

* * *

In the last chapter, we introduced various enterprise tools that can improve the developer experience by streamlining the development process, reducing cognitive load, and fostering collaboration among developers.

As we continue to explore the world of Developer Experience, this chapter will delve into powerful practices and new software delivery paradigms that can further enhance the developer experience. We will discuss topics such as microservices, monoliths, modern architecture patterns, and understanding the needs and desires of developers and how to address them as a leader.

Microservices is an architectural style that structures an application as a collection of small, loosely coupled services. Each service is responsible for specific functionality, can be developed and deployed independently, and communicates with other services via APIs. The benefits of adopting microservices include:

- Improved Scalability: Microservices can be scaled independently, allowing organizations to allocate resources more efficiently and handle varying workloads.
- Faster Development and Deployment: Smaller, independent services can be developed, tested, and deployed more quickly, leading to faster time-to-market and more frequent updates.
- Easier Maintenance: Microservices are easier to understand, debug, and maintain since each service is focused on a single responsibility.
- Technology Agnosticism: Each microservice can be developed using the most appropriate technology stack, providing developers more flexibility and options.

Monolithic applications, built as a single, unified system, can be challenging to maintain, scale, and update. One approach to transitioning from a monolithic architecture to a microservices-based one is the Strangler Pattern. This involves gradually replacing parts of the monolith with microservices, allowing for a smoother, more manageable transition.

In addition to microservices, several other modern architecture patterns can enhance the developer experience, such as the 12-Factor-Apps, Event-Driven Architecture, Serverless, and Containerization.

Microservices

* * *

In this chapter, we discuss the various paradigms of software delivery, starting with the issue of architectural complexity and the growing preference for microservices. Daniel J. Sturtevant, in his study for MIT, highlights the challenges and costs associated with architectural complexity in modern software systems.

Large software systems have become so complex that comprehending their entirety is daunting for developers. The engineering community recognizes the importance of architectural patterns, such as hierarchies, modules, and abstraction layers, in controlling complexity.

These patterns make systems easier to evolve, enabling distributed teams to work independently while jointly creating a coherent whole.

Sturtevant's study aimed to measure the relationship between architectural complexity and the costs incurred by a development organization. The study was conducted within a successful software firm, examining eight versions of its product.

It assessed significant cost drivers, including defect density, developer productivity, and staff turnover. The connection between cost and complexity was explored using various statistical techniques.

The study revealed that differences in architectural complexity could lead to a 50% drop in productivity, a three-fold increase in defect density, and an order-of-magnitude increase in staff turnover.

With the techniques developed in this study, firms can estimate the financial cost of complexity by assigning a monetary value to the decreased productivity, increased defect density, and increased turnover it causes. As a result, companies can more accurately estimate the potential dollar value of refactoring efforts to improve the architecture.

In light of these findings, the software industry has increasingly embraced microservices as an architectural pattern to address the complexity issue. Microservices involve breaking down a monolithic application into more minor, independent services that communicate through APIs. This approach allows development teams to focus on individual components, promoting better maintainability, scalability, and agility.

Microservices offer numerous benefits over monolithic architectures, such as:

- Improved modularity: By breaking down the application into more minor services, developers can create, maintain, and evolve each module independently.
- Enhanced scalability: Each service can be scaled independently, allowing for better resource allocation and management.
- Easier deployment and updates: Smaller services reduce the risk of failure during deployment and make it easier to roll out updates.
- Better fault isolation: If one service fails, it is less likely to affect the entire system, ensuring higher overall system resilience.

Organizations can effectively reduce architectural complexity by adopting microservices, leading to higher developer productivity, lower defect density, and reduced staff turnover. In essence, microservices serve as a powerful weapon in the digital transformation journey, enabling organizations to manage complexity and deliver high-quality software in a rapidly evolving technological landscape.

In conclusion, the study by Daniel J. Sturtevant for MIT underscores the importance of addressing architectural complexity in software systems. By embracing microservices as a preferred architectural pattern, organizations can harness the power of modularity and scalability, paving the way for a more efficient and successful digital transformation journey.

Benefits of Microservices

* * *

In this chapter, we will discuss the benefits of microservices and compare them with the traditional monolithic approach, highlighting the challenges and drawbacks associated with monolithic applications.

Too Large and Too Complex

Monolithic applications become large and complex over time, making them difficult to maintain and understand. As the codebase grows, developers often face challenges navigating the application, understanding its components, and making changes.

On the other hand, microservices break down the application into smaller, more manageable components, each responsible for specific functionality. This simplifies the development process, making it easier for developers to understand and maintain the codebase.

One Update Requires Testing and Redeploying Entirely

Changing a single component requires testing and redeploying the entire monolithic application. This process can be time-consuming and error-prone, increasing the risk of downtime and negatively impacting the developer experience.

Microservices, however, allow developers to update, test, and redeploy individual components independently, significantly reducing the time and effort required for updates and decreasing the risk of breaking the entire application.

Slow Start-up Time

Monolithic applications typically have a slower start-up time, as all components must be initialized together, which can lead to longer deployment times and increased resource consumption. On the other hand, Microservices enable faster start-up times by allowing individual components to initialize independently, resulting in a more efficient and responsive application.

One Bug Could Impact the Availability of the Application

A single bug can cascade in a monolithic application, potentially impacting the entire application's availability. Microservices offer better fault isolation, as each component runs independently. If a bug occurs in one microservice, it is less likely to affect other components, ensuring the overall application remains available and functional.

Conflict Resources Between Modules When Scaling

Scaling monolithic applications can be challenging, as increasing the resources for one module may lead to conflicts with other modules that share the same resources. Microservices allow for better resource management and scaling, as each component can be scaled independently based on its specific requirements, avoiding conflicts and ensuring optimal resource utilization.

Barriers to Adopting New Technologies

Monolithic applications often pose a barrier to adopting new technologies, as introducing new tools or frameworks may require significant refactoring of the entire application.

Microservices enable a more flexible approach to technology adoption, as each component can be developed using the most suitable technology for its specific needs. This allows developers to use new tools and frameworks without refactoring the entire application.

Conclusion

The shift from monolithic to microservices architecture has brought numerous benefits to the developer experience, including simplified codebases, faster start-up times, better fault isolation, improved resource management, and greater flexibility in technology adoption.

By adopting a microservices approach, developers can create more scalable, maintainable, and resilient applications, ultimately enhancing the overall developer experience and delivering greater user value.

Strangling Your Monolith

* * *

In the previous chapter, we discussed the downsides of monolithic applications and the benefits of adopting microservices. As organizations transition from monolithic to microservices architecture, it's essential to have a systematic approach to refactor and decompose the monolith.

In this chapter, we will explore the "Strangler Pattern" and outline a step-by-step guide on strangling your monolith effectively while minimizing risk and ensuring a smooth transition.

Define Boundaries and Modules

The first step in adopting microservices or function-as-a-service (FaaS) is to have clearly defined boundaries and modules within your monolithic application. Analyze the existing architecture, and identify logical components or functionalities that can be separated into individual services.

This modularization will reduce risk during the transition and ensure that each microservice has a well-defined purpose.

Find Bottlenecks

Identify bottlenecks within your monolithic application that may be causing performance issues, resource contention, or scalability challenges.

These bottlenecks can be potential candidates for the first services extracted from the monolith. Addressing them can bring immediate performance benefits and demonstrate the value of the microservices approach.

Identify Underperforming Modules

Using metrics, tracing, and analysis, pinpoint the modules within the monolith that are not meeting your performance needs. These underperforming components can also be prioritized for extraction into separate microservices, enabling focused optimization and performance improvements.

Translate Contracts

Before breaking out a module into a separate service, identify and document the contracts between the module and the rest of the monolithic application. These contracts define the interactions and dependencies between components and must be translated into web API contracts for the new microservices.

Convert Code Contracts into Web API Contracts

Once the contracts have been identified, translate them into web API contracts, such as RESTful APIs or gRPC. These new contracts will enable communication between the extracted microservices and the remaining monolith or other microservices, ensuring seamless integration and interoperability.

Break Out Service

After converting contracts, it's time to extract the module from the monolith:

6.1 Cut and Paste Module Code: Begin by cutting and pasting the module code into a new project dedicated to the new microservice. This process will separate the codebase and enable further development and optimization of the new service.

6.2 Wrap Module in API Implementation: Next, wrap the extracted module code in the API implementation defined earlier, such as a RESTful API or gRPC. This will allow the new microservice to communicate with the remaining monolith and other microservices using the defined web API contracts.

Refactor to Enable Horizontal Scaling

Once the module has been extracted and wrapped in an API implementation, refactor the new microservice to enable horizontal scaling. This may involve optimizing resource usage, implementing caching, or adopting event-driven architectures. By enabling horizontal scaling, the new microservice can better handle increased load and demand, further demonstrating the benefits of the microservices approach.

Conclusion

Strangling a monolith gradually decomposes a large monolithic application into smaller, more manageable microservices. By following this step-by-step guide, developers can minimize risk, maintain application functionality during the transition, and ultimately create a more scalable, resilient, and maintainable application.

Embracing the microservices architecture can significantly enhance the developer experience, providing greater flexibility and agility in the development process and delivering more value to users.

The 12-Factor App Architecture Model

* * *

In today's fast-paced software development landscape, it is essential to adopt methodologies that enhance developer productivity and provide an outstanding developer experience (DX). One such methodology is the 12-Factor App architecture model.

This model comprises a set of best practices for building scalable, maintainable, and portable applications, particularly in cloud-based environments. This chapter will explore the 12-Factor App model, its principles, and how it can improve developer productivity and experience.

Understanding the 12-Factor App Model

The 12-Factor App model is a set of principles designed to guide developers in building software-as-a-service (SaaS) applications that are easy to manage, scale, and deploy.

These principles address various aspects of application development, such as configuration management, dependency management, and log handling. By adhering to the 12-Factor App model, developers can create applications that are resilient, easy to maintain, and adaptable to different environments.

The following are the 12 factors of the 12-Factor App model and how they contribute to improved developer productivity and experience:

1. Codebase: Maintain a single codebase for each application, tracked in version control. This ensures consistency and reduces the likelihood of issues from managing multiple codebases.
2. Dependencies: Explicitly declare and isolate dependencies to ensure the application runs consistently across different environments. This practice simplifies dependency management and reduces the time spent troubleshooting dependency-related issues.
3. Config: Store configuration data, such as API keys and database URLs, separately from the codebase. This allows developers to quickly adapt the application to different environments without modifying the code.
4. Backing Services: Treat backing services, such as databases and messaging systems, as attached resources that can be swapped or replaced without affecting the application's code. This flexibility makes switching between service providers or migrating to new platforms more accessible.
5. Build, Release, Run: Separate the build, release, and run stages to enable a clear workflow and minimize potential errors. This separation ensures developers can focus on specific tasks and reduces the likelihood of deployment-related issues.
6. Processes: Execute the application as one or more stateless processes, simplifying horizontal scaling and improving application resilience. Stateless processes

enable developers to build applications that can easily scale to handle increased demand.
7. Port Binding: Expose services via port binding, allowing the application to become a self-contained unit that can be deployed without relying on runtime injection. This approach streamlines deployment and enables greater flexibility in hosting environments.
8. Concurrency: Scale the application by running multiple concurrent processes. By embracing concurrency, developers can create applications that effectively utilize available resources and handle the increased load without significant performance degradation.
9. Disposability: Build applications that can start quickly, shut down gracefully, and are resilient to sudden crashes. This characteristic minimizes downtime and ensures applications can recover quickly from unexpected events.
10. Dev/Prod Parity: Maintain consistency between development, staging, and production environments to minimize potential issues arising from differences between environments. This practice reduces the time spent troubleshooting environment-related problems and streamlines the deployment process.
11. Logs: Treat logs as event streams, allowing developers to collect, analyze easily, and store log data. By handling logs in this manner, developers can quickly identify and address issues in the application.
12. Admin Processes: Run administrative tasks as a one-off, separate from the application's regular processes. This separation ensures that administrative tasks do not interfere with the regular operation of the application and can be executed without affecting the application's runtime.

Next, we will explore how this methodology impacts the developer experience.

* * *

Embracing Modularity and Flexibility

One of the core tenets of the Twelve-Factor App methodology is to create modular, flexible applications that are easy to understand and maintain. This is achieved by breaking down the application into smaller, self-contained components, each with a well-defined purpose and interface.

This modular approach encourages reusable components and simplifies the overall development process. As a result, developers spend less time wrestling with complex codebases and more time focusing on delivering new features and improvements.

Encouraging a Clean Separation of Concerns

A clean separation of concerns is a key aspect of the Twelve-Factor App methodology, allowing developers to focus on individual components or aspects of the application without being overwhelmed by the complexity of the entire system.

By ensuring that each component is responsible for a single, well-defined function, developers can more easily understand, test, and maintain the application, leading to a more enjoyable and productive development experience.

Facilitating Scalability and High Availability

The Twelve-Factor App principles promote the creation of scalable and highly available applications by design. Developers working with these guidelines can build applications that can easily adapt to changing workloads and user demands.

This ensures the application performs well under various conditions, reducing the need for reactive measures like firefighting and emergency patches. Ultimately, this leads to a more stable and predictable development process.

Streamlining the Development-to-Deployment Process

The twelve-Factor App methodology emphasizes the importance of a smooth and automated development-to-deployment pipeline.

By adopting continuous integration and deployment practices, developers can ensure their code is regularly tested and deployed, reducing the risk of bugs and regressions. This, in turn, leads to faster development cycles, allowing developers to iterate more quickly and respond to user feedback more effectively.

Enhancing Collaboration and Communication

Following the Twelve-Factor App methodology, development teams can foster better collaboration and communication. The modular design and clear separation of concerns make it easier for team members to understand each other's work and coordinate their efforts.

Moreover, externalizing configuration data and using version control systems for both code and configuration ensure that changes can be tracked, reviewed, and discussed as needed, leading to more effective teamwork and a more enjoyable development experience.

In summary, the Twelve-Factor App methodology offers numerous benefits that can significantly improve the developer experience. By adhering to these principles, development teams can build flexible, maintainable, and scalable applications that are easier to understand, test, and deploy.

This leads to more efficient development processes and promotes a more enjoyable and productive experience for developers, resulting in better software for end users.

API-First Approach

* * *

The origin of the API First approach can be traced back to a bold mandate issued by Jeff Bezos, the founder and former CEO of Amazon, in the early 2000s. At that time, Amazon was evolving rapidly and expanding into new markets.

As the company grew, Bezos realized that the way software components and services were being developed and integrated within the company needed to change to keep up with its operations' increasing scale and complexity.

Bezos mandated that all Amazon software teams communicate and share data exclusively through APIs (Application Programming Interfaces). This directive transformed how Amazon developed its software and laid the foundation for the company's incredible success in the years to come.

The API First approach, born out of Bezos' mandate, has become a cornerstone of modern software development practices. It enables companies to accelerate their digital transformation journey and enhance the developer experience. Here are some Benefits of API First:

Enhanced Developer Experience

An API First approach puts the needs of developers at the forefront, ensuring that APIs are well-designed, easy to understand, and simple to use. This focus on developer experience leads to increased productivity, faster development cycles, and better collaboration between teams, all of which contribute to the success of your digital transformation efforts.

Improved Scalability and Flexibility

APIs enable the modularization and decoupling of software components, allowing individual services to evolve and scale independently. This architectural flexibility makes it easier to adapt to changing requirements and integrate new technologies, which is crucial for the success of any digital transformation journey.

Faster Time-to-Market

Adopting an API First approach can accelerate developing and deploying new software products and features. APIs enable seamless integration between different components, reducing the time and effort required to bring new solutions to market. This ability to quickly deliver new capabilities is a key competitive advantage in the fast-paced digital landscape.

Easier Integration with Third-Party Services

APIs provide a standardized way to interact with external services and data sources, making integrating with third-party platforms and tools easier. This seamless integration allows you to leverage best-of-breed solutions, enhancing your software products and driving innovation in your digital transformation journey.

Increased Innovation

The API First approach promotes a culture of innovation by encouraging developers to build reusable, modular components that can be easily combined in new and innovative ways. This approach fosters creativity and experimentation, creating more innovative and impactful software products.

Better Security and Compliance

Well-designed APIs can provide a more secure and controlled way to access and share data between different systems and services. By adopting an API First approach, you can implement security best practices and compliance measures more effectively, ensuring that your software products meet the necessary security and regulatory requirements.

Conclusion

API First has proven to be a game-changing approach in software development, as demonstrated by the incredible success of companies like Amazon. By embracing API First principles, you can significantly improve developer experience, accelerate innovation, and drive the success of your digital transformation journey.

By putting APIs at the core of your software development process, you can build a more agile, scalable, and adaptable foundation for your digital transformation efforts.

Event-Driven Architecture

* * *

In addition to microservices, several other modern architecture patterns, such as event-driven architecture, can enhance the developer experience. This pattern involves decoupling components of an application through asynchronous, event-based communication, allowing for greater scalability and adaptability.

Event-driven architecture is particularly useful for applications that handle many events or messages, such as real-time analytics, IoT systems, and notification services.

In an event-driven architecture, components (event producers) generate events representing state changes or significant occurrences within the system. These events are then sent to other components (event consumers) interested in those events.

Event consumers can process the events, update their internal state, and, if necessary, generate new events. This decoupled approach allows components to evolve independently and helps maintain the separation of concerns, as each component focuses on a specific task.

Key advantages of event-driven architecture include the following:

- Scalability: Event-driven systems can easily scale horizontally by adding more instances of event producers or consumers as needed. This enables the system to handle increasing workloads without major re-architecting efforts.
- Resilience: Since components are loosely coupled, the failure of one component does not necessarily cause the entire system to fail. Additionally, event-driven systems can be designed to handle message failures or delays, ensuring high availability gracefully.
- Flexibility: Event-driven architecture allows for greater flexibility in application design, as components can be added, removed, or modified without affecting the entire system. This makes it easier to adapt the system to changing business requirements or incorporate new technologies.
- Real-time processing: Event-driven systems can process events in real-time or near-real-time, enabling applications to respond quickly to changes in the environment or user actions.
- Improved maintainability: With a clear separation of concerns, event-driven systems are easier to understand, debug, and maintain. Each component's focused functionality simplifies the development and testing process.

By adopting event-driven architecture, developers can create more scalable, resilient, and flexible applications that adapt to changing needs and offer an improved developer experience.

The Power of Headless Systems

* * *

The rise of headless systems has brought forth a new paradigm in software development, enabling organizations to deliver highly engaging and customizable user experiences while simplifying the underlying infrastructure.

By decoupling the frontend user interface from the backend systems, headless architecture promotes greater flexibility, scalability, and extensibility, which are vital for a successful digital transformation journey. In this chapter, we will explore the benefits of headless systems in enhancing developer experience and accelerating digital transformation initiatives.

Benefits of Headless Systems

Headless systems enable developers to build highly customizable frontend experiences without being constrained by the backend systems.

This approach allows for greater freedom in designing user interfaces, ensuring that the end product meets the unique needs and expectations of the target audience. A headless architecture can deliver more engaging and tailored user experiences, driving higher customer satisfaction and engagement.

Faster Development and Deployment

By decoupling the front end from the backend, headless systems allow developers to work simultaneously on different aspects of the application. This parallel development process can significantly reduce development time, enabling faster deployment of new features and updates. By accelerating the development process, you can quickly respond to market demands and stay ahead of the competition in the digital landscape.

Improved Scalability

Headless systems enable easier scaling of the frontend and backend components independently. This separation of concerns allows you to scale the front and back end according to their specific requirements and resources, ensuring optimal performance even as your application grows in complexity and user base.

This improved scalability is essential for supporting the expanding needs of your digital transformation journey.

Enhanced Developer Experience

Headless systems can greatly improve the developer experience by simplifying the development process and allowing developers to leverage their preferred tools and technologies.

By decoupling the front and back end, developers can work with the frameworks and languages they are most comfortable with, leading to increased productivity and innovation. This improved developer experience is key to the success of your digital transformation initiatives.

Seamless Integration with Other Systems

Headless systems facilitate easy integration with other systems and services, as the front and back ends communicate through APIs. This API-driven communication allows for seamless connectivity with third-party services and platforms, enabling you to leverage best-of-breed solutions and further enhance your digital transformation efforts.

Future-Proofing Your Applications

Headless systems' decoupled nature means that your front and back end can evolve independently, ensuring your applications remain future-proof and adaptable to changing technologies and user expectations.

Adopting a headless architecture ensures that your software products remain relevant and up-to-date as new technologies emerge and the digital landscape continues to evolve.

Conclusion

Headless systems can significantly benefit your digital transformation journey, from improved developer experience and flexibility to better scalability and future-proofing.

By embracing headless architecture, you can create more engaging and responsive user experiences, accelerate development processes, and build a solid foundation for ongoing digital transformation success. This approach empowers developers to innovate and respond to changing market demands more effectively, ultimately driving growth and competitiveness in the digital age.

The MACH Architecture

* * *

In the previous chapters, we discussed the importance of microservices, API-first, cloud-native, and headless approaches in enhancing developer experience and driving digital transformation.

In this chapter, we will introduce the MACH Architecture concept, which combines all these elements to create a powerful and unified approach to software development and digital transformation. The MACH Architecture stands for Microservices, API-first, Cloud-native, and Headless, and it represents a comprehensive framework for modern software development that prioritizes flexibility, scalability, and adaptability.

The MACH Architecture Concept

The MACH Architecture concept unites the principles of microservices, API-first, cloud-native, and headless approaches to create an ecosystem that fosters innovation, agility, and seamless collaboration among developers.

This ecosystem empowers development teams to build software products adaptable to evolving technologies, user expectations, and market demands, ensuring long-term success in the digital landscape.

Let's explore how the MACH Architecture concept leverages these individual components to create a holistic approach to developer experience and digital transformation.

Microservices: Building Modular and Scalable Applications

The MACH Architecture promotes using microservices to develop modular and scalable applications that can easily adapt to changing requirements. By breaking down complex applications into smaller, independent services, development teams can work on different components simultaneously, accelerating the development process and reducing time-to-market.

* * *

API-first: Seamless Integration and Interoperability

In the MACH ecosystem, APIs are the backbone for communication and integration between various software components, services, and platforms.

By adopting an API-first approach, development teams can ensure seamless interoperability between different systems, enabling a more connected and collaborative development environment.

Cloud-Native: Leveraging the Power of the Cloud

The MACH Architecture emphasizes the importance of building cloud-native applications that can fully leverage the capabilities of cloud computing platforms.

Cloud-native development enables greater flexibility, scalability, and cost efficiency, ensuring that your software products can seamlessly adapt to the evolving needs of your digital transformation journey.

Headless: Delivering Customizable and Future-Proof User Experiences

Finally, the MACH Architecture integrates headless architecture to decouple the frontend user experience from the backend systems, enabling developers to create highly customizable and future-proof user interfaces.

By adopting a headless approach, development teams can deliver engaging and tailored user experiences that drive customer satisfaction and engagement, contributing to the success of your digital transformation initiatives.

The Synergy of the MACH Architecture

By combining the principles of microservices, API-first, cloud-native, and headless approaches, the MACH Architecture concept creates a synergistic ecosystem that enables development teams to build software products that are more flexible, scalable, and adaptable to change.

This synergy drives innovation and collaboration, leading to the development of impactful software products to propel your digital transformation journey forward.

Conclusion

The MACH Architecture concept presents a unified and comprehensive approach to developer experience and digital transformation, combining the best microservices, API-first, cloud-native, and headless development practices.

By embracing the MACH Architecture principles, organizations can create a flexible and adaptable software development environment that fosters innovation, accelerates time-to-market, and ensures long-term success in the rapidly evolving digital landscape.

The Rise of Serverless

* * *

As digital transformation progressed and organizations increasingly embraced cloud-native technologies, the need for more efficient and cost-effective ways to develop and deploy applications became apparent. Serverless architecture emerged as a groundbreaking approach to address these challenges.

In this chapter, we will embark on a journey that explores the evolution of serverless technology, starting with Amazon Web Services (AWS) and Lambda and continuing to modern platforms and the Knative project. Along the way, we will examine the benefits and challenges of adopting serverless architecture.

The Birth of Serverless: AWS Lambda

In 2014, AWS introduced a new service that would forever change the application development landscape: AWS Lambda. Lambda was the first serverless computing platform, allowing developers to run their code without provisioning or managing servers. Instead, AWS would manage the underlying infrastructure, enabling developers to focus solely on writing and deploying their code.

Lambda functions could be triggered by various AWS services or custom events, automatically scaling with the number of requests. Developers were only charged for their functions' computing time, making it a cost-effective solution for building and running applications.

The Serverless Ecosystem Expands

The success of AWS Lambda inspired other cloud providers to develop their serverless platforms, such as Google Cloud Functions, Microsoft Azure Functions, and IBM Cloud Functions.

As the serverless ecosystem expanded, new tools and frameworks emerged to support the development and deployment of serverless applications. These tools included the Serverless Framework, which provided a common interface for deploying serverless applications across multiple cloud providers.

Knative: Unifying the Serverless Landscape

As serverless architecture continued to gain traction, the need for a unified, open-source platform that could run on any Kubernetes cluster became apparent. Enter Knative, an open-source project launched in 2018 by Google in partnership with IBM, Pivotal, Red Hat, and SAP.

Knative aimed to provide a consistent developer experience across different Kubernetes environments, making it easier for developers to build, deploy, and manage serverless applications. Knative consists of three main components: Serving, Eventing, and Building. These components allow developers to create serverless applications that scale on demand, respond to events, and leverage a unified build system.

Conclusion

As we've seen throughout this chapter, serverless architecture has come a long way since the introduction of AWS Lambda. The technology has significantly impacted how organizations build, deploy, and manage applications in the cloud, offering numerous benefits that can enhance the developer experience.

Some key benefits of serverless architecture include cost efficiency, scalability, faster time-to-market, and simplified operations. These advantages allow developers to focus on writing code and delivering features more quickly, increasing productivity and innovation.

However, serverless architecture is not without its challenges. Developers and organizations must be mindful of potential drawbacks such as cold starts, vendor lock-in, limited customization, and the need for specialized monitoring and debugging tools. To successfully navigate these challenges, organizations should carefully evaluate their specific use cases and choose the serverless platform that best aligns with their needs.

In conclusion, serverless architecture has the potential to be a powerful tool in the digital transformation journey, enabling organizations to create more efficient, scalable, and cost-effective applications.

By understanding the benefits and challenges of serverless architecture, organizations can make informed decisions about whether and how to incorporate serverless technologies into their development processes.

As serverless continues to evolve, we expect to see even more exciting innovations and developments in this space, further enhancing the developer experience and empowering organizations to stay competitive in the ever-changing digital landscape.

Understanding What Developer Wants

* * *

A significant aspect of enhancing the developer experience revolves around understanding and addressing developers' needs and desires. In this chapter, we will explore the importance of offering developers various choices in various aspects of their work and the benefits of providing a worry-free infrastructure that allows them to focus on building high-quality applications.

Developers thrive when they can choose the tools, technologies, and methodologies that best align with their skills, preferences, and project requirements. This flexibility empowers them to be more productive and efficient while fostering innovation and creativity.

In the following sections, we will discuss the importance of offering developers a variety of choices in different areas.

Choice of Architectures

Allowing developers to choose from various architectural patterns, such as monolithic, microservices, or serverless, enables them to design applications that best suit their needs and requirements.

Offering a choice of architectures caters to developers' preferences and helps them adapt to different project constraints, scalability requirements, and performance expectations.

Choice of Programming Languages

Developers often prefer specific programming languages based on their skills, experience, and the problem domain.

By supporting a wide range of programming languages, organizations can attract diverse talent, encourage innovation, and accommodate the unique requirements of different projects. This flexibility is particularly important in digital transformation, allowing organizations to leverage the best tools for each use case.

For example, a data-driven organization might require developers skilled in Python or R for data analysis and machine learning. At the same time, a web development team might prefer using JavaScript, TypeScript, or Ruby. By offering a diverse range of supported languages, serverless platforms enable developers to work with their preferred tools, which can lead to higher levels of productivity and job satisfaction.

Moreover, the multi-language support offered by serverless platforms can facilitate collaboration between teams working on different project parts. For instance, a front-end team working on a web application may use JavaScript, while the back-end team might opt for Python or Java. With serverless platforms, these teams can seamlessly integrate their code without worrying about language compatibility issues.

Some popular serverless platforms and their supported languages include:

- AWS Lambda: Supports Node.js, Python, Ruby, Java, Go, and .NET Core.
- Microsoft Azure Functions: Offers support for JavaScript, TypeScript, C#, F#, Java, Python, and PowerShell.
- Google Cloud Functions: Provides Node.js, Python, and Go support.

By providing a wide range of programming languages, serverless platforms cater to developers' preferences and contribute to a more versatile and adaptable workforce.

This flexibility empowers organizations to tackle diverse challenges and explore new opportunities, ultimately driving innovation and success in their digital transformation journey.

Choice of Databases

Different databases serve different purposes and excel in distinct use cases. Providing developers with a choice of databases – such as relational, NoSQL, or graph databases – allows them to select the best fit for their application's data storage, retrieval, and processing needs.

This freedom results in more efficient and performant applications tailored to specific requirements.

Relational databases: These databases use a schema to define tables, columns, and relationships between tables. They are suitable for complex queries, data integrity, and transactional consistency applications. Some popular relational databases include PostgreSQL, MySQL, and Microsoft SQL Server.

Example: An e-commerce application might store information about products, customers, and orders using a relational database. The database would enable efficient querying and updating of data while maintaining referential integrity and transactional consistency.

NoSQL databases: NoSQL databases are designed for scalability, flexibility, and high performance. They do not adhere to a fixed schema and can store data in various formats, such as key-value, document, or column-family. Examples of NoSQL databases include MongoDB, Cassandra, and Redis.

Example: A social media application might use a NoSQL database to store user profiles, posts, and interactions. NoSQL databases' flexible schema and horizontal scalability make them well-suited for handling social media data's dynamic nature and growth.

Graph databases: Graph databases are designed to store and query data modeled as graphs, where nodes represent entities and edges represent relationships between entities. These databases excel at handling highly connected data and complex relationship queries. Some popular graph databases include Neo4j, Amazon Neptune, and OrientDB.

Example: A recommendation engine for a content platform could use a graph database to model relationships between users, their preferences, and content items. The graph database would facilitate efficient querying of connections and patterns to generate personalized recommendations.

By offering developers a variety of databases to choose from, organizations can empower them to create applications that best meet their specific needs. This flexibility contributes to a better developer experience and results in higher-quality, more efficient, and more scalable applications, ultimately supporting the organization's digital transformation goals.

Choice of Application Services

Developers often rely on application services, such as authentication, caching, or messaging, to build robust, feature-rich applications. Allowing them to choose from various application services enables them to leverage the most suitable tools for their specific use cases, resulting in a more productive and efficient development process.

Authentication services: These services handle user authentication and authorization, ensuring only authorized users can access specific application resources. Providing developers with multiple authentication services allows them to choose the most appropriate one based on their requirements, such as single sign-on (SSO), multi-factor authentication (MFA), or social media login. Examples of authentication services include Auth0, Okta, and Firebase Authentication.

Example: A mobile application might need to allow users to sign in with their Google or Facebook accounts. Using an authentication service that supports social media log-in, developers can quickly and easily implement this feature, enhancing the user experience.

Caching services: Caching services store frequently accessed data in memory to reduce data retrieval latency and improve application performance. Offering developers various caching services enables them to select the most suitable one based on data consistency, eviction policies, and distributed caching. Examples of caching services include Redis, Memcached, and Amazon ElastiCache.

Example: An online news portal might store and quickly serve popular articles using a caching service. By choosing a caching service that offers high performance and scalability, developers can ensure that the portal remains responsive even during traffic spikes.

Messaging services facilitate communication between application components through message queues or publish-subscribe patterns. Providing developers with a choice of messaging services allows them to select the best fit for their application's messaging needs, considering factors like reliability, message persistence, and delivery guarantees. Examples of messaging services include RabbitMQ, Apache Kafka, and Amazon SQS.

Example: An IoT application might require a messaging service to handle data ingestion from thousands of connected devices. Developers can build a robust and scalable data processing pipeline by selecting a messaging service that supports high throughput and fault tolerance.

By offering developers various application services, organizations empower them to create applications that best meet their needs. This flexibility contributes to a better developer experience and results in higher-quality, more efficient, and more scalable applications, ultimately supporting the organization's digital transformation goals.

Choice of Development Tools

Developers require various tools to facilitate their work, from integrated development environments (IDEs) and code editors to source control management and testing tools. Offering a choice of development tools enables them to select the ones that best complement their skills and workflow, ultimately enhancing their overall productivity and job satisfaction.

Integrated Development Environments (IDEs) and Code Editors: Developers often prefer specific IDEs and code editors based on language support, debugging capabilities, and ease of use. By offering a range of options, developers can choose the one that aligns with their needs and expertise. Popular IDEs and code editors include Visual Studio Code, JetBrains IntelliJ IDEA, and Sublime Text.

Example: A Java developer may prefer IntelliJ IDEA for its extensive Java-specific features, while a web developer might opt for Visual Studio Code due to its extensive support for JavaScript, HTML, and CSS.

Source Control Management (SCM) Tools: Source control management tools help developers collaborate on code, track changes, and manage project versions. By providing developers with options like Git, Mercurial, and Subversion, they can choose the SCM tool that best fits their workflow and collaboration requirements.

Example: A large, distributed team may prefer Git for its distributed architecture and flexible branching model. In contrast, a smaller team might find the simplicity of Subversion more suitable for their needs.

Continuous Integration and Continuous Deployment (CI/CD) Tools: CI/CD tools automate the building, testing, and deploying of code, helping to catch errors early and streamline the release process. Offering developers a choice of CI/CD tools, such as Jenkins, GitLab CI/CD, and Tekton, allows them to select the one that best aligns with their project's requirements and infrastructure.

Example: A team using Kubernetes for container orchestration might choose Tekton for its native Kubernetes support. Meanwhile, another team might prefer GitLab CI/CD for its tight integration with the GitLab platform.

Testing and Quality Assurance (QA) Tools: Testing and QA tools ensure that code is reliable, secure, and performant. They can select the tools that best fit their testing strategy and application requirements by providing developers with various options, such as JUnit, Playwright, and SonarQube.

Example: A team developing a web application might use Playwright for automated browser testing. A Java-based project might rely on JUnit for unit testing and SonarQube for code quality analysis.

By offering developers a variety of development tools to choose from, organizations create an environment that fosters productivity, creativity, and job satisfaction. This flexibility contributes to a positive developer experience, helping to attract and retain top talent while driving the organization's digital transformation goals.

Choice of Build and Deploy Workflows

Different projects and teams may have varying requirements for building and deploying workflows. By providing a range of options for continuous integration, continuous deployment, and release management, developers can choose the most suitable workflows for their needs, leading to smoother and more efficient development processes.

Continuous Integration (CI) Workflows: CI workflows automate merging code changes from multiple developers, ensuring the codebase is always in a releasable state. Different CI tools and platforms offer various features and integrations, allowing developers to choose the one that best aligns with their project's needs. Examples of CI tools include Jenkins, Travis CI, and Bamboo.

Example: A team working on an open-source project hosted on GitHub might prefer Travis CI due to its native GitHub integration and ease of use. An enterprise team might choose Jenkins for its extensive plugin ecosystem and customization options.

Continuous Deployment (CD) Workflows: After testing and approval, CD workflows automate deploying code to production environments. By providing developers with a choice of CD tools and platforms, such as Spinnaker, GitLab CI/CD, and Octopus Deploy, they can select the one that best suits their infrastructure and release strategy.

Example: A team using Kubernetes for container orchestration might opt for Spinnaker due to its native support for Kubernetes deployments. A team deploying to multiple cloud providers might choose Octopus Deploy for its cross-cloud capabilities.

Release Management Workflows: Release management workflows help teams plan, schedule, and track software releases, ensuring a smooth and coordinated release process. By offering developers a range of release management tools, such as Azure DevOps, Jira, and Release, they can choose the one that best fits their team's size, release cadence, and project complexity.

Example: A team following an Agile development process might use Jira to plan and track releases using sprints and epics. In contrast, a team with a more traditional release schedule might opt for Azure DevOps to manage their release pipeline and track progress.

Infrastructure as Code (IaC) Workflows: IaC workflows allow developers to manage and provision infrastructure using code, ensuring consistency and repeatability across environments. By providing a choice of IaC tools, such as Terraform, AWS CloudFormation, and Google Cloud Deployment Manager, developers can select the one that best aligns with their cloud provider and infrastructure needs.

Example: A team working primarily with AWS services might choose AWS CloudFormation to manage their infrastructure. A team using multiple cloud providers may prefer to Terraform for its provider-agnostic approach.

By offering developers various options for continuous integration, continuous deployment, and release management, organizations empower them to choose the most suitable workflows for their needs. This flexibility contributes to a positive developer experience, resulting in more efficient and streamlined development processes, ultimately supporting the organization's digital transformation goals.

Worry-Free Infrastructure

In addition to the freedom of choice, developers desire a worry-free infrastructure that allows them to focus on building high-quality applications without getting bogged down by infrastructure management tasks. This includes:

Seamless Scalability and High Availability: Developers should not have to worry about the infrastructure's ability to handle varying workloads and user demands. A worry-free infrastructure should provide seamless scalability and high availability, allowing applications to perform optimally under different conditions.

Example: A developer working on an e-commerce application should be able to trust that the infrastructure can handle sudden spikes in user traffic during sales events or seasonal demand without experiencing downtime or performance degradation.

Security and Compliance: Security and compliance are critical concerns for developers and organizations. A worry-free infrastructure should handle security aspects such as data protection, access control, and vulnerability management, ensuring that applications and data remain secure and compliant with relevant regulations.

Example: A developer working on a healthcare application that handles sensitive patient data should be able to rely on the infrastructure to automatically encrypt data at rest and in transit, manage access controls, and regularly scan for vulnerabilities, ensuring compliance with HIPAA or GDPR.

Monitoring and Observability: To diagnose issues and optimize application performance, developers require comprehensive monitoring and observability tools. A worry-free infrastructure should provide these capabilities out of the box, enabling developers to quickly identify and resolve issues without investing additional development time.

Example: A developer working on a microservices-based application should have access to monitoring tools that provide real-time insights into service performance, error rates, and latency, as well as distributed tracing capabilities to identify bottlenecks and diagnose issues across the entire application stack.

Automated Infrastructure Management: Developers should be able to rely on automation for infrastructure provisioning, configuration, and management. A worry-free infrastructure should support Infrastructure as Code (IaC) and other automation tools to minimize manual intervention and reduce human error, resulting in more efficient and reliable infrastructure.

Example: A developer working on a multi-cloud project should be able to use a tool like Terraform to define and manage infrastructure resources across different cloud providers, ensuring consistent and repeatable deployments.

By providing a worry-free infrastructure that addresses these key concerns, organizations can empower developers to focus on writing high-quality code and delivering value to the business. This, in turn, contributes to a better developer experience and supports the organization's digital transformation efforts.

Balancing Freedom of Choice with Leadership Oversight

* * *

While developers appreciate the freedom of choice in various aspects of their work, balancing autonomy and leadership oversight is crucial. In this chapter, we will discuss the importance of leadership in providing guidance, maintaining consistency, and ensuring the overall success of development projects, even when that means limiting some aspects of developers' freedom of choice.

Ensuring Consistency and Coherence

One of the primary reasons for leadership oversight in the development process is to ensure consistency and coherence across the organization. This includes:

* * *

1.1 Establishing Development Standards

Leadership is crucial in defining and enforcing development standards, such as coding conventions, design patterns, and best practices. These standards help maintain code quality and consistency, making it easier for developers to collaborate, understand, and maintain the codebase.

Example: A tech company might establish guidelines for using specific programming paradigms, such as object-oriented or functional programming, and enforce coding conventions like variable naming conventions and indentation styles. These standards improve code readability and make it easier for developers to onboard new team members and transition between projects.

1.2 Coordinating Technology Choices

While developers value the freedom to choose technologies, leadership must coordinate these choices across the organization. This coordination prevents technology sprawl, reduces the risk of duplication and redundancy, and ensures that resources are used effectively.

Example: A large organization with multiple development teams might decide to standardize on a single front-end framework, such as React or Angular, to streamline development efforts, reduce training costs, and ensure a consistent user experience across their applications.

1.3 Promoting Collaboration and Knowledge Sharing

Leadership oversight is vital for fostering collaboration and knowledge sharing among developers, ensuring that teams can effectively share insights, solutions, and best practices. This promotes the efficient use of resources and helps developers learn from each other, ultimately enhancing the overall developer experience.

Example: A company might establish an internal developer

portal or forum where developers can share code snippets, discuss problems and solutions, and collaborate on new ideas or techniques. This platform can also serve as a hub for hosting internal tech talks, workshops, and other learning opportunities, fostering a culture of continuous learning and improvement within the organization.

By focusing on these areas, leadership can ensure that the development environment remains consistent, coherent, and conducive to collaboration, ultimately supporting a positive developer experience and driving the organization's success.

Guiding Strategic Decision-Making

Leadership is responsible for guiding strategic decision-making, ensuring that development efforts align with the organization's goals and objectives. This includes:

2.1 Prioritizing Projects and Features

Leaders must prioritize projects and features based on business value, user needs, and resource availability. While developers may have preferences, leadership must make these decisions to ensure long-term success.

Example: In a financial services company, leadership may prioritize developing a new fraud detection system over adding new features to an existing product. This decision may be based on the potential business value of reducing fraud losses and the need to address regulatory requirements.

2.2 Navigating Trade-offs

Development projects often involve trade-offs, such as balancing performance, security, and maintainability. Leadership is vital in navigating these trade-offs, weighing the benefits and risks to make informed decisions that best serve the organization's interests.

Example: In an e-commerce application, leadership may prioritize performance improvements to ensure a faster user experience, even if this requires additional development resources or delays the implementation of other features. This decision could be based on the understanding that a better user experience can lead to increased customer satisfaction and higher sales.

2.3 Managing Risk and Uncertainty

Leadership is responsible for managing risk and uncertainty, including assessing the potential impact of technology choices on the organization's operations, security, and compliance. By providing oversight, leaders can help mitigate risks and ensure developers make decisions in the organization's best interest.

Example: A healthcare organization may consider adopting a new cloud-based data storage solution for sensitive patient data. Leadership must assess the potential risks associated with data security, privacy, and regulatory compliance before approving adoption of the new technology. This may involve consulting with legal and compliance teams, conducting risk assessments, and evaluating the cloud provider's security and privacy controls.

By focusing on these strategic decision-making areas, leadership can ensure that development efforts align with the organization's goals, navigate trade-offs effectively, and manage risk and uncertainty. This guidance supports a positive developer experience and drives the organization's success.

Ensuring Organizational Alignment

In addition to guiding strategic decision-making, leadership is critical in ensuring organizational alignment. This involves:

3.1 Communicating Vision and Goals

Leadership is responsible for clearly communicating the organization's vision and goals to developers, ensuring that they understand the broader context of their work and how it contributes to its overall success.

Example: At a tech startup focused on building a revolutionary mobile app, the leadership team regularly holds town hall meetings and shares updates via internal communication channels, ensuring that developers know the company's vision and how their work contributes to achieving it.

3.2 Facilitating Cross-Team Collaboration

Leadership is crucial in facilitating cross-team collaboration, breaking down silos, and promoting a culture of shared ownership and responsibility. Leaders can create a more cohesive and effective development environment by encouraging collaboration and communication.

Example: In a large software company, leaders may implement cross-functional teams, bringing together developers, designers, and product managers to work on specific projects. This approach encourages collaboration, fosters a sense of shared ownership, and helps ensure that projects are aligned with the organization's objectives.

3.3 Providing Resources and Support

Leaders are responsible for providing developers with the necessary resources and support, including training, mentoring, and access to tools and technologies. Leadership can help create a more positive and productive developer experience by ensuring developers have the needed resources.

Example: A growing tech company might establish a mentoring program in which experienced developers are paired with new hires to provide guidance, support, and knowledge sharing. This initiative helps new developers learn more quickly and fosters a culture of continuous learning and improvement throughout the organization.

By focusing on these aspects of organizational alignment, leadership can create a supportive environment for developers, encourage collaboration, and ensure that everyone is working towards the same goals. This alignment ultimately contributes to a positive developer experience and drives the organization's success.

Conclusion

While the freedom of choice is a vital aspect of the developer experience, balancing this autonomy with leadership oversight is essential.

By providing guidance, maintaining consistency, and ensuring organizational alignment, leaders can create an environment where developers can thrive while contributing to the organization's success.

Finding the right balance between freedom of choice and leadership oversight is crucial for fostering a positive developer experience and achieving long-term success.

Navigating the Remote, Hybrid, and Physical Debate

* * *

The world of work has been rapidly evolving, with remote, hybrid, and physical working models becoming popular topics of discussion. This shift has significantly impacted the developer experience and led to various opinions on the most effective model.

In this chapter, we will explore the pros and cons of remote, hybrid, and physical working environments, discuss how they impact developer experience, and provide guidance on how organizations can adapt to these changes to create the best possible working environment for their developers.

Remote Work

Remote work involves employees working from home or other locations outside of a traditional office environment. The COVID-19 pandemic, technological advancements, and a growing desire for more flexibility in the workplace have driven the rapid adoption of remote work.

***

Pros:

- Increased flexibility: Remote work allows developers to create a more flexible work schedule, improving work-life balance.
- Broader talent pool: Organizations can hire developers from different regions, expanding their talent pool and increasing diversity.
- Cost savings: Remote work can reduce overhead expenses, such as office space and commuting costs.

Cons:

- Collaboration challenges: Remote work may hinder collaboration and team cohesion, as face-to-face interactions are limited.
- Overworking: Developers may struggle with work-life balance as the boundaries between work and home become blurred.
- Isolation: Remote work can lead to feelings of isolation and loneliness, potentially affecting mental health and productivity.

Hybrid Work

Hybrid work combines the best remote and physical working models, allowing developers to work on-site and remotely. This approach aims to create a more balanced and flexible working environment.

***

Pros:

- Flexibility and balance: Hybrid work offers developers the flexibility of remote work while allowing in-person collaboration when needed.
- Increased employee satisfaction: Developers may experience higher job satisfaction due to the balance between remote and in-person work.
- Retention and recruitment: A hybrid work model can make organizations more attractive to potential hires and help retain current employees.

Cons:

- Inconsistency: A hybrid work model can lead to inconsistent schedules and work patterns, impacting productivity and team cohesion.
- Communication challenges: Coordinating between remote and in-person team members can be challenging, potentially leading to miscommunication and misunderstandings.
- Infrastructure requirements: Organizations must invest in tools and resources to support both remote and in-person work, which can be costly and complex.

Physical Work

Physical or traditional office work involves employees working in a centralized location, such as an office building. This working model has been the standard for many organizations for decades but has faced scrutiny recently due to its lack of flexibility.

Pros:

- Enhanced collaboration: Physical work enables face-to-face interactions, promoting collaboration and team cohesion.
- Clear boundaries: With a separate workspace, developers can maintain a clear distinction between work and home life.
- Networking opportunities: In-person work environments can provide developers valuable networking opportunities that may not be available in remote settings.

Cons:

- Lack of flexibility: Physical work offers limited flexibility for developers, potentially impacting work-life balance.
- Commuting: Traveling to and from the office can be time-consuming and expensive for developers.
- Limited talent pool: Organizations may be restricted to hiring developers who live within commuting distance, limiting their access to a broader talent pool.

Creating the Best Developer Experience

A positive developer experience is critical for the success of any organization, as it directly impacts productivity, job satisfaction, and employee retention. As organizations navigate the remote, hybrid, and physical work models debate, they must prioritize the developer experience to ensure their teams can thrive and deliver exceptional results.

To create the best developer experience amidst the remote, hybrid, and physical work model debate, organizations must consider several key factors:

1. Understand your developers' needs and preferences: Engage with them to understand their preferences regarding remote, hybrid, or physical work. This may involve conducting surveys or focus groups to gather input, allowing you to make informed decisions on the most suitable work model for your team.
2. Adopt a flexible approach: Recognize that one size does not fit all, and strive for a flexible approach that accommodates the unique needs of each developer. This may involve offering a range of remote, hybrid, and physical work options, enabling your developers to select the model that best suits their circumstances and preferences.
3. Prioritize communication and collaboration: Fostering a culture of open communication and collaboration is essential regardless of the work model chosen. Invest in tools and technologies that facilitate seamless communication, and establish processes that promote cross-functional collaboration and knowledge sharing.
4. Ensure equal opportunities: Ensure that all developers, regardless of their work model, have equal access to opportunities for growth and development. This may involve creating remote-friendly training and development programs and ensuring remote and hybrid team members are considered for promotions and advancement opportunities.
5. Foster an inclusive culture: Promote a culture of inclusivity and belonging, where all developers feel valued and supported, regardless of their work model preference. This can be achieved by offering flexible working hours, encouraging regular team-building activities, and establishing remote-friendly communication practices.

6. Reevaluate and adapt: Continuously reevaluate the effectiveness of your work model and be open to making changes based on feedback from developers and evolving business needs. Embrace a culture of continuous improvement to ensure your organization remains agile and responsive to the ever-changing workplace landscape.

The remote, hybrid, and physical work model debate presents challenges and opportunities for organizations seeking to create the best developer experience. By adopting a flexible and inclusive approach, prioritizing communication and collaboration, and continuously reevaluating and adapting to the needs of developers, organizations can create a working environment where developers can thrive and contribute to the organization's success.

Ultimately, the key to an optimal developer experience lies in striking the right balance between remote, hybrid, and physical work models tailored to your team's unique needs and preferences.

Finding Flow in Your Developer Experience

***

As a software developer, I have always wanted to create elegant, efficient, and effective code. Over the years, I have explored numerous methodologies and strategies to improve my Developer Experience (DX) and ultimately deliver better software.

One concept that truly resonated with me and transformed how I approach software development is "Flow," as described in Mihaly Csikszentmihalyi's seminal book, "Flow: The Psychology of Optimal Experience."

Csikszentmihalyi's work on flow opened my eyes to the importance of balancing challenges and skills to achieve complete immersion and focus while working on a task.

This state, known as flow, is characterized by heightened creativity, productivity, and satisfaction. I quickly realized that by harnessing the power of flow, I could dramatically enhance my DX and contribute more effectively to the success of my projects.

***

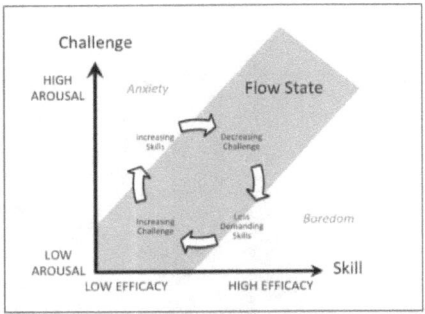

* * *

As I began incorporating the principles of flow into my daily work, I noticed significant improvements in my ability to tackle complex problems, collaborate with teammates, and maintain my motivation in the face of adversity.

The key to achieving flow was sharpening my technical skills and managing my cognitive load effectively.

So far, we have explored a range of software paradigms and discovered the power of microservices in managing cognitive load, ensuring that developers can deliver high-quality, creative, and passionate work. In this chapter, we will delve into the concept of Flow and investigate its correlation with cognitive load in software development.

The Essence of Flow

Flow is a powerful psychological state in which individuals become fully absorbed in the activity they are performing, entering a state of deep focus, enjoyment, and fulfillment. Mihaly Csikszentmihalyi, a pioneering researcher in positive psychology, has extensively studied this phenomenon, discovering that the key to achieving flow lies in striking a delicate balance between the challenges a task presents and the individual's skill set.

As a software developer, I have experienced the transformative power of flow in my work. Let me share some examples from my journey that illustrate the characteristics of flow as identified by Csikszentmihalyi:

Intense concentration on the present moment: I remember a time when I was working on a particularly challenging feature for our application. I became so deeply immersed in the task that all distractions and concerns about other projects vanished.

I was focused on the present moment, pouring all my energy and attention into solving the problem. This intense concentration allowed me to make significant progress and complete the feature more quickly and efficiently than anticipated.

Merging of action and awareness

I refactored a complex code to improve its performance and maintainability on another occasion. As I worked, I entered a state of flow where my thoughts, actions, and awareness seemed to merge seamlessly. It felt like I was an extension of the code, intuitively understanding its structure and behavior and effortlessly making the necessary modifications.

Loss of self-consciousness

During a particularly tight deadline, I was tasked with implementing a crucial integration between two systems. As I became fully engrossed in the task, I lost my sense of self and any concerns about my success or failure. My sole focus was overcoming technical challenges and delivering a robust solution to meet the project's requirements.

Sense of control

Despite facing numerous obstacles and complexities while developing a new software module, I felt a strong sense of control over my actions and the outcome of my efforts. This sense of control stemmed from my deep understanding of the problem domain, my confidence in my skills, and the support of my team. This empowered me to navigate the challenges effectively and deliver a successful solution.

Time distortion

There have been numerous instances where, while working on a complex task, I experienced time distortion—during these flow periods, hours seemed to pass like minutes, as I was entirely absorbed in my work. Conversely, there have been times when I was so deeply focused that even a short period felt much longer, as I made significant progress in what felt like an extended period.

* * *

These experiences have convinced me of the immense potential of flow in enhancing the Developer Experience. By understanding and cultivating the conditions that foster flow, we can empower ourselves and our teams to achieve greater productivity, creativity, and satisfaction in our work.

In the context of software development, achieving flow can have numerous benefits. Developers who can maintain a flow state will likely be more productive, as they can concentrate fully on their tasks without succumbing to distractions or interruptions.

Moreover, the heightened creativity accompanying flow enables developers to devise innovative solutions to complex problems, resulting in higher-quality software.

Furthermore, the sense of satisfaction and enjoyment that arises from the flow state can lead to increased job satisfaction and well-being as developers feel more connected to their work and more fulfilled by their accomplishments.

Creating an environment that balances the task's challenges and the developers' skills is essential to harness the power of flow in software development.

Organizations can empower their developers to achieve flow and unlock their full potential by providing appropriate resources, training, and support and fostering a culture that encourages collaboration and continuous improvement.

Balancing Cognitive Load and Flow

To understand the correlation between cognitive load and flow, it is essential to recognize that cognitive load can either facilitate or hinder the attainment of flow. When the cognitive load is optimally managed, developers can focus on the task without being overwhelmed by complexity, thus achieving flow. On the other hand, when the cognitive load becomes excessive, it can obstruct developers from entering a state of flow, leading to decreased productivity and satisfaction. Example: A Tale of Two Projects.

Let's consider the story of Alice, a talented software developer who has worked on two projects: a monolithic and a microservices-based application.

* * *

Monolithic Misery: On the monolithic project, Alice encountered a complex, intertwined codebase with numerous dependencies and a high cognitive load. Despite her skills and experience, Alice struggled to find flow in her work, as the overwhelming complexity of the project left her feeling perpetually stressed and unproductive.

Microservices Magic: On the microservices-based project, Alice discovered a well-organized, modular codebase with clear boundaries and reduced cognitive load. The manageable complexity of the project allowed Alice to fully engage with her work, effortlessly entering a state of flow. As a result, Alice experienced increased creativity, satisfaction, and productivity.

Strategies for Managing Cognitive Load and Achieving Flow

As a software development leader, harnessing the power of flow in our Developer Experience has been crucial to our team's success. To effectively manage cognitive load and enable our developers to reach a state of flow, I've adopted several strategies, some of which I'd like to share with you.

Break down tasks into manageable units: Large, complex tasks can be overwhelming and contribute to cognitive overload. By breaking tasks into smaller, more manageable units, we allow our developers to focus on one aspect at a time, reducing cognitive load and increasing the likelihood of experiencing flow.

For example, when we had to redesign a critical component of our application, we divided the project into subtasks such as UI design, backend API changes, and database updates. This allowed our developers to concentrate on specific aspects of the project, ultimately making it more manageable and enjoyable.

Encourage collaboration and knowledge sharing: Facilitating open communication and collaboration among team members can reduce cognitive load by allowing developers to leverage each other's expertise and experience.

Our team holds regular "brown bag" sessions where developers present a particular technology or concept they've mastered. This knowledge sharing not only helps other team members learn but also reduces the cognitive load for the presenter as they solidify their understanding of the topic.

Establish clear goals and priorities: Providing developers with well-defined goals and priorities helps them focus on the most important aspects of their work, reducing cognitive load by eliminating unnecessary distractions.

For example, our team holds weekly planning meetings to discuss and prioritize each developer's upcoming tasks. By clearly outlining their weekly priorities, our developers can focus on achieving these goals without the stress of juggling competing priorities.

Promote a healthy work-life balance: Encouraging developers to maintain a healthy work-life balance can help reduce cognitive load by preventing burnout and allowing them to recharge.

We've implemented flexible working hours and encourage our developers to take breaks and time off when needed. One of our developers, for instance, enjoys taking a mid-afternoon walk to clear their mind, which helps them return to their tasks with renewed focus and energy.

Foster a psychologically safe environment: A psychologically safe environment where developers feel comfortable sharing ideas, asking questions, and admitting mistakes, can help reduce cognitive load by alleviating the stress associated with fear of failure or judgment.

Our team encourages open and honest communication and celebrates failures as opportunities to learn and grow. This approach has helped create a supportive atmosphere where our developers can focus on their tasks without the added burden of self-doubt or fear.

By implementing these strategies, I've seen our developers flourish, experiencing flow more often and ultimately delivering high-quality work. Managing cognitive load effectively is a key component of a successful Developer Experience, and these techniques can help you and your team unlock your full potential.

Autotelism - Unlocking the Full Potential

As we've explored the concept of flow, we've discovered its impact on Developer Experience and its potential to elevate productivity, creativity, and satisfaction.

Another essential concept closely related to flow is *autotelism*, a term coined by Mihaly Csikszentmihalyi. Autotelism refers to intrinsically rewarding and motivating activities independent of external rewards or consequences.

Autotelism, a term derived from the Greek words "auto" (self) and "telos" (goal), is a concept in psychology that describes an activity performed for its inherent satisfaction rather than for a separate, external purpose or reward.

The idea behind autotelism is that individuals who engage in autotelic activities find them intrinsically rewarding and fulfilling, as the activity becomes the primary source of motivation and enjoyment.

In this chapter, we will delve into the power of autotelism and how, as a leader, understanding and embracing it can lead to cultivating more 10x developers and enhancing the Developer Experience.

The Pursuit of Intrinsic Rewards

Intrinsic motivation drives autotelic activities, leading individuals to engage in tasks for their inherent enjoyment, satisfaction, and sense of accomplishment.

This powerful force is rooted in personal interests, curiosity, and the desire for self-improvement, independent of external rewards or pressures. When developers find their work autotelic, they are more likely to experience flow and become deeply engaged with their tasks, unlocking their full potential and creativity.

The Role of Intrinsic Rewards in Developer Experience

Understanding the importance of intrinsic rewards and autotelic activities can be a game-changer for individual developers and development teams. When developers are intrinsically motivated, they are more likely to:

Exhibit heightened creativity

Intrinsic motivation fuels the creative process, allowing developers to think more expansively, explore novel solutions, and tackle complex problems with curiosity and excitement.

Pursue ongoing learning and development

Intrinsically motivated developers are more likely to seek opportunities to expand their skill set, learn new technologies, and stay up-to-date with industry trends, making them more valuable and adaptable in a rapidly evolving field.

Demonstrate persistence and resilience

Developers who find their work autotelic are more likely to persevere through challenges, setbacks, and failures, as they derive satisfaction from overcoming obstacles and are driven by a strong sense of personal accomplishment.

Foster a sense of ownership and accountability

When developers are intrinsically motivated, they are more likely to take ownership of their projects, exhibit a deep sense of responsibility, and hold themselves accountable for their work's quality and success.

Experience greater job satisfaction and well-being

Engaging in autotelic activities and experiencing the accompanying intrinsic rewards can contribute to a more positive work experience, increasing job satisfaction, reducing stress, and overall well-being.

By nurturing intrinsic motivation and promoting autotelic activities, leaders can unlock the full potential of their development teams, driving innovation, productivity, and overall Developer Experience to new heights. Embracing the power of intrinsic rewards sets the stage for a thriving development environment that fosters flow, creativity, and passion.

Harnessing Autotelism as a Leader

As a leader, understanding and leveraging the concept of autotelism can profoundly impact your team's Developer Experience. Here are some strategies to foster an autotelic environment and cultivate more 10x developers:

Encourage autonomy

Give your developers the freedom to choose their projects, set their own goals, and decide on the best approach to solving problems. This sense of autonomy can foster intrinsic motivation, making the work more engaging and autotelic.

Cultivate a culture of mastery

Encourage a culture that values continuous learning, growth, and improvement. Provide opportunities for developers to master new skills, experiment with new technologies, and tackle challenging projects. By fostering a growth mindset, you can help your team find intrinsic rewards in overcoming challenges and achieving mastery.

Align work with personal passions

Understand the passions and interests of your developers and align their work with these areas whenever possible. When developers are genuinely passionate about their projects, they are more likely to find them autotelic and experience flow.

Foster a sense of purpose

Help your developers see the bigger picture and understand how their work contributes to the overall goals and mission of the organization. When developers feel their work has purpose and meaning, they are more likely to be intrinsically motivated and find their tasks autotelic.

Recognize and celebrate achievements

While autotelic activities are driven by intrinsic motivation, acknowledging and celebrating your team's accomplishments can reinforce the inherent rewards they experience. Provide genuine feedback and praise to recognize your developers' hard work and dedication.

By embracing autotelism and fostering an environment that supports intrinsic motivation, you can create a culture where developers are more likely to experience flow and fully realize their potential.

As a leader, understanding and cultivating autotelism is a powerful tool in your arsenal to elevate Developer Experience, drive digital transformation, and create a thriving, innovative team of 10x developers.

Conclusion

Understanding the relationship between cognitive load and flow is critical to enhancing Developer Experience in your digital transformation journey. By managing cognitive load effectively, you can create an environment where developers can achieve flow, leading to increased productivity, creativity, and satisfaction.

By incorporating the lessons from Csikszentmihalyi's work on flow and the strategies outlined in this chapter, you can empower your developers to thrive, ensuring the success of your digital transformation projects.

Chapter 11
Anchored in Experience: Navigating Techniques

***

The Age of Discovery was a time of incredible courage, relentless exploration, and the indomitable spirit of adventurers like Bartolomeu Dias. Born in the picturesque region of the Algarve in southern Portugal, Dias began his career as a sailor and explorer at a young age.

Thirteen years before the discovery of Brazil, he was chosen by the king to lead an expedition to explore the western coast of Africa.

Dias faced numerous challenges throughout his journey, including ferocious storms, treacherous seas, and hostile native tribes. Yet, he persevered, driven by his expertise in navigation and unwavering determination. His resilience led him to the southern tip of Africa, which he aptly named the Cape of Good Hope.

Although Dias intended to continue eastward after rounding the Cape, his exhausted crew and depleted supplies forced him to decide to return to Portugal.

Dias's groundbreaking achievement not only marked a significant milestone in the Age of Discovery but also led to his involvement in

Pedro Álvares Cabral's expedition, where his navigation expertise would prove invaluable.

In this chapter, we draw inspiration from Bartolomeu Dias's extraordinary story to emphasize the importance of having the right expertise and techniques to achieve success.

Just as Dias's navigational skills and determination propelled him through the uncharted waters of the Age of Discovery, the knowledge and expertise of individuals will be crucial in navigating the complexities of the digital world.

Join me now as we embark on this exciting journey inspired by the tenacity and expertise of Bartolomeu Dias. Together, we will discover the power of having the right expertise and learn how to harness it in our quest for success in the ever-evolving digital landscape.

We will immerse ourselves in the fascinating world of battle-tested implementations and experience techniques spanning culture, technology, and people. Through real-world cases and hands-on examples, we will uncover the various aspects of enhancing developer experience, covering the entire software delivery lifecycle.

Beginning with onboarding, we will move through the discovery and planning phases, delving deep into the complexities of writing and maintaining code, testing, releasing, operating, and measuring. As we journey through these stages, we will reveal insights and valuable lessons from successful implementations that have brought significant change in organizations like yours.

Throughout our voyage, I aim to offer an engaging and accessible narrative that captures your interest, ignites your curiosity, and empowers you to make well-informed decisions as you guide your organization through its digital transformation journey.

By examining real-world examples and evidence-based strategies, you will be better prepared to evaluate the potential impact of these practices within your organization and identify the most effective course of action.

So, dear reader, let us embark on this exhilarating journey

together. As we delve into developer experience and its pivotal role in digital transformation, I encourage you to maintain an open mind, embrace innovative ideas, and, most importantly, savor the experience.

With anticipation and excitement, let us commence our adventure into the heart of developer experience and its transformative power in the digital age.

Accelerating Developer Experience through Effective Onboarding

* * *

The onboarding process is critical to enhancing the developer experience (DX) and accelerating your organization's digital transformation journey. A well-structured and efficient onboarding program can help developers get up to speed quickly and set the stage for long-term success and engagement. This chapter will explore the critical elements of effective developer onboarding and provide examples to illustrate best practices that can improve the developer experience.

* * *

1.1 Comprehensive Documentation and Knowledge Base

One of the most important aspects of developer onboarding is providing comprehensive documentation and maintaining an up-to-date knowledge base. This includes information on coding standards, architecture patterns, APIs, development tools, and other resources essential to the developers' day-to-day work.

Example: Consider maintaining a centralized and searchable repository where developers can quickly find answers to common questions, access documentation, and learn about new features or tools. This can minimize the learning curve and enable developers to be productive from day one.

1.2 Hands-on Training and Mentorship

Developers often learn best through hands-on experience and practical application. Training sessions, workshops, and opportunities to pair with experienced team members can help new developers quickly familiarize themselves with the organization's technology stack and development processes.

Example: Organize hands-on workshops where new developers can collaborate with experienced team members on real-world tasks. This helps build their technical skills and fosters relationships and team cohesion.

1.3 Clear Expectations and Goals

Establishing clear expectations and setting realistic goals for new developers during the onboarding process is vital. This includes providing them with an understanding of their roles, responsibilities, and how they fit within the organization's larger objectives.

Example: Conduct a one-on-one meeting with each new developer to discuss their role, set initial goals, and establish a timeline for achieving these objectives. This helps provide a sense of direction and purpose while ensuring that the developer and the organization are aligned in their expectations.

1.4 Building a Supportive and Inclusive Environment

Creating a supportive and inclusive environment ensures developers feel welcomed, valued, and motivated to contribute to the organization's success. Encourage open communication, collaboration, and knowledge sharing among team members to foster a sense of belonging and camaraderie.

Example: Establish regular team-building activities, such as weekly stand-ups, sprint reviews, or informal social events, to help developers feel connected and engaged with their colleagues. This helps create a positive work environment that promotes collaboration and collective success.

1.5 Regular Check-ins and Feedback

Maintaining open lines of communication and providing regular feedback is crucial for facilitating a smooth onboarding experience. Regular check-ins help identify any challenges or roadblocks developers may face and address them promptly.

Example: Schedule periodic one-on-one meetings with new developers to discuss their progress, address any concerns, and provide constructive feedback on their work. This demonstrates your commitment to their success and helps them grow and improve.

Conclusion

Organizations can significantly improve the developer experience and accelerate digital transformation by implementing effective onboarding practices. A well-executed onboarding program enables developers to quickly become productive and engaged, ultimately contributing to the organization's success. In the next chapter, we will explore other strategies for enhancing the developer experience and driving innovation within your organization.

The Importance of Well-Defined Service Ownership

* * *

This chapter will discuss the significance of well-defined service ownership in IT organizations and how it impacts developer experience. We will also explore the challenges organizations may face without clear service ownership.

Throughout my experiences in different organizations, I have often witnessed the challenges of transitioning to a DevOps model. One of the central tenets of DevOps is the "you build it, you run it" philosophy. However, this concept isn't always as smooth and accountable as we might hope.

In many cases, I've seen a troubling variation on this principle emerge: "You build it," and then "You run... away!" Instead of fostering a sense of ownership and responsibility, this approach creates an environment where developers can feel disconnected from the applications and services they create. As a result, they may be less inclined to address issues or optimize their work, which can negatively impact the organization.

This is why service ownership is so crucial. By emphasizing service ownership, we can ensure that developers are responsible for the entire lifecycle of their applications, from design and development to deployment and ongoing maintenance. This sense of ownership increases accountability and drives developers to create better, more reliable services.

Service ownership refers to the assignment of responsibility for developing, maintaining, and supporting a particular service within an organization. It encompasses many responsibilities, including planning, implementation, monitoring, and continuous improvement. When service ownership is well-defined, organizations can ensure a seamless flow of work, effective collaboration, and efficient problem-solving.

* * *

The Importance of Well-Defined Service Ownership

Accountability: Clear service ownership ensures that individuals or teams are accountable for the performance, reliability, and security of their assigned services. This fosters a sense of ownership, motivating them to proactively address issues and maintain high-quality standards.

Collaboration: When service ownership is well-defined, it fosters effective communication and collaboration between different teams. This enables teams to share knowledge, best practices, and resources, leading to faster issue resolution and overall improvement in developer experience.

Streamlined Processes: With clear service ownership, organizations can establish streamlined processes for development, deployment, and maintenance. This leads to reduced bottlenecks, improved efficiency, and faster delivery of new features and enhancements.

Continuous Improvement: Service owners are responsible for

identifying areas of improvement and implementing changes to optimize their services. This promotes a culture of continuous improvement, driving innovation and growth within the organization.

Challenges of Lacking Clear Service Ownership

Ambiguity and Confusion: Teams may face confusion and ambiguity regarding their roles and responsibilities without well-defined service ownership. This can result in duplicated efforts, miscommunication, and inefficient use of resources.

Slow Issue Resolution: Identifying and resolving issues can become time-consuming and cumbersome without clear service ownership. This can lead to prolonged downtimes, degraded user experiences, and increased costs.

Poor Quality and Reliability: When service ownership is not well-defined, there may be a lack of accountability for service performance, reliability, and security. This can result in poor quality, frequent outages, and reduced customer satisfaction.

Stunted Growth: Without a clear understanding of service ownership, it can be challenging for organizations to identify areas for improvement, implement changes, and innovate. This can hinder the organization's growth and ability from adapting to changing market conditions.

Pro tip: One effective way to encourage service ownership is by leveraging a developer portal. A well-designed developer portal can be a central hub for all the resources, tools, and documentation developers need to create, maintain, and optimize their services.

When combined with the short-lived campaign mechanism we'll discuss later in the book, a developer portal can be a powerful tool to drive ownership and engagement among your development team.

In conclusion, well-defined service ownership enhances developer experience and drives organizational success. Organizations can foster accountability, promote collaboration, streamline processes, and ensure continuous improvement by establishing clear roles and responsibilities.

On the other hand, lacking clear service ownership can lead to ambiguity, slow issue resolution, poor quality, and stunted growth. Organizations must prioritize establishing well-defined service ownership to optimize developer experience and drive innovation.

Mapping The Technology Landscape

* * *

This chapter will explore the importance of understanding an organization's various tools, platforms, languages, and techniques.

We will also discuss the concept of the Tech Radar by Thought-Works, an innovative framework that helps organizations make informed decisions about their technology landscape and drive better developer experiences.

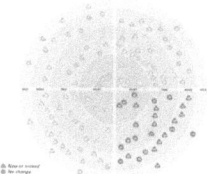

The Importance of a Clear Technology Landscape

Informed Decision-Making: Understanding the range of technologies used within an organization enables decision-makers to evaluate the effectiveness of current tools and processes.

This knowledge helps them identify areas for improvement and make informed decisions about adopting new technologies, retiring outdated ones, or consolidating redundant tools.

Efficient Collaboration: A clear picture of the technology landscape facilitates seamless team collaboration. When team members are familiar with the tools, platforms, languages, and techniques used across the organization, they can work together more effectively, leading to better results and a superior developer experience.

Enhanced Agility: A comprehensive view of the technology landscape allows organizations to adapt to changes in the market more rapidly. They can quickly adopt new technologies, respond to emerging trends, and innovate to stay ahead of competitors.

Skill Development and Knowledge Sharing: A clear understanding of the organization's technology landscape enables employees to identify gaps in their skill sets and pursue relevant training or mentorship opportunities. This fosters a culture of continuous learning and promotes the sharing of best practices across teams.

Introducing the ThoughtWorks Tech Radar

The ThoughtWorks Tech Radar is a robust framework designed to help organizations visualize and navigate their technology landscape. It enables organizations to assess and categorize their various tools, platforms, languages, and techniques, providing valuable insights to inform their technology strategy and improve developer experiences.

The Tech Radar is divided into four quadrants, each representing a distinct aspect of technology:

- Techniques: This quadrant encompasses practices and methodologies teams use to develop, maintain, and support software.
- Platforms: This quadrant covers the underlying infrastructure and technologies upon which software is built and deployed.
- Tools: This quadrant includes the software applications, libraries, and frameworks teams use to develop, test, and deploy their solutions.
- Languages and Frameworks: This quadrant represents the programming languages and frameworks teams utilize to create their software.

Within each quadrant, the Tech Radar identifies different "rings" that represent the maturity and adoption level of technology:

- Adopt: These technologies have been proven effective and are recommended for use within the organization.
- Trial: These technologies show promise and warrant further exploration and testing.
- Assess: These technologies are potentially helpful but require further investigation and evaluation.
- Hold: These technologies are not recommended for adoption due to concerns about their effectiveness, relevance, or support.

Leveraging the Tech Radar for Enhanced Developer Experience

By embracing the Tech Radar framework, organizations can gain valuable insights into their technology landscape and make data-driven decisions that enhance the developer experience:

Identify Opportunities for Improvement: The Tech Radar helps organizations identify areas where they can streamline processes, consolidate tools, or adopt new technologies to improve developer productivity and satisfaction.

Foster a Culture of Innovation: The Tech Radar encourages teams to experiment with new technologies and techniques, fostering a culture of innovation and continuous improvement.

Enable Effective Collaboration: By providing a shared understanding of the organization's technology landscape, the Tech Radar facilitates better team collaboration and helps developers quickly onboard new projects.

Support Skill Development: The Tech Radar can guide professional development, helping developers identify areas where they can expand their skill sets and stay current with industry trends.

In conclusion, understanding an organization's technology landscape is crucial for making informed decisions, fostering collaboration, enhancing agility, and promoting skill development.

The Power of Templates

* * *

In software development, templates are crucial in streamlining workflows and ensuring that code is written and maintained according to best practices.

Using templates, engineering leaders, platform engineers, and developers can benefit from increased efficiency, reduced risk, and a more enjoyable developer experience.

This chapter will explore the advantages of using templates for different roles within a development team.

Benefits of Templates for Engineering Leaders: De-risking Critical Workflows

Engineering leaders oversee the development process and ensure that projects are delivered on time, within budget, and to the highest quality standards. By leveraging templates, engineering leaders can de-risk critical workflows and ensure services are created correctly.

a. Consistency and Best Practices: Templates ensure that code is written according to established best practices and follows a consistent organizational structure. This reduces the likelihood of errors, making it easier for team members to understand, maintain, and troubleshoot the code.

b. Faster Onboarding: Templates enable new team members to quickly understand the organization's coding standards and project structure, speeding up the onboarding process and helping them become more productive.

c. Reduced Risk: By ensuring that code is correctly written the first time, templates help minimize the risk of errors or security vulnerabilities, which can be costly and time-consuming.

Example: An engineering leader might create a template for new microservices, ensuring that each service follows the organization's architectural patterns and security best practices, reducing the risk of errors or vulnerabilities.

Benefits of Templates for Platform Engineers: Operating with Leverage

Platform engineers are responsible for designing, building, and maintaining the infrastructure and tools developers rely on. By providing curated templates that codify best practices, platform engineers can operate with leverage and empower developers to build high-quality software.

a. Guardrails: Templates act as guardrails that help developers adhere to best practices and maintain a consistent codebase. This can reduce the need for platform engineers to intervene, freeing up their time to focus on other tasks.

b. Scalability: Templates can be easily updated and shared across the organization, ensuring that best practices and changes to infrastructure or tooling are consistently applied.

c. Knowledge Sharing: Templates can help capture and share the collective knowledge and expertise of the platform engineering team, making it easier for developers to access and learn from this information.

Example: A platform engineer might create a template for deploying applications to a Kubernetes cluster, ensuring that all applications follow a standardized deployment process and take advantage of the team's best configuration and resource management practices.

Benefits of Templates for Developers: Focusing on Impactful Features

Developers are at the heart of the software development process, and their primary goal is to write and ship impactful features. By using templates, developers can skip the boilerplate and bureaucracy associated with setting up new services and focus on what matters most: creating high-quality software.

a. Reduced Time to Market: Templates help developers get up and running quickly, reducing the time it takes to create, test, and deploy new features.

b. Improved Collaboration: When all developers work with the same templates and follow consistent coding practices, it becomes easier to collaborate and understand each other's work.

c. Lower Cognitive Load: By eliminating the need to remember and follow complex setup procedures or coding standards, templates help reduce developers' cognitive load, allowing them to focus on writing high-quality code.

Example: A developer might use a template for setting up a new API endpoint, allowing them to quickly scaffold the necessary code and focus on implementing the endpoint's business logic rather than spending time on boilerplate setup tasks.

Conclusion

In this chapter, we have explored the numerous benefits `o` of using templates for engineering leaders, platform engineers, and developers in the software development process.

By streamlining workflows, ensuring best practices, and enabling teams to focus on delivering impactful features, templates can be a powerful weapon in the journey toward digital transformation.

As we continue our exploration of Developer Experience, it is important to recognize templates' value to an organization. They provide a consistent foundation for collaboration, reduce the risk of errors, and enhance overall productivity.

Organizations can empower their development teams and accelerate digital transformation by embracing templates.

The Importance of Establishing Coding Standards and Conventions

* * *

In the previous chapter, we delved into the benefits of using templates to streamline workflows and ensure that best practices are followed across the organization.

Now, we focus on another crucial aspect of Developer Experience: establishing and enforcing coding standards and conventions. In this chapter, we will explore what coding standards are, how to enforce them, and address some typical fallacies surrounding their enforcement.

What Are Coding Standards and Conventions?

Coding standards and conventions are agreed-upon rules and guidelines that govern how code is written and organized within an organization. They encompass various topics, including naming conventions, indentation and formatting, commenting, and overall code structure. These standards and conventions not only improve code readability and maintainability but also foster a sense of consistency and coherence across the entire codebase. Enforcing coding standards and conventions can be achieved through several means:

Documentation

Develop concise documentation outlining the organization's coding standards and conventions. This documentation should be easily accessible to all developers and kept up-to-date. For example, create a shared repository or wiki page containing the organization's coding guidelines.

Ensure the documentation covers naming conventions, indentation rules, commenting styles, and language-specific best practices. Regularly review and update the documentation to keep it relevant and aligned with the latest industry standards.

Code Reviews

Incorporate coding standards and conventions into the code review process. Encourage team members to review each other's code for adherence to these guidelines and provide constructive feedback.

For example, during code reviews, reviewers can check if the submitted code follows the naming conventions, uses proper indentation, and adheres to the commenting guidelines. Reviewers can also provide suggestions to improve code readability and maintainability.

To facilitate this process, consider using a code review tool, like GitHub's pull request feature or GitLab's merge request feature, which allows developers to provide feedback and discuss changes in the code quickly.

Automated Tools

Utilize tools like linters and code formatters to check and enforce coding standards during development automatically. These tools can be integrated into the development environment or as part of the continuous integration pipeline. For example, tools like ESLint for JavaScript, Pylint for Python, and RuboCop for Ruby can be used to enforce coding standards and identify potential issues.

Code formatters, such as Prettier for JavaScript and Black for Python, can automatically format code to comply with the organization's conventions. Integrating these tools into the development workflow can help ensure that code adheres to the established guidelines without relying solely on manual code reviews.

Training and Workshops

Provide training and workshops to ensure developers are familiar with the organization's coding standards and conventions. This can minimize confusion and increase adherence to the guidelines.

For instance, hold regular training sessions or workshops focusing on specific aspects of coding standards, such as proper commenting techniques or best practices for naming variables and functions. Additionally, consider bringing in external experts to conduct workshops on the latest industry best practices, which can help keep the team up-to-date and informed.

By investing in the education and growth of developers, the organization can foster a culture of continuous improvement and adherence to coding standards.

The Typical Fallacies About Enforcing Standards

There are some common misconceptions and fallacies surrounding the enforcement of coding standards and conventions, including:

Fallacy 1: "Enforcing standards stifles creativity." Contrary to this belief, establishing and enforcing standards can enhance creativity by reducing the cognitive load on developers. With clear guidelines, developers can focus on solving problems and implementing features rather than debating code style and organization.

Fallacy 2: "Standards are one-size-fits-all." In reality, coding standards and conventions should be tailored to the specific needs and preferences of the organization. While some aspects may be universal, it is crucial to adopt standards to the unique context of the development team and the projects they work on.

Fallacy 3: "Enforcing standards is too time-consuming." Although the initial investment in establishing and enforcing coding standards may seem daunting, the long-term benefits far outweigh the initial effort. Improved code readability, maintainability, and consistency lead to more efficient development and reduced technical debt in the long run.

Conclusion

Establishing and enforcing coding standards and conventions is essential to Developer Experience. By implementing clear guidelines and using tools to enforce them, organizations can improve code quality, reduce technical debt, and foster a more efficient and cohesive development environment.

By debunking the fallacies surrounding the enforcement of standards, organizations can better understand the value that coding standards bring to their digital transformation journey.

Fighting Tech Debt with Short-Lived Campaigns

* * *

In the previous chapters, we've discussed the importance of templates and establishing coding standards and conventions to enhance the developer experience.

However, merely writing these standards and making them available somewhere, like in Confluence or SharePoint, may not be enough. Based on the principle "trust, but verify," we need a mechanism to verify that these standards are being followed.

Tech debt, or technical debt, is an ever-increasing problem that plagues many organizations, particularly as they scale and adapt to new technologies.

Technical debt is the accumulated cost of cutting corners, using outdated technologies, or implementing suboptimal solutions during software development. While saving time or resources in the short term, these shortcuts often lead to increased maintenance costs, reduced performance, and a slower pace of innovation in the long term.

One of the leading causes of technical debt is the pressure to deliver new features and functionality quickly. In the fast-paced world of software development, teams are often under immense pressure to meet deadlines and satisfy customer demands.

This may lead to shortcuts or "quick fixes" being applied, which may work in the short term but can create a tangled web of issues that need to be addressed later on.

As organizations grow, technical debt can accumulate at an alarming rate, making it increasingly difficult for development teams to maintain and improve their software.

This problem is exacerbated by the constant influx of new technologies and platforms, which can sometimes render previous solutions obsolete or incompatible. The result is a growing backlog of issues that require attention, ultimately slowing the pace of innovation and increasing the risk of software failures or security vulnerabilities.

Another factor contributing to the growth of technical debt is the lack of clear coding standards, documentation, and knowledge sharing within development teams. When developers have a limited understanding of the existing codebase or the rationale behind particular design decisions, building upon or modifying the existing code becomes more challenging.

This can lead to more technical debt as new code is added without understanding the underlying architecture or potential impacts on other software components.

Managing technical debt is an ongoing challenge for organizations, requiring a dedicated and proactive approach. Some strategies for addressing technical debt include allocating time and resources for regular refactoring, adopting a consistent set of coding standards and conventions, and fostering a culture of continuous improvement and learning within development teams.

By prioritizing technical debt management, organizations can create a more sustainable and efficient development process, ultimately leading to higher-quality software and a better overall developer experience.

Fighting Tech Debt with Short-Lived Campaigns

One solution I've come across recently is OpsLevel, a SaaS developer portal offering a campaign system to help enforce standards and guardrails. This campaign mechanism can potentially transform the development maturity of organizations.

A campaign in OpsLevel is a collection of changes or tasks related to a specific initiative or project. For example, a campaign could involve updating authentication across all microservices or upgrading all microservices to a new version of a programming language.

The campaign system allows teams to create a campaign, define the specific tasks or changes involved, and track progress toward completing those tasks. The platform provides visualizations and dashboards to help teams see how far along they are in a campaign, what work still needs to be done, and who is responsible for completing each task.

One aspect of OpsLevel that I find particularly interesting is the capability of automated guardrail checks. Instead of merely writing guardrails, you're now enforcing them via automated checks. The campaign mechanism can monitor these short-lived campaigns in real-time, providing complete visibility into the status of each campaign. Additionally, it has an automatic mechanism to ping and notify teams due to compliance with the guardrails.

Here are some examples of campaigns that could potentially be applied to your organization as well, starting with simple ones to help you adopt and become familiar with the process:

- Enforcing every repository has a code owner.
- Enforcing every repository has a README.md file.
- Enforcing every repository has a swagger file if it's an API type of service.
- Enforcing every repository has a metadata file classifying the type of service according to terms aligned by enterprise architecture.

- Enforcing every repository has an ESLint/Prettier configuration file.
- Enforcing every repository has a Dockerfile without outdated images.
- Enforcing every repository doesn't have any package.json Node.js version below 16.

Organizations can effectively enforce standards and guardrails by utilizing a platform like OpsLevel and its campaign system, resulting in improved compliance and a better developer experience overall. The automated checks and real-time monitoring of campaigns ensure that your team follows the established guidelines, ultimately leading to a more streamlined and efficient development process.

Running Short-Lived Campaigns to Increase Developer Maturity

* * *

In this chapter, we discuss short-lived campaigns as a mechanism to drive improvements in your engineering organization.

These campaigns are designed to roll out changes that require orchestrated effort across multiple teams, such as paying off technical debt, planning migrations or upgrades, and incrementally improving service maturity. Implementing these changes in a growing engineering organization demands significant managerial effort, which includes:

- Defining the required changes and actions
- Identifying the involved teams
- Communicating the necessary actions to the selected teams
- Measuring progress and driving the initiative forward through ongoing communication

To effectively run these campaigns, we suggest the following approach:

Define the required changes explicitly and measurably by creating checks that relevant service owners must complete as part of the campaign.

- Identify the in-scope services for a campaign using a filter.
- Schedule the campaign by setting a start and target date.
- Enable service owners to track their progress against the campaigns linked to their services from individual service pages.
- Allow campaign owners to monitor progress across all services from the campaign page.
- Empower campaign owners to send ad-hoc reminders via Slack or email to teams that have not completed the campaign.
- When the campaign ends, allow campaign owners to move checks to the Rubric, establishing them as ongoing standards for the organization.

By utilizing this mechanism, organizations can efficiently run short-lived campaigns that contribute to the overall maturity of their engineering teams. These campaigns enable systematic improvements, ensure effective communication, and create an environment that promotes continuous growth and development.

Writing Code Without Drama

* * *

This chapter will explore practical tips for creating a great developer experience when writing and dealing with code. As we have seen before, a positive developer experience increases productivity, better collaboration, and higher-quality software.

We must consider code readability, maintainability, efficient tooling, and a supportive environment to achieve this. This chapter will provide actionable advice for improving the developer experience while working with code.

Code Readability and Maintainability

Write clean, self-explanatory code: Prioritizing the creation of clean and easy-to-understand code is essential for reducing cognitive load on developers and improving overall code quality.

By focusing on readability and maintainability, developers can spend less time deciphering code and more time working on new features or improvements. Here are a few guidelines to follow when writing clean, self-explanatory code:

Use descriptive variable and function names: Choose meaningful and descriptive names for your variables and functions, which indicate their purpose and usage. This makes it easier for other developers to understand the intent behind the code without needing extensive comments.

Example: Instead of using ambiguous names like "x" or "temp," opt for more descriptive names such as "totalSales" or "averageTemperature."

Adhere to a consistent coding style: Consistency is crucial when writing clean code. Following a consistent coding style, whether established by your organization or based on widely accepted industry standards, helps make the code more readable and easier to maintain.

Example: If your team uses camelCase for variable names, consistently apply this convention throughout your code.

Follow best practices for the programming language being used: Each language has its own set of best practices and conventions. Please familiarize yourself with these guidelines and adhere to them while writing code. This improves the code quality and makes it easier for other developers familiar with the language to understand and work with your code.

Example: In Python, it's essential to follow PEP 8, the official Python style guide, which provides recommendations on topics like indentation, line length, and naming conventions.

Break down complex functions into smaller, more manageable pieces: Large, complicated functions can be challenging to understand and maintain. Instead, break down complex logic into smaller, more focused functions with a single responsibility. This approach makes the code more modular and easier to comprehend.

Example: If you have a function that retrieves data from an API, processes it, and writes it to a database, consider splitting it into three separate functions, each handling one of those tasks.

Write meaningful comments when necessary: While clean, self-explanatory code should minimize the need for comments, there are situations where comments can help explain complex logic or decisions that might not be evident from the code itself. When writing comments, ensure they are concise and provide valuable context.

Example: If you're using a specific algorithm to solve a problem, briefly explain the rationale behind choosing that algorithm and any potential trade-offs.

By following these guidelines, you can write clean, self-explanatory code that reduces the cognitive load on developers, making it easier to understand, maintain, and evolve the codebase over time.

Efficient Tooling and Workflows

Choose the right tools: Selecting appropriate tools for writing, debugging, and managing code is essential for reducing cognitive load and improving developer productivity. Integrated Development Environments (IDEs), version control systems, and code analysis tools can significantly enhance the developer experience. These tools should be tailored to the team's and the project's needs.

Example: A team working on a JavaScript project might choose Visual Studio Code as their IDE, Git for version control, and ESLint for code analysis to ensure code quality and maintainability.

Automate repetitive tasks: Automating repetitive or time-consuming tasks can greatly reduce cognitive load and free developers to focus on more critical aspects of their work. Utilize build tools, task runners, and Continuous Integration (CI) systems to automate code formatting, linting, and testing processes.

Example: A development team could use tools like Prettier for automatic code formatting, Webpack as a build tool and task runner, and Jenkins or GitHub Actions for setting up a CI pipeline to automate testing and deployment.

Optimize development environment: Customizing the development environment to suit personal preferences can significantly increase productivity and reduce cognitive load. Tailor the environment by setting up keyboard shortcuts, customizing the IDE, and using plugins or extensions that enhance the developer experience.

Example: A developer working in Visual Studio Code might set up custom keyboard shortcuts to quickly navigate between files, install the Material Theme extension for a visually appealing interface, and use the GitLens extension to view detailed Git history and annotations within the editor.

By choosing the right tools, automating repetitive tasks, and optimizing the development environment, developers can reduce cognitive load and focus on more valuable aspects of their work, ultimately leading to higher productivity and better outcomes.

Collaborative Coding Practices

Encourage code reviews: Implementing a code review process promotes collaboration, knowledge sharing, and continuous improvement. It is important to ensure that feedback is constructive, focused on the code rather than the individual, and offered in a supportive manner.

Example: A team might establish a policy that at least one other team member must review all pull requests before being merged. This ensures that everyone can learn from each other's work, discuss potential improvements, and maintain a high standard of code quality.

Pair programming and mob programming: Encouraging practices like pair programming and mob programming can lead to a more collaborative and productive work environment. In these setups, team members work together on code, sharing knowledge and learning from each other. This collaborative approach can lead to higher-quality code, fewer defects, and improved team dynamics.

Example: A development team might schedule regular pair programming sessions where team members rotate partners, allowing everyone to gain exposure to different parts of the codebase and work with various colleagues. Mob programming sessions could also be organized for particularly complex or high-impact tasks, ensuring that multiple perspectives are considered during development.

Foster a culture of learning and improvement: Encouraging team members to continually learn, share knowledge, and improve their coding skills is essential for a high-performing development team. This can be achieved through various means such as training, workshops, meetups, or informal knowledge-sharing sessions.

Example: A team might organize monthly tech talks, where members present on a topic they've recently learned about or a new technology they've been exploring. Additionally, the team could allocate a budget for each member to attend conferences or take online courses relevant to their work, ensuring continuous professional development.

By promoting code reviews, pair programming, mob programming, and fostering a culture of learning and improvement, DX teams can help reduce the cognitive load on developers, leading to better collaboration, increased productivity, and higher-quality software.

Supportive Environment and Continuous Feedback

Provide a supportive environment: Creating an environment where team members feel comfortable asking questions, seeking help, and sharing ideas are crucial for a healthy and productive team dynamic. Encourage open communication, collaboration, and a mutual respect and support culture.

Example: A team might implement regular "open space" meetings, where team members can bring up any issues, ideas, or questions they have. This creates a safe forum for discussion and problem-solving, ensuring everyone feels heard and supported. Additionally, team leads could try to be approachable and open to questions or concerns, fostering a sense of trust and openness within the team.

Encourage continuous feedback: Establishing a process for continuous feedback helps the team stay agile and responsive to changing needs and circumstances. By providing team members a platform to discuss coding practices, tools, and workflows and suggest improvements, potential issues can be identified and addressed early on, leading to a more enjoyable and productive developer experience.

Example: A team might introduce regular retrospectives, where team members can reflect on the previous development iteration, discuss what went well and what could be improved, and suggest actionable changes for the next iteration. This ongoing feedback loop helps the team stay adaptive and continually refine their processes for better efficiency and collaboration.

DX teams can create a positive atmosphere that fosters collaboration, innovation, and continuous improvement by providing a supportive environment and encouraging continuous feedback. This ultimately leads to a more productive and engaged team, delivering higher-quality software and contributing to the organization's success.

Conclusion

Improving the developer experience while writing and dealing with code requires clean, maintainable code, efficient tooling and workflows, collaborative practices, and a supportive environment. By implementing these practical tips, organizations can create a positive developer experience that promotes productivity, collaboration, and high-quality software.

Pair Programming and Code Reviews

* * *

In this chapter, we will delve into two widely used practices in software development: pair programming and code reviews. These practices have proven to improve the developer experience and accelerate the digital transformation journey. We will discuss the advantages of implementing these practices in detail, provide examples, and explore how they reduce cognitive load.

Pair Programming

Pair programming is a collaborative approach to software development where two developers work together on the same task using the same computer. One developer, called the "driver," writes the code, while the other, known as the "navigator," provides guidance, reviews the code, and suggests improvements.

The roles of driver and navigator are frequently switched, ensuring both developers stay actively engaged in the process.

Benefits of Pair Programming:

Improved Code Quality: Pair programming allows for continuous code review, which helps catch bugs and issues early in development. Two pairs of eyes are more likely to spot mistakes, and the collaboration between the developers often results in more efficient and elegant code.

Example: The driver might overlook a potential edge case in complex algorithm implementation. With their broader perspective, the navigator can identify the oversight and suggest a solution, preventing potential issues.

Enhanced Knowledge Sharing: Pair programming fosters a learning culture where developers can share their expertise, techniques, and insights. This knowledge transfer can lead to faster skill development, particularly for junior team members, who can learn best practices from their more experienced counterparts.

Example: A junior developer may not be familiar with specific design patterns or performance optimization techniques. By working closely with a senior developer in a pair programming session, they can learn these concepts more quickly and effectively than through independent study.

Faster Problem Solving: Pair programming enables developers to brainstorm and troubleshoot together, resulting in quicker problem resolution. The collaborative process allows them to bounce ideas off each other and explore multiple solutions before settling on the best one.

Example: When faced with a performance bottleneck, two developers working together can identify the root cause more rapidly and devise an effective solution by combining their insights and expertise.

Code Reviews

Code reviews involve systematically examining a developer's code by one or more colleagues to identify and resolve issues before the code is merged into the main codebase. The reviewing process can be either synchronous (conducted in real-time, with the reviewer and author present) or asynchronous (where the reviewer provides feedback at their convenience).

Benefits of Code Reviews:

Enhanced Code Quality: Code reviews help identify and fix bugs, vulnerabilities, and inefficiencies in the code, leading to more robust and maintainable software. Code reviews can also promote consistency across the codebase by ensuring the code adheres to the organization's coding standards and best practices.

Example: A developer submits a pull request for a new feature. During the code review process, another team member identifies a potential security vulnerability and suggests a fix, preventing the issue from reaching production.

Knowledge Sharing and Learning: Code reviews allow developers to learn from each other's work, understand different coding styles, and become familiar with various parts of the codebase. This shared understanding helps to create a more cohesive team and can lead to better collaboration in the future.

Example: A team member reviewing code may notice an innovative approach to a problem or clever use of a specific library. They can then apply this newfound knowledge to their future work, improving their skills and contributing to the overall skill set of the team.

Improved Collaboration and Communication: Code reviews foster open communication among team members, encouraging them to discuss potential issues and improvements. This collaborative environment helps to build trust within the team, and developers can become more receptive to feedback, knowing it is aimed at enhancing the overall quality of the software.

Example: During a code review, a developer may receive constructive feedback regarding their implementation. By discussing these suggestions openly, the developer can gain insights into alternative solutions and learn how to address similar issues in the future.

Accelerated Onboarding: Participating in code reviews can expedite the onboarding process for new team members. Reviewing others' code, they become familiar with the codebase, the organization's coding standards, and the overall project structure. This hands-on experience enables them to contribute more effectively and quickly integrate into the team.

Example: A new developer joins the team and begins participating in code reviews. Examining different parts of the codebase, they better understand the system's architecture, allowing them to start working on tasks and contributing to the project more rapidly.

Reduced Cognitive Load:

Code reviews, along with pair programming, help to reduce cognitive load for developers in several ways:

Shared Problem Solving: When developers collaborate on code reviews, they can collectively tackle problems and find optimal solutions. This shared approach reduces the cognitive burden on individual developers, as they can rely on the collective knowledge and expertise of the team.

Streamlined Decision Making: During code reviews, team members can discuss and evaluate different problem-solving approaches. This collaborative decision-making process helps to ensure that the best solutions are implemented, reducing the cognitive load associated with making complex decisions alone.

Improved Code Comprehension: As developers participate in code reviews, they become more familiar with various parts of the codebase and the coding styles of their colleagues. This increased understanding of the codebase can make it easier for developers to navigate and work with the code, reducing the cognitive effort required.

Early Detection and Resolution of Issues: By identifying and resolving issues early in the development process, code reviews help prevent problems from accumulating and becoming more complex. This proactive approach can reduce the cognitive load associated with debugging and fixing issues later in the development cycle.

In conclusion, both pair programming and code reviews are essential practices that can significantly enhance the developer experience and contribute to the success of your digital transformation journey. By implementing these practices, you can improve code quality, foster knowledge sharing, accelerate onboarding, and reduce cognitive load for your development team.

Unleashing the Power of Simplicity in Your Developer Experience

* * *

An exceptional Developer Experience (DX) is a cornerstone of successful digital transformation projects. DRY (Don't Repeat Yourself) and YAGNI (You Aren't Gonna Need It) are two guiding principles that can significantly enhance DX by reducing cognitive load.

This chapter will explore these principles, provide examples to illustrate their impact on cognitive load, and discuss how embracing DRY and YAGNI can lead to more straightforward, more effective software development.

DRY (Don't Repeat Yourself) Principle

The DRY principle emphasizes that each piece of knowledge or functionality should have a single, unambiguous representation within a system. By adhering to DRY, developers can create more accessible code to maintain, understand, and refactor.

Example: Imagine a project where multiple classes contain methods for calculating sales tax. Having this logic duplicated throughout the codebase increases cognitive load, as developers must remember the locations of these repeated code snippets and update them individually whenever a change is required.

By consolidating the sales tax logic into a single, reusable `TaxCalculator` class, developers can reduce cognitive load and create a more maintainable codebase, leading to a better DX.

YAGNI (You Aren't Gonna Need It) Principle

The YAGNI principle asserts that developers should only implement functionality when it is genuinely needed rather than trying to anticipate future requirements. This principle encourages simplicity and minimizes the risk of unnecessary complexity, which can lead to increased cognitive load and technical debt.

Example: In a content management system (CMS), a developer might be tempted to implement a complex tagging system to categorize content, even if there is no immediate requirement.

This additional complexity increases cognitive load, as developers must understand and maintain the tagging system, even if it's not being used.

By adhering to YAGNI, the developer can focus on implementing genuinely needed features, keeping the codebase simple, and reducing cognitive load for a more enjoyable DX.

Combining DRY and YAGNI for Maximum Impact

To harness simplicity's power, developers should consider combining the DRY and YAGNI principles. This combination allows them to create code that is both streamlined and easy to maintain, reducing cognitive load and fostering an exceptional DX.

Combined Example: In an online store, a developer might be tasked with implementing a feature that sends promotional emails to customers. Following the DRY principle, the developer could create a reusable EmailSender class to handle sending emails.

By adhering to YAGNI, the developer would only implement the specific functionality needed for sending promotional emails instead of over-engineering the solution with additional features that are not currently required. This combination of DRY and YAGNI results in a focused, reusable component that minimizes cognitive load and supports a superior DX.

Conclusion

Embracing the DRY and YAGNI principles can substantially reduce cognitive load, leading to a more enjoyable and efficient Developer Experience.

By creating code that is both streamlined and focused on current requirements, developers can concentrate on delivering high-quality features without being overwhelmed by complexity. In turn, this fosters greater productivity and collaboration, ensuring the success of digital transformation projects.

Building a Solid Architecture

* * *

A solid architecture is essential for successful digital transformation, and it enables developers to create efficient, reliable, scalable systems that meet users' expectations and drive business growth.

This chapter delves into the importance of balancing cost, performance, and failure characteristics, creating an event-driven architecture, and enforcing standardization to optimize the developer experience.

Balancing Cost, Performance, and Failure Characteristics

Balancing cost, performance, and failure characteristics is crucial when designing a system. These trade-offs should be made deliberately to avoid pitfalls and ensure the system operates efficiently.

For instance, incremental performance improvements can be expensive and may not consistently deliver proportional benefits.

Over-engineering for higher performance than users expect can lead to increased costs without a noticeable impact on user experience. To avoid this, assess the system's requirements and user expectations to make informed decisions on performance optimization.

Creating an Event-Driven Architecture

An event-driven architecture (EDA) is a powerful approach to building scalable and resilient systems, as it fosters modularity and adaptability. This architectural style is centered around the flow of events, which are generated by various components within the system.

In an EDA, services react to events rather than relying on direct communication. This results in loose coupling between services, which allows for several key benefits.

Independent Evolution: With loose coupling, services can evolve independently without affecting other system parts. This means that updates, bug fixes, and feature additions can be performed on individual services without necessitating changes across the entire system. This flexibility accelerates development and reduces the risk of unintended consequences due to system-wide changes.

Efficient Communication: An event-driven architecture enables efficient communication between services using asynchronous messaging. This means that services can send and receive messages without waiting for responses, thus reducing latency and improving overall system performance. Messaging protocols like publish-subscribe and message queues also allow for better handling traffic spikes and system failures.

Developing skills in microservices techniques is crucial for creating robust event-driven architectures. Some of these techniques include:

Service Mesh: A service mesh is a dedicated infrastructure layer that manages service-to-service communication. It provides features like load balancing, traffic management, and security, enabling developers to focus on building the application logic without worrying about the underlying communication details.

Circuit Breaker Patterns: The circuit breaker pattern is a fault-tolerance mechanism that prevents cascading failures in a distributed system. When a service fails to respond or takes too long, the circuit breaker trips and further requests are prevented from reaching the failed service. This allows the system to continue functioning without being impacted by the failed service and provides time for the service to recover.

Caching: Caching is a technique that stores frequently used data in memory, reducing the need to repeatedly fetch the same data from the source. In an event-driven architecture, caching can improve performance by reducing latency and minimizing the load on services that generate data.

Service Discovery: Service discovery is a mechanism that enables services to locate each other in a distributed system. Service discovery allows services to dynamically update their locations, making managing and scaling the system easier.

Working with skilled partners can help organizations effectively implement these microservices techniques. Collaborating with experts ensures a smooth transition to an event-driven architecture, as they bring valuable experience and best practices.

This collaboration enhances the developer experience and accelerates digital transformation by ensuring that the architectural foundation is solid and capable of supporting future growth.

Enforcing Architecture with Standardized Services

Standardization is critical to solid architecture, as it brings consistency and uniformity to the development process. Organizations can streamline their development efforts by enforcing standardized services and reap numerous benefits.

Improved Developer Experience: When standardized services are in place, developers can concentrate on domain logic rather than design patterns. This frees them from the need to reinvent the wheel for each project, allowing them to focus on implementing business-specific functionality. As a result, the developer experience is significantly improved, leading to higher productivity and job satisfaction.

Accelerated Development Cycles: Standardized services enable faster development cycles by providing reusable components and templates that developers can build upon. This reduces the time spent on boilerplate code and architectural decisions, allowing teams to deliver features and enhancements more rapidly. This accelerates digital transformation and enables organizations to respond more swiftly to changing market conditions.

Reduced Likelihood of Errors: Using standardized services minimizes the risk of errors by providing well-tested and proven components. Developers can confidently leverage these components, knowing they have been designed and tested to meet specific quality standards. This reduces the likelihood of errors and ensures the system remains stable and reliable.

Real-Time Performance Metrics: Standardized instrumentation facilitates the collection of real-time performance metrics, providing valuable insights into system health. By monitoring these metrics, teams can quickly identify bottlenecks, performance issues, and potential points of failure. This proactive approach to monitoring allows organizations to address problems before they escalate, ensuring optimal system performance and user satisfaction.

Efficient Troubleshooting: With standardized services, troubleshooting becomes a more streamlined process. Since developers are familiar with standardized components, they can more easily pinpoint issues and implement solutions. This efficiency reduces downtime and mitigates the impact of system failures on the end users.

Driving Business Growth: By enabling developers to deliver high-quality solutions more quickly, standardized services contribute to business growth. Faster development cycles and reduced errors translate to more frequent releases and improvements, resulting in better products and services that satisfy customer needs and drive revenue growth.

In conclusion, standardization is crucial in creating a solid architecture for digital transformation initiatives. Organizations can improve the developer experience by implementing standardized services, accelerating development cycles, reducing errors, and enabling efficient monitoring and troubleshooting. These benefits ultimately drive business growth and ensure the success of digital transformation efforts.

Building a solid architecture is a powerful weapon in your digital transformation journey. By balancing cost, performance, and failure characteristics, embracing event-driven architectures, and enforcing standardization, organizations can optimize the developer experience and drive business success. Investing in a robust architecture improves development efficiency and lays the foundation for scalable and resilient systems that support long-term growth.

SOLID Principles: Reducing Cognitive Load

* * *

In today's fast-paced world of software development, reducing cognitive load is essential for creating an exceptional Developer Experience (DX). One way to achieve this is by employing the SOLID principles—design guidelines that promote maintainable, scalable, and robust code.

This chapter will examine the SOLID principles, read examples that showcase their impact on cognitive load, and discuss how they can revolutionize your software development process.

Single Responsibility Principle (SRP)

The Single Responsibility Principle states that a class should have only one reason to change, meaning each class should be responsible for a single functionality or concern. Adhering to SRP allows developers to create modular code, which is easier to understand, test, and maintain.

Consider a project where a class named `UserManager` handles user authentication and data retrieval from a database. Combining these responsibilities in a single class increases cognitive load, as developers must mentally process unrelated tasks simultaneously. By separating the responsibilities into two classes, `UserAuthenticator` and `UserDataRetriever`, developers can focus on one task at a time, reducing cognitive load and enhancing DX.

Open/Closed Principle (OCP)

The Open/Closed Principle asserts that software entities (classes, modules, functions, etc.) should be open for extension but closed for modification. This means that existing code should not be altered when adding new functionality; developers should extend the codebase by adding new components.

Imagine a notification system that sends messages through various channels like email, SMS, and Slack. If developers modify the core `NotificationSender` class each time they add a new channel, they must constantly reevaluate the existing code, increasing cognitive load. By designing the `NotificationSender` class to be extensible, developers can easily add support for new channels without modifying existing code, thereby reducing cognitive load and improving DX.

Liskov Substitution Principle (LSP)

The Liskov Substitution Principle states that objects of a derived class should be able to replace objects of the base class without affecting the correctness of the program. In simpler terms, subclasses should be substitutable for their base classes without altering the program's functionality.

Consider a media player application that supports different media formats, such as MP3, WAV, and FLAC. If developers create a base class called AudioFile and derived classes for each design, adhering to LSP ensures they can treat all audio file objects uniformly. This reduces cognitive load by allowing developers to focus on shared behavior and avoid constantly checking for specific file types.

Interface Segregation Principle (ISP)

The Interface Segregation Principle encourages creating smaller, more focused interfaces rather than large, monolithic ones. It asserts that clients should not be forced to depend on interfaces they do not use. By applying ISP, developers can achieve greater flexibility and modularity in their code.

In a restaurant management system, a single `IRestaurantOperations` interface that includes methods for managing orders, inventory, and reservations might overwhelm developers who only need specific functionality. By breaking down the interface into smaller interfaces, such as `IOrderManager`, `IInventoryManager`, and `IReservationManager`, developers can choose the interfaces they need, leading to reduced cognitive load and a more enjoyable DX.

Dependency Inversion Principle (DIP)

The Dependency Inversion Principle (DIP) promotes the idea that high-level modules should not depend on low-level modules; both should depend on abstractions. Additionally, abstractions should not rely on details; details should depend on abstractions. Applying DIP leads to a more flexible and decoupled architecture, making it easier to modify and extend the system without causing ripple effects throughout the codebase.

Consider a simple e-commerce application with a Checkout class responsible for processing payments. Without adhering to DIP, the `Checkout` class might directly depend on a specific payment gateway implementation, such as `StripePaymentGateway`.

This direct dependency increases cognitive load as developers must understand the intricacies of the specific gateway implementation whenever they work on the `Checkout` class. Moreover, introducing support for a new payment gateway, such as `PayPalPaymentGateway`, would require modifying the `Checkout` class, further increasing cognitive load.

By applying DIP, developers can introduce an abstraction layer, such as an `IPaymentGateway` interface, which both the `Checkout` class and specific payment gateway implementations depend on. Now, the `Checkout` class only needs to understand the `IPaymentGateway` interface, significantly reducing cognitive load.

When adding support for new payment gateways, developers can create a new implementation of the `IPaymentGateway` interface without modifying the existing `Checkout` class, thereby minimizing cognitive load and enhancing the overall Developer Experience.

Conclusion

In conclusion, adhering to the SOLID principles can substantially reduce cognitive load in software development, leading to a more enjoyable and efficient Developer Experience.

By creating modular, extensible, and decoupled code, developers can focus on their tasks without being overwhelmed by complexity, allowing for greater productivity and collaboration in their digital transformation journey.

Mastering Test Automation for Exceptional Developer Experience

* * *

In this chapter, we delve into the foundational aspects of test automation, focusing on mastering the basics that can significantly enhance the quality of your software development process.

We will explore the differences between functional and non-functional requirements and how understanding these distinctions can create more robust and resilient applications.

By gaining a solid understanding of test automation practices and the various types of testing, you will be better equipped to ensure that your code is efficient and effective.

Furthermore, we will discuss the importance of assessing organizational maturity and taking action to address areas that need improvement. A mature organization is better positioned to deliver high-quality software and provide a positive developer experience.

We will explore various techniques for evaluating your organization's maturity, including using maturity models and benchmarking.

By proactively assessing and improving your organization's maturity, you can foster an environment that supports continuous growth, innovation, and success in your digital transformation journey.

In today's fast-paced software development world, delivering high-quality code while maintaining speed and agility is crucial. Test automation is a powerful practice that can significantly contribute to the developer experience (DX) by reducing cognitive load, ensuring code resiliency, and preventing technical debt accumulation.

As a DX leader, mastering test automation is essential for creating an environment that fosters quality, efficiency, and innovation. This chapter will explore traditional test automation practices and discuss their benefits for engineering teams.

Test Automation Fundamentals

*** * ***

1.1 Unit Testing: Unit testing involves testing individual components or functions in isolation, ensuring that each part of the code works as intended. By writing and maintaining unit tests, developers can catch bugs early, simplify debugging, and ensure the correctness of their code.

Example: A developer working on a payment processing system creates unit tests to validate the correct calculation of tax rates, ensuring that the system accurately handles different tax scenarios.

1.2 Integration Testing: Integration testing focuses on verifying that different components of an application work together correctly. This practice helps identify communication and data exchange issues between components, ensuring the system functions as expected.

Example: In a content management system, integration tests are created to verify that the user authentication component correctly interacts with the database and the content editing component, ensuring that users can securely access and modify content.

1.3 End-to-End Testing: End-to-end testing simulates user interactions with an application, validating that the entire system functions as expected from a user's perspective. This practice helps identify user experience, performance, and functionality issues.

Example: An e-commerce website implements end-to-end tests to simulate user interactions, such as browsing products, adding items to the cart, and completing the checkout process, ensuring a seamless shopping experience for customers.

Test Automation Best Practices

2.1 Continuous Integration: Continuous integration (CI) involves regularly merging code changes into a shared repository and automatically running tests to validate the integrity of the codebase. CI helps detect integration issues early, reduce the risk of breaking changes, and maintain a consistent level of quality.

Example: A mobile app development team sets up a CI pipeline that automatically runs the unit, integration, and end-to-end tests every time a developer pushes code to the repository, ensuring any issues are detected and resolved quickly.

2.2 Test-Driven Development (TDD): Test-driven development (TDD) is a software development methodology that involves testing before writing the actual code. This approach encourages developers to think about the desired behavior and requirements of the code, leading to more robust and maintainable solutions.

Example: A developer working on a data processing module writes tests describing the expected behavior, such as data validation and transformation, before implementing the code to satisfy those tests.

2.3 Code Coverage: Code coverage is a metric that measures the proportion of code exercised by tests. High code coverage indicates that most of the codebase is tested, reducing the likelihood of undetected bugs and improving overall code quality.

Example: A web application team strives to achieve at least 80%

code coverage, ensuring their automated test suite tests and verifies most of their code.

The Impact of Test Automation on Developer Experience

* * *

By adopting and mastering test automation practices, DX leaders can significantly improve the developer experience in several ways:

3.1 Reduced Cognitive Load: Test automation enables developers to focus on writing high-quality code, knowing that the automated tests will catch errors and ensure correctness. This reduces cognitive load, allowing developers to be more productive and innovative. They can confidently change the codebase, knowing their tests will help identify any issues. As a result, developers can spend more time on creative problem-solving and designing better solutions.

Example: A development team working on an e-commerce platform can focus on implementing new features and optimizing performance, knowing that their comprehensive test suite will catch any regressions or potential issues.

3.2 Code Resiliency: Automated tests help ensure that code is resilient to changes and can adapt to new requirements without breaking existing functionality. With a robust test suite, developers can confidently make changes, knowing that the tests will catch any unintended consequences. This leads to a more flexible and maintainable codebase that can evolve without accumulating technical debt.

Example: A software company upgrading its API to support new data formats can rely on its test suite to ensure that existing functionality remains intact, allowing for a smooth transition and minimizing the risk of downtime or user issues.

3.3 Faster Feedback Loop: Test automation accelerates the feedback loop by providing developers with rapid insights into the impact of their changes. This allows them to identify and fix issues quickly, leading to shorter development cycles and more frequent releases. The faster feedback loop also promotes a culture of continuous improvement, where developers can iteratively refine their code and respond to changing requirements more effectively.

Example: An agile development team using test automation and continuous integration can quickly identify issues and iterate on their code, ensuring that each release is more stable and feature-rich than the previous one.

3.4 Enhanced Collaboration: Test automation encourages collaboration among developers, testers, and other team members by promoting a shared understanding of the code's functionality and expected behavior.

Well-written tests serve as living documentation, helping team members understand the code's intent and ensuring everyone is on the same page. This shared understanding fosters better communication and collaboration, leading to a more cohesive and effective development team.

Example: A cross-functional team working on a complex distributed system can use test automation to ensure that all team members understand the system's various components and their interactions, enabling them to collaborate more effectively on design, implementation, and troubleshooting tasks.

Understanding Functional and Non-Functional Testing

* * *

As software development has evolved, so needs comprehensive testing strategies that ensure the quality and performance of our applications.

Two significant testing categories have emerged: functional testing and non-functional testing. In this chapter, we will explore the differences between functional and non-functional tests, with real-world examples that highlight the importance of each.

Functional Testing: Ensuring Correctness

Functional testing focuses on verifying that an application performs as expected, meeting the requirements outlined in the specification. It involves testing individual features, components, and user interactions to ensure they function as intended. Functional tests are crucial for catching bugs, validating user stories, and confirming that the application meets the needs of its users.

* * *

Example 1: Jane's Online Store - Imagine Jane, an entrepreneur who has recently launched an online store. Her development team has created a feature that allows customers to add items to their shopping carts. To ensure that this feature works correctly, the team writes functional tests to verify that:

- Items can be added to the shopping cart with the correct quantity
- The shopping cart displays the correct total price for all items
- Items can be removed from the shopping cart
- The shopping cart updates appropriately when items are added or removed

By conducting functional tests, Jane's team can ensure that the shopping cart feature behaves as expected, providing a seamless user experience for her customers.

Non-Functional Testing: Assessing Quality Attributes

Non-functional testing focuses on evaluating the quality attributes of an application, such as performance, reliability, usability, and security.

These tests help ensure the application functions correctly and meets the desired quality and user experience standards. Non-functional tests are essential for identifying bottlenecks, optimizing performance, and ensuring the application can withstand real-world conditions.

* * *

Example 2: Sam's Video Streaming Service - Sam, the founder of a video streaming service, wants to ensure that his platform delivers a smooth and enjoyable user experience. His development team conducts non-functional tests to assess various aspects of the application's quality:

- Load testing to evaluate the platform's ability to handle a large number of simultaneous users
- Usability testing to determine the ease of use and intuitiveness of the user interface
- Security testing to identify potential vulnerabilities and protect user data
- Accessibility testing to ensure that the platform is usable by individuals with disabilities

By performing non-functional tests, Sam's team can identify areas for improvement and optimize the video streaming service to deliver a high-quality experience for all users.

Conclusion

Both functional and non-functional testing play critical roles in ensuring the quality and performance of an application. As developers and software testers, balancing these two testing categories is essential.

By conducting comprehensive functional tests to validate features and non-functional tests to assess quality attributes, we can build applications that meet their users' needs and deliver exceptional user experiences.

In the next chapter, we'll dive deeper into specific testing techniques and best practices to help you further enhance your application's quality and developer experience.

Assessing Organizational Maturity and Ensuring Quality Improvement

* * *

The previous chapter delved into various test automation methods and best practices for enhancing application quality and developer experience. In this chapter, we will discuss how leaders can assess the maturity of their organization and ensure continuous improvement in the organization's quality rather than just focusing on the code.

Run Automated Checks

Regularly running automated checks on different aspects of the organization, such as development practices, security, and performance, can help leaders monitor progress and identify improvement areas.

* * *

1.1 Code Quality Metrics: Automated code analysis tools can measure code quality metrics such as cyclomatic complexity, code coverage, and technical debt. By regularly monitoring these metrics, leaders can ensure that the organization maintains high code quality standards and promptly addresses potential issues.

* * *

1.2 Security Vulnerability Scans: Conducting automated security scans to identify potential vulnerabilities in applications, infrastructure, and third-party dependencies is essential for maintaining a secure environment. Leaders should prioritize addressing identified vulnerabilities to minimize the risk of security breaches and data leaks.

Create a Maturity Report

Creating a maturity report involves compiling a comprehensive assessment of the organization's strengths and weaknesses. This report can help leaders identify areas for improvement and track progress over time, ensuring that the organization continues to grow and evolve. Example: An Organization's Maturity Report.

Imagine a software development company that wants to assess its maturity and identify opportunities for improvement. The company's leadership team decides to create a maturity report that covers several key areas, such as development practices, security, and performance.

* * *

2.1 Maturity Model: Utilizing a maturity model like the Capability Maturity Model Integration (CMMI) helps the company assess its processes, practices, and tools. The CMMI model consists of five levels, from Level 1 (Initial) to Level 5 (Optimizing).

Each level represents a different stage of maturity, with higher levels indicating more mature and efficient processes.

Example: Applying CMMI to the Organization

The company's leadership team evaluates its development practices using the CMMI model and discovers it is currently at Level 2 (Managed). This indicates that the organization has established processes but lacks consistency and optimization.

The company can create a roadmap for achieving higher CMMI maturity levels and enhancing its overall efficiency by identifying the areas that need improvement, such as project management and quality assurance.

2.2 Benchmarking: Benchmarking involves comparing the organization's performance against industry standards or similar organizations to understand its relative position and identify areas where it lags. This information can be invaluable in prioritizing improvement initiatives and allocating resources effectively. Example: Benchmarking against Competitors.

The software development company benchmarks its performance against other companies in its industry. It evaluates various aspects of its operations, such as development cycle times, defect rates, and customer satisfaction.

By comparing these metrics to industry averages, the company discovers that its development cycles are longer than its competitors' defect rates are higher.

Armed with this information, the company can prioritize efforts to shorten development cycles and reduce defect rates, ensuring it remains competitive.

By regularly benchmarking its performance, the company can continuously identify areas for improvement and track its progress toward becoming a more mature and efficient organization.

Define Service Levels

Establishing clear service level objectives (SLOs) and service level agreements (SLAs) can help set expectations and ensure that the organization delivers consistent, high-quality services to its users.

* * *

3.1 SLOs and SLAs: Define SLOs and SLAs for different aspects of the organization's services, such as availability, performance, and response times. Regularly monitor and report on these service levels to ensure the organization meets its commitments and continuously improves quality.

3.2 Incident Management: Implement a robust incident management process to quickly identify, respond to, and resolve incidents that impact service levels. By continuously improving incident management practices, leaders can minimize the impact of incidents on users and the organization's reputation.

Visibility

Enhancing visibility into the organization's processes, practices, and performance can help leaders make informed decisions, identify trends, and drive continuous improvement.

4.1 Dashboards and Reporting: Create dashboards and reports that provide real-time insights into the organization's performance across various dimensions, such as code quality, security, and service levels. These insights can help leaders identify trends, spot issues, and make data-driven decisions.

4.2 Feedback Loops: Establish feedback loops with stakeholders, including users, developers, and other team members, to gather input on the organization's performance and areas for improvement. By incorporating this feedback into the improvement process, leaders can ensure that the organization continuously adapts to changing needs and expectations.

Conclusion

By assessing the maturity of their organization and focusing on continuous improvement, leaders can drive excellence in the quality of the organization itself, not just the code.

Implementing automated checks, creating maturity reports, defining service levels, and enhancing visibility are critical steps to achieving this goal. As the organization matures, leaders will see the benefits in increased efficiency, better collaboration, and a more positive developer experience.

Pro Tips for Releasing Software and Managing Environments

* * *

In this chapter, we'll dive into pro tips for releasing software and managing environments, focusing on various strategies to help you streamline your development experience. By following these guidelines, you'll be better equipped to create and maintain a robust and scalable software system.

Ephemeral Environments

Ephemeral environments are temporary, short-lived instances created for specific tasks, such as testing or debugging. These environments provide numerous benefits that can significantly improve your software development process.

First and foremost, temporary environments ensure a clean slate for every test. When you begin a new test or debugging session, you start with a fresh environment, free from any lingering artifacts or states from previous tests.

This eliminates potential conflicts or inconsistencies arising from prior tests and reduces the risk of false positives or negatives.

Ephemeral environments enable you to catch issues early in the development process by preventing the accumulation of unwanted artifacts and states. This is crucial for maintaining high-quality software, as it allows you to identify and fix defects before they go to production.

The sooner you can detect and address problems, the more time and resources you can save.

Ephemeral environments also promote collaboration and parallelization among developers. Because each environment is isolated and independent, multiple team members can work on different tasks simultaneously without affecting each other's work. This speeds up the development process and reduces the potential for bottlenecks.

To create and manage temporary environments efficiently, it's essential to adopt containerization technologies like Docker and Kubernetes. Docker allows you to package your application and its dependencies into a lightweight, portable container.

This makes it easy to create and destroy environments on demand, ensuring that your application runs consistently across various stages of the development process.

Kubernetes, on the other hand, is a container orchestration platform that automates containerized applications' deployment, scaling, and management. By leveraging Kubernetes, you can quickly spin up and tear down ephemeral environments as needed, making it an ideal solution for managing temporary instances.

Pro Tip: To further streamline the creation and management of temporary environments, consider using tools like Helm for Kubernetes, which simplifies the deployment of applications by providing a package manager and templating system.

This lets you define your application's desired state using a declarative configuration file, allowing you to spin up temporary environments with minimal manual intervention quickly.

By incorporating ephemeral environments into your development process, you can improve the quality and reliability of your software, minimize the risk of deploying faulty code to production, and foster a more efficient and collaborative development experience.

Everything as a Service

Treating all infrastructure components, including databases, message queues, and caches, as services are crucial in modern software development. This approach brings numerous benefits to your development process and system architecture.

You can decouple components from your application code and scale them independently by treating components as services.

This allows you to handle the increased demand for a specific component without affecting the entire system's performance. For example, if your application experiences a sudden surge in user traffic, you can scale your database service to accommodate the increased load without modifying the rest of your infrastructure.

When components are treated as services, they can be designed and built with fault tolerance in mind. By isolating the failure domain of individual components, you can prevent a single point of failure from causing a system-wide outage.

For instance, if a message queue service goes down, your application can continue running and processing user requests while the underlying platform automatically recovers the queue service.

Managing resources consistently across different components become more accessible when treated as services. This enables you to adopt standardized practices, tools, and conventions for monitoring, logging, and configuration management, streamlining your development and operations processes.

Pro Tip: Leverage cloud platforms and managed services to access a wide range of scalable, ready-to-use services.

Cloud platforms, such as AWS, Azure, and Google Cloud Platform, offer a wealth of managed services that can be utilized in your infrastructure. These services abstract away the underlying complexities of managing components, allowing you to focus on your application's core functionality.

Managed services are designed to be highly available, scalable, and fault-tolerant by default, so you can rely on them to provide a robust foundation for your infrastructure. Some popular managed services include Amazon RDS for databases, Google Cloud Pub/Sub for message queues, and Azure Cache for Redis caching.

By leveraging cloud platforms and managed services, you can accelerate your development process and create a more resilient, scalable, and manageable infrastructure.

Additionally, adopting the "everything as a service" mindset can help minimize operational overhead, reduce costs, and improve your system's reliability and performance.

Consistent Approach

Ensuring consistency across all environments—development, staging, and production—is fundamental to a smooth and efficient software development lifecycle.

Maintaining consistency can reduce the likelihood of encountering environment-specific issues, leading to costly downtime, bugs, or deployment failures.

When environments are inconsistent, it's more likely that developers will encounter issues when deploying code or migrating changes between environments. By ensuring that all settings are as close to identical as possible, you can minimize the risk of environment-specific issues and improve the overall reliability of your application.

Consistency across environments also streamlines the deployment process, simplifying the process of promoting code from one environment to the next. Developers can have greater confidence that their code will function as expected in each environment, which reduces the time and effort required for testing and troubleshooting.

Pro Tip: Use Infrastructure as Code (IaC) tools like Terraform or Crossplane to maintain consistency across your environments.

Infrastructure as Code (IaC) tools ensure consistency across environments. These tools allow you to define the desired state of your infrastructure in a declarative manner using code or configuration files.

Doing so allows you to version control your infrastructure configuration and apply changes consistently across all environments. Some popular IaC tools include:

Terraform: A widely-used IaC tool that enables you to define and provision infrastructure across various cloud providers using a consistent, declarative language called HCL (HashiCorp Configuration Language). Terraform supports many cloud providers and services, making it versatile for managing infrastructure.

Crossplane: An open-source IaC tool that extends Kubernetes to manage external infrastructure resources. Crossplane allows you to define your infrastructure using Kubernetes custom resources, which makes it easy to integrate with existing Kubernetes-based workflows and tooling.

By utilizing IaC tools like Terraform or Crossplane, you can automate the provisioning and management of your infrastructure across different environments.

This ensures consistency and increases the speed and reliability of deployments, reducing the potential for human error and manual intervention.

Maintaining consistency across development, staging, and production environments is crucial for minimizing the risk of environment-specific issues and streamlining the deployment process. IaC tools like Terraform or Crossplane can help you achieve this goal and significantly improve your software development lifecycle's efficiency and reliability.

Use it Like You're Paying for It

Developing a cost-conscious mindset when using resources is essential for optimizing your infrastructure and reducing expenses.

This applies to production and non-production environments like development, staging, or testing. By closely monitoring usage and optimizing resource allocation, you can minimize costs and improve overall efficiency.

Regularly review and analyze resource usage in your environments to identify areas where resources can be optimized or scaled back. This includes monitoring CPU, memory, storage, and network utilization to ensure you only use the needed help.

Once you've identified areas for improvement, optimize your resource allocation by adjusting your infrastructure configuration. This may involve resizing virtual machines or containers, consolidating services, or implementing auto-scaling policies to ensure that resources are only provisioned when needed.

Pro Tip: Implement budget alerts and cost monitoring tools to keep your resource usage in check.

Set up budget alerts to notify you when resource usage or costs approach predefined thresholds. This will help you stay on top of your spending and prevent unexpected expenses.

Many cloud providers, such as AWS, Azure, and Google Cloud Platform, offer built-in budget alert features you can easily configure.

Utilize cost monitoring tools to gain insights into your resource usage and spending patterns. These tools can help you identify inefficiencies, spot trends, and make data-driven decisions about resource allocation. Some popular cost-monitoring tools include:

AWS Cost Explorer: A powerful tool for visualizing and analyzing your AWS spending.

Google Cloud Cost Management: Provides detailed cost breakdowns and recommendations for optimizing your Google Cloud Platform spending.

Azure Cost Management: Offers comprehensive cost analysis and optimization features for your Azure resources.

Declarative GitOps

GitOps is a modern approach to managing infrastructure and application configuration that leverages the popular version control system, Git.

This powerful method simplifies the management of complex systems by treating the entire system state as code, enabling easy rollbacks and fostering collaboration across teams. By implementing GitOps, organizations can ensure their infrastructure is reliable, scalable, and easy to maintain.

Declarative Configuration: GitOps relies on a declarative approach, meaning that the system's desired state is defined in configuration files. This makes it easier to understand, maintain, and track changes in the system state over time.

Version Control: Using Git as the single source of truth, GitOps ensures that the entire system is version-controlled. This allows for easy rollbacks, audit trails, and the ability to recreate past configurations as needed.

Collaboration: GitOps promotes collaboration across teams by utilizing a shared repository for system configurations. This allows team members to contribute and review changes, ensuring everyone is on the same page and reducing the likelihood of conflicts.

Continuous Deployment: GitOps enables continuous deployment by automatically applying configuration changes to the system when updates are pushed to the Git repository. This ensures the system is always in sync with the desired state, reducing human error and manual intervention.

Pro Tip: Implement GitOps with Tools like Flux or ArgoCD

To fully leverage the benefits of GitOps, choosing the right tools to automate your deployment processes is essential. Two popular tools for implementing GitOps are Flux and ArgoCD:

Organizations can automate their deployment processes by implementing GitOps with tools like Flux or ArgoCD, reducing the time and effort required to maintain and update their systems.

This results in a more resilient, scalable, and efficient infrastructure that can adapt to the ever-changing needs of the business.

Consistent Logging, Tracing, and Metrics

Establish a consistent logging, tracing, and metrics approach across all services and environments. This will help you troubleshoot issues quickly and efficiently and provide valuable insights into your system's performance.

Pro Tip: Utilize log aggregation and monitoring tools like Elasticsearch, Logstash, Kibana (ELK stack), or Prometheus and Grafana for comprehensive observability.

Visible-Ops: Observability by Default

Ensure your systems and services are observable by default, providing comprehensive visibility into their behavior and performance. This will help you identify and resolve issues before they escalate.

Pro Tip: Incorporate tools like OpenTelemetry or Jaeger to standardize tracing and monitoring across your services.

Provide Guardrails and Get Out of the Way

Establish guardrails that enforce best practices and compliance without hindering your development team's productivity. This allows teams to innovate and experiment within defined boundaries, balancing autonomy and risk management.

Pro Tip: Implement automated policies and checks using tools like Open Policy Agent (OPA) or Azure Policy.

Strict Criteria for Production

Define strict criteria that must be met before deploying code to production. This could include passing integration tests, code reviews, and performance benchmarks. By enforcing these standards, you can reduce the risk of introducing defects or performance issues into your production environment.

Pro Tip: Use continuous integration and continuous deployment (CI/CD) pipelines to automate testing and enforce strict criteria throughout your development process.

Incorporating these pro tips into your software release process and environmental management will create a more efficient, reliable, cost-effective development experience. Embrace the power of automation, consistency, and observability to maximize the value and stability of your software systems.

Comparing Traditional and Cloud-Native CI/CD in Platform Engineering

* * *

In software development, Continuous Integration (CI) and Continuous Deployment (CD) have become essential practices that enable teams to build, test, and deploy their applications more rapidly and efficiently.

As organizations move towards cloud-native architectures and adopt Kubernetes for managing containerized applications, it's crucial to understand the differences between traditional and cloud-native CI/CD approaches.

This chapter will explore these differences and explain why cloud-native CI/CD is the preferred choice for platform engineering teams.

Traditional CI/CD

Traditional CI/CD solutions, such as Jenkins, were designed for virtual machines and often required significant IT operations overhead for maintaining the CI engine. Critical characteristics of traditional CI/CD include:

- Plugins are shared across the CI engine, which can lead to version conflicts and security vulnerabilities.
- Plugins dependencies have undefined update cycles, causing potential issues with compatibility and stability.
- No interoperability with Kubernetes resources, limiting the ability to integrate with modern container orchestration platforms.
- Administrators manage persistence, adding a layer of complexity and potential risk.
- Configuration is baked into the CI engine container, making it less flexible and harder to change or scale.

Cloud-Native CI/CD

Cloud-native CI/CD platforms like Tekton and OpenShift Pipelines are explicitly designed for containers and Kubernetes. They offer several advantages over traditional CI/CD solutions:

- Pipeline as a service, removing the operational overhead of managing CI engines.
- Pipelines are fully isolated from each other, eliminating the risks of cross-contamination and enhancing security.
- Everything is lifecycle-managed as a container image, promoting consistency and streamlining deployment.
- Native Kubernetes resources enable seamless integration with container orchestration platforms.
- The platform manages persistence, reducing complexity and administrative overhead.
- Configuration is managed via Kubernetes ConfigMaps, making it more flexible and easier to manage.

Advantages of Cloud-Native CI/CD in Platform Engineering

The following benefits make cloud-native CI/CD the preferred choice for platform engineering teams:

- Scalability: Cloud-native CI/CD solutions can quickly scale horizontally, adapting to increasing workloads and resource demands without affecting performance or stability.
- Flexibility: Using Kubernetes resources and ConfigMaps allows for easy configuration changes, promoting agility and adaptability.
- Security: The isolation of pipelines and container images reduce the risk of security vulnerabilities and ensures a more secure development environment.
- Resiliency: Native integration with Kubernetes and container orchestration platforms allows for self-healing and fault-tolerant CI/CD processes.
- Portability: Containerized CI/CD pipelines can be easily deployed across different environments, ensuring consistency and simplifying migration processes.
- Easier collaboration: Cloud-native CI/CD platforms enable better collaboration between development and operations teams, streamlining workflows and reducing bottlenecks.
- Reduced operational overhead: By offloading the management of persistence and CI engines, cloud-native CI/CD solutions reduce the burden on IT operations teams.

Conclusion

In the context of platform engineering, cloud-native CI/CD platforms offer significant advantages over traditional CI/CD solutions. They provide greater scalability, flexibility, security, and resiliency while reducing operational overhead and promoting team collaboration.

As organizations continue to adopt Kubernetes and containerization, cloud-native CI/CD platforms like Tekton and OpenShift Pipelines will become increasingly essential for managing the development and deployment of modern applications.

Feature Flags: An Adaptable Practice

* * *

In the ever-evolving world of software development, adapting quickly and efficiently to changes is crucial for a successful digital transformation. Using feature flags is one practice that has gained significant traction in recent years and has proven instrumental in enhancing developer experience.

Also known as feature toggles or feature switches, feature flags offer a powerful way to manage the release of new features while minimizing risk and ensuring a seamless user experience.

In this chapter, we'll delve into the concept of feature flags, explore their benefits, and discuss best practices for implementing them in your development process.

What are Feature Flags?

Feature flags are a technique used in software development that allows developers to enable or disable specific features of an application during runtime without requiring a code change or redeployment.

This is achieved by wrapping the new feature or functionality in a conditional statement that checks the status of a corresponding flag. The quality of the flag can be controlled remotely, allowing developers to turn features on or off for different users, environments, or situations.

Benefits of Feature Flags

Incremental rollout: Feature flags enable developers to release new features gradually, allowing them to test the functionality with a small group of users before rolling it out to a larger audience.

This approach helps identify and address any issues or bugs before they affect the entire user base, minimizing the risk of deploying new features.

A/B testing and experimentation: Feature flags provide a straightforward way to run A/B tests and experiments by selectively enabling features for different user segments.

This enables developers to gather valuable feedback on new features' effectiveness and user experience, leading to more informed decision-making and better product development.

Simplified rollback: In case of unforeseen issues or negative user feedback, feature flags allow for an easy and immediate rollback. Instead of reverting the entire codebase or deploying a hotfix, developers can disable the problematic feature using the feature flag, minimizing downtime and ensuring a seamless user experience.

Separation of concerns: Feature flags decouple feature releases from code deployment, allowing developers to focus on writing and testing code without worrying about the impact of releasing new features on users. This separation of concerns helps streamline the development process and reduces the likelihood of errors and deployment-related issues.

Enhanced collaboration: Feature flags foster a more collaborative development environment by enabling different teams to work on features independently without affecting the stability of the main codebase. This promotes parallel development and ensures that teams can work efficiently without stepping on each other's toes.

Best Practices for Implementing Feature Flags

Choose a robust feature flag management system: Opt for a feature flag management system that offers granular control over feature flag statuses, supports multiple environments, and provides an intuitive interface for managing flags. Some popular feature flag management tools include LaunchDarkly, Split.io, and Rollout.

Keep feature flags short-lived: Feature flags should ideally be used as a temporary mechanism for managing the release of new features. Once the quality has been thoroughly tested and is deemed stable, the flag should be removed, and the code should be refactored to ensure maintainability.

Establish a consistent naming convention: Adopt a clear and consistent naming convention for your feature flags to ensure that they're easily identifiable and manageable. This will help developers quickly understand the purpose of a flag and minimize confusion during development and maintenance.

Monitor and log feature flag usage: Keep track of feature flag usage by monitoring and logging any changes to flag statuses. This will help identify potential issues or unintended consequences arising from using feature flags and ensure that any necessary adjustments can be made promptly.

Complementary Practices

Feature toggles not only enhance the developer experience but also complement and simplify the implementation of several practices, such as A/B testing, canary releases, dark launches, and the design of experiments. These practices involve selectively enabling new features or versions for specific user segments, and feature toggles are essential in achieving this goal. This section will explore how feature toggles can be effectively utilized in these practices.

A/B Testing

A/B testing, also known as split testing, involves comparing two or more variations of a feature, design, or functionality to determine which performs better. Feature toggles can activate different variations of a part for other user groups.

Developers can make informed decisions about which variation should be permanently implemented by gathering and analyzing data on user engagement, conversion rates, and other performance metrics.

Using feature toggles in A/B testing simplifies the process and allows greater control over the test environment. It also enables developers to run multiple tests simultaneously without any interference, leading to faster and more accurate results.

Canary Releases

A canary release is a deployment technique where a new feature or version of an application is rolled out to a small subset of users before being released to the entire user base.

This gradual rollout helps identify potential issues or bugs, minimizing the risk of deploying new features. Feature toggles can activate the new feature or version for the selected group of users, making it easy to manage and monitor the canary release.

By incorporating feature toggles into the canary release process, developers can quickly toggle the new feature on or off, adjust the rollout percentage, and, if necessary, roll back the release with minimal effort.

Dark Launches

A dark launch releases new features or functionality to a subset of users without their knowledge, primarily to test and gather performance data.

Feature toggles play a crucial role in dark launches by enabling the new feature for specific user segments while keeping it hidden from the rest of the user base.

By leveraging feature toggles in dark launches, developers can validate new features' scalability, performance, and reliability before officially launching them. This ensures that issues are addressed proactively, minimizing the risk of negative user experiences and potential downtime.

Design of Experiments

Design of experiments is a systematic approach to planning, conducting, analyzing, and interpreting experiments to optimize processes, products, or systems.

It involves testing various factors and their interactions to determine the optimal conditions for achieving desired outcomes. Feature toggles can be employed in designing experiments to activate different feature or functionality variations for distinct user segments or under other conditions.

Utilizing feature toggles in the design of experiments enables developers to execute experiments in a controlled and efficient manner. This, in turn, leads to more accurate results and helps identify the most effective solutions to improve the overall user experience.

In conclusion, feature toggles not only enhance developer experience but also serve as a vital tool in implementing complementary practices like A/B testing, canary releases, dark launches, and the design of experiments.

By incorporating feature toggles into these practices, developers can manage feature rollouts more effectively, reduce risks, and make data-driven decisions to optimize their products and services.

Hackathons For Fun and Profit

*　*　*

I remember the first time I decided to participate in a hackathon – I was nervous and excited. But little did I know that this single decision would change the course of my professional journey, leading me to embrace hackathons as powerful tools for enhancing developer experience and organizational culture.

Over the years, I've participated in and even hosted numerous hackathons, innovation days, and other themed sessions that have brought people together to dream, explore, and innovate.

One of the most significant benefits of participating in hackathons is the opportunity for personal development. During these events, I honed my technical skills, learned new programming languages, and explored cutting-edge technologies. I've also had the chance to work closely with other talented individuals, learning from their expertise and expanding my horizons.

Hackathons are not for the faint-hearted. The tight deadlines, high-pressure environment, and demanding challenges force participants to push themselves to their limits. This intense environment has helped me grow professionally, causing me to think creatively and work more efficiently to deliver results.

Hackathons are fertile grounds for innovation, where diverse groups develop new ideas and solutions for pressing problems. Hackathons have led to the creation of groundbreaking products and technologies that have the potential to transform industries and even address social issues.

Hackathons foster an environment where new ideas can flourish by bringing together people from different backgrounds and diverse skill sets. I've seen firsthand how these events can spark innovative ideas and solutions that would have been impossible to conceive in isolation.

Overcoming Hackathon Challenges

Despite the numerous benefits of hackathons, there are some challenges that participants and organizers alike must navigate.

This chapter will explore these challenges and strategies for overcoming them, ensuring that hackathons continue to be a powerful force for innovation, collaboration, and growth.

One of the most common challenges hackathon organizers faces is the perception that these events are exclusively for hackers or highly skilled developers.

This misconception can lead to potential participants feeling intimidated or excluded, ultimately hindering the diversity and creativity that hackathons thrive on.

To address this issue, organizers need to promote hackathons as inclusive events open to people with varying skill sets and backgrounds. Emphasize the value of interdisciplinary collaboration and highlight that hackathons are an opportunity for learning, experimentation, and networking, regardless of one's current skill level.

The fast-paced nature of hackathons can be both a blessing and a curse. While time constraints can drive creativity and rapid problem-solving, they can also cause stress and make it difficult for participants to develop their ideas fully.

To mitigate this challenge, organizers can provide participants with ample resources, mentorship, and guidance before and during the event. This support can help participants better prepare for the hackathon, allowing them to make the most of the time available. Additionally, providing clear expectations and guidelines can help participants focus their efforts and avoid becoming overwhelmed.

A significant challenge for hackathon participants is sustaining the energy and excitement built up during the event. All too often, once the hackathon concludes, participants go back to their daily routines, leaving the projects they worked on during the hackathon behind.

Creating a supportive environment for continued collaboration and development of hackathon projects is crucial to address this issue. This can be achieved by establishing communication channels and platforms for participants to stay in touch, share updates, and seek help or feedback on their projects.

Additionally, organizations can encourage the progress of these projects by offering resources, mentorship, and opportunities for showcasing the work done during the hackathon. Participants can maintain the momentum and enthusiasm generated during the event by providing a clear pathway for the continued development and integration of hackathon projects into the organization's broader goals.

Communities of Practice

* * *

In the ever-evolving landscape of technology, developer experience is crucial to ensuring productivity and satisfaction. One way to improve the developer experience is through communities of practice – groups of professionals who share a common interest or passion and who collaborate, learn, and support each other in their pursuit of growth and excellence.

This chapter will delve into the concept of communities of practice, how they can enhance developer experience, and provide examples of various themes within these communities.

The Importance of Communities of Practice

Communities of practice play a vital role in enhancing developer experience for several reasons:

Knowledge Sharing: Developers can share their expertise, best practices, and experiences, helping others to learn and grow. This collaborative environment fosters a culture of continuous improvement and innovation, ultimately leading to increased productivity and satisfaction.

Networking: Participating in communities of practice allows developers to expand their professional networks, creating opportunities for collaboration on projects, mentorship, and even career advancement.

Problem-Solving: By engaging with peers with diverse perspectives and skills, developers can find novel solutions to complex problems, improving individual and collective performance.

Emotional Support: Communities of practice provide a platform for developers to share their challenges, frustrations, and successes, offering emotional support and encouragement in a safe and understanding environment.

Themes and Examples

There are numerous themes and areas of focus within communities of practice. Some examples include:

Agile Development: This community of practice focuses on the principles and practices of Agile methodologies, such as Scrum and Kanban. Developers can share experiences, discuss challenges, and explore ways to improve their Agile implementation.

DevOps: A community of practice centered on DevOps explores the intersection of development and operations, aiming to streamline processes and enhance collaboration between these essential functions. Members can share their experiences implementing DevOps principles and tools, such as continuous integration and deployment.

Programming Languages and Frameworks: Communities of practice dedicated to specific programming languages (e.g., Python, JavaScript, Java) or frameworks (e.g., React, Angular, Django) allow developers to learn from each other, share tips and tricks, and stay up-to-date on the latest developments in their chosen technologies.

Software Architecture: A community of practice focused on software architecture explores the design, development, and maintenance of robust, scalable, and secure systems. Participants can discuss architectural patterns, best practices, and trade-offs to make informed project decisions.

Code Quality and Testing: These communities of practice emphasize the importance of writing maintainable, efficient, and bug-free code. Developers can share experiences with various testing methodologies, tools, and techniques, ultimately improving the overall quality of their work.

Encouraging Participation in Communities of Practice

To fully realize the benefits of a community of practice, it is crucial to actively engage and motivate members to participate in discussions and knowledge sharing. This chapter will explore strategies for encouraging involvement in communities of practice, ensuring the community becomes a thriving and valuable resource for all members.

Promoting a community of practice through various channels is essential, ensuring that as many potential members as possible know its existence. Some methods for promoting a community of practice include:

- Emails: Send announcements to relevant mailing lists or group addresses.
- Team calls: Share information about the community during regular team meetings or conference calls.
- Mobile apps: Use company-approved mobile applications or communication tools to spread the word.
- Meeting invites: Include details about the community of practice in the invitations for relevant meetings or events.

Utilizing multiple avenues for promotion increases the likelihood of attracting a diverse and engaged group of members.

* * *

Fostering a Gradual Progression of Participation

It is natural for new members to progress through various stages of engagement in a community of practice. They may begin by lurking (observing without participating), then move on to consuming content (reading and learning from others), and finally contribute their insights and experiences. To encourage this progression, community leaders should:

- Monitor participation: Monitor new members and identify those needing encouragement or support to move from lurking or consuming to contributing.
- Offer mentoring and enablement: Leverage the community as a platform for mentorship and learning, pairing experienced members with newcomers to help them feel more comfortable engaging in discussions.
- Celebrate contributions: Acknowledge and appreciate the contributions of all members, regardless of their level of expertise, to create a positive and supportive atmosphere.

One effective way to attract attention and interest in a community of practice is by inviting well-respected or influential individuals from within the organization to speak at launch events or meetings. These speakers can share their experiences, insights, and support for the community, providing credibility and sparking interest among potential members.

- Plan speaker engagements: Identify and invite respected individuals within the organization who can offer valuable perspectives or expertise related to the community's focus.

- Promote speaker events: Use the various promotional channels mentioned earlier to advertise the speaker event, highlighting the importance and relevance of the topic and speaker.
- Encourage interaction: During the event, encourage attendees to ask questions and engage with the speaker, fostering a sense of community and active participation.

Encouraging participation in a community of practice is essential for creating a vibrant, thriving environment where members can learn, grow, and support each other.

By effectively promoting the community, fostering a gradual progression of engagement, and inviting influential speakers, community leaders can ensure that their community of practice becomes a valuable resource for all members.

Conclusion

Communities of practice offer developers a valuable opportunity to learn from their peers, build networks, and find innovative solutions to challenges. By participating in these communities, developers can enhance their experience, increasing productivity and satisfaction.

As the digital transformation journey continues, fostering a culture of collaboration and continuous learning through communities of practice will be a crucial driver of success for developers and organizations.

Measuring and Monitoring

In the following chapters, we will investigate the importance of measuring developer experience (DX) and its impact on your organization's digital transformation journey.

We will begin by discussing various methods for measuring DX, such as conducting surveys with a comprehensive repository of questions and tracking key performance indicators (KPIs) across multiple categories.

We will also explore how to act on the data obtained from these measurements and empower teams by providing them with actionable insights to drive continuous improvement. Examples of developer experience surveys and techniques for analyzing the results and tracking progress will be presented to demonstrate the practical application of these methods in real-world scenarios.

Next, we will explore the significance of building dashboards and KPIs to monitor and enhance developer experience effectively. This section will cover various charts that can be incorporated into a DX dashboard, categorized by productivity, stability, onboarding, and anecdotal experience.

We will also discuss the role of KPIs in driving measurable

improvements in developer experience and present several examples to illustrate their practical use. By creating a comprehensive dashboard that captures critical aspects of DX, organizations can foster a data-driven culture and promote continuous improvement in their development processes.

Finally, we will examine the role of the DevOps Research and Assessment (DORA) metrics in measuring developer experience and supporting your digital transformation journey. These metrics, which include deployment frequency, lead time for changes, mean time to recover, and change failure rate, serve as fundamental indicators of your organization's development performance and can inform your DX strategy.

By incorporating DORA metrics into your DX measurement framework, you can gain valuable insights into your development processes, identify areas for improvement, and drive meaningful progress in your digital transformation efforts.

Throughout this chapter, we will provide practical examples and guidance to help you effectively measure and enhance developer experience within your organization.

Measuring Developer Experience for Data-Driven Decision Making

* * *

In this chapter, we will delve into the importance of measuring developer experience (DX) and using data-driven decision-making to optimize and enhance the overall experience for developers.

We will discuss various aspects of measuring DX, including the importance of regular assessments, measurement methods, and actionable insights.

Importance of Regular Measurements

Measuring developer experience should be a recurrent process, ideally conducted every quarter. Regular assessments allow organizations to identify trends, track improvements, and detect issues before they escalate.

Organizations can proactively address potential challenges by consistently monitoring DX and refining their processes for a better developer experience.

How to Measure Developer Experience

Several methods to measure DX offer unique insights into different aspects of the developer experience. These methods include:

Surveys: Distribute questionnaires to developers to gather their feedback on various aspects of their experience. Surveys can be distributed through email lists or communication apps like Slack and Microsoft Teams.

Additionally, banners or links to surveys can be placed on platforms frequently used by developers, such as Github, StackOverflow (Enterprise), Jira, and Confluence. When designing surveys, consider using a mix of quantitative (e.g., rating scales) and qualitative (e.g., open-ended questions) questions to capture both objective and subjective feedback from developers.

Automated Data Collection: Utilize automated data collection techniques to capture data on developer activities, such as code commits, pull request reviews, and build times. This method allows organizations to analyze trends in developer productivity and identify bottlenecks or inefficiencies in the development process.

Tools like Git Analytics, Jenkins, and Travis CI can be employed to gather this data, providing valuable insights into the developer workflow.

Integrated Data Sources: Leverage tools like Workplace Analytics to gather information about developers' deep work focus time and use DORA (DevOps Research and Assessment) metrics to analyze developer productivity and performance.

By integrating data from multiple sources, organizations can gain a holistic view of the developer experience, identify correlations between different factors, and develop targeted improvement initiatives.

eNPS (Employee Net Promoter Score): Assess developers' overall satisfaction and loyalty towards the organization by measuring their eNPS. This metric is derived from a simple question asking developers how likely they are to recommend the organization as a great workplace, typically on a scale from 0 to 10.

The NPS is calculated by subtracting the percentage of detractors (those who score 0-6) from the percentage of promoters (those who score 9-10). This metric offers a quick and straightforward way to gauge developers' overall sentiment toward the organization and track changes over time.

* * *

Importance of Acting on the Measured Data

Collecting data is the first step; organizations must act on the insights gathered to drive meaningful improvements in the developer experience. Analyze the data to identify trends, address concerns, and implement changes to enhance developer satisfaction, productivity, and overall experience.

Empowering Teams with Data Visibility

Make the collected data visible to teams, enabling them to take ownership of their performance and act on the results. Transparent data sharing fosters a culture of continuous improvement and empowers teams to address issues and improve proactively.

Two critical types of metrics in measuring DX are sentiments and workflows. Sentiment metrics focus on developers' feelings and attitudes toward their work environment, tools, and processes. On the other hand, workflow metrics track the efficiency and effectiveness of development processes.

Areas of the Questionnaire

To gather comprehensive insights into the developer experience, consider including the following areas in the DX questionnaire, along with relevant examples for each:

Demographics: Capture developers' roles, teams, and organizational tenure information. Examples of questions include:

- "What is your primary role?"
- "Which domain or area do you belong to?"
- "How long have you been with the organization?"

General Experience: Assess developers' overall satisfaction with their work environment, tools, and processes. Example questions could include:

- "How satisfied are you with the development tools provided?"
- "How effective is the onboarding process for new developers?"
- "How easy is it to access necessary resources and documentation?"
- "How well do the provided tools and platforms meet your needs for daily tasks?"
- "How comfortable is your physical work environment (desk setup, office space, etc.)?"
- "How satisfied are you with the level of support provided by your team and organization?"
- "How effective is the communication between different teams within the organization?"
- "How well do the resources (tutorials, guides, etc.) help you learn new technologies or tools?"
- "How satisfied are you with the balance between innovation and maintenance in your work?"

- "How well do the organization's processes support work-life balance and personal well-being?"

Requirements Gathering: Evaluate the effectiveness of processes for gathering and managing project requirements. Example questions include:

- "How clear are the project requirements when you begin working on them?"
- "How effective is the communication between product owners and developers?"
- "How easy is it to prioritize tasks based on the provided requirements?"
- "How often are requirements updated or modified during development?"
- "How well does the organization handle scope changes or new feature requests?"
- "Do you feel you have adequate input and influence over project requirements?"

Software Development: Examine the efficiency and quality of the software development lifecycle. Sample questions might include:

- "How well do the development processes support collaboration between team members?"
- "How effective is the code review process?"
- "How easy is it to maintain and refactor existing code?"
- "How satisfied are you with the available libraries and frameworks for development?"
- "Do you feel the development process supports high-quality code output?"
- "How well does the organization balance technical debt and new feature development?"

Test and Integration: Assess the processes for testing and integrating code changes. Example questions could include:

- "How easy is it to write and maintain tests for your code?"
- "How effective is the continuous integration process?"
- "How frequently do you encounter issues with merging code changes?"
- "How satisfied are you with the available testing tools and frameworks?"
- "Do you feel that the test coverage is adequate for ensuring software quality?"
- "How well do the testing processes catch potential issues before deployment?"

Deployment: Evaluate the effectiveness of deployment processes and tools. Sample questions might be:

- "How easy is it to deploy your code to production?"
- "How confident are you in the deployment process's ability to catch potential issues?"
- "How well do deployment tools support rollback and recovery in case of issues?"
- "How satisfied are you with the speed and reliability of the deployment process?"
- "Do you feel the organization has a good balance between manual and automated deployment processes?"
- "How well does the organization handle deployment-related incidents and post-mortems?"

Operationalization and Maintenance: Examine the processes for monitoring, maintaining, and optimizing deployed software. Example questions include:

- "How effective are the monitoring and alerting tools?"

- "How easy is it to diagnose and resolve production issues?"
- "How well do the processes in place support continuous improvement of the deployed software?"
- "How satisfied are you with the documentation and knowledge sharing related to operational tasks?"
- "How well does the organization handle incident management and post-mortems?"
- "Do you feel that there are adequate resources and support for maintaining and optimizing software in production?"

Team Processes: Assess the effectiveness of team collaboration, communication, and decision-making. Sample questions could be:

- "How well do your team members communicate and collaborate?"
- "How effective are the team's decision-making processes?"
- "How well does your team handle and resolve conflicts?"
- "How satisfied are you with the level of autonomy and trust within your team?"
- "How well does the organization support cross-functional collaboration and knowledge sharing?"
- "Do you feel that your team's goals and objectives are clearly defined and aligned with the organization's overall strategy?"

eNPS: Measure developers' loyalty and willingness to recommend the organization as a great workplace. The NPS question is typical: "On a scale of 0-10, how likely are you to recommend this organization as a great place to work for a friend or colleague?"

Analyzing the Results

Once you've collected the survey responses, analyze the data to identify trends and areas for improvement. Consider the following steps:

Calculate response rates and representativeness: Determine if your sample size is large enough to draw meaningful conclusions. Assess the response rate by comparing the number of respondents to the total number of developers in your organization. Evaluate the representativeness of your sample by comparing the demographics of respondents to the overall developer population.

Analyze quantitative data: Calculate averages, medians, and percentages for closed-ended questions to identify patterns and trends. Use visual aids, such as graphs and charts, to help illustrate the findings. Compare the results against previous surveys to track changes and progress over time.

Review qualitative data: Categorize open-ended responses into themes, and identify common sentiments and suggestions. Use qualitative analysis techniques, such as thematic or content analysis, to systematically review the comments. Use word clouds or other visual representations to display common themes and keywords.

Identify strengths and weaknesses: Highlight areas where developers are satisfied and areas that need improvement. Take note of any significant differences in satisfaction levels between various demographic groups or teams, which may indicate specific challenges or successes within certain organization segments.

Prioritize areas for action: Based on the analysis, identify the most critical areas for improvement and prioritize them according to their potential impact on developer experience. Consider the severity of the issues identified and the resources required to address them.

Share the results: Present the findings to relevant stakeholders, including team leads, managers, and executives. Use clear, concise language and visual aids to communicate the key takeaways. Ensure that the results are accessible to all developers in the organization, fostering transparency and promoting a culture of continuous improvement.

Develop an action plan: Based on the insights gained from the survey, collaborate with stakeholders to develop an action plan for addressing the identified areas for improvement. Establish clear goals, assign responsibilities, and set timelines for implementing changes.

Monitor progress and iterate: Regularly track progress against the action plan and adjust as needed. Continue to measure developer experience periodically to assess the effectiveness of implemented changes and identify new areas for improvement.

Taking Action

After analyzing the results, prioritize the areas that require attention and develop a plan to address them. This may involve:

Improving tools and technologies: Evaluate the current tools and technologies used by developers and consider upgrading or replacing them with more efficient, user-friendly options. Please consult with the development team to ensure their needs and preferences are considered.

Enhancing documentation and support resources: Identify gaps in existing documentation and create or update materials to better support developers. Offer centralized and easily accessible repositories for documentation, code samples, and best practices.

Offering additional training or mentorship programs: Provide developers with opportunities to expand their skills through targeted training, workshops, or mentorship programs. Encourage knowledge sharing and continuous learning within the team.

Streamlining onboarding processes: Review and optimize the onboarding process for new developers, ensuring they have the necessary resources and support to become productive team members quickly.

Promoting collaboration and communication: Foster a culture of open communication and cooperation within the team by implementing regular meetings, code reviews, and feedback sessions. Encourage developers to share their ideas, challenges, and successes.

Ensure you communicate the survey findings and planned improvements with the development team to demonstrate their feedback is valued and taken seriously.

* * *

Tracking Progress

As stated before, surveys should not be a one-time event. To measure the effectiveness of your improvements, periodically conduct follow-up surveys and track changes in developer experience over time. This will help you gauge the impact of your efforts and identify new areas for enhancement.

Regularly compare the results of the follow-up surveys with the baseline data to assess progress and make data-driven decisions. Adjust your action plan as needed, and continue to involve developers in enhancing their experience.

By consistently monitoring and acting upon feedback, you can create a culture of continuous improvement that benefits both developers and the organization.

In conclusion, measuring developer experience is crucial for making data-driven decisions and driving continuous improvement in the development process.

By regularly assessing DX, organizations can identify trends, address challenges, and refine their processes for a better developer experience.

* * *

Recently, I stumbled upon an innovative solution that automates certain aspects of survey methodology for measuring developer experience (DX). The platform, getdx.com, offers an impressive suite of tools and resources to help organizations gauge and improve DX. I recommend exploring their offerings and considering their services, especially if your organization lacks robust research and data analytics capabilities in-house.

Getdx.com can be a valuable partner in your journey to enhance the developer experience within your organization. By leveraging their expertise and cutting-edge technology, you can gain insights into your developers' needs, preferences, and pain points. Don't hesitate to contact them for assistance in understanding and improving your team's DX, ultimately leading to a more productive and successful work environment.

Building Dashboards and KPIs for Developer Experience

***

Dashboards and KPIs are crucial in measuring developer experience and showcasing the progress made after implementing improvements. They help track and visualize various aspects of the development process, making it easy for teams and stakeholders to understand current trends.

After measuring developer experience, assessing the data, and taking action, it is crucial to showcase improvements to prove that the changes made have been effective.

This chapter will focus on building dashboards and KPIs to visualize the progress made in the development process, including productivity, building and tools, testing, onboarding, stability, risk and compliance, anecdotal experience, and collaboration metrics.

Productivity

Monitoring productivity metrics helps identify areas where developers excel, and improvements are needed. These metrics also provide insights into the effectiveness of tools and processes implemented. Some potential charts for the productivity dashboard include:

- Deployments per day: Indicates the rate of changes being pushed to production, reflecting the agility and responsiveness of the development process.
- Lead Time: Measures when a task is created to when it is deployed, offering insights into overall efficiency.
- Build time: Captures the time required to compile, test, and package the code, providing insights into tool performance and build process optimization.
- Pull Request lifetime: Tracks the duration from when a pull request is opened to when it is merged, reflecting the efficiency of the code review process.
- Release frequency: Measures the cadence of software releases, providing insights into the organization's ability to deliver value to customers.
- Code review time: Captures the time spent reviewing code changes, reflecting the thoroughness of the code review process and the engagement of team members.
- Lifetime of git branches: Indicates the duration of feature or bugfix branches, reflecting the speed of development and integration.
- Local development easiness: Measures the ease of setting up and working with local development environments, providing insights into tooling and documentation quality.
- Deep work time: Captures the amount of uninterrupted, focused work time available to developers, indicating the effectiveness of the work environment in supporting productivity.

* * *

Building and tools

Monitoring building and tools metrics helps evaluate the performance and stability of the development environment, providing insights into potential bottlenecks and areas for improvement. Some likely charts for the building and tools dashboard include:

- Build stability: Measures the success rate of build processes, offering insights into the codebase's quality and the build pipeline's effectiveness.
- Build time: Captures the duration of the build process, providing insights into the tools' performance and the build pipeline's efficiency.

Testing related

Monitoring testing metrics helps evaluate the effectiveness of the testing processes, providing insights into the quality of the codebase and the team's ability to identify and fix issues. Some potential charts for the testing dashboard include the following:

- Test coverage: Measures the percentage of code covered by tests, reflecting the thoroughness of the testing process.
- Test flake rate: Captures the rate of inconsistent test results, indicating the reliability of the test suite.
- Test execution time: Tracks the time required to run the test suite, providing insights into the testing infrastructure's performance and the test suite's efficiency.

Onboarding

Monitoring onboarding metrics helps evaluate the effectiveness of the onboarding process, providing insights into the team's ability to integrate new developers and empower them to contribute quickly. Some potential charts for the onboarding dashboard include the following:

- Time to 1st and 10th PR: Measures the time it takes for a new developer to submit their first and tenth pull requests, reflecting their ability to become productive quickly.
- Time to 1st impactful PR: Captures the time it takes for a new developer to submit their first significant contribution, offering insights into the onboarding process and the developer's understanding of the codebase.

Stability

Monitoring stability metrics helps evaluate the performance and reliability of the deployed software, providing insights into the team's ability to maintain and operate the system effectively. Some potential charts for the stability dashboard include:

- Incidents by severity: Tracks the number and severity of incidents, reflecting the overall reliability and stability of the deployed software.
- Mean Time To Recovery (MTTR): Measures the average time it takes to recover from incidents, offering insights into the team's ability to respond to and resolve issues.
- Error budgets: Monitors the acceptable threshold for errors and downtime, helping the team balance feature development with system reliability.

- Change failure rate: Captures the percentage of changes that result in incidents or require rollback, reflecting the risk associated with deployments.
- Open Post-Mortem Actions (PMAs): Tracks the number of outstanding action items from incident post-mortems, indicating the team's commitment to learning from incidents and improving system stability.

Risk and Compliance

Monitoring risk and compliance metrics helps ensure the development process adheres to security and regulatory requirements, protecting the organization from potential risks. Some likely charts for the risk and compliance dashboard include the following:

- Risk score: Measures the overall risk associated with the software development process, providing insights into potential vulnerabilities and threats.
- Vulnerabilities: Tracks the number of known security vulnerabilities in the codebase, reflecting the effectiveness of security practices and tools.
- Deviation from golden paths: Monitors the extent to which developers follow established best practices and guidelines, helping to maintain code quality and consistency.

Anecdotal Experience

Monitoring anecdotal experience metrics helps capture qualitative aspects of developer experience, providing insights into team dynamics, collaboration, and overall satisfaction. Some potential charts for the anecdotal experience dashboard include:

- Ways of Working: Measures developers' satisfaction with team processes and methodologies, providing insights into potential areas for improvement.
- Support: Evaluate the quality of support and resources available to developers, reflecting the organization's effectiveness in empowering developers.
- Happiness: Captures developers' overall happiness and job satisfaction, indicating the success of efforts to create a positive and fulfilling work environment.

Collaboration Metrics

Monitoring collaboration metrics helps evaluate the effectiveness of team communication and collaboration, providing insights into team dynamics and the organization's ability to work together effectively. Some potential charts for the collaboration dashboard include the following:

- Jira and Atlassian metrics: Track the usage and effectiveness of Jira and other Atlassian tools in facilitating project management, communication, and collaboration.
- StackOverflow Enterprise metrics: Monitor the engagement and effectiveness of the StackOverflow Enterprise platform in fostering knowledge sharing and problem-solving within the organization.
- GitHub Enterprise metrics: Capture the usage and performance of GitHub Enterprise in facilitating code collaboration, review, and integration.

Suggested KPIs for a Developer Experience Organization:

Developer Satisfaction Score: A metric that captures developers' overall satisfaction with their work environment, tools, and processes, based on survey responses or other feedback mechanisms. This KPI helps the organization understand the impact of its efforts and identify areas for further improvement.

Time-to-Productivity: The time it takes for a new developer to become productive, measured from their start date to their first significant contribution or the completion of their onboarding. Organizations can evaluate their onboarding processes' effectiveness by monitoring this KPI and identifying enhancement opportunities.

Tool Adoption Rate: The percentage of developers using recommended tools and best practices daily. This KPI helps organizations ensure developers have access to the best tools and resources, enabling them to work more efficiently and effectively.

Documentation Usage: The frequency and depth of developers accessing and engaging with documentation and support resources. Tracking this KPI can help organizations identify gaps in documentation, understand which resources are most valuable to developers, and prioritize improvements to support materials.

Code Quality: Metrics such as code complexity, code maintainability index, or static analysis results that measure the overall quality of the codebase. By monitoring code quality, organizations can ensure that their development processes promote best practices and maintain high performance and security standards.

Developer Retention Rate: The percentage of developers who remain with the organization over a specified period. This KPI can provide insights into developers' overall satisfaction and loyalty, helping organizations identify potential issues and opportunities for improvement to retain top talent.

Collaboration Score: A metric that measures the effectiveness of team collaboration based on factors like code review participation, meeting attendance, and cross-team communication. Tracking this KPI can help organizations understand how well their teams work together, identify areas for improvement in communication and collaboration, and foster a culture of teamwork and shared success.

By leveraging these dashboards and KPIs, developer experience organizations can monitor their progress and showcase improvements resulting from their efforts. Regularly reviewing and updating these dashboards and KPIs will help ensure that the organization continues to evolve and provide an exceptional developer experience.

Leveraging DORA Metrics

* * *

In the quest to improve developer experience (DX), measuring the impact of the implemented changes is crucial. A metrics-driven transformation is an approach that uses data to inform decisions, monitor progress, and drive continuous improvement.

This chapter will explore the DORA (DevOps Research and Assessment) metrics derived from the book "Accelerate" by Nicole Forsgren, Jez Humble, and Gene Kim. These metrics provide a solid foundation for assessing the effectiveness of your DX initiatives and guiding your transformation journey.

DORA metrics consist of four key performance indicators (KPIs) that measure software delivery performance. These KPIs provide a comprehensive view of your development process, capturing speed, stability, and efficiency.

a) Deployment Frequency (DF): The number of times code is deployed into production. This metric reflects the speed at which new features and bug fixes are delivered to users, and higher DF typically indicates a more agile and responsive development process.

b) Lead Time for Changes (LT): The time it takes for a code change to move from commit to deployment in production. Shorter lead times suggest developers are more productive and can deliver value to users faster.

c) Change Failure Rate (CFR): The percentage of fail deployments requiring a rollback or hotfix. Lower CFR indicates better code quality and more stable releases.

d) Time to Restore Service (TRS): The time it takes to recover from a failure and restore service to regular operation. Shorter TRS demonstrates the team's ability to quickly identify, address, and resolve issues.

Establish baselines for each metric to leverage the DORA metrics in your DX transformation. This will provide a snapshot of your current performance and serve as a benchmark for improvement. Collect data from your development processes, tools, and monitoring systems to determine your baselines.

Next, set realistic and achievable goals for each metric. These goals should align with your organization's strategic objectives and be informed by industry benchmarks or best practices. Ensure the purposes are communicated clearly to the development team and encourage a shared sense of ownership and accountability.

Implementing Changes and Monitoring Progress

With goals in place, identify and implement changes to drive improvements in your DORA metrics. This may involve:

- Streamlining and automating your deployment process to increase deployment frequency
- Adopting agile methodologies to reduce lead time for changes
- Improving code quality through testing, code reviews, and automated tools to decrease the change failure rate

- Enhancing monitoring, alerting, and incident management processes to minimize time to restore service
- Monitor your DORA metrics regularly to track progress toward your goals. Use data visualization tools like dashboards to make the data easily accessible and understandable for your team.

Learning and Adapting

Metrics-driven transformation is an iterative process. Regularly review your DORA metrics and analyze the data to identify trends, patterns, and areas for improvement. Celebrate successes, but also learn from setbacks.

Encourage a culture of continuous learning and experimentation. Foster open communication and collaboration, allowing developers to share their experiences, insights, and ideas for improvement. Adjust your goals and strategies based on your metrics and evolving organizational priorities.

Expanding Beyond DORA Metrics

While the DORA metrics provide valuable insights into your development process, it's essential to consider additional metrics that capture other aspects of developer experience; please see more in the Measuring Developer Experience chapter.

Leveraging Pelorus to Collect DORA Metrics

* * *

In this chapter, we will explore how Pelorus, an open-source tool developed by Red Hat, can be utilized to collect DevOps Research and Assessment (DORA) metrics and improve developer experience (DX) in an automated manner.

By leveraging Pelorus, organizations can gain valuable insights into their development processes, identify areas for improvement, and drive meaningful progress in their digital transformation efforts.

We will begin by providing an overview of Pelorus and its capabilities, followed by a step-by-step guide on how to set up and configure the tool to collect DORA metrics. Finally, we will discuss best practices for using Pelorus to enhance developer experience and drive continuous improvement within your organization.

Pelorus Overview

Pelorus is a comprehensive tool that provides real-time visibility into software delivery performance by automatically collecting DORA metrics from various data sources, such as CI/CD pipelines, source code repositories, and issue trackers.

By aggregating and visualizing this data in an easy-to-understand format, Pelorus enables organizations to track key performance indicators (KPIs) critical to their success in the digital transformation journey. Some of the main features of Pelorus include:

- Integration with popular CI/CD tools, source code management systems, and issue trackers.
- Customizable dashboards for visualizing DORA metrics.
- Extensible architecture that allows for adding custom metrics and data sources.
- Setting Up and Configuring Pelorus

* * *

To leverage Pelorus for collecting DORA metrics, follow these steps:

1. Deploy Pelorus: Deploy Pelorus on a Kubernetes or OpenShift cluster using the Helm charts or OpenShift templates provided. Detailed deployment instructions can be found in the Pelorus documentation.
2. Configure Data Sources: Connect Pelorus to your CI/CD pipelines, source code repositories, and issue trackers by configuring the relevant integrations. Pelorus supports many tools, such as Jenkins, GitLab, GitHub, and Jira.
3. Customize Dashboards: Customize the provided Pelorus dashboards or create your own to visualize DORA metrics and other KPIs relevant to your organization. Dashboards can be tailored to display data for individual teams, projects, or the entire organization.

Best Practices for Enhancing Developer Experience with Pelorus

By leveraging Pelorus to collect and visualize DORA metrics, organizations can gain valuable insights into their development processes and identify areas for improvement. Here are some best practices for using Pelorus to enhance developer experience:

Review DORA metrics regularly: Establish a cadence for reviewing DORA metrics with your team to identify trends, detect anomalies, and discuss areas for improvement.

Set targets and track progress: Set goals for each DORA metric based on industry benchmarks or your organization's unique context. Use Pelorus to track progress towards these targets and celebrate successes.

Encourage continuous improvement: Foster a culture where developers are encouraged to experiment, learn from failures, and continuously improve their processes. Use the insights provided by Pelorus to identify and prioritize improvement initiatives.

Collaborate and share knowledge: Encourage collaboration and learning sharing among teams by using Pelorus as a platform for discussing and understanding software delivery performance.

Conclusion

Pelorus offers a powerful solution for organizations seeking to improve their developer experience and drive digital transformation through automated data collection and visualization of DORA metrics.

By deploying, configuring, and leveraging Pelorus effectively, you can gain valuable insights into your development processes, identify areas for improvement, and foster a culture of continuous improvement within your organization. In this chapter, we have provided an overview of Pelorus, a guide on setting up and configuring the tool, and best practices for using it to enhance the developer experience.

Browser-Based IDE

* * *

Browser-Based Integrated Development Environments (IDEs) are web-based platforms that provide developers with comprehensive tools for coding, debugging, and deploying applications directly from a web browser. This approach simplifies the setup and maintenance of development environments and enables real-time collaboration among developers. Key features of browser-based IDEs include:

- Simplified setup and onboarding: Browser-based IDEs significantly streamline the process of setting up a development environment for new developers. They eliminate the need to install and configure various tools and dependencies on local machines, reducing the time spent getting started.
- Consistent development environment: Browser-based IDEs provide a uniform development environment across the entire team, regardless of individual developers' machines and operating systems. This consistency helps

prevent issues arising from differing configurations and reduces the "it works on my machine" problem.
- Real-time collaboration: One of the significant benefits of browser-based IDEs is the ability to collaborate in real-time with team members. Developers can share code, work on duplicate files simultaneously, and discuss issues without switching between tools.
- Reduced reliance on local resources: Since browser-based IDEs run on remote servers, they offload resource-intensive tasks from developers' local machines. This reduces the need for powerful hardware and ensures the development environment remains responsive even when working with large projects.
- Accessibility: Browser-based IDEs are accessible from any device with a modern web browser and an internet connection. This lets developers work from anywhere and easily switch between devices without losing work progress.

Downsides of using Browser-Based IDEs:

- Internet dependency: One significant drawback of browser-based IDEs is their reliance on a stable Internet connection. Developers with limited or unreliable internet access might face difficulties using browser-based IDEs.
- Limited customization: Browser-based IDEs often provide a predefined set of tools and plugins, which might not cover a development team's specific needs. Although many browser-based IDEs offer extensibility, the customization options might not be as extensive as those in traditional desktop IDEs.

- Performance concerns: While browser-based IDEs offload resource-intensive tasks to remote servers, the performance of these environments can still be affected by network latency, bandwidth limitations, or server-side issues. In some cases, desktop IDEs might provide better performance and responsiveness.
- Security and privacy concerns: Storing code and other sensitive information on remote servers can raise security and privacy concerns. Organizations must ensure the browser-based IDE provider has robust security measures to protect their data.
- Potential costs: Although many browser-based IDEs offer free tiers, organizations with large development teams or resource-intensive projects might need to opt for paid plans. These costs can add up over time and should be considered when evaluating browser-based IDEs.

In summary, browser-based IDEs can significantly improve the developer experience by simplifying setup, fostering collaboration, and providing consistent development environments.

However, organizations must also consider the downsides, such as internet dependency, limited customization, performance concerns, security and privacy issues, and potential costs. Weighing the advantages and disadvantages, organizations can decide whether browser-based IDEs fit their development teams.

Chapter 12
The Journey's End

* * *

In this chapter, we chart a course to help you sail toward becoming a world-class Developer Experience (DX) organization. By anchoring your strategies to the expertise of research companies and staying current with the latest studies and evidence-based methodologies from respected navigators in the field, you can confidently steer your organization through the ever-changing waters of technology.

With a keen eye on these authoritative sources and a steady hand on the helm, you'll be well-equipped to embrace innovative practices and technologies, ensuring a seamless and exceptional DX voyage.

One key resource to monitor is the Gartner Hype Cycle, specifically the technology trigger stage, which highlights emerging topics related to Developer Experience. Some notable subjects in this area include GitOps, Browser-Based IDEs, Platform Engineering, Performance Engineering, Inner-sourcing, AI Augmented Software Engineering, and Cloud Native architecture.

The Gartner Hype Cycle assists organizations and decision-makers in navigating the hype surrounding new technologies, comprehending their expectations, and assessing their potential impact on the industry. By staying abreast of such insights, your organization can maintain its course as a world-class DX organization, ready to face the ever-changing technological seas. The Gartner Hype Cycle consists of five key stages:

1. Technology Trigger: This initial phase introduces a new technology, innovation, or concept. There is a spark of interest as the potential benefits of the technology are recognized, but practical applications and products are not yet available.
2. The peak of Inflated Expectations: Early publicity and high expectations increase hype and excitement during this stage. Some early adopters may experience success with the technology, but there may also be failures and disappointments as the technology's limitations become evident.
3. Trough of Disillusionment: As the initial excitement fades, the technology's shortcomings and challenges become more apparent. Many implementations fail to deliver the expected results, leading to disappointment and disillusionment. Some companies may abandon the technology at this stage, while others continue to refine and improve it.
4. The slope of Enlightenment: In this phase, the technology's potential starts to be better understood, and practical use cases emerge. Companies invest in technology and begin to develop methods to overcome its limitations. As more organizations adopt the technology and share their experiences, knowledge about its application and benefits grows.
5. Plateau of Productivity: The technology reaches mainstream adoption and becomes an industry-

established part. Its capabilities and limitations are well understood, and organizations can reliably achieve the benefits promised by the technology. At this stage, the hype has subsided, and the technology's true value is recognized.

The Gartner Hype Cycle helps organizations navigate emerging technologies' often complex and uncertain landscape. It can guide them in making informed decisions about when to adopt a technology, how to allocate resources, and how to manage expectations throughout the technology's lifecycle.

By focusing on these emerging technologies and practices, your organization can align itself with the best-in-class DX organizations and stay ahead of the curve in the rapidly evolving software development landscape.

Throughout this book, we have already touched on some of these topics. By understanding in detail the connections between these cutting-edge practices and the success of top-tier DX organizations, you will be better equipped to prioritize your efforts and investments, ensuring that your organization remains at the forefront of the industry and consistently delivers exceptional Developer Experience.

Here is an expanded list of reliable sources and communities related to developer experience and platform engineering:

Platform Engineering Meetups

Meetups provide an excellent opportunity to connect with like-minded professionals, share knowledge, and learn about new trends and technologies. Attending platform engineering meetups, both in-person and virtual, can help you expand your network, gain insights from industry experts, and stay informed about the latest developments in the field.

Platform Engineering Slack

Slack communities have become popular for fostering collaboration and knowledge sharing among professionals. The Platform Engineering Slack group is a hub for platform engineers to discuss best practices, troubleshoot issues, and stay updated on the latest industry news. Joining this community can help you gain valuable insights from your peers and contribute to the collective knowledge.

PlatformEngineering.org

PlatformEngineering.org is a comprehensive online resource dedicated to platform engineering. The website offers articles, case studies, and tutorials that cover various aspects of platform engineering, such as infrastructure as code, containerization, and monitoring. By regularly visiting this resource, you can stay updated on the latest trends and best practices in platform engineering.

Platformweekly.com

Platformweekly.com is an online newsletter that curates content related to platform engineering, developer experience, and DevOps. Subscribing to this newsletter will provide you with regular updates on the latest news, articles, and resources in the field, ensuring you stay well-informed and ahead of the curve.

PlatformCon.com

Platformcon.com is an annual conference focused on platform engineering and developer experience. The event brings together industry leaders, practitioners, and enthusiasts to share knowledge, discuss challenges, and explore new ideas. By attending Platformcon, you can gain insights from expert speakers, participate in hands-on workshops, and network with other professionals in the field.

In conclusion, engaging with these resources and communities can help you maintain a growth mindset, stay updated on the latest technologies and trends, and ultimately enhance your expertise in developer experience and platform engineering. You will be better equipped to drive innovation and create value for your organization by continuously learning and adapting.

Creating a World-Class Software Engineering Organization

* * *

With top talent now on board your organization's ship and an arsenal of powerful tools and expertise techniques at your disposal, the next voyage lies in charting a course to create a world-class software engineering organization.

This organization should consistently hoist the sails of exceptional digital products, services, and experiences that customers treasure and that the business considers indispensable. Having been a part of a world-class software engineering organization, I can attest to the incredible knowledge and work-life balance it offers.

It's where you're excited to go to work every day, driven by passion and a commitment to excellence. In this chapter, I will share some key characteristics that define such organizations, drawing from my experiences and observations.

A world-class software engineering organization is characterized by the following:

Developers who are excited to work and driven by passion

In the world-class organization I belonged to, we had a team of highly motivated and passionate developers who genuinely loved what they were doing.

This contagious excitement created an environment where everyone was driven to push their limits and achieve exceptional results. We were given the autonomy and trust to explore new technologies, develop innovative solutions, and continuously improve our processes to deliver outstanding customer products and services.

Example: Our organization encouraged developers to spend some of their time on passion projects, allowing them to explore new technologies and ideas that could benefit the company. This helped keep developers engaged and excited about their work and led to several innovative solutions that became integral to our products.

Work that drives significant business value

A world-class software engineering organization aligns deeply with the business's goals and priorities. The work we did was not only technically challenging but also had a direct impact on the company's bottom line. Our projects were carefully selected and prioritized to ensure our efforts focused on delivering maximum value to the business.

Teams that consistently exceed expectations

A hallmark of a world-class software engineering organization is consistently surpassing expectations. In my previous organization, our teams were made up of highly skilled professionals committed to excellence in everything they did.

We constantly pushed ourselves to improve, seeking feedback, learning from our mistakes, and iterating on our processes and products.

Example: Our organization had a strong culture of continuous improvement, and we regularly held retrospectives to identify areas for growth and opportunities to enhance our processes.

This relentless pursuit of excellence enabled us to consistently exceed expectations, delivering high-quality products and services that delighted our customers and drove significant value for the business.

To create a world-class software engineering organization, consider the following key strategies:

Foster a culture of innovation: Encourage your team to think outside the box and embrace a culture of continuous improvement. This helps you stay ahead of the competition and fosters a stimulating and rewarding work environment that motivates developers to give their best.

Implement agile methodologies: Agile methodologies have proven highly effective in driving rapid and iterative product development. Adopting agile practices enables your teams to respond quickly to changing customer needs, ensuring that your digital products and services remain relevant and valuable to your customers.

Focus on collaboration and communication: A world-class software engineering organization is built on effective collaboration and communication. Encourage open and transparent communication within and across teams, promoting knowledge sharing and fostering a culture of mutual support.

Develop clear goals and metrics: Establish clear goals and metrics that help you measure the performance of your software engineering organization. This enables you to track progress and identify areas for improvement and ensures that your teams have a shared understanding of what success looks like.

Invest in professional development: Help your developers grow and advance their skills by providing ample opportunities for professional development. This can include training, mentorship, and access to industry conferences and events. Investing in your developers' growth improves your organization's overall capabilities and creates an environment where developers feel valued and appreciated.

Emphasize customer-centricity: Keep your customers at the heart of everything you do. By prioritizing customer needs and delivering exceptional customer experiences, your teams will be better positioned to create digital products and services that resonate with your target audience and drive business value.

Celebrate success and learn from failure: Recognize and celebrate your teams' achievements while learning from setbacks and disappointments. By fostering a culture of learning and growth, you create an environment where developers are not afraid to take risks and push the boundaries of innovation.

By implementing these strategies, you can transform your organization into a world-class software engineering powerhouse that consistently delivers exceptional digital products, services, and experiences. This helps you drive business value and creates an environment where developers are excited to work and your teams consistently exceed expectations.

The journey to create a world-class software engineering organization is undoubtedly challenging. Still, the rewards are well worth the effort as you pave the way for your organization's success in the digital transformation journey.

Leadership, Resilience, and Innovation

* * *

Maintaining a world-class organization is a complex and demanding endeavor, with numerous challenges that must be overcome. At the beginning of this book, we drew inspiration from the story of the intrepid Portuguese navigators who braved the unknown to chart new territories.

Their tale imparts a potent message about the importance of resilience, exploration, and an unwavering commitment to change whenever the situation calls for it. Such qualities are crucial for organizations striving to excel in today's competitive landscape, particularly when enhancing the developer experience (DX).

Throughout the book, we examined various obstacles and mental model shifts within the industry, highlighting their impact on the evolution of DX. We discussed the importance of staying informed about the latest trends and breakthroughs and understanding how they can shape the future of DX.

By closely examining recent developments and assessing the current state of DX, we can derive valuable insights that will help organizations adapt and thrive in this ever-changing environment. In doing so, we can foster a culture of innovation and continuous improvement, much like the pioneering spirit exhibited by the Portuguese navigators of old.

This mindset will enable organizations to navigate the complexities of DX with confidence, ultimately leading to success in a constantly evolving industry.

Following our exploration of the challenges organizations face, we turned our attention to the significance of adopting the right mindset for leading an organization through a transition towards a product-oriented approach. Emphasizing innovation in the development process is key to fostering a thriving DX environment. To achieve this, it is essential to understand what developers want, cater to their needs, and provide them with the support and guidance necessary to excel in their work.

* * *

Effective leadership is crucial in steering the organization toward a more productive and satisfying workplace. Leaders must be empathetic, decisive, and proactive in addressing issues that might hinder developers' progress. By fostering an environment of open communication, collaboration, and continuous learning, leaders can empower their teams to achieve their full potential.

To successfully chart the course of a new DX organization, it is vital to equip teams with the right set of tools, practices, and cultural values.

We explored the importance of implementing modern development methodologies, leveraging cutting-edge technologies, and embracing agile principles to maximize efficiency and productivity. Additionally, cultivating a culture of innovation, adaptability, and collaboration ensures that teams remain motivated, engaged, and prepared to tackle the challenges of an ever-evolving landscape.

By adopting the right mindset and focusing on the critical

elements of a successful DX organization, leaders can guide their teams toward a product-oriented approach, ultimately creating an environment that fosters growth, innovation, and exceptional developer experiences.

The formation of specialized teams and departments, such as Platform Engineering, is a highly effective approach to software development and meeting the needs of top talent.

These dedicated teams work on creating and maintaining a robust platform infrastructure that enables developers to focus on delivering high-quality products and features. Platform Engineering teams help reduce complexity, streamline workflows, and increase efficiency by centralizing platform management and standardizing tools and processes.

Addressing cognitive load is essential for enhancing the developer experience. Throughout the book, we explored various technical practices and innovative solutions that target cognitive load from different perspectives.

By simplifying processes, providing clear documentation, and adopting the right software paradigms, organizations can help developers focus on their core tasks and reduce mental strain. This, in turn, leads to increased productivity, better decision-making, and overall job satisfaction.

By implementing the strategies and insights shared in this book, your organization will be on the path to building an exceptional DX environment. This includes fostering a culture that encourages collaboration, innovation, and success.

As teams work together seamlessly, share ideas, and embrace cutting-edge solutions, your organization will be well-positioned to navigate the complexities of software development and deliver outstanding results. Ultimately, this creates a virtuous growth cycle, attracting top talent and driving the organization toward even more significant achievements.

By demonstrating a steadfast commitment to continuous improvement and maintaining an unwavering focus on addressing the needs of developers, your organization can set itself apart as a world-class DX leader.

Embracing the core principles of resilience and exploration, which have underpinned human innovation and progress throughout history, is crucial to achieving this distinction. These values serve as guiding lights, enabling your organization to navigate the complexities of the rapidly evolving tech landscape.

Incorporating these principles into your organization's DNA will ensure that it is not only prepared to tackle the challenges of today but also primed to excel in the ever-changing landscape of tomorrow.

By fostering a culture that values adaptability, learning, and growth, you create an environment where developers can continuously hone their skills and contribute to the organization's success. This forward-looking approach, combined with a deep understanding of developers' needs, will ensure that your organization remains at the cutting edge of innovation and maintains its status as a world-class DX leader.

As you continue to learn from past experiences and embrace new ideas, your organization will be well-equipped to navigate the shifting tides of the tech industry.

By remaining agile, responsive, and focused on the needs of your developers, you will cultivate a resilient organization that is not only prepared for the challenges of today but also poised to seize the opportunities of tomorrow, ensuring long-term success in an ever-evolving world.

The Journey's End

* * *

As we end this journey, I'm filled with an overwhelming sense of optimism for the boundless potential within the developer community.

As a driving force behind digital transformation, we must nurture leaders who embody the right mindset, attitude, and robust technical expertise to forge resilient organizations capable of delivering outstanding experiences to their customers.

This book synthesizes shared experiences, research, delivery practices, tools, principles, paradigms, and correlations. It is designed to guide you toward becoming an increasingly relevant player in the dynamic and ever-changing world of digital transformation.

It is a story of overcoming challenges, pursuing growth, and fostering a resilient mindset in the face of the complex landscape of software development and developer behavior.

As a first-time author, my ambition with this book has been to cast a light on developer experience. In this realm, limited knowledge and evidence-based information are available. I invite developers, managers, and leaders to adopt a growth mindset and elevate their careers, equipped with the knowledge and expertise shared within these pages.

Furthermore, I urge developers to strive for excellence in their field and to nurture self-awareness, identifying and addressing counterproductive behaviors such as self-victimization and accepting less than we deserve.

It's time for us to rise, come together, adopt a forward-thinking approach, and educate future generations on the benefits of living in a digital world. United, we can spark a revolution of remarkable experiences for ourselves and the broader universe.

I sincerely thank the incredible crew of developer experience engineers, platform engineers, software developers, and everyone whose work has been referenced in this book.

Your contributions to the field have been a tremendous source of inspiration and knowledge, and I am honored to be a part of this passionate and dedicated fleet of professionals.

This community's collective wisdom, experience, and innovation have played a crucial role in charting the course of this book. Through the exchange of ideas, collaboration, and our shared commitment to excellence, we can continue to steer the industry forward and make a lasting impact in the world of digital transformation.

To every one of you, thank you for your contributions, passion, and unwavering dedication to the craft. Your work serves as a guiding lighthouse for us all, and I am truly grateful for the opportunity to learn from and build upon your collective expertise.

I hope this book has proven to be an entertaining and enlightening voyage. I am deeply grateful for your time and engagement and thank you for joining me on this nautical adventure. I trust that the knowledge and insights shared within these pages will be a valuable compass as you continue to play a role in charting the future of digital transformation.

Thank you for reading. I, Marcus Maestri, am truly appreciative of your support. I am profoundly grateful for the opportunity to share my story with you—a story that bears witness to the power of passion, resilience, and an unwavering commitment to lifelong learning.

As I mentioned at the beginning of this book, my journey began with humble origins and the pursuit of self-taught programming. I navigated the ever-evolving software development landscape, embracing new opportunities and overcoming obstacles.

Along the way, I discovered the importance of cultivating a deep understanding of the technical and human aspects of the developer experience. This invaluable insight enabled me to unlock my true potential and contribute meaningfully to the industry.

I hope that by sharing my experiences and the knowledge I have gained, you will be inspired to embrace your journey of growth, resilience, and lifelong learning. As we collectively strive for excellence, we can continue to shape the future of digital transformation and create remarkable experiences for ourselves and the world.

Bibliography

Patterns of Developer Experience. (2012, June 26). Patterns of Developer Experience. https://softwareas.com/patterns-of-developer-experience/

The Art Of Saying No. (2016, October 20). Gartner. https://www.gartner.com/smarterwithgartner/the-art-of-saying-no

Humble, Kim, & Forsgren. (2018, March 27). Accelerate: The Science of Lean Software and DevOps: Building and Scaling High Performing Technology Organizations Paperback – Illustrated, March 27, 2018.

Graziotin, & Fagerholm. (2019, April 16). Happiness and the productivity of software engineers.

Pais, & Skelton. (2019, September 17). Team Topologies. IT Revolution Press.

100 Days of Developer eXperience. (2019, November 6). 100 Days of Developer eXperience. https://100daysDX.com/

4 approaches to cut physicians' mental workload—and burnout. (2021, March 29). American Medical Association. https://www.ama-assn.org/practice-management/physician-health/4-approaches-cut-physicians-mental-workload-and-burnout

Krohn, R. (2022, April 6). Autonomy is the future of software development - Work Life by Atlassian. Work Life by Atlassian. https://www.atlassian.com/blog/software-teams/state-of-the-developer-2022

Orr, E. (2022, May 9). Council Post: Why Developer Experience Belongs In The C-Suite. Forbes. https://www.forbes.com/sites/forbesbusinesscouncil/2022/05/09/why-developer-experience-belongs-in-the-c-suite/

W. (2022, August 30). GitHub - workos/awesome-developer-experience: A curated list of DX (Developer Experience) resources. GitHub. Retrieved April 5, 2023, from https://github.com/workos/awesome-developer-experience

Galloway, M. (2022, October 14). Your Platform Org needs a purpose. Here's how to find it. Medium. https://medium.com/@michael.roy.galloway/your-platform-org-needs-a-purpose-heres-how-to-find-it-64874b082d80

of the Cloud, M. T. (2022, October 24). What is Platform Engineering? Medium. https://medium.com/@mike_tyson_cloud/what-is-platform-engineering-e8f4e2257063

Galloway, M. (2022, November 27). Your Platform Org needs a vision. Here's how to get started. Medium. https://medium.com/@michael.roy.galloway/your-platform-org-needs-a-vision-heres-how-to-get-started-7e571d54db13

Pratomo, A. (2022, December 8). Notes from building internal developer platform— Part 3: Managing platform as product. Medium. https://adityop.medium.com/notes-from-building-internal-developer-platform-part-3-managing-platform-as-product-33b3946678d3

Ghosh, B. (2022, December 21). What is platform engineering and how it reduce cognitive load on developers. Medium. https://medium.com/@bijit211987/what-is-platform-engineering-and-how-it-reduce-cognitive-load-on-developers-ac7805603925

Galante. (2023, January 13). What is platform engineering? What Is Platform Engineering? Retrieved April 4, 2023, from https://platformengineering.org/blog/what-is-platform-engineering

Platform Engineering 101: What You Need to Know about This Hot New Trend. (2023, January 24). InfoQ. Retrieved April 5, 2023, from https://www.infoq.com/articles/platform-engineering-primer/

Unlock your business potential with open leadership. (2023, January 30). Unlock Your Business Potential With Open Leadership. https://www.redhat.com/blog/unlock-your-business-potential-with-open-leadership

Charissis, L. (2023, February 7). Platform Engineering KPIs. Medium. https://medium.com/wise-engineering/platform-engineering-kpis-6a3215f0ee14

E. (2023, February 14). The ****ing amazing way to improve your Github code. eFinancialCareers. https://www.efinancialcareers.se/news/2023/02/github-swearing

Bansal. (n.d.). Create an Exceptional Developer Experience Unblock, Your Software Engineers to Transform DevOps. https://harness.io/. Retrieved April 5, 2023, from https://assets-global.website-files.com/6222ca42ea87e1bd1aa1d10c/62fd33214535a45ee352b994_Harness_Ebook_DeveloperExperiences.pdf

Whitepaper: State of Platform Engineering Report Volume 1 | Humanitec. (n.d.). Whitepaper: State of Platform Engineering Report Volume 1 | Humanitec. https://humanitec.com/whitepapers/state-of-platform-engineering-report-volume-1

Cognitive Loadometer. (n.d.). Open Practice Library. https://openpracticelibrary.com/practice/cognitive-loadometer/

Consult the Board: Creating Best-in-class Developer Experience. (n.d.). Gartner. https://www.gartner.com/en/documents/4006223

Innovation Insight for Internal Developer Portals. (n.d.). Gartner. https://www.gartner.com/en/documents/4010078

How Netflix unified their engineering experience with a federated platform console | Brian Leathem. (n.d.). How Netflix Unified Their Engineering Experience With a Federated Platform Console | Brian Leathem. https://platformengineering.org/talks-library/netflix-platform-console-to-unify-engineering-experience

The top 10 fallacies in platform engineering | Humanitec. (n.d.). The Top 10 Fallacies in Platform Engineering | Humanitec. https://humanitec.com/blog/top-10-fallacies-in-platform-engineering

Red Hat. (n.d.). Digital Transformation, the open source way. https://www.redhat.com/rhdc/managed-files/cm-digital-transformation-open-source-ebook-f25290-202011-en.pdf

Pais. (n.d.). Platform as a Product - PlatformCon 2022. https://www.youtube.com/watch?v=b8YHCDMxqfg

ThoughtWorks. (n.d.). Technology Radar Vol.16. https://www.thoughtworks.com/content/dam/thoughtworks/documents/radar/2017/03/tr_technology_radar_vol_16_en.pdf

The History of DevOps Reports | Puppet by Perforce. (n.d.). Puppet by Perforce. https://www.puppet.com/resources/history-of-devops-reports

Download the 2021 State of DevOps Report | Puppet by Perforce. (n.d.). Download the 2021 State of DevOps Report | Puppet by Perforce. https://www.puppet.com/resources/state-of-devops-report

Stack Overflow Developer Survey 2022. (n.d.). Stack Overflow. Retrieved April 5, 2023, from https://survey.stackoverflow.co/2022

Open Practice Library. (n.d.). Open Practice Library. https://openpracticelibrary.com/

Dev Experience team. (n.d.). Dev Experience Team. https://handbook.sourcegraph.com/departments/engineering/teams/dev-experience/

Principles of Developer Experience. (n.d.). Principles of Developer Experience | Christoph Nakazawa. https://cpojer.net/posts/principles-of-devx

Red Hat Open Innovation Labs is a consulting engagement for teams. (n.d.). Red Hat Open Innovation Labs Is a Consulting Engagement for Teams. https://www.redhat.com/en/services/consulting/open-innovation-labs

Developer Experience Whitepaper | DX. (n.d.). Developer Experience Whitepaper | DX. https://getdx.com/developer-experience-management-paper

Developer portals: 10 things you need to know to maximize your investment. (n.d.). Thoughtworks. https://www.thoughtworks.com/insights/articles/developer-portals--10-things-you-need-to-know-to-maximize-your-i

Whitepaper: State of Platform Engineering Report Volume 1 | Humanitec. (n.d.). Whitepaper: State of Platform Engineering Report Volume 1 | Humanitec. https://humanitec.com/whitepapers/state-of-platform-engineering-report-volume-1

Create an Exceptional Developer Experience. (n.d.). Harness.io. https://www.harness.io/resources/exceptional-developer-experience

Open Leadership Enablement Program. (n.d.). Open Leadership Enablement Program. https://www.redhat.com/engage/open-leadership-enablement-program

Home | OpenGitOps. (n.d.). Retrieved April 26, 2023, from https://opengitops.dev/

Sourcegraph. (n.d.). Sourcegraph. https://sourcegraph.com/

Cortex | Help Engineering Teams Drive Microservices Best Practices. (n.d.). Cortex | Help Engineering Teams Drive Microservices Best Practices. https://www.cortex.io/

A. (n.d.). Compass | Mission control for your distributed architecture. Atlassian. https://www.atlassian.com/software/compass

Welcome to Pelorus. (n.d.). Welcome to Pelorus - Pelorus Docs. https://pelorus.readthedocs.io/en/latest/

Self-managed | SonarQube. (n.d.). Self-managed | SonarQube | Sonar. https://www.sonarsource.com/products/sonarqube/

The meaning of manager - Management Excellence at Microsoft: Model, Coach, Care Video Tutorial | LinkedIn Learning, formerly Lynda.com. (n.d.). LinkedIn.

https://www.linkedin.com/learning/management-excellence-at-microsoft-model-coach-care/the-meaning-of-manager-14492917

Backstage by Spotify | Supercharged developer portals. (n.d.). Backstage by Spotify | Supercharged Developer Portals. https://backstage.spotify.com/

Dynamic Reteaming | Heidi Helfand. (n.d.). Dynamic Reteaming | Heidi Helfand. https://www.heidihelfand.com/dynamic-reteaming/

Kubernetes: the origin story. (n.d.). Kubernetes: The Origin Story. https://www.linkedin.com/pulse/kubernetes-origin-story-steve-libbey

Project to Product: How to Survive and Thrive in the Age of Digital Disruption With the Flow Framework: Kersten, Mik: 9781942788393: Amazon.com: Books, 2018

Learn More

dx-book.com

www.ingramcontent.com/pod-product-compliance
Lightning Source LLC
LaVergne TN
LVHW091610070526
838199LV00044B/746